THE NEIGHBOURS OF THE
EUROPEAN UNION'S NEIGHBOURS

The Neighbours of the European Union's Neighbours

Diplomatic and Geopolitical Dimensions beyond the European Neighbourhood Policy

Edited by
SIEGLINDE GSTÖHL
College of Europe, Belgium

and

ERWAN LANNON
College of Europe and Ghent University, Belgium

LONDON AND NEW YORK

First published 2014 by Ashgate Publishing

2 Park Square, Milton Park, Abingdon, Oxfordshire OX14 4RN
711 Third Avenue, New York, NY 10017

Routledge is an imprint of the Taylor & Francis Group, an informa business

First issued in paperback 2018

British Library Cataloguing in Publication Data
A catalogue record for this book is available from the British Library

The Library of Congress has cataloged the printed edition as follows:
The neighbours of the European Union's neighbours : diplomatic and geopolitical dimensions beyond the European neighbourhood policy / edited by Sieglinde Gstöhl and Erwan Lannon.
    pages cm
  Includes bibliographical references and index.
  ISBN 978-1-4724-1777-0 (hardback)
1. European Neighbourhood Policy (Program) 2. European Union countries – Foreign relations. 3. European Union countries – Foreign relations – Middle East. 4. Middle East – Foreign relations – European Union countries. 5. European Union countries – Foreign relations – Africa. 6. Africa – Foreign relations – European Union countries. 7. European Union countries – Foreign relations – Asia, Central. 8. Asia, Central – Foreign relations – European Union countries. I. Gstöhl, Sieglinde, 1964- author, editor of compilation. II. Lannon, Erwan, 1968- author, editor of compilation.
  JZ1570.A5N45 2015
  341.242'2 – dc23

                                                                                        2014023403
ISBN 978-1-4724-1777-0 (hbk)
ISBN 978-1-138-36089-1 (pbk)

Contents

List of Figures, Maps and Tables

Figures

Maps

Tables

List of Abbreviations and Acronyms

AA	Association Agreement
ACG	Azeri-Chirag-Guneshli oil fields
ACP	Africa, Caribbean and Pacific countries
AFISMA	Africa-led International Support Mission to Mali
AMIS	African Union Mission in Sudan
AMISOM	African Union Mission in Somalia
AMU	Arab Maghreb Union
APF	African Peace Facility
APSA	African Peace and Security Agenda/Architecture
AQAP	al-Qaeda in the Arabian Peninsula
AQIM	al-Qaeda in the Islamic Maghreb
AU	African Union
AUHIP	African Union High Level Implementation Panel
BMENA	Broader Middle East and North Africa
BOMCA	Border Management Programme in Central Asia
bpd	barrels per day
BRICs	Brazil, Russia, India and China
BSEC	Black Sea Economic Cooperation
BTC	Baku–Tbilisi–Ceyhan pipeline
CADAP	Central Asia Drug Action Programme
CAGP	Central Asia–China Gas Pipeline
CEFTA	Central European Free Trade Agreement
CEMAC	Economic and Monetary Community of Central Africa
CFSP	Common Foreign and Security Policy
CIS	Commonwealth of Independent States
CMR	Critical Maritimes Routes
CNPC	China National Petroleum Corporation
COMESA	Common Market for Eastern and Southern Africa
COREPER	Comité des représentants permanents (Committee of Permanent Representatives)
CPC	Caspian Pipeline Consortium
CSDP	Common Security and Defence Policy
CSP	Country Strategy Paper
CSTO	Collective Security Treaty Organization
DCFTA	Deep and Comprehensive Free Trade Area
DCI	Development Cooperation Instrument
DG	Directorate-General

DG DevCo	Directorate-General for Development and Cooperation – EuropeAid
DG ECHO	Directorate-General for Humanitarian Aid and Civil Protection
EAC	East African Community
EaP	Eastern Partnership
EBA	Everything but Arms initiative
ECCAS	Economic Community of Central African States
ECHO	European Community Humanitarian Office
ECOWAS	Economic Community of West African States
EDF	European Development Fund
EEA	European Economic Area
EEAS	European External Action Service
EEC	European Economic Community
EED	European Endowment for Democracy
EFTA	European Free Trade Association
EIB	European Investment Bank
EIDHR	European Instrument for Democracy and Human Rights
EMAA	Euro-Mediterranean Association Agreement
EMP	Euro-Mediterranean Partnership
ENI	European Neighbourhood Instrument
ENP	European Neighbourhood Policy
ENPI	European Neighbourhood and Partnership Instrument
EPA	Economic Partnership Agreements
ESAIO	Eastern and Southern Africa and Indian Ocean
ESF	East African Stand-by Force
EU	European Union
EUCAP NESTOR	EU Regional Maritime Capacity Building Mission in the Horn of Africa and the Western Indian Ocean
EUCAP SAHEL	EU civilian CSDP mission in Niger
EUJUST LEX	European Union Integrated Rule of Law Mission for Iraq
EU NAVFOR	European Union Naval Force
EurAsEC	Eurasian Economic Community
EUSR	European Union Special Representative
EUTM	EU Training Mission
EUAVSEC	European Union Aviation Mission in South Sudan
FAO	Food and Agriculture Organization
FDI	Foreign Direct Investments
FPI	Service for Foreign Policy Instruments
FTA	Free Trade Agreement
FYROM	Former Yugoslav Republic of Macedonia
GAFTA	Greater Arab Free Trade Area

GCC	Gulf Cooperation Council
GNP	Gross National Product
GSP	Generalized System of Preferences
GSPC	Groupe Salafiste pour la Prédication et le Combat
HR/VP	High Representative/Vice President
IAEA	International Atomic Energy Agency
ICC	International Criminal Court
ICI	Financing Instrument for Cooperation with Industrialized Countries
IEA	International Energy Agency
IfS	Instrument for Stability
IGAD	Inter-Governmental Authority on Development
IMB	International Maritime Bureau
IMF	International Monetary Fund
IMU	Islamic Movement of Uzbekistan
INOGATE	Interstate Oil and Gas Pipeline Management
IOC	Indian Ocean Commission
IPA	Instrument for Pre-Accession Assistance
IR	International Relations
IRGC	Islamic Revolutionary Guard Corps
IRISL	Islamic Republic of Iran Shipping Lines
ISAF	International Security Assistance Force
JAES	Joint Africa-EU Strategy
LDC	Least Developed Country
LNG	Liquefied Natural Gas
LRRD	Link Relief, Rehabilitation and Development
MDGs	Millennium Development Goals
MENA	Middle East and North Africa
MICEMA	Mission de la Cedeao au Mali
MINUSMA	Integrated Stabilization Mission in Mali
MNLA	Mouvement National de Libération de l'Azawad
MoU	Memorandum of Understanding
MPCs	Mediterranean Partner Countries
MUJAO	Mouvement pour l'Unicité et le Jihad en Afrique de l'Ouest
NATO	North Atlantic Treaty Organization
NEC	Neighbourhood Economic Community
NGO	Non-governmental organization
NIP	National Indicative Programme
OECD DAC	Organization for Economic Co-operation and Development Development Assistance Committee
OIC	Organization of Islamic Cooperation
OPEC	Organization of Petroleum Exporting Countries
PCA	Partnership and Cooperation Agreement

PI	Partnership Instrument
PRC	People's Republic of China
PSC	Political and Security Committee
PSI	Pan-Sahel Initiative
PSO	Peace Support Operations
REC	Regional Economic Communities
RIP	Regional Indicative Programme
RMCB	Regional Maritime Capacity Building
RSP	Regional Strategy Paper
SCO	Shanghai Cooperation Organization
SHARE	Supporting Horn of Africa Resilience
SNA	Somali National Army
SPMME	Strategic Partnership with the Mediterranean and the Middle East
SWF	Sovereign Wealth Fund
TACIS	Technical Assistance to the Commonwealth of Independent States
TANAP	Trans-Anatolian Pipeline
TEU	Treaty on European Union
TFEU	Treaty on the Functioning of the European Union
TFG	Transitional Federal Government
TMC	Third Mediterranean Countries
TRACEA	Transport Corridor Europe Caucasus Asia
TSCTP	Trans-Sahara Counterterrorism Partnership
UAE	United Arab Emirates
UfM	Union for the Mediterranean
UK	United Kingdom
UKMTO	United Kingdom Maritime Trade Operation
UN	United Nations
UNAMID	United Nations-African Union Hybrid Mission in Darfur
UNIFIL	United Nations Interim Force in Lebanon
UNMIK	United Nations Interim Administration Mission in Kosovo
UNSC	United Nations Security Council
US	United States
WMD	Weapons of Mass Destruction
WTO	World Trade Organization

Notes on Contributors

Andrew Bower was an Academic Assistant in the Department of EU International Relations and Diplomacy Studies at the College of Europe in Bruges (2011–13) and a visiting research fellow in the Middle Eastern and Mediterranean Department at King's College London when he wrote his contribution for this book. He has since then been working at the European Commission in the Directorate-General for Humanitarian Aid and Civil Protection, and has previously also worked for the Directorate-General for External Relations of the European Commission (2010) and the European Institute for Research on Euro-Arab Cooperation (2010–11). Andrew Bower holds an MA in Middle Eastern and Mediterranean Studies from King's College London (2009) and a BA in International Studies with Spanish from the University of Birmingham (2008).

Maike Christiansen holds an MA in Interdisciplinary European Studies from the College of Europe in Natolin (Warsaw) and an MA in Geography, Geomatics and Law from Humboldt University Berlin. She worked on urban environmental planning and climate change at the United Nations Human Settlements Programme (UN-Habitat) and the United Nations Environment Programme (UNEP) in Nairobi and Paris. Between 2011 and 2013 she coordinated the programme to improve energy efficiency in the housing sector at the United Nations Economic Commission for Europe (UNECE) in Geneva. Currently, she works for Greenpeace Germany in Hamburg.

Silvia Colombo is a researcher at the International Affairs Institute (IAI) in Rome. She is an expert on Middle Eastern politics, transatlantic relations in the Mediterranean, Euro-Mediterranean relations and politics in the Arab world. She holds an MA in Near and Middle Eastern Studies from the School of Oriental and African Studies (SOAS) in London. Silvia Colombo is a PhD candidate in Political Science at the Istituto Italiano di Scienze Umane/Scuola Normale Superiore of Pisa where she is working on a research project on political transitions in the Arab world. Her recent publications include *Regional Dynamics in the Mediterranean and Prospects for Transatlantic Cooperation*, Mediterranean Paper Series, The German Marshall Fund of the United States, July 2013, and 'The GCC and the Arab Spring: A Tale of Double Standards', *The International Spectator*, 47(4), 2012.

Francesca Fenton was an Academic Assistant in the Department of EU International Relations and Diplomacy Studies at the College of Europe in Bruges (2011–12) when she wrote her contribution for this book. She has since then joined the British Embassy in Paris as a policy analyst. Francesca Fenton holds an MA in EU International Relations and Diplomacy Studies from the College of Europe (2011) and an MA in Political Science from the University of Edinburgh (2009), including an exchange with Sciences Po Paris. Prior to her studies, Francesca Fenton worked in China and for a London-based charity.

Sieglinde Gstöhl is Director of the Department of EU International Relations and Diplomacy Studies at the College of Europe in Bruges. She has been fulltime professor at the College since 2005. From 1999 to 2005 she was Assistant Professor of International Relations at the Institute of Social Sciences at Humboldt University Berlin. She was a research fellow at the Liechtenstein-Institut in Liechtenstein and at the Center for International Affairs at Harvard University. Sieglinde Gstöhl holds a PhD and an MA in International Relations from the Graduate Institute of International and Development Studies in Geneva as well as an MA in Public Affairs from the University of St. Gallen. She also acquired professional experience in European affairs (e.g. EFTA Secretariat, national referendum campaign). Her books inter alia include *Reluctant Europeans: Sweden, Norway, and Switzerland in the Process of Integration* (2002), *European Union Diplomacy: Coherence, Unity and Effectiveness* (2012, edited with D. Mahncke), *Europe's Near Abroad: Promises and Prospects of the EU's Neighbourhood Policy* (2008, edited with D. Mahncke).

Stephan Keukeleire is Jean Monnet Professor of European Foreign Policy at the Institute for International and European Policy and coordinator of the Jean Monnet Centre of Excellence 'The EU, Foreign Policy and Global Governance' at the University of Leuven. He was Chairholder of the TOTAL Chair of EU Foreign Policy in the Department of EU International Relations and Diplomacy Studies at the College of Europe in Bruges (2011–13). He has been a Visiting Professor at the College of Europe since 2001. In the past he gained experience with the practice of EU foreign policy when working at the cabinet of the Belgian Minister of Foreign Affairs and at the European Parliament. Stephan Keukeleire is a graduate of the Universities of Leuven, Hull and Strasbourg. His many publications in the field of the EU foreign policy and diplomacy include in particular *The Foreign Policy of the European Union* (with T. Delreux, 2013; 2008 edited with J. MacNaughtan).

Erwan Lannon is Professor in the Department of EU International Relations and Diplomacy Studies at the College of Europe in Bruges and since 2002 Professor in European Law at the Faculty of Law of Ghent University. He has been a Visiting Professor at the College of Europe since 2004 and was Director of European Interdisciplinary Studies at Natolin (Warsaw) from 2009 to 2011. Erwan Lannon holds an MA in International Politics and Strategic Studies from the Université Libre de Bruxelles and a PhD in European Law from the University of Rennes I. He worked as a (senior) researcher at Ghent University, as an expert for the EU institutions and for various Euromed networks, as head of the Brussels office of the EU Institute for Security Studies (EUISS), and as consultant for the United Nations and the European International Movement. His books include *The European Neighbourhood Policy's Challenges* (ed., 2012), *Les défis de l'adhésion de la Turquie à l'Union européenne* (edited with J. Lebullenger, 2006), and *The EU's Enlargement and Mediterranean Strategies: A Comparative Analysis* (edited with M. Maresceau, 2001).

Sir Michael Leigh is a consultant and senior adviser to the German Marshall Fund in Brussels, where he focuses on the European Neighbourhood Policy (ENP), post-Lisbon Europe, China's growing role and the EU's relations with the Middle East. He became EU Director-General for Enlargement in 2006 after serving for three years as external relations Deputy Director-General with responsibility for the ENP, relations with Eastern Europe, Southern Caucasus, Central Asia, Middle East, and the Mediterranean countries. Michael Leigh began his current role after more than 30 years in EU institutions, including as a cabinet member for various Commissioners and as director in the Task Force for the EU Accession Negotiations. He was admitted to the Order of St Michael and St George (United Kingdom) as Knight Commander in 2012.

Alexander Mattelaer is Assistant Director of the Institute for European Studies at the Vrije Universiteit Brussel. His research interests include European defence policy (CSDP/NATO), civil–military relations and strategic-level operations planning. He holds a PhD from the Vrije Universiteit Brussel, an MA in European Politics from the University of Bath and an MA in Germanic Languages from the University of Leuven. He is also a graduate of the Belgian Royal High Institute for Defence and the Belgian Advanced Staff College. Alexander Mattelaer has in addition acquired work experience in the Policy Planning Unit of the Private Office of the NATO Secretary-General, the Security and Defence Agenda and the International Peace Information Service. His publications include *The Politico-Military Dynamics of European Crisis Response Operations* (2013) and the European Parliament study *A Coherent EU Strategy for the Sahel* (with L. Simon and A. Hadfield, 2012).

Raphaël Metais was Research Assistant for the TOTAL Chair of EU Foreign Policy and Academic Assistant in the Department of EU International Relations and Diplomacy Studies at the College of Europe in Bruges (2011–13) when he wrote his contribution for this book. He has since then joined the French Ministry of Foreign Affairs. Raphaël Metais holds an MA in EU International Relations and Diplomacy Studies from the College of Europe (2011) and an MA in European Politics and Public Management from the University of Strasbourg (2010). He is a graduate of the Institut d'Etudes Politiques de Strasbourg and spent an academic year in Turkey. Raphaël Metais worked as an intern in Dakar (public policy auditing), Tehran (journalism), Brussels (European Parliament) and Paris (French General Secretariat for European Affairs).

David O'Sullivan is the Chief Operating Officer of the European External Action Service in Brussels. Before joining the EEAS, he was Director-General for Trade (2005–10), Secretary General of the European Commission (2000–05), Head of Cabinet of Commission President Romano Prodi and Director-General for Education and Training. He started his career in the Irish Foreign Ministry and spent four years in the Commission Delegation in Tokyo in the 1980s. He also has extensive experience in EU social and employment policy. David O'Sullivan has a background in economics, graduating from Trinity College Dublin and having completed postgraduate studies at the College of Europe in Bruges. He holds an honorary doctorate from the Dublin Institute of Technology. He is also a Member of the Consultative Board of the Institute for International Integration Studies at Trinity College.

Ahmed Soliman is Researcher on the Horn of Africa at Chatham House in London. He works in the Africa Programme producing policy-driven research that influences thinking on the Horn of Africa. His area of expertise is the politics of Somalia, the Sudans and Ethiopia. Ahmed Soliman is a co-author of *The EU Strategic Framework for the Horn of Africa: A Critical Assessment of Impact and Opportunities*, a report published in September 2012 by the European Parliament's Committee on Foreign Affairs. He produces briefings on the politics of the region and is often interviewed by the media, including the BBC, *The Economist*, *The Wall Street Journal*, *The Guardian* and *The Telegraph*.

Clément Therme is an Associate Fellow at the Centre d'analyse et d'intervention sociologiques (CADIS) at the School for Advanced Studies in Social Sciences (EHESS) and a postdoctoral Research Fellow at the Institut de Recherche Stratégique de l'École Militaire in Paris. He has also taught in the Department of Politics, Languages and International Studies at the University of Bath. He holds a PhD in International Relations from the Graduate Institute of International and Development Studies in Geneva and in Sociology from the EHESS. His articles have appeared in *Politique étrangère*, *Maghreb-Machrek* and *Politique américaine*, and he is the author of *Les relations entre Téhéran et Moscou depuis 1979* (2012) and the co-editor of *Iran and the Challenges of the Twenty-First Century* (2013).

Jonatan Thompson is since April 2013 Academic Assistant in the Department of EU International Relations and Diplomacy Studies at the College of Europe in Bruges. He holds an MA in European Affairs from Sciences Po Paris and a BA in Social and Political Sciences from the University of Cambridge. He has previous work experience in EU affairs in Brussels, including as an intern in the General Secretariat of the Council of the EU.

Alex Vines is Head of the Africa Programme and Research Director for Area Studies and International Law at Chatham House in London. From 2005 to 2007 he chaired the UN Panel of Experts on Côte d'Ivoire and from 2001 to 2003 was a member of the UN Panel of Experts on Liberia. He was a UN election officer for both UNOMOZ in Mozambique in 1994 and UNAVEM II in Angola in 1992. He is also a Senior Lecturer at Coventry University and in 2012–13 was a Visiting Lecturer at Bradford University. Alex Vines has worked for Human Rights Watch and held affiliations with a number of universities and research institutes, including Oxford, King's College London, the British Institute in Eastern Africa and the Nigerian Institute of International Affairs. He serves on the editorial board of several leading academic journals on Africa, is regularly interviewed by international media on African peace and security issues and has testified to various European parliaments and to the US Congress. He has written extensively on EU-Africa relations, including contributing to the European Parliament reports *The EU Strategic Framework for the Horn of Africa: A Critical Assessment of Impact and Opportunities* (2012), *Implementing the EU Concept on Mediation: Learning from the Cases of Sudan and the Great Lakes* (2011), and *Options for the EU to Support the African Peace and Security Architecture* (2008).

Alexander Warkotsch is a freelance security consultant in Berlin. Previously, he worked as a NATO civilian consultant at the ISAF Headquarters in Kabul. Between 2007 and 2009 he was a Lecturer for European Studies at King's College London and a Postdoctoral Fellow at the University of Western Australia in Perth. Alexander Warkotsch holds a diploma in economics as well as an MA and a PhD in political science from the University of Würzburg. He has published widely on Europe's relations with Central Asia and is the editor of *The European Union and Central Asia* (2011).

Claudia Zulaika was an Academic Assistant in the Department of EU International Relations and Diplomacy Studies at the College of Europe in Bruges (2011–13) when she wrote her contribution for this book. She has since then joined the Delegation of the European Union in Liberia as Junior Professional. Claudia Zulaika holds a postgraduate diploma in Development Cooperation and Humanitarian Aid from the National University for Long-Distance Education of Spain (UNED, 2012), an MA in EU International Relations and Diplomacy Studies from the College of Europe (2011), an MA in Diplomacy and International Relations from the Diplomatic School of Madrid (2007) and a Joint LLB/Master 1 degree in Spanish and French Law from the Complutense University of Madrid and the University of Paris 1 (2006). She also worked as a trainee at the Embassy of Spain in Nairobi (2007–08).

Foreword

The Neighbours of the European Union's Neighbours[1]

David O'Sullivan, Chief Operating Officer, EEAS

The concept of neighbourhood, when applied to international relations, can get quite complicated. In looking at the neighbours of our neighbours, the focus of this book goes far beyond Europe's natural frontiers and immediate sphere of influence. It presents the broader interdependencies which characterize our world, and the need for us to look at developments around us through an increasingly wider angle.

In speaking about neighbours and neighbourhood, the ideal is often linked to harmony and mutual support. Scriptures call on us to 'love Thy neighbour'. Sadly, this harmonious view of neighbourhood has not always reflected reality. Rivalries and animosities have repeatedly plunged neighbours into conflicts, which have often spread far beyond their immediate region. The spill-over effects of social injustice and even crime are felt thousands of kilometres away. Paradoxically, distance is diminished in the modern world but the local is still hugely important. Conflicts in Africa are felt in Europe, as are the consequences of instability in Central Asia. The events of 11 September 2001 offers a tragic reminder of the wide-ranging repercussions on security worldwide from state failure in a seemingly faraway region.

The European Union (EU) is itself a reaction to conflict between neighbours. After the most catastrophic war in human history, visionary European leaders understood that the continent could no longer sustain traditional geopolitical rivalries, nor Westphalian approaches to international relations. Shared control of coal and steel, the fundamental resources at the time needed for waging war, was a first step. Out of this grew the process of European integration, which has made war between the nations of our continent a virtual impossibility. Age old enemies joined hands in tying themselves to ever closer cooperation and joint governance, based on shared values of democracy, the rule of law and a functioning and integrated social market economy. The benefits of this approach were progressing, extended across the continent and, in 2012, the European Union received the Nobel Peace Prize for this process.

---

1   Based on the keynote address delivered at the conference 'The Neighbours of the EU's Neighbours: Diplomatic and Geopolitical Dimensions beyond the ENP' at the College of Europe in Bruges on 15 November 2012.

Even if this Nobel Prize was not awarded for external action, the reasons for which it was given underpin our efforts both in the EU's neighbourhood and beyond. The lessons of the importance of democracy, the rule of law, good governance and interdependent cooperation have led to a firm European value system which has become part of our own DNA. It is based on these values that we approach the world in search of sustainable win-win solutions. To have realized that, in today's interconnected world, the best way to retain sovereignty is to share it, is one of the most far-sighted lessons Europe could offer to the rest of the world.

It is on this belief that Europe devised its European Neighbourhood Policy (ENP), which was launched in 2003–04, in response to both the EU's interests and the wishes of our eastern neighbours to come closer to the EU. In the end, this policy evolved to cover the entire neighbourhood, both in the East and in the South, constituting a strong toolbox for the Union to support its closest partners. This choice was also particularly fortunate, as in 2011 it enabled us to respond rapidly to the important changes taking place in the Southern Mediterranean with the so-called 'Arab Spring'.

The ENP was built on the analysis of the world and goals set out in the European Security Strategy of 2003. This document, which assessed the EU's strategic interests and objectives, underlined the longer-term aim of promoting a 'ring of well governed countries' at the Union's borders.[2] The then Commission President Romano Prodi quite aptly spoke about a 'ring of friends'.[3]

This conceptual formulation highlighted the values-interests nexus underpinning EU external action. The ENP thus became at the same time a means to safeguard Europe's security interests and a policy to promote our core values of democracy, the rule of law and respect for human rights. It is a fundamentally strategic policy based on security and on the values we wish to share with our neighbours, and which many of them have publicly committed to uphold either as part of their European or their national aspirations. In a way, one could even say that in the ENP we aligned our values and our interests. Their realization – we believed and continue to believe – would guarantee the wellbeing and human security of the citizens of our neighbours, and in this manner bring predictability and sustainable stability to our own environment.

The launch of the ENP also coincided with what many called the 'big bang' of EU enlargement in 2004, when 10 new Member States joined the Union. This moved the borders of the EU dramatically further east, reunifying through European integration those countries with which for centuries our peoples had had deep cultural, social and political links. In this context, the ENP had a key role to play in addressing relations between the enlarged EU and those countries which remained outside it. Many of these countries had talked about their own European

---

2   European Council 2003. *European Security Strategy, 'A Secure Europe in a Better World'*, Brussels, 12 December 2003, 8.

3   Prodi, R. 2002. *A Wider Europe – A Proximity Policy as the Key to Stability*, Speech/02/619, Sixth ECSA-World Conference, Brussels, 5–6 December 2002, 4.

aspiration. We responded to this by an extended hand of policies designed to assist their own domestically driven efforts to come closer to EU standards and to build modern European societies. Fundamentally, we sought to promote stability, prosperity and security in our eastern neighbourhood from Ukraine and Belarus to Armenia and Azerbaijan, and our southern Rim from Morocco and Tunisia to Lebanon and Syria.

The approach we were following with countries around Europe was about maximizing our effectiveness without the tool which at least until then had been seen as the most effective one – enlargement. The EU offer to its neighbours included 'everything but institutions'.[4] The ENP was from the outset clearly distinct from enlargement, even if it had been made clear to our European neighbours that it would not prejudge possible further developments. Despite the fact that membership as such had not been discussed, the ENP did provide a robust transition tool, building also on lessons learned from the enlargement policies.

Still, it soon became clear that this policy was not always that easy to understand for our neighbours. It was not about any geopolitical location, but about domestic reforms. A representative of a eastern neighbourhood country once made a comparison between the EU approach and that of Russia. He noted that Russia tended to make offers which one could not refuse, while the EU made offers one could not understand!

True, the ENP is complex. However, this complexity should not mean ineffectiveness. Thanks to the ENP, much valuable work has been done in many fields. In line with the basic approach of the policy, this work has been done as much for our own benefit as it has been for the benefit of our neighbours. Legislative approximation is a good example of this. We have helped our partners shaping their legislation in key areas such as environmental protection. This is a clear, shared win-win. For European business, the approximation of environmental standards helps to reduce costs on regulatory compliance of exports outside the EU.

On the whole, trade with our ENP partners has undergone a steady increase since 2004. It now totals over €240 billion. To promote this even further, and to harmonize our standards, we have launched, or are planning to launch, negotiations on Deep and Comprehensive Free Trade Areas (DCFTAs) with several of our neighbours. For the so-called Eastern Partnership countries, DCFTAs are inherent to all Association Agreements negotiated between the EU and those neighbours which are members of the World Trade Organization. These are truly ambitious agreements, as they do not only focus on the abolition of tariffs, but also on regulatory convergence.

The DCFTA approach is therefore one of market access in return for concrete and verifiable reforms. A country's political will to undertake a serious reform course is measured by a number of aspects in the way its society functions. We can only enter into a closer association with a country that respects certain criteria of democratization and rule of law, and respects human rights values and

---

4   Ibid., p. 6.

freedom of expression. We have, for instance, concluded the negotiation of an Association Agreement and DCFTA with Kyiv. In late 2012, the Foreign Affairs Council called for determined action and tangible progress in addressing areas of EU concerns, including selective justice and judicial reform.[5] This sends a clear message of the importance the EU attaches to its value base in its relations with partners.

Another key area of cooperation is energy. The EU is supporting its neighbours in enhancing energy efficiency and introducing broader use of renewable energy sources. Our eastern neighbours have become either members or observers of the Energy Community Treaty. On the southern shores of the Mediterranean, we are working with our partners towards the development of a Maghreb-wide energy market. At the same time, we are also developing a more efficient energy infrastructure network, as well as infrastructure connections between the Trans-European Transport network and the transport networks of our neighbours to facilitate the circulation of goods and people between our neighbours and the EU.

Since the late 1990s, the Common Foreign and Security Policy has played an increasing role in the EU's engagement with its neighbourhood. The Union's long-standing active participation in the Middle East Peace Process Quartet is a case in point. Furthermore, the EU's role – under the French EU Council Presidency – contributed to resolve in 2008 the dramatic conflict between Russia and Georgia. The Union took the lead in the post-conflict situation as well, deploying in record time an EU Monitoring Mission to Georgia, to ensure the swift implementation of the ceasefire. The EU continues to lead diplomatic efforts towards a sustainable solution to issues arising from the conflict. Since 2005, the EU has also been actively involved in the so-called '5+2' format aimed at finding a viable political settlement to the Transnistrian conflict in the Republic of Moldova.

The deployment of various missions plays a key role in our engagement in conflicts. We are helping manage borders between the occupied Palestinian territories and Egypt, as well as between Ukraine and Moldova, especially as regards the border segment between Ukraine and the Moldovan breakaway region of Transnistria. EU advisers have also played a key role in providing high-level training to Palestinian police officers.

Finding solutions to separatist conflicts requires a heavy focus on trust. In this vein, the EU has invested and continues to invest considerable resources in supporting confidence-building measures, bringing populations together around shared interests. Much of our support in this field has gone to Transnistria and to efforts in the context of the EU's non-recognition and engagement policy towards the Georgian regions of Abkhazia and South Ossetia. While the EU is as such not involved in the Minsk Group around the Nagorno-Karabakh conflict, we remain strongly committed to supporting eventual positive dynamics here too, with a robust confidence-building measures package.

---

5   Council of the European Union 2012. 3209th Council meeting Foreign Affairs, Press Release, 17438/1/12 REV 1, PRESSE 516, Brussels, 10 December.

The EU through its policies has contributed to making the neighbourhood a better, safer and more prosperous place. At the same time, one needs to admit that the ENP cannot take credit for any ground-breaking transformations in the neighbourhood. In reality, successful transition is always domestically driven and at best externally supported.

It is too early to say where the changes brought by the 'Arab Spring' in the Southern Mediterranean will lead. We have seen great hopes, but also worrying signs.

What is clear is that the transformations, which started in 2011, are indicative of an on-going paradigm shift. It would be too simplistic to look at the current changes in the global order merely through questions of whether the West is in decline or not. What we are in essence witnessing is a re-distribution of power which is not only vertical, but – perhaps even more fundamentally – horizontal. Power is being diffused across states and geographical regions. Most crucially, it is being re-distributed inside states. We are living in an era of empowerment of the individual, of ordinary people, not least through the extraordinary explosion of social networking media.

What we are seeing is people getting together and challenging authoritarian regimes and systems of governance, both at the domestic and international levels. Globalization and the new means of communication have altered the meaning of distance. Processes starting thousands of kilometres away from Europe's shores can have an effect on Europe almost in real time. The concept of neighbourhood has changed. While our immediate neighbours remain central, their neighbours – or the neighbours of our neighbours – will be equally central in the EU's external action.

There are so many variables to be taken into consideration in dealing with our modern-day world, with its increasingly complex challenges. How, for instance, do we address the pressing demands for human dignity, democratic freedoms and more accountable governments rising from the 'Arab street' or elsewhere? How do we address the challenges and potential dangers posed by failing states, or states struggling to counter the scourge of rising organized crime and militant fundamentalism, be it in the Sahel or the Horn of Africa? These are existential questions. However, no less important is to try to manage relations where our neighbours feel that they neither share – nor aspire to share – our values. Belarus is a telling example of this challenge.

In finding responses to many of these questions, we also need to look at the fundamental relationship we have with Russia, which for the EU is both a neighbour and a strategic partner. We need to be able to work together in addressing challenges of our common neighbourhood, but also far beyond. History continues to haunt the EU–Russia relationship. We have much work ahead in building trust between us. This will require an ability to listen with empathy, to understand each other. It is only through building trust that we can surmount traditional zero-sum thinking, and work together towards mutually beneficial outcomes.

The 'Arab Spring' was a trigger to review the ENP or – to be more precise – review the review which had already been completed to bring the policy in line with the realities of the Lisbon Treaty's external relations architecture. It became clear that a thorough re-think was needed for a number of reasons.

First and foremost, we needed to move towards a truly tailor-made approach towards our partners. This had been the goal from the outset, but we felt that in reality we ended up with a 'one-size-fits-all' approach. This was no longer acceptable or even feasible in the heterogeneous landscape of the globalized world, which also characterized our own neighbourhood. In line with a strong understanding that reforms could not be imposed from the outside, but needed to be based on domestic ownership, we understood that we needed to be able to better support those governments which truly demonstrated political will to reform.

This understanding lies at the heart of the so-called 'more-for-more' approach and the concept of 'mutual accountability'. Through these, the EU is trying to develop a real spirit of partnership and joint ownership of reforms with its partner countries. Building on the goal of promoting stability, prosperity and security and 'deep democracy', the EU is working towards a more tailor-made approach within the ENP. This approach is based on a balance between conditionality and the needs and aspirations of our partners, and perhaps more importantly of their societies. We are talking about partnering with entire societies.

The test of this new approach lies in its implementation. We fully understand that even when the political will for reforms is there, transition does not happen over night. We are committed for the long haul. However, I am confident that this policy will bring results. In the meantime, in 2011–12 the EU devoted an additional €600 million to economic development, health and reconstruction in our southern neighbourhood, as well as a further €350 million to governance and socio-economic development. This is a significant commitment, especially as it comes over and above earlier committed resources.

The changes taking place in our neighbourhood also coincided with the establishment of the European External Action Service (EEAS), in the context of the implementation of the Lisbon Treaty. The aim of the Treaty was to develop the capacity and capability of the EU's external action to better meet the challenges and requirements of the modern, increasingly complex world. The EEAS was established to bring more coherence and consistency to our external policy, through harnessing all of the EU's tools in a co-ordinated manner. Developing and consolidating this comprehensive approach is a crucial priority for both High Representative/Vice President (HR/VP) Catherine Ashton and the EEAS.

The High Representative has been consistent in her message that the establishment of the EEAS was not meant as a grab for power, but as a grab for efficiency. It is not there to replace the diplomatic services of the EU Member States nor the European Commission. As its staff composition bringing together EU officials and Member States' diplomats suggests, the EEAS is there to integrate and complement actions earlier taken in a vacuum from each other. Its main task is to help forge a more cohesive and effective European presence on the global scene. Another message often voiced by the High Representative is that the EEAS is not about speaking with a single voice but about helping to deliver a single and integrated European form of 'joined-up government'. Its major asset is a worldwide diplomatic network of 139 embassies (the sixth largest diplomatic network in the world).

The EEAS has the ability to draw from a very extensive toolbox. This provides the Service's strength, but also its complexity. While it has strongly developed the EU's capabilities in the traditional field of foreign policy, it has also built on the external relations instruments of trade, development aid and humanitarian assistance. In finding the right mix between these, tailored for a specific situation, the EEAS is attempting to provide a sophisticated response to complex, multi-faceted and evolving challenges.

The 'Task Force Concept' for the countries of the Southern Mediterranean is a distinctive example of the added value which the EEAS can bring. The Task Forces, chaired by the High Representative together with the Foreign Minister of the concerned partner country – with a key role played by the EU Special Representative for the Southern Mediterranean –, assemble together the donor community, civil society and the private sector as a catalyst for providing financial support and restoring investor confidence. Such meetings have, for instance, been organized with Tunisia, Jordan and Egypt.

The establishment of the EEAS has enabled us to take a more strategic look at the priorities, interests and goals of the EU. With the Service, and led by the High Representative personally, the EU is in the forefront of efforts to tackle major international crises, both in the neighbourhood and in the neighbourhood of our neighbourhood.

One of the priorities for the HR/VP in this respect has been facilitating the dialogue between Belgrade and Pristina. Between March 2011 and February 2012 the EEAS has led a process that culminated with Serbia obtaining EU candidate status. In the fall of 2012 (following a hiatus due to the Serbian elections/new government formation) the dialogue was upgraded with the personal involvement of the High Representative.

The next milestone is a possible opening of accession negotiations for Serbia and of negotiations for a Stabilization and Association Agreement with Kosovo. Should this target be reached, the overall involvement of the EU in the normalization of this relationship will have to continue. Given the EU perspective for the Western Balkans, and the unique EU leverage that stems from this, it would be difficult not to continue to play a central role in the Serbia–Kosovo future relationship.

In the Middle East Peace Process, we play an active role with our participation in the Quartet. The on-going tragic situation in Syria remains a focus, with efforts to rally the international community to work towards ending the killing of innocent civilians and getting the country on track towards democratic transition. The role of the League of Arab States and the efforts of United Nations special envoy Lakhdar Brahimi are crucially important in this context, and are strongly supported by the EU.

Countering the threat posed by a potential Iranian nuclear programme is a key priority and an issue where the EU plays a particular role, with the High Representative in the lead. Iran continues to expand its nuclear activities and international concerns are high. The High Representative, together with the 'E3/ E3+3',[6] continues to lead intensive diplomatic efforts to engage Iran in a process of substantial talks which will restore the confidence in the exclusively peaceful nature of the Iranian nuclear programme. Here, we have a dual track approach of diplomatic engagement and pressure. EU sanctions will remain in place until Iran creates conditions to bring these sanctions to an end by engaging in serious negotiations aimed at restoring confidence in the exclusively peaceful nature of its nuclear programme and by complying with all its international obligations.

Africa is another priority, and one which is being responded to also through an increased focus on regional strategies, which have been agreed for both the Horn of Africa and the Sahel. The EU had started developing a comprehensive 'Strategy for the Security and Development in the Sahel' already some years back.[7] Its objective is to support national and regional strategies aimed at restoring regional and state authority and conditions for stability in the region. This global approach is currently being implemented in Mauritania, Niger and Mali, in close coordination with Algeria. It takes a truly comprehensive approach, including support to security forces and border services, as well as development cooperation.

In the coming period, the restoration of security and stability in Mali will continue to occupy an important place in EU activities in the Sahel region albeit always as part of an overall comprehensive approach. The EU training mission in Mali will help improve the military capacity of the Malian Armed Forces in order to allow, under civilian authority, the restoration of the country's territorial integrity. In parallel, the EU will continue to work with international actors, including ECOWAS, to provide support for the African-led International Support Mission to Mali and eventual further stabilization measures.

The Horn of Africa is a region where the EU has adopted a truly holistic approach. Here, attention has been placed on achieving a well-balanced and coherent mix of diplomatic, crisis management, development and humanitarian assistance tools. Particular mention needs to be given to the EU NVFOR Atalanta maritime mission, which is countering piracy off the coast of Somalia. This mission has been successful, as witnessed by a significant drop in the number of attacks by pirates. In parallel to our own naval presence, the EU is building regional maritime capacity to fight piracy. In Somalia, we are also supporting governance, the rule of law and security, by providing training to police and judges, as well

---

6　The 'E3' refer to France, Germany and the United Kingdom, while the 'E3+3' includes as well China, Russia and the United States.

7　Council of the European Union 2011. *Strategy for Security and Development in the Sahel*, Annex to the Council Conclusions on a European Union Strategy for Security and Development in the Sahel, Brussels, 21 March.

as supporting the development of Somalia's security capacities and the African Union peacekeeping forces. While the situation in the region remains volatile, the comprehensive approach of the strategy is bearing fruit, and gives a good basis for long-term involvement.

The picture of the neighbours of the EU's neighbours would not be complete without a few words on Central Asia. This region is a growing priority. We have had a Central Asia Strategy in place since 2007.[8] The establishment of the EEAS has further assisted us in its implementation in a more coherent manner, bringing to bear the EU's entire toolbox. Following the High Representative's visit to Central Asia in late 2012, we decided to launch a 'High Level Security Dialogue' with all the countries of the region. Our engagement has strengthened in the increasingly important area of counter-terrorism with a recently agreed 'Joint Plan of Action' with all five Central Asian countries for the implementation of the UN Counter-Terrorism Strategy in Central Asia.[9] We are active in countering narcotics trafficking, and have agreed an updated 'EU-Central Asia Drug Action Plan'.[10] The EU is also visibly and importantly engaged on border management. Structured human right dialogues have also been put in place with all five countries, complemented by regional and bilateral civil society seminars involving local and European NGOs. The EU is the only external actor dealing with these issues in the region. Focus is also being placed on water resources management, energy, education and the rule of law. The EU Special Representative for Central Asia has been in the lead in coordinating EU efforts in the region.

Summing up and concluding my contribution to this important publication, I need to admit that the challenges of our neighbourhood, both in the narrower and broader senses of the term, are complex, and at times even daunting. At the same time, the implementation of the Lisbon external relations architecture is still in its early stages. However, already now, we can look at the steps we have taken in responding to these challenges with a sense of satisfaction, at times even pride. Success in facing the challenges of the early twenty-first century will not – but also probably cannot – be immediate or easy. We can be satisfied of the fact that we are well on the way forward. Moreover, we can safely say, as an old Frank Sinatra song says, that the best is yet to come.

What we know is that we stand here on the threshold of a new kind of world. This world is both fast-moving and interconnected. It moves in real time and often gives us very little time to reflect. It is certainly a much more challenging and complex world than any generation before ours has known. It is not based on the monopoly of state actors. Neither is it based solely on so-called Western leadership.

---

8 Council of the European Union 2007. *European Union and Central Asia: Strategy for a New Partnership*, 10113/07, Brussels, 2 May.

9 United Nations 2011. Joint Plan of Action, 30 November, http://www.un.org/en/terrorism/ctitf/pdfs/final_joint_action_plan_en.pdf [accessed: 5 November 2012].

10 Council of the European Union 2009. *2009–2013 Action Plan on Drugs between the EU and Central Asian States*, 9961/09, Brussels, 19 May.

The time immediately after the end of the Cold War when many thought that Western values had won out on the global level had passed. We needed to learn more humility.

The challenges we are facing, and the responses I have described above, demonstrate that the changes in the EU's foreign policy architecture brought about by the Lisbon Treaty were very timely. They were necessary to enable the EU to become an adaptive twenty-first century global actor. Not only do we have to be more agile than before, but we need to be able to continue doing what we do best, in the most efficient manner: finding cooperative win-win solutions, based on good governance, benefiting from our entire toolbox in a coherent and holistic manner. I am personally convinced that this remains the best way to advance security and stability in our neighbourhood, with our neighbours' neighbours, and globally.

Bibliography

Council of the European Union 2007. *European Union and Central Asia: Strategy for a New Partnership*, 10113/07, Brussels, 2 May.

Council of the European Union 2009. *2009–2013 Action Plan on Drugs between the EU and Central Asian States*, 9961/09, Brussels, 19 May.

Council of the European Union 2011. *Strategy for Security and Development in the Sahel*, Annex to the Council Conclusions on a European Union Strategy for Security and Development in the Sahel, Brussels, 21 March.

Council of the European Union 2012. 3209th Council meeting Foreign Affairs, Press Release, 17438/1/12 REV 1, PRESSE 516, Brussels, 10 December.

European Council 2003. *European Security Strategy, 'A Secure Europe in a Better World'*, Brussels, 12 December 2003.

Prodi, R. 2002. *A Wider Europe – A Proximity Policy as the Key to Stability*, Speech/02/619, Sixth ECSA-World Conference, Brussels, 5–6 December 2002.

United Nations 2011. Joint Plan of Action, 30 November, http://www. un.org/en/terrorism/ctitf/pdfs/final_joint_action_plan_en.pdf [accessed: 5 November 2012].

Preface

This edited volume builds on the presentations and discussions at the international conference 'The Neighbours of the EU's Neighbours: Diplomatic and Geopolitical Dimensions beyond the European Neighbourhood Policy' which gathered scholars and practitioners to reflect on the European Union's broader neighbourhood at the College of Europe in Bruges, Belgium, in November 2012. The presentations were subsequently revised and updated, while new contributors joined the project.

The concept of the 'neighbours of the neighbours' of the European Union, introduced by the European Commission in the framework of the European Neighbourhood Policy (ENP), refers mainly to countries in Saharan Africa, the Middle East and Central Asia. This book explores this concept and examines the EU's relations with the neighbours of the ENP countries and other EU neighbours not included in the ENP framework as well as the current and potential bridges between the EU, its 'immediate' and 'broader neighbourhood'. It is the first full length study of this kind. The contributions to this volume were largely completed in late 2013 and thus before Russia's occupation of Crimea in March 2014 and the political crisis in eastern Ukraine.

We gratefully acknowledge the financial support of the European Commission for this project.

Sieglinde Gstöhl and Erwan Lannon
Bruges, June 2014

Chapter 1

Introduction: The 'Neighbours of the EU's Neighbours', the 'EU's Broader Neighbourhood' and the 'Arc of Crisis and Strategic Challenges' from the Sahel to Central Asia

Erwan Lannon

Introduction

We are currently witnessing the rapid development of a new 'arc of crisis and strategic challenges' from the Sahel to Central Asia. A sort of 'second ring' has been emerging around the 'EU's immediate neighbourhood circle', that Romano Prodi, the then President of the European Commission, described as a 'ring of friends' when the European Neighbourhood Policy (ENP) was launched.[1] Obviously the current destabilization of some of the 'neighbours of the EU's neighbours' has and will have a strong impact on the stability and security of the EU and its neighbours.

Indeed, it is impossible today to properly address the situation in Libya without referring to the situation in Mali and in the Sahel at large or the one in Egypt without mentioning the role played by Saudi Arabia or Qatar.[2] The evolution of the civil war in Syria is unfortunately a very good example where all neighbours of this country, as well as external actors/powers, play a role in or are affected by the conflict. These are just a few examples among many others in the EU's broader southern neighbourhoods. In the East, the Russian Federation is an EU neighbour but also a neighbour of EU neighbours included in the ENP like Ukraine or the Southern Caucasus countries. Russia is also a direct neighbour of Kazakhstan and Turkmenistan via the Caspian Sea.[3]

---

1   Prodi, R. 2002. *A Wider Europe – A Proximity Policy as the Key to Stability*, Sixth ECSA-World Conference, Brussels, 5–6 December, SPEECH/02/619, http://europa.eu/rapid/press-release-SPEECH-02-619-en.htm [accessed: 22 March 2014].

2   See Chapter 6 by Silvia Colombo and Chapter 5 by Andrew Bower and Raphaël Metais.

3   See Maps I and IV in the Annex.

The neighbours of the enlarged EU are thus European, African and Asian and are located in a particular regional environment that must be taken into consideration in order to reach the three general objectives of the ENP: stability, security and prosperity. Good neighbourly relations are a key principle enshrined in Article 8 of the Treaty on European Union (TEU), the current legal basis for developing a 'special relationship with neighbouring countries'.[4]

The main objective of this contribution is to introduce the concepts of the 'neighbours of the EU's neighbours' and of the 'EU's broader neighbourhood' and to identify and categorize, as clearly as possible, the countries and (sub-)regions which are at the heart of the analyses conducted in this volume. These two notions are in fact quite difficult to circumscribe. For instance, China is a neighbour of an EU neighbour (Russia) but is not taken into consideration as such in this analysis but as one of the 'global players in the EU's broader neighbourhood'.[5] Also, if one considers all EU maritime borders, this could lead us to the Arctic and the Pacific Ocean via the US, Norway, Canada and Russia. It is thus important to limit, as clearly as possible, the scope of the analysis to countries and regions that can be relatively well identified and that do belong to the same geopolitical areas. This is not an easy task as, for example, a neighbour of the EU might not necessarily be included (yet) in the European Neighbourhood Policy framework (Libya, Switzerland or Turkey). Moreover, some partners of the EU which are included in the ENP are not necessarily direct neighbours of EU Member States, geographically speaking (Armenia, Azerbaijan and Jordan).[6]

In 2006 the European Commission introduced the concept of the neighbours of the EU's neighbours at a time when the ENP was just about to become fully operational.[7] However, since then not much has been achieved despite the war in Mali and its repercussions in Algeria and Libya, the further regionalization of the Syrian conflict or the deterioration of the human rights situation in some Central Asian countries.[8] It is true that the EU, notably in Africa, has designed sub-regional

---

4   Article 8 of the TEU states: '1. The Union shall develop a special relationship with neighbouring countries, aiming to establish an area of prosperity and good neighbourliness, founded on the values of the Union and characterised by close and peaceful relations based on cooperation. 2. For the purposes of paragraph 1, the Union may conclude specific agreements with the countries concerned. These agreements may contain reciprocal rights and obligations as well as the possibility of undertaking activities jointly. Their implementation shall be the subject of periodic consultation'. See also Hanf, D. 2012. The European Neighbourhood Policy in the Light of the New 'Neighbourhood Clause' (Article 8 TEU), in Lannon, E. (ed.), *The European Neighbourhood Policy's Challenges/Les défis de la politique européenne de voisinage*. Brussels: Peter Lang, 109–23.

5   See Chapter 12 by Jonatan Thompson in this volume.

6   See Map I in the Annex.

7   The European Neighbourhood and Partnership Instrument (ENPI) entered into force on 1 January 2007.

8   See Chapter 8 by Francesca Fenton in this volume.

initiatives[9] and that several missions and operations under the Common Security and Defence Policy (CSDP) have been launched but it is still difficult to identify a long-term and comprehensive EU strategy regarding the 'neighbours of its neighbours' or some kind of 'broader neighbourhood strategy'. It is therefore urgent to draw the attention of decision-makers to this strategic deficit. The necessity of updating the EU's approach is obvious in the light of the consolidation of this 'arc of crisis and strategic challenges' and implies identifying the means and instruments at the disposal of the EU to tackle all kinds of transnational factors of destabilization.[10] It is also fundamental to look for potential areas of transnational cooperation and to consider this geopolitical area not only as a threat, but also as an opportunity for further linkages and cooperation across the traditional EU frameworks for cooperation.

In order to introduce these challenges and concepts, we will address three main points:

1. the consolidation of an 'arc of crisis and strategic challenges' from the Sahel to Central Asia via the Horn of Africa[11] and the Arabian Gulf;
2. the EU's neighbours and their neighbours; and
3. the emergence of the concept of the 'neighbours of our neighbours'.

The Consolidation of an 'Arc of Crisis and Strategic Challenges' from the Sahel to Central Asia via the Horn of Africa and the Arabian Gulf

Since the launching of the present project on the neighbours of the EU's neighbours in 2012,[12] the situation has dramatically evolved. The perception of the development of an arc of crisis and instability surrounding the EU's neighbours is now shared by the Secretary General of the North Atlantic Treaty Organization (NATO), Anders Fogh Rasmussen, who declared at the Munich Security Conference in February 2013: 'when I look at our world, I see an arc of crises stretching from the Sahel to Central Asia'.[13] In October 2013, the annual report of the European Parliament on the Common Foreign and Security Policy (CFSP) also referred to an 'arc of strategic challenges stretching from Central Asia to the Middle East and from the

---

9 See notably the contributions of David O'Sullivan (Foreword), Alexander Mattelaer (Chapter 3), Alex Vines and Ahmed Soliman (Chapter 4) and Claudia Zulaika (Chapter 2) in this volume.

10 Terrorism, organized crime, illegal immigration, etc.

11 See Chapter 4 by Alex Vines and Ahmed Soliman in this volume.

12 See College of Europe 2012. *The Neighbours of the EU's Neighbours: Diplomatic and Geopolitical Dimensions beyond the ENP – Conference Summary*. Bruges: College of Europe, 15–16 November. https://www.coleurope.eu/sites/default/files/uploads/page/conference-summary.pdf [accessed: 22 March 2014].

13 NATO 2013. *NATO after ISAF – staying successful together*, Remarks by NATO Secretary General Anders Fogh Rasmussen at the Munich Security Conference, 2 February, http://www.nato.int/cps/en/natolive/opinions-94321.htm [accessed: 22 March 2014].

Horn of Africa across the Sahel'.[14] It is proposed, in this introduction, to combine the 'strategic' and 'political' approaches to work on the concept of an 'arc of crisis and strategic challenges' that take stock of the existing and potential crises in this area while, at the same time, calling for a more proactive policy to tackle the challenges the EU is facing. The impact of the successive and interlinked wars in Libya, Mali and Syria extends far beyond the Sahel, the Horn of Africa and the Gulf, while, at the same time, the EU's direct neighbours are confronted with serious, if not critical, challenges; Libya, Syria and Ukraine being at a crossroad in the first quarter of 2014.

This concept of an 'arc of crisis and strategic challenges' should not be confused with what Zbigniew Brzezinski described in January 1979, in a Cold War context, as a 'crescent of crisis' stretching 'along the shores of the Indian Ocean, with fragile social and political structures in a region of vital importance to us threatened with fragmentation'.[15] Still in 1979 and in the same vein, George Lenczowski published in *Foreign Affairs* an article entitled 'The Arc of Crisis: Its Central Sector'.[16] His argument was that the Middle East constituted the core of this arc of crisis:

> Its strategic position is unequalled: it is the last major region of the Free World directly adjacent to the Soviet Union, it holds in its subsoil about three-fourths of the proven and estimated world oil reserves, and it is the locus of one of the most intractable conflicts of the twentieth century: that of Zionism versus Arab nationalism. Moreover, national, economic and territorial conflicts are aggravated by the intrusion of religious passions in an area which was the birthplace of Judaism, Christianity and Islam, and by the exposure, in the twentieth century, to two competing appeals of secular modernization: Western and communist.[17]

This specific concept of a 'crescent/arc of crisis', developed in 1979, aimed in fact mainly at destabilizing the Soviet Union during the Cold War. Bernard Lewis updated this approach in 1992 for the post-Cold War era and the 'crescent of

---

14   The European Parliament stressed in its Resolution on the Annual Report from the Council to the European Parliament on the Common Foreign and Security Policy that 'negotiations with Iran' and the 'EU-facilitated dialogue between Kosovo and Serbia' should be considered as 'examples of leadership and priority-setting' and 'should be applied further in the EU's candidate and potential candidate countries and in its neighbourhood, and in response to an arc of strategic challenges stretching from Central Asia to the Middle East and from the Horn of Africa across the Sahel'. European Parliament 2013. *Annual Report from the Council to the European Parliament on the Common Foreign and Security Policy*, Committee on Foreign Affairs, Rapporteur: Elmar Brok, A7–0330/2013, Brussels, 15 October.

15   Brzezinski, Z. 1979. Iran: The Crescent of Crisis. *TIME Magazine*, 15 January, http://content.time.com/time/magazine/article/0,9171,919995,00.html#ixzz2tHbAjOuO [accessed: 22 March 2014].

16   Lenczowski, G. 1979. The Arc of Crisis: Its Central Sector. *Foreign Affairs*, Spring, http://www.foreignaffairs.com/articles/32309/george-lenczowski/the-arc-of-crisis-its-central-sector [accessed: 22 March 2014].

17   Ibid.

crisis' reappeared a year later as a 'crescent-shaped Islamic bloc of nations from the bulge of Africa to central Asia' in the famous article of Samuel Huntington entitled 'The Clash of Civilizations?'.[18] Interestingly, the concept of an 'arc of crisis' resurfaced more recently in the 2008 French White Paper on Security and Defence that identified among the major threats for French security an 'arc of crisis from the Atlantic to the Indian Ocean':

> This region is not a homogeneous entity. Each country has its own identity and its own history, its own political, social, economic and human dynamics. Regional subsets have their own logic. That of the Sahel, from Mauritania to Somalia, is clearly distinguishable from the borders of the Mediterranean, the Near East and the Arabian-Persian Gulf or from Afghanistan and Pakistan. But, in this part of the world, in the vicinity of Europe, in the heart of strategic interests to global security, essential changes modify the security of France and Europe. The development of radical Islam, the antagonisms between Sunnis and Shiites, the Kurdish question and the fragility of political regimes are an explosive mixture. The new risk of a connection of conflicts emerges between the Near and the Middle East and the regions of Pakistan and Afghanistan.[19]

Some analysts across the Atlantic are now even referring to a '2.0 arc of crisis',[20] but what about the European Union? Is this 'arc of crisis and strategic challenges' not even more critical for the EU than for the US? Yet, the EU should avoid launching

---

18   Lewis, B. 1992. Rethinking the Middle East. *Foreign Affairs*, Fall. It is also interesting to quote the paragraph of Samuel Huntington while pointing out his own quote of Bernard Lewis (at 32): 'In Eurasia the great historic fault lines between civilizations are once more aflame. This is particularly true along the boundaries of the *crescent-shaped Islamic bloc of nations from the bulge of Africa to central Asia*. Violence also occurs between Muslims, on the one hand, and orthodox Serbs in the Balkans, Jews in Israel, Hindu in India, Buddhists in Burma and Catholics in the Philippines. Islam has bloody borders'. [emphasis added]. Huntington, S.P. 1993. The Clash of Civilizations? *Foreign Affairs*, 72(3), 22–49.

19   Présidence de la République Française – Commission du livre blanc sur la défense et la sécurité nationale 2008. *Défense et sécurité nationale – Le Livre Blanc*. Paris: Odile Jacob and La Documentation Française, juin, 43–4, http://www.ladocumentationfrancaise. fr/var/storage/rapports-publics/084000341/0000.pdf [accessed: 22 March 2014] [author's translation]. Note that the White Paper was prefaced by the then French President Nicolas Sarkozy. In the still provisional 2013 edition, prefaced by President François Hollande, it is emphasized that France should have the military capabilities to engage in priority zones of action like the 'European periphery', the 'Mediterranean Basin', parts of Africa 'from the Sahel to equatorial Africa', the 'Arabian-Persian Gulf' and the 'Indian Ocean'. Présidence de la République Française – Commission du livre blanc sur la défense et la sécurité nationale 2013. *Défense et sécurité nationale – Le Livre Blanc 2013*. Paris: La Documentation Française, 135–6 [accessed: 22 March 2014].

20   Rehman, I. 2013. Arc of Crisis 2.0? *National Interest*, 7 March, http://nationalinterest.org/commentary/arc-crisis-20–8194?page=2 [accessed: 22 March 2014].

a strategy whose only aim would be to fill a gap or to react to a third country initiative. This is more or less what happened with the Strategic Partnership with the Mediterranean and the Middle East (SPMME) which was more a reaction to the Bush Administration's so-called 'Greater Middle East approach'[21] than a genuine long-term and comprehensive EU strategy.[22]

Addressing the consolidation of this 'arc of crisis and strategic challenges' is indeed a major challenge for the EU and its Member States, not only because of the seriousness of the security situation but also because of the heterogeneity of relationships established between the EU, its neighbours and their neighbours.

The European Union's Neighbours and their Neighbours

In order to apprehend properly this complex situation, it is important to proceed with a systematic approach starting with the neighbours of the European Union, most of which are linked (or not) to the EU via different agreements and frameworks.[23]

The EU's Neighbours

The first EU's neighbours to be examined here are those included, or to be included in the ENP framework.

The EU's Neighbours Included (or to Be Included) in the ENP Framework

The EU partners that are fully included in the ENP framework benefiting from a Partnership and Cooperation Agreement (PCA) or an Association Agreement (AA) and an ENP Action Plan can be divided into three categories:

1. the Southern and Eastern Mediterranean countries: Morocco, Tunisia, Egypt, Palestinian territories, Israel and Jordan;
2. the Southern Caucasus countries: Armenia, Georgia and Azerbaijan; and
3. the Eastern European countries: Moldova and Ukraine.

Hence, 11 countries from three different regions have to be taken into consideration in this category. In fact, three of them are not direct neighbours of the EU,

---

21   Followed by the G8 2004 'Broader Middle East and North Africa (BMENA) initiative'.

22   See Carothers, T. and Ottaway, M. 2004. Greater Middle East Initiative: Off to a False Start. *Carnegie Policy Outlook*, no. 29, 18 March, http://carnegieendowment.org/files/Policybrief29.pdf; and Sharp, J.M. 2005. The Broader Middle East and North Africa Initiative: An Overview. *CRS Report for Congress*. Washington, DC: Library of Congress, 15 February, https://www.fas.org/sgp/crs/mideast/RS22053.pdf [accessed: 22 March 2014].

23   See Map I in the Annex.

geographically speaking, be it from a maritime or terrestrial point of view (Armenia, Azerbaijan and Jordan). What is striking is that Armenia and Azerbaijan are in fact neighbours of an EU neighbour that is not included in the ENP framework (Turkey). Another interesting case is Jordan which is a neighbour of Syria, Israel and the Palestinian territories (the West Bank) and is fully included in the ENP although this country does not share a common border with the EU. In other words, the European Union obviously followed a geopolitical rather than a strictly geographical approach in the design of the ENP. This is not a 'new approach' as Jordan has been, since the 1970s, considered by the EEC as belonging to the so-called 'Third Mediterranean Countries' (TMC) group, although it has no direct access to the *Mare Nostrum*. One should also note that the three Caucasus countries were included in the ENP framework only in 2004, after Russia refused to participate.[24] If in the future, Turkey would join the EU, Armenia and Azerbaijan would then become direct geographical neighbours of the EU, but the same would then also apply to Iraq and Iran. Jordan will, however, remain a specific case. Also, theoretically speaking, it could be possible for Iraq to join the Mediterranean Partner Countries group (MPCs).

The countries that are supposed to be addressed by the EU through the ENP framework but have not yet concluded an Association Agreement or an ENP Action Plan are the following:

- Algeria (concluded an Association Agreement, but only in 2012 did Algiers decide to negotiate an ENP Action Plan);
- Belarus (the PCA ratification has been frozen and there is no ENP Action Plan);[25]
- Libya (has no contractual relations with the EU and no ENP Action Plan);[26]

---

24   In 2002–03 the three Southern Caucasus states were not included in the ENP. The European Commission made that proposal in 2004 after Russia's refusal to take part of the ENP despite the fact that Russia was the primary target of the original ENP plans. See European Council 2002. *Presidency Conclusions*, 12 and 13 December, point 24; and European Commission 2004. Communication from the Commission. *European Neighbourhood Policy – Strategy Paper*, COM(2004) 373 final, Brussels, 12 May, 7.

25   According to Directorate-General Trade: 'In response to Belarus' lack of commitment to democracy and political and civil rights, the EU has not yet ratified the bilateral Partnership and Cooperation Agreement concluded with Belarus in 1995. The bilateral trade and economic relations therefore remain covered by the Trade and Cooperation Agreement – concluded by the European Community with the Soviet Union in 1989 and subsequently endorsed by Belarus'. European Commission 2014. Belarus, http://ec.europa.eu/trade/policy/countries-and-regions/countries/belarus [accessed: 22 March 2014].

26   According to DG Trade the negotiations for a 'Framework Agreement between the EU and Libya started in November 2008'. The aim was to include a 'Free Trade Agreement covering trade in goods, services and investment' (with a focus on 'services and establishment, public procurement and gas and oil markets'). However, 'following the events in early 2011 in Libya, negotiations were suspended in February 2011'. http://ec.europa.eu/trade/policy/countries-and-regions/countries/libya [accessed: 22 March 2014].

•   Syria (the EMAA has not been signed and there is no ENP Action Plan).

Algeria could leave this category immediately if the negotiations of the ENP Action Plan are finalized but the three other countries might stay much longer in this 'ENP grey area'.

The EU's Neighbours Not Included in the ENP Framework

Among the other European neighbours of the EU which are not included in the ENP framework, Russia and Turkey are two powers deserving special attention by the EU on account of their geopolitical importance.

Russia is one of the most important EU neighbours which is not included in the ENP. It is worthwhile to stress that originally the ENP was precisely designed to deal with the potential impact of the 'big bang' enlargement (2004–07) on the so-called 'new neighbours' and, first of all, Russia. However, Russia refused to be fully included in the ENP but was nevertheless listed among the beneficiaries of the European Neighbourhood and Partnership Instrument (ENPI).[27] The EU-Russia Strategic Partnership and the four Common Spaces now shape the EU-Russia relationship and Russia is not included in the list of beneficiaries of the new European Neighbourhood Instrument (ENI).[28]

Turkey is also a very important regional power with global ambitions[29] and included in the EU's pre-accession strategy (as a 'negotiating country') but not in the ENP framework. It therefore benefits from the Instrument for Pre-accession Assistance (IPA). In 2006 the European Commission stressed, however, that at the level of regional cooperation with the 'partner countries around the Black Sea', the EU should be 'fully inclusive, whatever the formal context of its bilateral relations with these countries',[30] referring explicitly to Turkey and Russia.

---

27   European Parliament and of the Council of the European Union 2006. *Regulation (EC) No 1638/2006 of the European Parliament and of the Council of 24 October 2006 laying down general provisions establishing a European Neighbourhood and Partnership Instrument.* OJ L 310/1, 9 November.

28   Beneficiaries of the 2014–2020 ENI are: Algeria, Armenia, Azerbaijan, Belarus, Egypt, Georgia, Israel, Jordan, Lebanon, Libya, Moldova, Morocco, occupied Palestinian territory (oPt), Syria, Tunisia, Ukraine. See Annex of the Proposal for a Regulation of the European Parliament and the Council establishing a European Neighbourhood Instrument, COM(2011) 839 final. See also Adomeit, H. 2012. *Russia: ENP Competitor,* in Lannon, E. (ed.), *The European Neighbourhood Policy's Challenges/Les défis de la politique européenne de voisinage.* Brussels: Peter Lang, 381–409.

29   Evin, A. et al. 2010. *Getting to ZERO: Turkey, Its Neighbors and the West.* Washington, DC: Transatlantic Academy, August, http://www.transatlanticacademy.org/sites/default/files/publications/GettingtoZeroFINAL.pdf [accessed: 22 March 2014].

30   European Commission 2006. *Communication from the Commission to the Council and the European Parliament on Strengthening the European Neighbourhood Policy,* COM(2006)726 final, Brussels, 4 December, point 3.6.

Other European countries which are not included in the ENP framework and not taken into consideration in the chapters of this volume, but which are also neighbours of the EU, include:[31]

- In the Balkans:[32] Albania is included in the Euro-Mediterranean Partnership (EMP) since 2007 and the in the UfM, Kosovo (remains a special case)[33], Serbia ('negotiating country' since January 2014), Bosnia Herzegovina, the Former Yugoslav Republic of Macedonia (FYROM) and Montenegro are potential candidates[34] and Bosnia Herzegovina and Montenegro are also members of the UfM;
- Iceland,[35] Liechtenstein and Norway are, as members of the European Free Trade Association (EFTA), included in the European Economic Area (EEA);
- Switzerland, a member of EFTA, is linked to the EU via a large number of bilateral sectoral agreements;[36]
- the specific cases of Andorra (Cooperation Agreement in force since 2005 and Customs Union Agreement in force since 1991); Monaco (included in the UfM[37] and in a Customs Union with the EU through its Customs Union with France),[38] San Marino (Cooperation Agreement and Customs Union agreement in force since 2002) and the Holy See have also to be mentioned here. All four small-sized countries have also concluded monetary agreements or conventions with the EU.[39]

The conclusion is clear: the concept of the EU's neighbours is a 'variable geometry concept' that is not based on a purely geographical analysis. There are obviously strategic and economic interests at work that pushed the EU to go beyond a pure geographical approach in favour of a geopolitical one.

---

31   See Maps I and II in the Annex.

32   See the state of play of bilateral agreements on Map I in the Annex.

33   See European Commission 2013. Kosovo, 2 June, http://ec.europa.eu/enlargement/countries/detailed-country-information/kosovo/index-en.htm [accessed: 22 March 2014].

34   See the website of the Commission's Directorate-General Enlargement, http://ec.europa.eu/enlargement/index-en.htm [accessed: 22 March 2014]; and Map I in the Annex.

35   According to the European Commission: Iceland is a 'candidate country, accession negotiations started in July 2010 and were put on hold by the Icelandic government in May 2013'. European Commission 2014. Iceland, 11 March, http://ec.europa.eu/enlargement/countries/detailed-country-information/iceland/index-en.htm [accessed: 22 March 2014].

36   Because of the negative outcome of the December 1992 referendum, Switzerland is not taking part in the EEA.

37   See Map II in the Annex.

38   Council of the European Union 2011. *Relations entre l'UE et la Principauté d'Andorre, la République de Saint-Marin et la Principauté de Monaco*, Brussels, 14 June, http://register.consilium.europa.eu/doc/srv?l=FRandf=ST%2011466%202011%20INIT [accessed: 22 March 2014].

39   Ibid.

In the following part we will try to evaluate whether or not a similar, flexible approach can be developed vis-à-vis the neighbours of the EU's neighbours.

The 'Neighbours of the EU's Neighbours' and the 'EU's Broader Neighbourhood'

If one considers that the concept of the 'EU's neighbours' can be extended to countries not necessarily sharing any terrestrial or maritime border with an EU Member State but belonging to the ENP geopolitical framework, we have three main regions to take into consideration – Africa, the Arabian Gulf and Central Asia – in order to identify the neighbours of the EU's neighbours.[40] Thus, two approaches can be envisaged: a strictly geographical approach in terms of the 'neighbours of the EU's neighbours'; and a broader geopolitical approach covering the 'EU's broader neighbourhood'.

The Geographical Approach: The 'Neighbours of the EU's Neighbours'

The following neighbours of the EU's neighbours are obviously at the heart of the analyses of this volume:[41]

- in Africa: (Western Sahara), Mauritania, Mali, Niger, Chad, and Sudan;
- in the Middle East: Iraq, Iran, and Saudi Arabia; and
- in Central Asia: Kazakhstan and Turkmenistan.

Hence, 10 countries and a territory listed by the UN as a 'Non-Self-Governing Territory'[42] – the Western Sahara – can be identified as 'neighbours of the EU's neighbours'. Note that all Asian neighbours of Russia are in principle direct neighbours of the EU's neighbours (China, Japan, Mongolia) but they obviously belong to another East Asian geopolitical framework.

The Geopolitical Approach: The 'EU's Broader Neighbourhood'

Another possibility is to consider a wider regional approach that can be called the 'EU's broader neighbourhood'. In this case three 'macro-regions' can be distinguished. The first macro-region is Africa. On the one hand, the African continent is a potential framework of EU cooperation given the relationships established between the African Union[43] (AU), and the EU and the Africa-EU

---

40   See Map III in the Annex.

41   Ibid.

42   United Nations 2014. *Non-Self-Governing Territories*, http://www.un.org/en/decolonization/nonselfgovterritories.shtml. See also United Nations 2014. *UN Documents for Western Sahara*, http://www.securitycouncilreport.org/un-documents/western-sahara; and the UN map of Western Sahara at: http://www.un.org/Depts/Cartographic/map/profile/wsahara.pdf [accessed: 22 March 2014].

43   See Map III in the Annex.

Strategic Partnership is part of the so-called African 'continental approach'.[44] On the other hand, the EU has developed two additional major frameworks for cooperation: the ENP framework for North Africa and the Cotonou framework for the rest of the African countries.[45] The contributors of this volume also look at two sub-regions: the Sahel in a large sense[46] and the Horn of Africa more specifically.[47]

The second macro-region is the Middle East. It includes the Arabian Peninsula (the GCC and Yemen), Iraq and Iran[48] but also the Near East that is covered by the ENP (with the exception of Syria, for the time being). Linkages between the Horn of Africa and Yemen have also been identified.[49] In the Arabian Gulf, a free trade agreement (FTA) with the EU[50] has been on the EU-GCC agenda for a while but despite the design in June 2004 of a Strategic Partnership with the Mediterranean and the Middle East,[51] not much has been achieved in the Euro-Arab relations until a few years ago when the channel between the EU and the League of Arab States was (re-)activated. In Table 1.1 all members of the Arab League are mentioned, with the exception of Djibouti and Comoros. They can,

---

44   Council of the European Union 2007. *The Africa-EU Strategic Partnership – A Joint Africa-EU Strategy*, Lisbon, 9 December, 16344/07 Press 291, http://www.consilium. europa.eu/uedocs/cms-data/docs/pressdata/en/er/97496.pdf; European External Action Service 2014. *Africa: The Continental Approach*, http://eeas.europa.eu/africa/continental/ index_en.htm [accessed: 22 March 2014].

45   See the contributions of Andrew Bower and Raphaël Metais (Chapter 5), David O'Sullivan (Foreword) and Claudia Zulaika (Chapter 2) in this volume and Map III in the Annex.

46   See the contributions of Alexander Mattelaer (Chapter 3), David O'Sullivan (Foreword) and Claudia Zulaika (Chapter 2) in this volume. For the EEAS: 'The three core Sahelian states, and the focus of this Strategy (for Security and Development in the Sahel), are Mauritania, Mali and Niger, though the geographical conditions – and therefore challenges – also affect parts of Burkina Faso and Chad'. Council of the European Union. 2011. *Strategy for Security and Development in the Sahel*, Annex to the Council Conclusions on a European Union Strategy for Security and Development in the Sahel, Brussels, 21 March. The Horn of Africa includes Djibouti, Eritrea, Ethiopia, Somalia (see Map VI in the Annex). It seems also difficult to exclude South Sudan and the northern part of the Central African Republic from the picture although they do not belong to the Sahel region or the Horn of Africa (see Map III in the Annex).

47   Council of the European Union 2009. *EU policy on the Horn of Africa – Towards a comprehensive strategy*, Brussels, 10 December. See Chapter 4 by Alex Vines and Ahmed Soliman in this volume.

48   See Chapter 7 by Clément Therme in this volume.

49   See Chapter 5 by Andrew Bower and Raphaël Metais and Chapter 2 by Claudia Zulaika in this volume.

50   See the Chapter 6 by Silvia Columbo as well as Chapter 5 by Andrew Bower and Raphaël Metais in this volume.

51   European Council 2004. *Final Report: EU Strategic Partnership with the Mediterranean and the Middle East*, June. http://consilium.europa.eu/uedocs/cmsUpload/ Partnership%20Mediterranean%20and%20Middle%20East.pdf [accessed: 22 March 2014].

however, be added as well because Djibouti is a 'strategic platform' for France and the US to intervene in the region[52] and also because of its membership of the Arab League and of the African Union. They are thus briefly covered in two contributions of this volume.[53] The lack of coherence generated by a fragmented EU approach towards the members of the Arab League[54] through so many different cooperation frameworks will hopefully be reduced by the development of the new EU-Arab League dynamic encompassing the 28 EU Member States and the 22 Members of the Arab League in one single framework.[55] One should recall that originally the SPMME was introduced as a means of 'Strengthening the EU's Partnership with the Arab World'.[56] At the same time, there is an obvious interest for the EU to reactivate the SPMME as it includes members of the Arab League like Iraq and Yemen, which are both linked to the EU via bilateral agreements, but not the Arab countries in the group of the African, Caribbean and Pacific (ACP) countries. Iran, Israel and Turkey – three non-Arab powers in the Middle East – deserve particular attention by the EU in the design of any regional strategy as fundamental variables of the Middle East equation which are also covered by the SPMME.

The third macro-region is Central Asia. It includes Kazakhstan and Turkmenistan but also the Caspian Sea area[57] as well as Kyrgyzstan, Tajikistan and Uzbekistan. The EU's Central Asia 'Strategy for a New Partnership' adopted in June 2007[58] is the EU's main framework for cooperation with this region. The EU institutions frequently link Eastern Europe and Central Asia. For instance, in the 2010 'Joint Progress Report by the Council and the European Commission on the implementation of the EU Strategy for Central Asia' it was underlined that 'with EU enlargement, the inclusion of the Southern Caucasus into the European Neighbourhood Policy and the Black Sea Synergy Initiative, Central Asia and the EU are moving closer together'.[59] This is a very important point.

---

52   See Map VI in the Annex.

53   See Chapter 5 by Andrew Bower and Raphaël Metais and Chapter 2 by Claudia Zulaika in this volume and Map VI in the Annex.

54   See Map V in the Annex.

55   Council of the EU 2012. *High Representative Catherine Ashton inaugurates EU funded Crisis Room at League of Arab States*, A 510/12, Cairo, 13 November, http://www.consilium.europa.eu/uedocs/cms-Data/docs/pressdata/EN/foraff/133466.pdf [accessed: 22 March 2014].

56   Patten, C., Solana, J. and Prodi, R. 2003, *Paper for the attention of Franco Frattini, President of the Council, Strengthening the EU's partnership with the Arab world*, D(2003) 10318, Brussels, 4 December, http://www.consilium.europa.eu/uedocs/cms_data/docs/pressdata/en/misc/78358.pdf [accessed: 22 March 2014].

57   See Chapter 9 by Alexander Warkotsch in this volume.

58   See Chapter 8 by Francesca Fenton in this volume, and Council of the European Union 2007. *European Union and Central Asia: Strategy for a New Partnership*, 10113/07, Brussels, 2 May.

59   Ibid., 4.

Obviously, the 2004 decision to include these three Caucasus states in the ENP framework changed the scope of the ENP and enabled the EU to potentially 'connect' three seas: the Mediterranean, the Black Sea and the Caspian Sea. One should not forget that, with the accession of Romania and Bulgaria to the EU in 2007, the EU's terrestrial and maritime borders' reached the Black Sea and the EU consolidated its influence on the edge of the emerging Eurasian Economic Community (EurAsEC).

Strategic energy interests are obviously at stake in this geopolitical design. This was clearly stated in the 2004 ENP 'Strategy Paper':

> Enhancing our strategic energy partnership with neighbouring countries is a major element of the European Neighbourhood Policy. This includes security of energy supply and energy safety and security. The European Union ... is surrounded by the world's most important reserves of oil and natural gas (Russia, the Caspian basin, the Middle East and North Africa). It will increasingly depend on imports, from its current level of 50% to 70% by 2030, on present projections. Neighbouring countries play a vital role in the security of the EU's energy supply. Many countries seek improved access to the EU energy market, either as current or future suppliers (for instance, Russia, Algeria, Egypt, Libya) or as transit countries (Ukraine, Belarus, Morocco, Tunisia). The Southern Caucasus countries are also important in this respect in terms of new energy supplies to the EU from the Caspian region and Central Asia. Improving energy network connections between the EU and its partners, as well as legal and regulatory convergence, are thus strong mutual interests. Moreover, increased energy cooperation provides mutual business opportunities and can also contribute to socio-economic development and improvement to the environment.[60]

---

60 European Commission 2004. *European Neighbourhood Policy Strategy Paper*, COM(2004) 373 final, Brussels, 12 May, 17, 'Connecting the neighbourhood'. This was stated again in the 2008 Report on the Implementation of the European Security Strategy: 'Greater diversification, of fuels, sources of supply, and transit routes, is essential, as are good governance, respect for rule of law and investment in source countries. EU policy supports these objectives through engagement with Central Asia, the Caucasus and Africa, as well as through the Eastern Partnership and the Union for the Mediterranean. Energy is a major factor in EU–Russia relations. Our policy should address transit routes, including through Turkey and Ukraine'. Council of the EU 2008. *Report on the Implementation of the Council of the EU 2008, European Security Strategy – Providing Security in a Changing World*, S407/08, Brussels, 11 December, 5, http://www.consilium.europa.eu/ueDocs/cms-Data/docs/pressdata/EN/reports/104630.pdf [accessed: 22 March 2014].

Within this logic, Central Asian countries were, in 2010, 'invited to participate in regional programmes under the European Neighbourhood Policy in priority areas such as energy, transport, education, environment and water'.[61]

Some authors also address Afghanistan and Pakistan in this volume.[62] Obviously these countries cannot be totally disconnected from the Middle East or Central Asian equations. It is worth noting that the US does take into account these countries in its own MENA (Middle East North Africa) design. Finally, the range of piracy attacks in the Indian Ocean is also playing a role.[63]

Considering only the EU's neighbours and their neighbours and the main EU frameworks for cooperation it is possible to identify more precisely the scope of the analysis in a series of synthetic tables.

Table 1.1   The EU's neighbours and their neighbours: Frameworks of cooperation with the Arab world

Countries and Regions	Main (Sub-) Regional Integration Frameworks	Relations with the European Union		Main EU Financial Instruments
		Multilateral Framework	Bilateral Framework	
Arab League Member Countries (Maghreb, Mashreq, Gulf)				
Maghreb				
Algeria	AMU, GAFTA, AU	SPMME, UfM, (not yet full ENP partner)	EMAA	ENPI/ENI
Libya	AMU, GAFTA, AU	SPMME, UfM, (not yet included in the ENP)	-	ENPI/ENI
Morocco	Agadir, AMU, GAFTA	SPMME, UfM, ENP	EMAA, Advanced status	ENPI/ENI
Mauritania	AMU, AU	SPMME, UfM, (joined the EMP), EU-Africa Strategic Partnership	Cotonou Agreement	EDF
Tunisia	Agadir, AMU, GAFTA, AU	SPMME, UfM, ENP	EMAA Preferential Partnership	ENPI/ENI
Mashreq				
Egypt	Agadir, GAFTA, AU	SPMME, UfM, ENP	EMAA	ENPI/ENI
Jordan	Agadir, GAFTA	SPMME, UfM, ENP	EMAA Advanced status	ENPI/ENI
Iraq	GAFTA	SPMME	PCA signed 11/05/2012	DCI

---

61   Council and European Commission 2010. *Joint Progress Report by the Council and the European Commission to the European Council on the implementation of the EU Strategy for Central Asia*, Brussels, 14 June, Annex, 5, http://register.consilium.europa.eu/pdf/en/10/st11/st11402.en10.pdf [accessed: 22 March 2014].

62   See Chapter 8 by Francesca Fenton, Chapter 5 by Andrew Bower and Raphaël Metais as well as Chapter 12 by Jonatan Thompson in this volume.

63   See Map VI in the Annex.

Lebanon	GAFTA	SPMME, UfM, ENP	EMAA	ENPI/ENI
Palestinian Territories	GAFTA	SPMME, UfM, ENP	Interim EMAA	ENPI/ENI
Syria	GAFTA	SPMME, UfM (not included in ENP)	Old AA[1] suspended	ENPI/ENI but under restrictions

Arab Gulf Countries

Saudi Arabia	GCC, GAFTA	SPMME	EEC-GCC Cooperation Agreement	DCI/ICI/PI
Bahrain	GCC, GAFTA	SPMME	EEC-GCC Cooperation Agreement	ICI/PI
United Arab Emirates	GCC, GAFTA	SPMME	EEC-GCC Cooperation Agreement	ICI/PI
Kuwait	GCC, GAFTA	SPMME	EEC-GCC Cooperation Agreement	ICI/PI
Oman	GCC, GAFTA	SPMME	EEC-GCC Cooperation Agreement	DCI/ICI/PI
Qatar	GCC, GAFTA	SPMME	EEC-GCC Cooperation Agreement	ICI, PI
Yemen	GAFTA	SPMME	Cooperation Agreement	DCI

Other Arab League Member Countries included in the ACP Countries Group (excl. Mauritania, Djibouti and Comoros)

Somalia		EU-Africa Strategic Partnership	Not a signatory of Cotonou yet but in 2013 Somalia's request for observership and subsequent accession to the Cotonou Agreement was approved.[2]	EDF
Sudan	GAFTA	EU-Africa Strategic Partnership	Signatory of Cotonou, did not ratify the 2005 revised Cotonou Agreement	EDF (9th)[3]

Notes: 1   Note that this agreement although entitled 'cooperation agreement' is in fact an 'association agreement' based on the former article 238 of the EEC Treaty.
2   ACP-EU Council of Ministers 2013. S*atisfactory outcome; Good compromise on EDF*;
3   See European Commission 2009. Non-ratification of the revised Cotonou Agreement by Sudan FAQ, Brussels, August, http://ec.europa.eu/development/icenter/repository/ sudan_final_non-ratification_faq_200908.pdf [accessed: 22 March 2014]. *Welcome to Somalia*, Brussels, ACP Press Release, 7 June, http://www.acp.int/fr/node/1991 [accessed: 22 March 2014].

In Table 1.1 the countries were chosen on the basis of their affiliation with the
Arab League in order to understand the complexity of the EU-Arab relationships.
Table 1.2 illustrates the diversity of the relationships established with non-Arab
countries in the Sahel and in the Middle East.

**Table 1.2   The EU's neighbours and their neighbours: Frameworks
of cooperation with non-Arab African and Middle
Eastern countries**

African, Non-Arab ACP Countries				
Mali	ECOWAS	EU-Africa Strategic Partnership	Cotonou Agreement	EDF
Niger	ECOWAS	EU-Africa Strategic Partnership	Cotonou Agreement	EDF
Chad	CEMAC	EU-Africa Strategic Partnership	Cotonou Agreement	EDF
Other Non-Arab Countries in the Middle East				
Iran	SCO	SPMME		(DCI)
Israel	–	UfM, ENP, SPMME, EMP	EMAA	ENPI/ ENI
Turkey	BSEC	SPMME, UfM, founding member of the EMP (not included in the ENP)	Association agreement incl. a customs union	IPA

**Table 1.3   The EU's neighbours and their neighbours: Frameworks
of cooperation with Eastern European and Central
Asian countries**

Eastern European and Southern Caucasus Countries				
Russia	CIS, EurAsEC, BSEC		PCA, Strategic Partnership – Four Common Spaces	ENPI
Armenia	CIS, EurAsEC (accession negotiations), BSEC	ENP, EaP	PCA	ENPI/ ENI
Azerbaijan	CIS, EurAsEC	ENP, EaP	PCA	ENPI/ ENI

Belarus	CIS, EurAsEC	Not included in the ENP, EaP specific arrangements	(PCA) ratification frozen	(ENPI)
Georgia	CIS, BSEC	ENP, EaP	PCA, AA signed in 2014	ENPI/ ENI
Moldova	CIS, CEFTA, BSEC	ENP, EaP	PCA, AA signed in 2014	ENPI/ ENI
Ukraine	Declared its intention to leave the CIS in March 2014, BSEC	ENP, EaP	PCA, AA signed in 2014	ENPI/ ENI
Central Asian Countries				
Kazakhstan	CIS, EurAsEC, SCO	EU Strategy for Central Asia	PCA	DCI
Kyrgyz Republic	CIS, EurAsEC, SCO	EU Strategy for Central Asia	PCA	DCI
Turkmenistan	CIS	EU Strategy for Central Asia	PCA	DCI
Uzbekistan	CIS, EurAsEC (suspended), SCO	EU Strategy for Central Asia	PCA	DCI
Tajikistan	CIS, EurAsEC, SCO	EU Strategy for Central Asia	PCA	DCI

Table 1.3 includes Eastern European and Central Asian countries for which the European Commission advocated to build new bridges.

The tables above illustrate the complexity of the situation. One has to go back to the 2006, 2007 and 2011 Communications of the European Commission (and the High Representative) to understand how the concept of the 'neighbours of the EU neighbours' was first introduced, given the obvious heterogeneity of the relations established with these EU partners.

The Emergence of the Concept of the 'Neighbours of the EU's Neighbours'

The European Neighbourhood Policy was progressively shaped from 2003 on by a series of European Commission Communications. In December 2006, the Commission, in its Communication on the 'Strengthening of the European Neighbourhood Policy' proposed to 'look beyond the Union's immediate neighbourhood' and to work with 'the neighbours of our neighbours'.[64] The Communication continued:

> [i]n Central Asia, for example, or in the Gulf, the new instruments (both ENPI and DCI) will be able to fund regional cooperation activities including countries in both regions – this could be of particular importance in sectors such as energy, transport, environment and research policy.[65]

Hence, it is worth underlining that the Commission mentioned, from the outset, the importance of transnational areas of cooperation as well as specific geographical financial instruments. The European Commission went on to stress that:

> [s]imilar considerations also apply beyond the North African ENP countries, in the context of the EU-Africa Strategy, where broader regional cooperation programmes and cooperation in areas like migration, infrastructure, energy and peace and security will be of great interest. Looking beyond such regional cooperation activities, consideration might also be given to building a comparable agenda for dialogue and reform with Kazakhstan, in response to their expressed interest.[66]

Moreover, the European Commission identified two 'action points' of special interest to our topic for such 'regional cooperation':

- The 'Black Sea Synergy, including Foreign Ministers dialogue and intensified cooperation with BSEC, taking account of existing regional cooperation such as the Baku Initiative on energy and transport';
- 'Strengthened cooperation with "the neighbours of our neighbours", e.g. on energy, transport, the fight against illegal immigration'.[67]

All in all, the 2006 Communication identified six main sectors for cooperation: energy, transport, environment, research policy, the fight against illegal immigration and peace and security,[68] and three main regions: Africa, Central Asia and the Arabian Gulf. Beyond regional cooperation activities, the European Commission also referred explicitly to Kazakhstan.

Later on, in 2007, within the framework of a second Communication entitled 'A Strong European Neighbourhood Policy', the European Commission stressed that 'the Black Sea Synergy has been launched to complement the EU's mainly bilateral policies in the region: the ENP, the Strategic Partnership with the Russian

---

64   COM(2006) 726 final, op. cit., 11.
65   Ibid., 11.
66   Ibid.
67   Ibid., 12.
68   Ibid., 11.

Federation and the accession negotiations with Turkey', adding that 'similarly, possible synergies will be explored with the EU Strategy for Central Asia and the Joint EU-Africa Strategy'.[69] Then, in a section devoted to 'Sectoral reform and modernisation', the Communication identified two specific initiatives:

1. the 'Baku Process (Black Sea/Caspian/Central Asia)'; and
2. the 'Sharm-el-Sheik EU-Africa-Middle East energy conference, particularly on development of the Arab Gas Pipeline'.[70]

The March 2011 Joint Communications of the High Representative and the European Commission on the 'Partnership for democracy and shared prosperity with the southern Mediterranean'[71] – which was in fact the first answer to the so-called 'Arab Spring'[72] – and the May 2011 Communication on the revision of the ENP entitled 'A new response to a changing Neighbourhood'[73] make almost no references to the neighbours of the EU's neighbours. In the first one, however, a tentative link was made between the Maghreb and sub-Saharan Africa in addressing the problem of the refugees from Libya.[74] A year later, another Joint Communication entitled 'Delivering on a new European Neighbourhood Policy' acknowledged that 'countries such as Russia and Turkey have the potential to make an important contribution to regional stability'.[75] However, one can regret the absence, in the 2011 Joint Communication on the revision of the ENP, of any concrete proposal to develop a strategic dialogue with those countries sharing common neighbourhoods with the EU. Less than two years later, in March

---

69　European Commission 2007. *Communication from the Commission. A Strong European Neighbourhood Policy*, COM(2007) 774 final, Brussels, 5 December, 4–5, '2.3. Regional processes'.

70　COM(2006) 726 final, op. cit., 12.

71　European Commission and High Representative 2011. *Joint Communication to the European Parliament – A partnership for democracy and shared prosperity with the Southern Mediterranean*, COM(2011) 200 final, Brussels, 8 March.

72　See Lannon, E. 2012. L'Union européenne et la nouvelle donne géopolitique en Méditerranée, *EuroMeSCo Papers*, 15/2012, April, Barcelona: IEMED, http://www.euromesco.net/images/papers/papersiemed15.pdf [accessed: 22 March 2014].

73　European Commission and High Representative 2011. *Joint Communication to the European Parliament on a new response to a changing Neighbourhood*, COM(2011) 303, Brussels, 25 May.

74　'Vigilance is necessary as the humanitarian crisis threatens to escalate to neighbouring countries both in the Maghreb and sub Saharan Africa as people flee from Libya. The Commission will increase financial support if needs on the ground so require it and we encourage EU Member States to continue to respond in a similar fashion'. COM(2011) 200 final, op. cit., 3–4.

75　European Commission and High Representative 2012. *Joint Communication to the European Parliament on delivering on a new European Neighbourhood Policy*, JOIN(2012) 14 final, Brussels, 15 May, 16.

2014, the European Council 'strongly condemn(ed) the unprovoked violation of Ukrainian sovereignty and territorial integrity by the Russian Federation and call(ed) on the Russian Federation to immediately withdraw its armed forces to the areas of their permanent stationing, in accordance with the relevant agreements',[76] while Poland activated article 4 of the Washington Treaty establishing NATO.[77]

Conclusion

This introductory chapter aimed at clarifying the concepts of the 'neighbours of the EU's neighbours', the 'EU's broader neighbourhood' and of the 'arc of crisis and strategic challenges'. There is obviously a need for developing research in these areas and to identify opportunities in terms of cooperation and economic integration.[78] This is one of the key aims of this volume. According to the Lisbon Treaty, the 'Member States shall ensure, through the convergence of their actions, that the Union is able to assert its interests and values on the international scene' (Article 32 TEU) whereas the preamble clearly states that the implementation of the CFSP, including the 'progressive framing' of a 'common defence policy, which might lead to a common defence' would reinforce the 'European identity and its independence in order to promote peace, security and progress in Europe and in the world'. The 2008 Russian military intervention in Georgia changed the map of Europe, at least on the ground, and the decision of the 'Crimean Regional Assembly' to declare Crimean independence on 11 March 2014 as a first step before joining the Russian Federation could lead to a further redrawing of the borders of the EU's neighbours, even if the annexation is not internationally recognized. This Crimean case is certainly a litmus test for the enlarged EU.

As a matter of fact, there has been a lack of convergence between Member States in the ENP as various Member States have promoted the launching of sub-regional initiatives like the Union for the Mediterranean or the Eastern Partnership (EaP) that have proven to be relatively inefficient as they were mainly based on intergovernmental methods and on particular interests. The consistency – and sometimes the credibility – of the ENP as a whole have been affected. Although the EaP was more integrated into the ENP framework than

---

76   European Council 2014. *Statement of the Heads of State or Government on Ukraine*, Brussels, 6 March, http://www.consilium.europa.eu/uedocs/cms_data/docs/pressdata/en/ec/141372.pdf [accessed: 22 March 2014].

77   Article 4 states that 'the parties will consult whenever, in the opinion of any of them, the territorial integrity, political independence, or security of any of the parties is threatened'. This article precedes the collective defence clause of Article 5. NATO 2014. *Statement by the North Atlantic Council following meeting under article 4 of the Washington Treaty*, Brussels: NATO, http://www.nato.int/cps/en/natolive/news_107716.htm [accessed: 22 March 2014].

78   See the Conclusion by Sieglinde Gstöhl in this volume.

the original Union *of* the Mediterranean, its link with the Black Sea Synergy – an initiative emanating from the European Commission – has never been entirely clear.[79] At the same time, the creation of some sort of EaP was necessary as no multilateral framework was in place for the EU's Eastern neighbours, contrary to the Mediterranean partners which benefited, after November 1995, from the 'Barcelona Process', the multilateral track of the Euro-Mediterranean Partnership. What is obvious is that the European Security Strategy needs another urgent update and that the relationship between the different components of the EU's numerous proximity strategies should be clarified and improved. If the promotion of Member States' national interests was clearly counter-productive, at EU level the institutions and bodies sometimes address regions or regional groupings in a quite technocratic way and 'administrative boundaries' do not always match geography or geopolitics.[80] In 2003 Romano Prodi, Javier Solana and Christopher Patten, in a letter addressed to the EU Council Presidency on the 'Strengthening the EU's partnership with the Arab world', asserted that:

> [f]rom a strictly political point of view, relations with the ACP belong to a different set of problems. There will then be two main lines of action for the EU in its relations with the Arab countries, the Mediterranean line and the Wider Middle East.[81]

What happened in Mali, Sudan or Somalia is sufficient to advocate that the EU's relations with the ACP and the ENP countries located in North Africa, the Sahel and the Horn of Africa do not belong to a completely 'different set of problems'. Each of those countries has of course its own distinct characteristics, its own identity and challenges, but they also all share common challenges and have the potential to develop transnational cooperation in many areas.

The overall lesson that can be drawn is clear: one should avoid this kind of dispersed approach in the future. It is time to return to a more comprehensive approach for the sake of the general interest of the EU and its partners. It is also essential to define a 'long-term strategy' with a clear 'end goal', as the Neighbourhood Economic Community (NEC) remains a quite vague concept. That does not mean that an intergovernmental forum for political dialogue should

---

79   According to the 2007 Communication: 'In response to calls for the establishment of a regional cooperation framework in the East, the Black Sea Synergy has been launched to complement the EU's mainly bilateral policies in the region: the ENP, the Strategic Partnership with the Russian Federation and the accession negotiations with Turkey'. COM(2007) 774, op. cit., 4.

80   See also Chapter 11 by Stephan Keukeleire in this volume.

81   Patten, C., Solana, J. and Prodi, R. 2003. *Strengthening the EU's partnership with the Arab world*, Paper for the attention of Franco Frattini, President of the Council, D(2003) 10318, Brussels, 4 December, 7, http://register.consilium.europa.eu/doc/srv?l=ENandt=PDF andgc=trueandsc=falseandf=ST%2015945%202003%20INIT [accessed: 22 March 2014].

not be developed or created. What is crucial is that those intergovernmental fora for political dialogue should not interfere with the cooperation frameworks which are to be managed in the general interest by the European Commission and the European Investment Bank in close cooperation with the High Representative chairing the Foreign Affairs configuration of the Council of Ministers. Instruments and programmes for developing cooperation should be more clearly identified for cross-fertilization and synergies.

It is absolutely essential that partners have credible ownership of any EU initiative in which they take part. Building a 'spirit of partnership' is a precondition for the success of EU strategies. And this means that the perceptions of countries like Russia and Turkey have at least to be taken seriously into consideration and discussed, as any EU initiative against their interests will be, in one way or another, counteracted.

Is a new 'Broader Neighbourhood Policy Framework' or a new EU strategy necessary to develop the concept of the 'neighbours of the neighbours'? Or should the EU continue to promote a more flexible (but relatively fragmented) approach based on the creation of new sub- regional initiatives like in the Sahel or the Horn of Africa? These are pressing questions addressed in this volume,[82] but if academics can provide the analysis and propose options it is up to decision-makers to take their responsibilities.

The EU and its Member States cannot afford to witness passively the consolidation of an 'arc of crisis and challenges' beyond their immediate neighbourhood which directly affects their stability, security and prosperity. The EU and its Member States should therefore be more proactive and develop an appropriate answer to these alarming developments. It will be crucial to avoid any strategy perceived as an attempt to 'Balkanize' or 'Lebanize' the Arab or the Muslim world or as an attempt to consolidate the so-called 'Fortress Europe'. On the contrary, the approach must be as inclusive as possible and based on the respect for and promotion of 'universal values' and the 'rule of law'. The implementation of these principles and the development of a real 'spirit of partnership' are the most important preconditions for successfully developing a genuine EU approach vis-à-vis its broader neighbourhood.

Bibliography

ACP-EU Council of Ministers 2013. *Satisfactory outcome; Good compromise on EDF; Welcome to Somalia,* Brussels, ACP Press Release, 7 June, http://www.acp.int/fr/node/1991 [accessed: 22 March 2014].

Adomeit, H. 2012. Russia ENP competitor, in Lannon, E. (ed.), *The European Neighbourhood Policy's Challenges/Les défis de la politique européenne de voisinage.* Brussels: P.I.E Peter Lang, 381–409.

---

82   See the Conclusion by Sieglinde Gstöhl in this volume.

Brzezinski, Z. 1979. Iran: The Crescent of Crisis, *TIME Magazine*, 15 January, http://content.time.com/time/magazine/article/0,9171,919995,00. html#ixzz2tHbAjOuO [accessed: 22 March 2014].

Carothers, T. and Ottaway, M. 2004. Greater Middle East Initiative: Off to a False Start, *Carnegie Policy Outlook*. Washington, DC: Carnegie, 18 March.

College of Europe 2012. *The Neighbours of the EU's Neighbours: Diplomatic and Geopolitical Dimensions beyond the ENP – Conference Summary*. Bruges: College of Europe, 15–16 November.

Council of the European Union 2007. *European Union and Central Asia: Strategy for a New Partnership*, 10113/07, Brussels, 2 May.

Council of the European Union 2007. *The Africa-EU Strategic Partnership – A Joint Africa-EU Strategy*, Lisbon, 9 December.

Council of the European Union 2008. *Report on the Implementation of the Council of the EU 2008, European Security Strategy – Providing Security in a Changing World* S407/08, Brussels, 11 December, 5, http://www.consilium.europa. eu/ueDocs/cms-Data/docs/pressdata/EN/reports/104630.pdf [accessed: 22 March 2014].

Council of the European Union 2009. *EU policy on the Horn of Africa – Towards a comprehensive strategy*, 17383/09, Brussels, 10 December.

Council of the European Union and European Commission 2010. *Joint Progress Report by the Council and the European Commission to the European Council on the Implementation of the EU Strategy for Central Asia*, Brussels, 14 June, http://register.consilium.europa.eu/pdf/en/10/st11/st11402.en10.pdf [accessed: 22 March 2014].

Council of the European Union 2011. *Relations entre l'UE et la Principauté d'Andorre, la République de Saint-Marin et la Principauté de Monaco*, Brussels, 14 June, http://register.consilium.europa.eu/doc/srv?l=FR&f=ST%20 11466%202011%20INIT [accessed: 22 March 2014].

Council of the European Union 2012. *High Representative Catherine Ashton inaugurates EU funded Crisis Room at League of Arab States*, Cairo, 13 November, A 510/12, http://www.consilium.europa.eu/uedocs/cms_Data/ docs/pressdata/EN/foraff/ 133466.pdf [accessed: 22 March 2014].

Council of the European Union 2011. *Strategy for Security and Development in the Sahel*, Annex to the Council Conclusions on a European Union Strategy for Security and Development in the Sahel, Brussels, 21 March.

European Commission 2004. *Communication from the Commission to the Council and the Parliament, European Neighbourhood Policy Strategy Paper*, COM(2004) 373 final, Brussels, 12 May.

European Commission 2006. Communication from the Commission to the Council and the Parliament on *Strengthening of the European Neighbourhood Policy*, COM(2006) 726 final, Brussels, 4 December.

European Commission 2007. Communication from the Commission. *A Strong European Neighbourhood Policy*, COM(2007) 774 final, Brussels, 5 December.

European Commission 2009. *Non-ratification of the revised Cotonou Agreement by Sudan FAQ*, August, http://ec.europa.eu/development/icenter/repository/sudan_final_non-ratification_faq_200908.pdf.

European Commission 2011. *Proposal for a Regulation of the European Parliament and the Council establishing a European Neighbourhood Instrument*, COM(2011) 839 final, Brussels, 7 December.

European Commission 2013. *Kosovo*, Brussels, 2 June, http://ec.europa.eu/enlargement/countries/detailed-country-information/kosovo/index_en.htm [accessed: 22 March 2014].

European Commission 2014. Belarus, http://ec.europa.eu/trade/policy/countries-and-regions/countries/belarus [accessed: 22 March 2014].

European Commission and High Representative 2011. Joint Communication of the Commission and High Representative to the European Parliament. *A partnership for democracy and shared prosperity with the Southern Mediterranean*, COM(2011) 200 final, Brussels, 8 March.

European Commission and High Representative 2011. *Joint Communication of the Commission and High Representative to the European Parliament, A new response to a changing Neighbourhood*, COM(2011) 303, Brussels, 25 May.

European Commission and High Representative 2012. Joint Communication of the Commission and High Representative to the European Parliament. *Delivering on a new European Neighbourhood Policy*, JOIN(2012) 14 final, Brussels, 15 May.

European Council 2002. *Presidency Conclusions*, Brussels, 12–13 December.

European Council 2004. *Final Report: EU Strategic Partnership with the Mediterranean and the Middle East*, June. http://consilium.europa.eu/uedocs/cmsUpload/Partnership%20Mediterranean%20and%20Middle%20East.pdf [accessed: 22 March 2014].

European Council 2007. *The EU and Central Asia: Strategy for a New Partnership*, Brussels, 22 June.

European Council 2014. *Statement of the Heads of State or Government on Ukraine*, Brussels, 6 March, http://www.consilium.europa.eu/uedocs/cms-data/docs/pressdata/en/ec/141372.pdf [accessed: 22 March 2014].

European Parliament 2013. *Annual Report from the Council to the European Parliament on the Common Foreign and Security Policy*. Committee on Foreign Affairs, Rapporteur: Elmar Brok. A7–0330/2013, Brussels, 15 October.

European Parliament and Council of the European Union 2006. *Regulation (EC) No 1638/2006 of the European Parliament and of the Council of 24 October 2006 laying down general provisions establishing a European Neighbourhood and Partnership Instrument*. OJ L 310/1, 9 November.

Evin, A. et al. 2010. *Getting to ZERO Turkey, Its Neighbors and the West*, Washington, DC: Transatlantic Academy, August, http://www.transatlanticacademy.org/sites/default/files/publications/GettingtoZeroFINAL.pdf [accessed: 22 March 2014].

Hanf, D. 2012. The European Neighbourhood Policy in the Light of the New 'Neighbourhood Clause' (Article 8 TEU), in Lannon, E. (ed.), *The European Neighbourhood Policy's Challenges/Les défis de la politique européenne de voisinage*, Brussels: P.I.E Peter Lang, 109–23.

Huntington, S.P. 1993. The Clash of Civilizations? *Foreign Affairs*, 72(3), 22–49.

Lannon, E. 2012. L'Union européenne et la nouvelle donne géopolitique en Méditerranée. *EuroMeSCo Papers*, Barcelona: IEMed, 15 April, http://www.euromesco.net/images/papers/papersiemed15.pdf [accessed: 22 March 2014].

Lenczowski, G. 1979. The Arc of Crisis: Its Central Sector. *Foreign Affairs*, Spring 1979, http://www.foreignaffairs.com/articles/32309/george-lenczowski/the-arc-of-crisis-its-central-sector [accessed: 22 March 2014].

NATO 2013. *NATO after ISAF – staying successful together. Remarks by NATO Secretary General Anders Fogh Rasmussen at the Munich Security Conference*, 2 February, http://www.nato.int/cps/en/natolive/opinions_94321.htm [accessed: 22 March 2014].

NATO 2014. *Statement by the North Atlantic Council following meeting under article 4 of the Washington Treaty*, Brussels, 4 March: NATO, http://www.nato.int/cps/en/natolive/news-107716.htm [accessed: 22 March 2014].

Patten, C., Solana, J. and Prodi, R. 2003. *Paper for the attention of Franco Frattini, President of the Council – Strengthening the EU's partnership with the Arab world*, D(2003) 10318, Brussels, 4 December.

Présidence de la République Française – Commission du livre blanc sur la défense et la sécurité nationale 2008. *Défense et sécurité nationale – Le Livre Blanc*. Paris: Odile Jacob & La Documentation Française, juin, http://www.ladocumentationfrancaise.fr/var/storage/rapports-publics/084000341/0000.pdf [accessed: 22 March 2014].

Présidence de la République Française – Commission du livre blanc sur la défense et la sécurité nationale 2013. *Défense et sécurité nationale – Le Livre Blanc 2013*. Paris: La Documentation Française, Paris, http://www.ladocumentationfrancaise.fr/var/storage/rapports-publics/134000257/ 0000.pdf [accessed: 22 March 2014].

Prodi, R. 2002. *A Wider Europe – A Proximity Policy as the Key to Stability, Peace, Security and Stability International Dialogue and the Role of the EU*, Sixth ECSA-World Conference, SPEECH/02/619, Brussels, 5–6 December.

Rehman, I. 2013. Arc of Crisis 2.0? *National Interest*, 7 March, http://nationalinterest.org/commentary/arc-crisis-20–8194?page=2 [accessed: 22 March 2014].

Sharp, J.M. 2005. The Broader Middle East and North Africa Initiative: An Overview, *CRS Report for Congress*. Washington, DC: Library of Congress, 15 February.

PART I
Geopolitical Dimensions beyond the ENP's South: Sahel and Horn of Africa

Chapter 2

State of Play: The EU, the African Parties to the Cotonou Agreement and the ENP

Claudia Zulaika

Introduction: The EU's Relations with its Southern Neighbours and beyond

The notions of 'Sahel' and 'Horn of Africa' have evolved from their original geographical meaning to become two generally recognized geopolitical systems. Reflecting both of these aspects, the European Union (EU) approaches these areas in two distinct ways. On the one hand, the EU acknowledges the natural boundary separating its neighbouring Southern Mediterranean countries from sub-Saharan Africa – the Arabic word *sāḥil* actually means 'shore' or 'coast', suggesting a description of the Sahara desert as a sea of sand.[1] On the other hand, those two sub-regions are components of a broader political framework for the EU's external action: that of the African, Caribbean and Pacific (ACP) group of countries. Indeed, in the last decades of the twentieth century the Sahel and the Horn of Africa have developed common traits with this ACP group and also among themselves; maybe this explains why traditionally the EU has not dealt with them through specific distinguished policies. Actually, the EU's interest even seemed to be on the wane in the late 1990s and at the beginning of the 2000s, until the increasingly visible needs and vulnerability of the region called for a more proactive stance. As the threats of conflict and violent spill-over not far from the European doors slowly materialized, the EU's renewed interest in the problems of the Sahel and the Horn of Africa took the shape of various specific initiatives set out below.[2] However, at the same time, the EU was devising tools for its relations with its immediate neighbours in the Maghreb region – eventually grouped under the European Neighbourhood Policy (ENP). As a result, the policies proliferated and the potential risk of inconsistencies arose.

In this context, the present chapter examines the EU's action towards the Sahel and the Horn of Africa, in link with the EU's relations with the African countries of its immediate neighbourhood in the Maghreb. In order to do so, the chapter starts by depicting the challenges ahead for the two sub-regions in focus, within the broad ACP framework. It then draws a general outlook of the structures

---

1 See Maps IV and VI in the Annex.
2 See also Chapter 3 by Alexander Mattelaer and Chapter 4 by Alex Vines and Ahmed Soliman in this volume.

shaping the EU's relations with the African countries situated along the Sahara and connects them to the countries of the EU's immediate neighbourhood. On the basis of this analysis, it is argued that some mechanisms are available that could allow the EU to maximize its assets and avoid inefficiencies in order to globally enhance its action. Consequently, the final part of the chapter reflects on the ways in which the EU could further upgrade its policies towards its southern neighbours and their neighbours; an endeavour which regains significance in the present times of economic crisis and rationalization.

Multifaceted Challenges for the EU beyond its Immediate Neighbourhood

The Cotonou Agreement covers the two regions that are of interest for this chapter: the Sahel and the Horn of Africa. However, it also goes beyond these regions and encompasses all the countries forming the so-called 'ACP group', brought together by the Georgetown Agreement of 1975. The association of the three geographical components of this group[3] has increasingly been contested, with some authors observing that 'the pan-African organizations – the African Union (AU) – or regional organizations (for example, ECOWAS) appear to have gained more legitimacy and credibility in dealing with continental and regional political and security issues [than the ACP forum]'.[4] Still, the internal coordination and cooperation of the group is effective in many fields where the ACP countries face common challenges.

These challenges are, first, of a socioeconomic nature: high poverty rates with an unequal distribution of resources and access to basic services (health, education), stagnant economic growth, a lack of structural transformation and high levels of unemployment (affecting predominantly the large category of young people aged between 14 and 25)[5]. Second, and despite being spread over three continents, all members of the ACP group are confronted with serious climate threats in various forms such as exposure to tropical storms and floods (the Caribbean), sea level rise (islands in the Pacific Ocean) and droughts, deforestation, soil fertility depletion and desertification (sub-Saharan Africa). In this context, the insufficient means and policies for preparation and adaptation to climate change result in 53 out of

---

3   Out of 79 countries in this group (soon to become 80 as South Sudan joins the configuration), 48 belong to sub-Saharan Africa, 16 to the Caribbean and 15 to the Pacific. Cuba has not signed the Cotonou Agreement and the membership of Somalia and South Sudan is still pending.

4   Laporte, G. 2012. What future for the ACP and the Cotonou Agreement? Preparing for the next steps in the debate. *ECDPM Briefing Note*, no. 34, Maastricht: ECDPM, April.

5   The availability of data on (un)employment in the region is particularly limited, as an extremely high percentage of the economy is typically informal in these countries. See OECD 2012. *African Economic Outlook 2012: Promoting Youth Employment*. Paris: OECD, table at http://dx.doi.org/10.1787/888932600374 [accessed: 20 January 2014].

79 ACP countries suffering from an 'acute vulnerability' to the expected impact of climate change in the coming decades.[6] Especially in Africa, malnutrition, hunger, migration and sometimes conflict have come hand in hand with these environmental events.

These threats are yet another element feeding into a third major common challenge for many ACP countries: fragile statehood, widening social inequality, corruption and crime which prevent the consolidation of stable, well governed democratic systems. In many territories on which fratricidal wars left vacuums of power, extremist and criminal movements have slowly developed roots and now profit from trading weapons, raw materials and human beings. One outstanding security problem for some ACP governments on both shores of the Atlantic is the 'occupation' of West African vulnerable states (Guinea Bissau, Sierra Leone, Liberia) by transnational drug trafficking networks coming from South America and transiting through the Caribbean. After reaching West Africa, the loads of cocaine are shipped by sea (mainly through the ports of Spain and the Netherlands) or air to Europe, the second-largest cocaine market in the world after the United States. Since 2004, this phenomenon has caught the attention of the international community on the regional and global level, including that of the Economic Community of West African States (ECOWAS), the Economic Community of Central African States (ECCAS), the broader AU and the United Nations (UN). As a result, the role of West Africa in drug trafficking from South America to Europe was dramatically reduced between 2007 and 2009 if judged from seizures only. However, other indications suggest that traffickers have just changed their tactics (for example by flying deeper inland and landing in remote areas of the region) but in 2011 still channelled around 13 per cent of the cocaine reaching Europe through West Africa.[7] While doing so, moreover, they have established cooperation patterns with different terrorist or anti-government forces in the Sahel (such as 'al-Qaeda in the Islamic Maghreb', AQIM), which escort them northward through the Sahara desert.

The challenges outlined above and common to most ACP countries become outstanding when looking at the two sub-regions in the focus of this chapter. There, the indicators are shocking even compared to the ACP average: unemployment is chronic, the percentage of population below 14 years old ranges from 35 per cent

---

6   See DARA International Foundation 2012. *Climate Vulnerability Monitor 2nd Edition – A Guide to the Cold Calculus of a Hot Planet*. Madrid: DARA, 72–97. The vulnerability of the remaining 26 ACP countries is reckoned either *high* or *severe*, and in all but seven ACP countries (Gambia, Guinea Bissau, Sierra Leone, Liberia, Burkina Faso, Equatorial Guinea and Somalia) it is gauged to be 'increasing'.

7   See United Nations Office on Drugs and Crime 2011. *World Drug Report 2011*. Vienna: United Nations Publications, http://www.unodc.org/documents/data-and-analysis/ WDR2011/ – World_Drug_Report_2011_ebook.pdf [accessed: 3 January 2014].

in Djibouti to up to 49 per cent in Niger[8] and the whole area is troubled with recurrent and exacerbated humanitarian crises,[9] appalling food insecurity,[10] crime and weapon proliferation, social tensions and political uncertainty. The situation has further deteriorated following the upheavals of the Libyan revolution and the Tunisian and Egyptian 'Arab Spring', which have spilled over and destabilized all southern neighbours. The violent unrests in Niger (July 2011) and Mali (March 2012) seemed only further pieces of evidence to recognize an 'arc of crisis' unfolding in Africa from the Atlantic to the Indian ocean, along the Sahel Strip.

The EU, by drafting its strategies for the Sahel and the Horn of Africa, formulated its own definition of a cross-continental configuration embracing 13 African ACP countries (Mauritania, Mali, some parts of Burkina Faso, Niger, Chad, the two Sudans, Ethiopia, Eritrea, Djibouti, Uganda, Kenya and Somalia) belonging to the two sub-regions.[11] Within this area, the set of challenges with which the EU finds itself confronted consist in 'persisting problems as well as sudden shocks'.[12] This is why the EU shall, firstly, direct its efforts at supporting poverty reduction, economic growth, job creation and sustainable development as key prerequisites for a long-lasting peace in this 'arc of crisis'. Secondly, the EU shall be prepared to undertake swift actions and tackle abrupt security outbursts such as the Tuareg rebellion in Mali. But what tools does the EU have at its disposal to channel such responses?

European Strategies and Frameworks for the Relations with its Neighbours and their Direct Neighbours

Prior to the emergence of this new arc of instability, the traditional keystone of the EU's policy towards the broad ACP region was development aid, governed first

---

8   Figures compiled for 2012 by the World Bank, on the basis of the *World Population Prospects* published by the United Nations Population Division, http://data.worldbank.org/indicator/SP.POP.0014.TO.ZS.

9   North Sudan, Somalia, Kenya, Uganda and Chad are among the top 15 countries in the world giving asylum or residence to refugees, asylum-seekers, internally displaced and stateless persons, according to the United Nations High Commissioner for Refugees (UNHCR) 2011. *Statistical Yearbook 2010 – Trends in Displacement, Protection and Solutions: Ten Years of Statistics*. Geneva: UNHCR Publications, Annex, 62.

10   See the FAO *Regional Strategic Response Framework* for the 2012 food and nutrition crisis in the Sahel, and the FAO monthly *Updates on the Horn of Africa Crisis*.

11   See Council of the European Union 2011. *Strategy for Security and Development in the Sahel*, Annex to the Council Conclusions on a European Union Strategy for Security and Development in the Sahel, Brussels, 21 March; and Council of the European Union 2011. *A Strategic Framework for the Horn of Africa*, Annex to the Council Conclusions on the Horn of Africa, 3124th Foreign Affairs Council meeting, Brussels, 14 November.

12   Simon, L., Mattelaer, A. and Hadfield, A. 2012. *A Coherent EU Strategy for the Sahel*. Brussels: European Parliament (DG External Policies PE 433.778), 5.

by the two Yaoundé Conventions (1964–75), then by the four Lomé Conventions (1975–2000) and finally overhauled by the Cotonou Partnership Agreement (2000–20; reviewed in 2005 and 2010). The latter covers all main fields of development cooperation and goes well beyond them by also setting the basis for both the political dialogue and the trade relations between the EU and the ACP countries. Thus, right after its entry into force in 2000, a first Africa-EU Summit was held in Cairo, where the political dialogue between the two parties was institutionalized. An Africa-EU Strategic Partnership followed in 2007, paving the way for a joint definition of long-term policy orientations for both continents on the basis of a shared vision and common principles such as equality, ownership, joint responsibility and mutual accountability.[13] In the same way, deriving from the provisions of the Cotonou Agreement, negotiations were officially launched in 2002 to redefine the EU-ACP trade regime through Economic Partnership Agreements (EPAs). This comprehensiveness explains why the Cotonou system has been deemed 'the world's largest and most advanced financial and political contractual framework for North-South cooperation'.[14]

Still, towards the end of the decade more and more voices claimed that this tool had become insufficient. The EU institutions and Member States became visibly concerned about their own security in a twenty-first century context where transnational forms of crime blurred the traditional boundaries between domestic and external security imperatives.[15] The conviction emerged that, as the EU's 'southern geopolitical border … any instability [in the Sahel region] will eventually find its way into the European neighbourhood and Europe itself'.[16] In need for a more inclusive and multidirectional response to the rapidly evolving developments in the Sahel and the Horn of Africa, the EU had to both mobilize old tools (such as the Lomé/Cotonou setting) and provide itself with innovative diplomatic and technical means.

The starting point to that process was the adoption in 2009 of an 'EU Policy on the Horn of Africa', further developed in an EU 'Strategic Framework for the Horn of Africa' in 2011, and of a 'Strategy for Security and Development in the Sahel' in 2011.[17] Through these documents, the EU consolidated its new

---

13   See European Commission 2005. *EU Strategy for Africa: Towards a Euro-African Pact to Accelerate Africa's Development.* COM(2005) 489 final, Brussels, 12 October, 18–19.

14   Gavas, M. 2012. Reviewing the evidence: How well does the European Development Fund perform? *Overseas Development Institute/ONE Discussion Paper.* London: ODI, January, 3.

15   See, as one of the first authors to write on this subject, Ferruccio, P. 2001. Reconciling the Prince's two 'arms': Internal-external security policy coordination in the European Union. *European Union Institute for Security Studies Occasional Paper*, no. 30, Paris: EUISS, October.

16   Simon, Mattelaer and Hadfield, op. cit., 1.

17   Council of the European Union, *Strategy for Security and Development in the Sahel*, op. cit.; and Council of the European Union, *A Strategic Framework for the Horn of Africa*, op. cit.

stand on the existence of a 'development-security nexus' – a concept which has allegedly become a trend in the EU's development policy.[18] Moreover, the two regional strategies were to serve as roadmaps for the EU's action towards these sub-regions, and as such they called for a much wider European involvement, drawing on the EU's 'array of means':

> development co-operation through the European Development Fund (EDF) and Member States' bilateral programmes ... joint programming in the ... countries where appropriate, relevant EU budget lines, trade instruments, conflict prevention and crisis response, including the CSDP [Common Security and Defence Policy], diplomacy, EU Special Representatives (EUSRs), co-operation and dialogue through the Cotonou Agreement ... [as well as] humanitarian assistance.[19]

Consequently, an EU Special Representative for Sudan and South Sudan (Rosalind Marsden) took office as from September 2010 and a new EUSR for the Horn of Africa (Alexander Rondos) was appointed as from January 2012.[20] The two are meant to cooperate closely, so as to enhance the 'coherence, quality, impact and visibility of the EU's action in the region'.[21] One year later, the EU also followed the example of the UN[22] and nominated a specific envoy for the Sahel region (Michel Dominique Reveyrand-de Menthon).[23] Furthermore, three CSDP civilian missions were created in June and July 2012 to reinforce the EU action towards the area: EUAVSEC South Sudan, in charge of strengthening aviation security at Juba International Airport, EUCAP SAHEL Niger, mandated to support the fight against organized crime and terrorism in the Sahel region, and

---

18   See, for instance, Furness, M. and Gänzle, S. 2012. The European Union's Development Policy: A Balancing Act between 'A More Comprehensive Approach' and Creeping Securitisation. *ISL Working Paper*, no. 11, Kristiansand: University of Agder, November.

19   Council of the European Union. *A Strategic Framework for the Horn of Africa*, op. cit., 13.

20   Council of the European Union 2010. *Decision 2010/450/CFSP of 11 August 2010 appointing the European Union Special Representative for Sudan*. OJ L 211/42, 12 August; and Council of the European Union 2011. *Decision 2011/819/CFSP of 8 December 2011 appointing the European Union Special Representative for the Horn of Africa*. OJ L 327/62, 9 December.

21   Council of the European Union 2011. *Conclusions on the Horn of Africa*, 3124th Foreign Affairs Council meeting, 14 November, 2.

22   Ban Ki-Moon appointed Romano Prodi as his Special Envoy for the Sahel in October 2012. See UN Department of Public Information 2012. *Secretary-General Appoints Romano Prodi of Italy as Special Envoy for Sahel*, http://www.un.org/News/Press/docs/2012/sga1377.doc.htm [accessed: 3 January 2014].

23   Council of the European Union 2013. *Decision 2013/133/CFSP of 18 March 2013 appointing the European Union Special Representative for the Sahel*. OJ L 75/29, 19 March.

EUCAP NESTOR, a maritime capacity-building mission in the Horn of Africa, complementary with the EU NAVFOR/Atalanta mission and the EU Training Mission in Somalia (EUTM).[24] In January 2013 an EUTM was established for Mali too.[25]

Certainly, the vision underpinning these recent initiatives is more comprehensive and wide-ranging than ever before: first, because the EU now envisages the various dimensions of the regions' realities in an integrated fashion, and second, because it recognizes the unbreakable links between the countries in and beyond these regions, increasingly treating the EU's own Mediterranean neighbours and their southern neighbours as part of a broader geopolitical system. Indeed, the problems affecting the Sahel and Horn countries impact on their adjoining states (those of the Maghreb, most evidently, but also on others such as Nigeria or Yemen). This connection between countries has been found strong enough for the EU to consider devising a new category besides that of the 'EU's neighbours': the group of states 'neighbouring the EU neighbours'.[26]

But despite the emerging commonalities in this 'arc' of countries, the EU still addresses the region through a series of intertwined tools which place the countries of the Sahel and of the Horn of Africa in different relationships with Europe. The example of Mauritania is, perhaps, the greatest exponent of this complexity: the country is both a signatory to the Cotonou Agreement and a member of the Euro-Mediterranean Partnership, but it does not take part in the ENP, unlike the other countries of the Arab Maghreb Union (AMU: Algeria, Libya, Morocco and Tunisia). At the other end of the 'arc of crisis', Yemen is also a paradoxical case: the EU links this country to the African continent through the policy on the Horn of Africa but Yemen also belongs to the Middle East as a neighbour to the countries of the Gulf Cooperation Council (GCC) and a member of the Arab League. Djibouti, Comoros, Mauritania, Somalia and Sudan also form part the Arab League, together with the countries of the AMU. Another special case is the one of the few ACP countries that have either not signed or not ratified the

---

24 Council of the European Union 2012. *Decision 2012/312/CFSP of 18 June 2012 on the European Union Aviation Security CSDP Mission in South Sudan (EUAVSEC-South Sudan)*. OJ L 158/17, 19 June; Council of the European Union 2012. *Decision 2012/389/ CFSP of 12 July 2012 on the European Union Mission on Regional Maritime Capacity Building in the Horn of Africa (EUCAP NESTOR)*. OJ L 306/17, 17 July; Council of the European Union 2012. *Decision 2012/392/CFSP of 16 July 2012 on the European Union CSDP mission in Niger (EUCAP Sahel Niger)*. OJ L 187/48, 17 July; and Council of the European Union 2010. *Decision 2010/197/CFSP of 31 March 2010 on the launch of a European Union military mission to contribute to the training of Somali security forces (EUTM Somalia)*. OJ L 87/33, 7 April.

25 Council of the European Union 2013. *Decision 2013/34/CFSP of 17 January 2013 on a European Union military mission to contribute to the training of the Malian Armed Forces (EUTM Mali)*. OJ L 14/19, 18 January.

26 European Commission 2006. *Communication on Strengthening the European Neighbourhood Policy*. COM(2006) 726, Brussels, 6 December, 11.

Cotonou Agreement or its revisions: both Sudans and Somalia (as well as Cuba and Equatorial Guinea). The implications of this non-signature or non-ratification are significant, as these countries are excluded from the mandate of the European Investment Bank (EIB), and therefore from its lending. In Somalia, a neighbour to the EU's southern neighbours, the absence of government institutions prevented the country from signing the Cotonou Agreement. However, it still received assistance under this ACP scheme because a special provision allowed for it.[27] In June 2013 the joint ACP-EU Council of Ministers approved Somalia's request for accession and observer status.[28] Sudan, in turn, signed the Agreement but did not ratify its first revision in 2005, as the government of Al-Bashir opposed the new clause on cooperation with the International Criminal Court (ICC). This prevented the European Commission from using the 'Cotonou funding instrument', the 10th European Development Fund (EDF), for activities in Sudan, but the country still receives funding from the previous 9th EDF. The same mechanism is used for South Sudan which currently enjoys observer status, pending its ratification of the Cotonou Agreement.

This fragmented landscape shows that, despite having sketched a conceptual framework for the neighbours of its southern neighbours, the EU is still far from designing a coherent, homogeneous policy for the region. For such an overarching structure to become operational, the various EU instruments applicable should be reassessed and reconciled.

The Quest for Coherence: Bridging the EU's Tools in its Wider Southern Neighbourhood

With effectiveness being the primary public and institutional demand in times of economic crisis and budgetary constraints, the EU is bound to make the most out of its resources in the coming years. In order to do so, it needs to find a balanced link between the latest 'hard security responses' provided through CFSP/CSDP missions and its work on the root causes of instability and slow development in the 'arc of crisis'. This equilibrium can only rest on the potential synergies between the existing EU tools for the region and beyond. These could help lay the foundations of a wider, more harmonized and effective policy, but the modalities which allow combining the relevant instruments (and their funding mechanisms) remain largely unexplored. The following paths are worth considering.

---

27   See article 93.6 of the Cotonou Agreement, which provides for support to countries which, in the absence of established government institutions, have not been able to sign or ratify the Agreement.

28   ACP Secretariat 2013. ACP-EU Council of Ministers: Satisfactory outcome; Good compromise on EDF; Welcome to Somalia. *ACP Press Release*, Brussels: ACP Secretariat, 7 June, http://www.acp.int/fr/node/1991 [accessed: 27 March 2014].

First, certain clauses of the legal documents can in all likelihood be used as 'gateways' to bridge several EU instruments. Article 58 of the Cotonou Agreement, for instance, indicates that not only the ACP countries are eligible for the financing provided for by the treaty, but also the 'regional or inter-State bodies to which one or more ACP States belong, including the African Union or other bodies with non-ACP State members, which are authorised by those ACP States'.[29] As a result, the EDF now includes three financial envelopes: one covering bilateral cooperation with individual ACP countries, a second one covering relations with ACP regions as such and a third one addressing the common challenges facing ACP states that transcend geographical criteria. The appropriate financial arrangements have also been envisaged in the second revision of the Cotonou Agreement (2010): while the EDF, an extra-budgetary tool subject to specific administrative and decision-making rules,[30] shall finance actions in the ACP countries, the participation of non-ACP states (such as those of the ENP South) in Pan-African programmes and activities will be financed from non-EDF instruments. Accordingly, both the Development Cooperation Instrument (DCI) and the European Neighbourhood and Partnership Instrument (ENPI) Regulations foresee this possibility as does the Regulation establishing a new European Neighbourhood Instrument (ENI) for the period 2014–20.[31]

A second interesting path to examine could be cross-border cooperation, which aims, in the context of the ENP, at promoting cooperation between EU Member States and partner countries along the Union's external borders. Could such a model not be imagined to strengthen the ties between the ENP countries and their immediate non-EU neighbours? Of course, the major advantage provided by the ENPI is that the programmes involving regions on both sides of the EU's border share common management structures and one single budget, which today is not the case of the southern ENP countries and their southern neighbours. Still, this methodology could be worth exploring in the future.

---

29   Cotonou Agreement, article 58.1 (b), under the conditions of article 58(2) and in combination with article 6 of Annex IV to the Agreement.

30   For more details, see the EDF Financial Regulations and Annual Reports, http://ec.europa.eu/budget/biblio/documents/FED/fed_en.cfm#disp_fin [accessed: 20 January 2014]. For an older but still valid summary of the debate around a possible 'budgetization' of the EDF, see Mackie, J. Frederiksen, J and C. Rossini 2004. Improving ACP-EU Cooperation: Is 'budgetising' the EDF the answer? *ECDPM Discussion Paper*, Maastricht: ECDPM, no. 5.

31   See European Parliament and Council of the European Union 2006. *Regulation (EC) 1905/2006 establishing a financing instrument for development cooperation.* OJ L 378/41, 27 December, articles 31 and 36; European Parliament and Council of the European Union 2006. *Regulation (EC) 1638/2006 laying down general provisions establishing a European Neighbourhood and Partnership Instrument.* OJ L 310/1, 9 November, articles 21.2 and 27.1; and European Parliament and Council of the European Union 2014. *Regulation (EU) No 232/2014 of the European Parliament and of the Council of 11 March 2014 establishing a European Neighbourhood Instrument.* OJ, L 77/27, 13 March, article 16.

Third, the EPAs (meant to replace the trade cooperation chapter of the Cotonou Agreement as of 2008) could also be a tool for more consistency between the EU-ACP framework and the ENP framework. Indeed, those agreements aim at creating free trade areas between the EU and different groupings of ACP countries, including those of the Sahel and the Horn of Africa. Four different EPA groupings apply to these two sub-regions: West Africa (including Mauritania, Mali, Burkina Faso, Niger), Central Africa (to which Chad belongs), Eastern and Southern Africa (covering the Sudans, Ethiopia, Eritrea, Djibouti) and the East African Community (including Kenya and Uganda). The negotiations have surely been sluggish and arduous, and none of the countries just cited has yet (as of January 2014) signed its corresponding Interim EPA. However, if the disagreements are ever overcome and the EPAs finally enter into force, economic integration could act as a 'building block' and significantly trigger convergence between the Maghreb ENP countries and their southern ACP neighbours.

Fourth, the EU-Africa Strategic Partnership is also worth considering. Launched in 2007 as the overarching long-term roadmap for cooperation between the two continents, the EU views this framework as particularly useful in that it identifies precise thematic areas for joint action in a broader regional space, in fields such as 'migration, infrastructure, energy and peace and security'.[32] The progress, however, has been slow and uneven across the different domains, with some of the partnerships virtually stalling.

Nevertheless, this overview shows that there is some room to build bridges and foster synergies between the numerous initiatives. As a matter of fact, the EU has already sought to enhance the overall consistency of its vision on fragile states and regions at the highest conceptual level; an endeavour that has not gone unnoticed:

> At the policy level, recognition that while development and security are interdependent measures to pursue them may be counterproductive has led to efforts to improve the coherence of policy frameworks and the creation of tailored instruments ... This process has had a positive influence on the EU's effectiveness and reputation as a development actor, especially in Africa.[33]

Examples of such possible 'tailored instruments' already exist. The first one can be found in the functioning of the EDF itself. This framework, while being the main source of EU funding to the ACP countries, 'is credited by the OECD DAC for its flexibility and adaptability to changes in the political and economic climate'.[34] Such flexibility comes both from the division of funds into two elements (envelope A for the regular support and envelope B to cover unforeseen needs – humanitarian or others), thus 'promoting links from relief to long-term

---

32   COM(2006) 726, op. cit., 11.
33   Furness and Gänzle, op. cit., 25.
34   Gavas, op. cit., 16–17.

development programmes',[35] and from the European Commission's Vulnerability FLEX instrument (V-FLEX), which since 2010 helps ACP countries to cope with the impact of the economic downturn and maintain their level of public spending in priority areas. The 'Arab Spring' revealed that swift crisis management may also be required in the Maghreb. Thus, why not imagine that this versatility (which has been ameliorated in the successive editions of the instrument) could somehow be replicated for the EDF funds available to non-ACP countries? In such a scenario, the EDF would fit similar short-term needs both of the ACP regions (Sahel and Horn of Africa) and of their ENP neighbours.

A second interesting example of a 'tailored instrument' is that of the umbrella framework of the EU-Africa Strategic Partnership, financed by blended funding from various tools both specific to the ACP countries, the EDF, and beyond them: the DCI in its geographical and thematic components, the 7th Framework Programme for Research and Technological Development, the schemes managed by the European Investment Bank (such as the Africa-EU Infrastructure Trust Fund), the ENPI, the European Instrument for Democracy and Human Rights (EIDHR) and the Instrument for Stability (IfS). The latter is actually a 'bridging' mechanism in itself, strategically created for actions halfway between security and development promotion and whose characteristics make it extremely accommodating:

> The main objective is to support measures aimed at safeguarding or re-establishing the conditions under which the partner countries of the EU can pursue their long term development goals. The Instrument complements existing EU geographic and thematic instruments and policies, Common Foreign and Security Policy actions, regional and international organizations and bilateral programmes carried out by EU Member States. The Instrument brings added value as it fills gaps where geographical or other development instruments cannot be used; and can be used to address trans-regional threats to security, which cannot be done through traditional development instruments.[36]

Hence, the IfS can benefit very varied entities, including, among others, partner countries and regions, joint bodies (of the partner regions and the EU) and international organizations, and serve different yet complementary purposes, given its two components enabling to allocate funds either to short-term or to long-term assistance. One example of a trans-regional initiative funded under the IfS is the programme 'Supporting the fight against organised crime on the Cocaine Route', launched in 2009 and aimed at strengthening the anti-drugs capacities at selected airports and seaports in West Africa, Latin America and the Caribbean, and at helping these regions tackling transnational organized crime and money laundering. Another example is the Critical Maritimes Routes Programme (CMR),

---

35 Ibid.

36 European Commission 2013. *New EU initiative to combat piracy in the Gulf of Guinea*. Press release, IP/13/14, Brussels, 10 January, 2.

consisting of five projects in different geographical areas (including the Western Indian Ocean and the Gulf of Guinea) which address the problems of the security and safety of maritime routes by putting emphasis on capacity building (providing legal assistance and training) at regional and national levels. All in all, this instrument illustrates how innovative means may allow the EU to construct transregional policies where needed.

However, more adjustments will be necessary to make these new formulae successful. Certainly, in spite of the improvements, 'the EDF ... continue[s] to face the challenge of being flexible enough to re-programme funds and to respond to crises, whilst at the same time ensuring long-term funding to strengthen security, development and humanitarian linkages'.[37] As for the Africa-EU Strategic Partnership, many experts believe that two key drivers of the Strategy are still missing: political steering and a long-term direction.[38] Furthermore, when it comes to its coordination with the other EU instruments, the parties themselves acknowledge a need 'to ensure coherence between activities pursued within the framework of the Joint Strategy and those within the framework of other co-operation frameworks such as the ACP and ENPI'.[39]

In the long run, only political will can ensure that more flexible bridges are devised to promote the current EU mechanisms.

Conclusion

This chapter has sought to analyse the EU's policy towards the Sahel and the Horn of Africa in connection with the policies devoted to the African countries of the ENP. Taking into account the wider dimension of the challenges affecting the two sub-regions and the policy tools currently in place, it was argued that some bridges can be used to further enhance the consistency and efficiency of the EU's action towards both its neighbouring countries and their southern neighbours. The analysis has shown that the EU pursues two main objectives in the Sahel and the Horn of Africa: development cooperation and a stabilization resulting in the assurance of the EU's domestic security. Now two threats can hamper these aspirations in particular: the politicization of the EU's development policy in the shape of excessive securitization, and the inconsistency among policies for countries and regions which cannot be isolated from each other. As regards the first threat of mismanaging the development-security nexus:

---

37   Gavas, op. cit., 20.

38   Goertz, S. 2012. JAES: We have a strategy, now we need a strategic partnership. *ECDPM blog 'Talking Points'*, 27 April, http://www.ecdpm-talkingpoints.org/jaes-we-have-a-strategy-now-we-need-a-strategic-partnership [accessed: 25 February 2013].

39   Council of the European Union 2010. *14th Africa-EU Ministerial Meeting.* Luxembourg: 9041/10 (Presse 92), 26 April, 11.

[t]he European engagement through different, at times uncoordinated and overlapping, channels does not always make for a consistent approach and underlines a profound gap between what has come to be a generally accepted diagnostic – that international insecurity is caused, or at least facilitated, by weak states – and the remedies applied by the EU. While Europe increasingly perceives Africa's weak governance as a security threat, it remains unwilling to engage politically and on a longer-term basis on the continent.[40]

The danger of securitization, however, has been contained by the belief that 'decisions to allocate resources cannot always be reduced to considerations of whether the partner represents a security risk to Europe, to its neighbours or to itself', and consequently, '[t]o the extent that the Commission has promoted and enacted the securitization of foreign aid, this has been, on balance, an effort to improve the coherence of security and development policy at the EU level'.[41]

As for the second threat (the lack of broader geographical tools to consistently tackle some geopolitical realities), the initiatives stressing the links between the EU neighbours and their own neighbours have proliferated in recent years, but their contour lines are not always clear and, more importantly, they do not (yet) put sufficient stress on addressing those two regions together. For this reason, their implementation still risks creating inconsistencies and foregone synergy effects.

In such a complex picture, the question of how exactly the European Union should work with 'the neighbours of its southern neighbours' remains to be seen. As highlighted by Ehrhardt and Petretto in their study on Somalia, the most evident starting point to prevent and solve conflict in these countries may be that 'the [Somali] people – supported by the EU – get their act together in a bottom-up political process and find a solution acceptable to all sides'.[42] This idea became a strong guideline for the reform of the ENP after the 'Arab Spring', and it should help devise future Euro-Mediterranean relations based on a strengthened engagement with and ownership of civil societies. Arguably, this same approach must be endorsed towards the Sahel and the Horn of Africa if the EU's policies are to be coherent across regions. Furthermore, a habit of designing 'geopolitical' EU policy tools rather than national or sub-regional ones seems desirable, too, as far as the 'neighbours of the EU's neighbours' are concerned: the unrest in the Central African Republic in late 2013 and early 2014 clearly shows that these fragile countries can also be destabilized by spill-over effects from the next 'concentric circle', further south of their boundaries.

---

40 Gibert, M.V. 2009. The Securitisation of the EU's Development Agenda in Africa: Insights from Guinea-Bissau. *Perspectives on European Politics and Society*, 4(10), 621.

41 Furness and Gänzle, op. cit., 24–5.

42 Ehrhart, H-G. and Petretto, K. 2012. The EU, the Somalia Challenge and Counter-piracy: Towards a Comprehensive Approach? *European Foreign Affairs Review*, 17(2), 283.

Bibliography

ACP Secretariat 2013. ACP-EU Council of Ministers: Satisfactory outcome; Good compromise on EDF; Welcome to Somalia. *ACP Press Release*, Brussels: ACP Secretariat, 7 June, http://www.acp.int/fr/node/1991 [accessed: 27 March 2014].

Council of the European Union 2010. *Decision 2010/197/CFSP of 31 March 2010 on the launch of a European Union military mission to contribute to the training of Somali security forces (EUTM Somalia)*. OJ L 87/33, 7 April.

Council of the European Union 2010. *14th Africa-EU Ministerial Meeting*. Luxembourg: 9041/10 (Presse 92), 26 April.

Council of the European Union 2010. *Decision 2010/450/CFSP of 11 August 2010 appointing the European Union Special Representative for Sudan*. OJ L 211/42, 12 August.

Council of the European Union 2011. *Strategy for Security and Development in the Sahel*, Annex to the Council Conclusions on a European Union Strategy for Security and Development in the Sahel, Brussels, 21 March.

Council of the European Union 2011. *A Strategic Framework for the Horn of Africa*, Annex to the Council Conclusions on the Horn of Africa, 3124th Foreign Affairs Council meeting, Brussels, 14 November.

Council of the European Union 2011. *Conclusions on the Horn of Africa – 3124th Foreign Affairs Council Meeting*, Brussels, 14 November.

Council of the European Union 2011. *Decision 2011/819/CFSP of 8 December 2011 appointing the European Union Special Representative for the Horn of Africa*. OJ L 327/62, 9 December.

Council of the European Union 2012. *Decision 2012/312/CFSP of 18 June 2012 on the European Union Aviation Security CSDP Mission in South Sudan (EUAVSEC-South Sudan)*. OJ L 158/17, 19 June.

Council of the European Union 2012. *Decision 2012/389/CFSP of 16 July 2012 on the European Union Mission on Regional Maritime Capacity Building in the Horn of Africa* (EUCAP NESTOR). OJ L 306/17, 17 July.

Council of the European Union 2012. *Decision 2012/392/CFSP of 16 July 2012 on the European Union CSDP mission in Niger (EUCAP Sahel Niger)*. OJ L 187/48, 17 July.

Council of the European Union 2013. *Decision 2013/34/CFSP of 17 January 2013 on a European Union military mission to contribute to the training of the Malian Armed Forces (EUTM Mali)*. OJ L 14/19, 18 January.

Council of the European Union 2013. *Decision 2013/133/CFSP of 18 March 2013 appointing the European Union Special Representative for the Sahel*. OJ L 75/29, 19 March.

DARA International Foundation 2012. *Climate Vulnerability Monitor 2nd Edition online. A Guide to the Cold Calculus of a Hot Planet*. Madrid: DARA, http://daraint.org/climate-vulnerability-monitor/climate-vulnerability-monitor-2012/report [accessed: 1 March 2013].

Ehrhart, H-G. and Petretto, K. 2012. The EU, the Somalia Challenge and Counter-piracy: Towards a Comprehensive Approach? *European Foreign Affairs Review*, 17(2), 261–83.

European Commission 2005. *EU Strategy for Africa: Towards a Euro-African Pact to Accelerate Africa's Development*, COM(2005) 489 final, Brussels, 12 October.

European Commission 2006. *Communication on Strengthening the European Neighbourhood Policy*, COM(2006) 726, Brussels, 4 December.

European Commission 2013. *New EU initiative to combat piracy in the Gulf of Guinea. Press release*, IP/13/14, Brussels, 10 January, http://europa.eu/rapid/press-release_IP-13-14_en.htm [accessed: 25 February 2013].

European Parliament and Council of the European Union 2006. *Regulation (EC) 1638/2006 of European Parliament and of the Council of 24 October 2006 laying down general provisions establishing a European Neighbourhood and Partnership Instrument*. OJ L 310/1, 9 November 2006.

European Parliament and Council of the European Union 2006. *Regulation (EC) 1905/2006 of European Parliament and of the Council of 18 December 2006 establishing a financing instrument for development cooperation*. OJ L 378/41, 27 December.

European Parliament and Council of the European Union 2014. *Regulation (EU) No 232/2014 of the European Parliament and of the Council of 11 March 2014 establishing a European Neighbourhood Instrument*. OJ L 77/27, 13 March.

Ferruccio, P. 2001. Reconciling the Prince's two 'arms': Internal-external security policy coordination in the European Union. *European Union Institute for Security Studies Occasional Paper*, no. 30, Paris: EUISS, October.

Furness, M. and Gänzle, S. 2012. The European Union's Development Policy: A Balancing Act between 'A More Comprehensive Approach' and Creeping Securitisation. *ISL Working Paper*, no. 11, Kristiansand: University of Agder, November.

Gavas, M. 2012. Reviewing the evidence: How well does the European Development Fund perform? *Overseas Development Institute/ONE Discussion Paper*. London: ODI, January, http://www.odi.org.uk/sites/odi.org.uk/files/odi-assets/publications-opinion-files/8218.pdf [accessed: 15 December 2013].

Gibert, M.V. 2009. The Securitisation of the EU's Development Agenda in Africa: Insights from Guinea-Bissau. *Perspectives on European Politics and Society*, 4(10), 621–37.

Goertz, S. 2012. JAES: We have a strategy, now we need a strategic partnership. *ECDPM blog 'Talking Points'*, 27 April, http://www.ecdpm-talkingpoints.org/jaes-we-have-a-strategy-now-we-need-a-strategic-partnership [accessed: 25 February 2013].

Laporte, G. 2012. What future for the ACP and the Cotonou Agreement? Preparing for the next steps in the debate. *ECDPM Briefing Note*, no. 34, Maastricht: ECDPM, April, http://www.ecdpm.org/Web-ECDPM/Web/Content/Download.nsf/0/A80840C540D36BE8C12579D000311896/$FILE/

BN34-What%20f.uture%20f.or%20the%20ACP-FINAL.pdf [accessed: 15 December 2013].

Mackie, J., Frederiksen, J. and Rossini, C. 2004. Improving ACP-EU Cooperation: Is 'budgetising' the EDF the answer? *ECDPM Discussion Paper*, no. 5, Maastricht: ECDPM http://www.ecdpm.org/Web_ECDPM/Web/Content/Download.nsf/0/3FE1F3B83D3F2538C1256E220035BAFB/$FILE/04-51-jm_jf_cr.pdf [accessed: 20 January 2014.

OECD 2012. *African Economic Outlook 2012: Promoting Youth Employment*. Paris: OECD, table at http://dx.doi.org/10.1787/888932600374 [accessed: 20 January 2014].

Simon, L., Mattelaer, A. and Hadfield, A. 2012. *A Coherent EU Strategy for the Sahel*. Brussels: European Parliament (DG External Policies PE 433.778).

United Nations Department of Public Information 2012. *Secretary-General Appoints Romano Prodi of Italy as Special Envoy for Sahel*. http://www.un.org/News/Press/docs/2012/sga1377.doc.htm [accessed: 3 January 2014].

United Nations Food and Agriculture Organization (FAO) 2012. *The food and nutrition crisis in the Sahel Regional Strategic Response Framework: Urgent action to support the resilience of vulnerable populations*. Rome, July. http://www.fao.org/fileadmin/user-upload/emergencies/docs/Programme%20document-Sahel%20crisis-ENGLISH.pdf [accessed: 15 December 2013].

United Nations High Commissioner for Refugees 2011. *Statistical Yearbook 2010 – Trends in Displacement, Protection and Solutions: Ten Years of Statistics*. Geneva: UNHCR Publications.

United Nations Office on Drugs and Crime 2011. *World Drug Report 2011*. Vienna: United Nations Publications. http://www.unodc.org/documents/data-and-analysis/ WDR2011/World_Drug_Report_2011_ebook.pdf [accessed: 3 January 2014].

Chapter 3

The EU's Growing Engagement in the Sahel: From Development Aid to Military Coordination

Alexander Mattelaer

Introduction

The Sahel region has recently become a focal point of the foreign policy of the European Union (EU).[1] As a result of rising instability throughout the southern neighbourhood, European engagement in this region has been on the increase for several years. This trend not only manifested itself in the traditional areas of EU external action – development assistance and humanitarian aid – but also expanded into the realm of security policy. Inspired by counterterrorism and other strategic concerns, the Sahel developed into a growth region of an otherwise stagnating Common Security and Defence Policy (CSDP). Furthermore, the adoption of a regional strategy in 2011 set a major institutional precedent in the workings of the EU foreign policy system. The 'Strategy for Security and Development in the Sahel' constituted the first flagship of the newly established European External Action Service (EEAS) trying to synchronize the EU's various policy instruments.[2] But it was the implosion of the Malian state in 2012 that truly catapulted the region to the forefront of the EU's foreign policy agenda. Given that the Malian crisis was intimately related to developments in Libya and Algeria, it rapidly became clear that Europe was confronted with a geopolitical chess game on its very doorstep. Since the United States, as part of its pivot to the Asia-Pacific region, encourages European leadership in the southern neighbourhood, the EU framework is slowly emerging as the central mechanism for addressing the broader crisis in the Sahel region.

This chapter intends to take stock of the growing engagement of the EU in the Sahel and to offer an assessment of its logic. It argues that this engagement has over time acquired a strategic dimension, involving the use of various instruments of power at the service of the political debate at the highest level. This follows from a careful consideration of common, though asymmetrically distributed, European interests. Yet in spite of its increased role in the region, the EU operates within the narrow confines of Member State consensus. European foreign policy cooperation

---

1 See Map III in the Annex.

2 Council of the European Union 2011. *Strategy for Security and Development in the Sahel*, Annex to the Council Conclusions on a European Union Strategy for Security and Development in the Sahel, Brussels, 21 March.

therefore consists in an uneasy combination of EU activities and complementary national policies undertaken by (primarily) France and other Member States. In that sense, one must maintain a healthy scepticism about the degree of autonomy of European actions: although the product of complex decision-making processes, the EU's Sahel Strategy can perhaps best be described as the lowest common denominator of European support for French designs in the region. Having said that, a clear case can be made that wider European interests and values are being promoted by the same effort.

The chapter is structured as follows. The first section sets out the broad context required for understanding the geopolitical dynamics of the Sahel region. The second section provides an overview of the EU's policy responses to the challenges the region faces. This is organized around the adoption of the EU's Sahel Strategy in 2011. The third section zooms in the implosion of the Malian state that was triggered by the insecurity fallout from the conflict in Libya. The fourth section analyses the various interventions that have been undertaken to mitigate the security vacuum that emerged in Mali, paying particular attention to the central role of the European crisis response in this regard. Finally, the concluding section takes stock of the various elements discussed and sets forth the overall assessment of the growing EU engagement in the region. In methodological terms, this chapter draws heavily on an analysis of European policy documents and a series of research interviews conducted in the context of a study undertaken earlier at the request of the European Parliament.[3] It is also informed by the discussions held at a number of policy workshops and conferences.[4]

State Fragility in Europe's Southernmost Neighbourhood

Geographically, the Sahel region encompasses the southern edges of the Saharan desert. The exact delineation of the region is subject to some dispute. The EU's Sahel Strategy refers to Mauritania, Mali and Niger as the core Sahelian states, but recognizes that parts of Burkina Faso and Chad are part of the region as well. Yet many scholars prefer to focus on the broader Sahara region into which these

---

3   See Simon, L., Mattelaer, A. and Hadfield, A. 2012. *A Coherent EU Strategy for the Sahel*. Brussels: European Parliament (DG External Policies PE 433.778). The author wishes to thank all interviewees for sharing their valuable insights and his colleague Luis Simon for commenting on an earlier draft of this text. The responsibility for any errors lies of course solely with the author.

4   Apart from the conference 'The Neighbours of the EU's Neighbours: Diplomatic and Geopolitical Dimensions' held at the College of Europe in Bruges on 15–16 November 2012, the conference 'The Sahel Crisis: Where do European and African Perspectives Meet?' jointly organized by the Institute for European Studies at the Vrije Universiteit Brussel and the Egmont Institute on 27 February 2013 needs to be mentioned.

countries are embedded.[5] Given its strong interdependence with developments in North Africa, the analysis presented here adopts the view that the Sahel constitutes Europe's southernmost neighbourhood. The Sahelian states as defined by the EU are not neighbouring countries in a strict sense but constitute the geopolitical frontier south of the Mediterranean, dividing North Africa from sub-Saharan Africa. As such their enduring instability has multiple knock-on effects on Europe's own borders.

The main characteristic of the Sahel is the general fragility of state structures. The Sahel states are geographically vast, extremely poor and politically turbulent. They have to cope with harsh climate conditions and challenging demographics. The region as a whole suffers from frequent food crises and chronic underdevelopment. Individual countries struggle to control their borders and ensure territorial control. Political transitions are typically bound up with armed rebellions or *coups d'état*. The inadequacy of state capacity implies that a relative vacuum of governance endures in the peripheral regions of the Sahel states, giving rise to a breeding ground for all types of illicit activities.

Local economies are heavily reliant on the exports of primary materials. These include, for example, iron ore in Mauritania, gold in Mali, uranium in Niger and oil in Chad.[6] Low levels of agricultural productivity combined with a harsh climate (long dry seasons and short and irregular rainy seasons) imply that subsistence farming is the general rule – leading to recurring famines in dry years.[7] In spite of significant inflows of humanitarian and development aid from the international donor community, the Sahel countries are all situated at the bottom of the Human Development Index and struggle to make any progress towards the Millennium Development Goals.[8] These problems are amplified by demographical trends. Sahelian populations – roughly doubling in size every 20 years – are growing at rapid rates that outpace economic growth. Unsurprisingly, the situation of chronic poverty and unemployment that these young populations find themselves mired in gives rise to turbulent politics.

5   See, for example, Lacoste, Y. 2011. Sahara, perspectives et illusions géopolitiques. *Hérodote*, 142(3), 12–41; and Lacher, W. 2012. *Organized Crime and Conflict in the Sahel-Sahara Region*. Carnegie Papers – Middle East, Washington, DC: Carnegie Endowment for International Peace.

6   See, for example, Augé, B. 2005. Les nouveaux enjeux pétroliers de la zone saharienne. *Hérodote*, 142(3), 183–205; Grégoire, E. 2011. Niger : Un État à forte teneur en Uranium. *Hérodote*, 142(3), 206–25; Deltenre, D. 2012. *Gestion des ressources minérales et conflits au Mali et au Niger. Note d'Analyse*, Brussels: GRIP.

7   See Kandji, T., Verchot, L. and Mackensen, J. 2006. *Climate Variability and Climate Change in the Sahel Region: Impacts and Adaptation Strategies in the Agricultural Sector*. Nairobi: United Nations Environment Programme and World Agroforestry Centre.

8   Chad, Mali, Mauritania and Niger respectively occupy position 184, 182, 155 and 186 on the 2012 Human Development Index. See Human Development Report 2013. *The Rise of the South: Human Progress in a Diverse World*. New York: United Nations Development Programme, 143.

Although the Sahelian states attempt to engage in democratic politics, their history is riddled by frequent rebellions and *coups d'état*. The quasi-permanent challenge to establish a governmental monopoly on the use of violence and the effective rule of law implies that local political establishments are characterized by fraught civil–military relations as well as by a security-centric approach to governance. Whether the result of corruption and patronage, or of sheer governmental incapacity, the political concerns in geographically peripheral regions often go unaddressed and lead to long-standing grievances. Most notably, the nomadic Tuareg community in northern Mali and northern Niger has frequently engaged in armed rebellion as a means to press for political reform.[9] The near absence of regional political cooperation and bilateral suspicions about foreign support for rebel groups give rise to frequent proxy wars amongst the states in the Sahel. Throughout recent history, both Libya and Algeria as the regional powerhouses on the northern flank of the Sahara played important roles in engaging in and arbitrating these regional power plays.[10] The demographical trends mentioned earlier also entailed the existence of large foreign diaspora of Sahelian populations in North Africa (and to a lesser extent in Europe). These migrant communities generate a constant flow of foreign remittances and support.

The limited ability of the Sahel states to police their large and mostly inhospitable territories gives rise to a political vacuum along their northern edges, where most of the subterranean natural resources are concentrated. The thousands of kilometres of desert borders have little to do with local geography or ethnicity and are notoriously porous. Thus emerges a sanctuary for all sorts of illicit activities. These range from various types of smuggling – building on the centuries old tradition of trans-Saharan desert caravans – to a geographical space offering strategic depth to armed rebellions and terrorist groups.[11] Sahel smuggling networks account for one of the main drug trafficking routes into Europe, in particular as far as cocaine imports from Latin America are concerned.[12] Illegal arms trade and human trafficking – including the trading of kidnapped Westerners – constitute

---

9   See, for example, Lecocq, B. 2010. Disputed Desert: Decolonisation, Competing Nationalisms and Tuareg Rebellions in Northern Mali. Leiden: Brill; Raffray; and M. 2013. Les rebellions touarègues au Sahel. Paris: Centre de Doctrine d'Emploi des Forces (Cahier du RETEX).

10   See Chena, S. 2011. Portée et limites de l'hégémonie algérienne dans l'aire sahélo-maghrébine. *Hérodote*, 142(3), 108–24.

11   See, for example, Lohmann, A. 2011. *Who Owns the Sahara? Old Conflicts, New Menaces: Mali and the Central Sahara between the Tuareg, Al Qaida and Organized Crime*. Friedrich Ebert Stiftung, Regional Office Abuja; Tisseron, A. 2011. Enchevêtrements géopolitiques autour de la lutte contre le terrorisme dans le Sahara. *Hérodote*, 142(3), 98–107.

12   See Julien, S. 2011. Le Sahel comme espace de transit des stupéfiants : Acteurs et conséquences politiques. *Hérodote*, 142(3), 12–41.

yet other components of these networks.[13] These swathes of ungoverned space are used by criminal gangs, locally inspired rebellions and foreign groups alike. The infamous presence of 'al-Qaeda in the Islamic Maghreb' (AQIM) is, for example, the reincarnation of the *Groupe Salafiste pour la Prédication et le Combat* – itself a remnant of the Algerian civil war in the 1990s that relocated to northern Mali to evade Algerian counterterrorism efforts.[14] In a great strategic paradox, the near anarchical environment that is the Sahel-Saharan core qualifies a key determinant of the political stability in North Africa, West Africa and the countries along the northern coast of the Gulf of Guinea.

Throughout recent years, the Sahel Strip has increasingly become a 'belt of instability'. Long-standing challenges in terms of socioeconomic developments were ever more frequently complemented by security concerns. This manifested itself in a rise in kidnappings of foreign nationals, religious radicalization, a consolidation of terrorist groups such as AQIM and efforts by both local governments and foreign sponsors to increase the capacity of local security forces.[15] Although one can argue that the fragility of the Sahelian states tended to be deeply intertwined with local politics, the principal diagnosis of the international community was that a lack of state control was the root of the problem, and therefore had to be addressed by capacity-building efforts. It is in this scheme that the EU came to play an ever more prominent role.

Initial Responses: The EU Sahel Strategy

As the long-standing challenges the Sahel region faces were increasingly fused with emerging security threats, various elements within the EU's foreign policy machinery became active in formulating a policy response. This ultimately led the Foreign Affairs Council on 21 March 2011 to adopt the 'Strategy for Security and Development in the Sahel'.[16] This document – the first of its kind – aimed to synchronize the use of the EU's various policy instruments in line with the implicit ambition of addressing the brewing Sahel crisis at the preventive stage. This section describes the policy process that produced this document, analyses

---

13   See, for example, Berghezan, G. 2013. Côte d'Ivoire et Mali, au coeur des traffics d'armes en Afrique de l'Ouest. Brussels: GRIP.

14   See Boukraa, L. 2010. Du Groupe Salafiste pour la Prédication et le Combat (GSPC) à Al-Qaida au Maghreb Islamique (AQIM). *African Journal on Terrorism Studies*, 1, 35–57.

15   The 'war on terror' that followed the 11 September 2001 attacks on the United States also featured an uptick of counterterrorism efforts in the Sahel. See, for example, Ellis, S. 2004. Briefing: The Pan-Sahel Initiative. *African Affairs*, 103(412), 459–64. In turn, various Arab regimes are said to have contributed to the spread of Salafism in the region, displacing the indigenous Sufi tradition of Islam.

16   Council of the European Union, Strategy for Security and Development in the Sahel, op. cit.

its main thrust and suggests that its effective implementation was undermined by internal discord and an acceleration of negative security trends as a result of the conflict in Libya in 2011.

Concern for the Sahel region was first put on the EU's foreign policy agenda during the French Presidency in 2008. Various elements such as the Tuareg uprising in northern Niger in 2007–08, the cancellation of the 2008 Dakar rally out of concern for terrorist attacks in northern Mali, the reporting by the EU Delegations in Sahel countries and the particularly vocal concerns formulated by the EU's Counterterrorism Coordinator Gilles de Kerchove all contributed to a growing appreciation of security threats in the Sahel. Most emblematically, the Malian government already in 2009 requested military assistance from the EU in order to be able to retain control over its northern territories. Under the 2009 Swedish and 2010 Spanish Presidencies, the European Commission and the Council Secretariat dispatched multiple fact-finding missions to Mali, Niger, Mauritania and Algeria. Their findings were incorporated into a joint report finalized in October 2010.[17] Continued unrest in the region (as manifested by multiple kidnappings, assassinations of European nationals and a *coup d'état* in Niger in February 2010) led a group of Member States to press the High Representative for intensified European engagement.[18]

The Foreign Affairs Council of 25 October 2010 tasked the newly established EEAS to draft a strategy for the Sahel.[19] In response to this request, a dedicated Sahel task force was set up under the auspices of the Director for West and Central Africa Manuel López Blanco. Apart from EEAS staff, this task force featured officials from the Directorate-General of Development and Cooperation (DG DevCo), the Directorate-General for Humanitarian Aid and Civil Protection (DG ECHO), the office of the Counter-Terrorism Coordinator and the Commission's new Service for Foreign Policy Instruments (FPI) in charge of managing the Instrument for Stability (IfS). This task force coordinated the allocation of the €450 million originally foreseen in the 10th European Development Fund for Mali, Mauritania and Niger, an additional €150 million made available by DG DevCo and the development of various IfS-funded capacity-building programmes. As such its work constituted an unprecedented exercise of knitting different strands of EU action together in an all-encompassing policy document.[20] Following consultations with Member States, the Sahel Strategy was officially approved by the Foreign Affairs Council of 21 March 2011.

---

17   Council of the European Union 2010. *Final Report on the Sahel Security and Development Initiative*, doc 14361/1, Brussels, 1 October.

18   See Gros-Verheyde, N. 2010. Au Sahel, pas de mission PeSDC pour l'instant, mais une mission quand même. *Bruxelles2*, 22 October.

19   Council of the European Union 2010. *Foreign Affairs Council Conclusions*, doc 15350/10, Brussels, 25 October.

20   See López Lucia, E. 2012. *The EU Foreign Policy after Lisbon: The case of the European Strategy for Security and Development in the Sahel*, paper presented at the GR:EEN First Annual Conference 'The Nature of the EU as a Global Actor', Milan, 13–14 February.

The Sahel Strategy identified four strategic lines of action: (1) development, good governance and internal conflict resolution, (2) political and diplomatic action, (3) security and rule of law, and (4) the fight against violent extremism and radicalization. In consultation with the various partner countries, the EEAS developed a plan that continued existing EU engagement and proposed new initiatives (see Figure 3.1 below). The most prominent strand of EU engagement in the Sahel – with historical roots stretching back to the first Yaoundé Convention of 1963 – is that of development cooperation. With over €500 million earmarked for development spending, the first line of action accounts for the financial lion's share of the European engagement in the region.[21] Yet this traditional engagement was now complemented by an increase in quiet diplomacy – as demonstrated by discrete ministerial visits – and a variety of projects pertaining to the third and fourth line of action.[22] These include IfS-funded initiatives such as the Counter-Terrorism Sahel programme (providing assistance to civilian law enforcement actors) and the West Africa Police Information System (linking the police networks of Benin, Ghana, Mali, Mauritania and Niger with INTERPOL) as well as projects aimed at strengthening regional security capacities in the ECOWAS framework. In short, the Sahel Strategy constituted an ambitious attempt at operationalizing the EU much-vaunted 'comprehensive approach', bridging the gap between security and development policies.

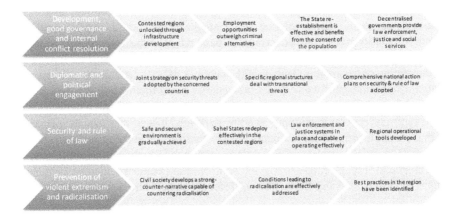

Figure 3.1   EU Strategic Lines of Action in the Sahel
Source: Reproduced from Simon, Mattelaer and Hadfield 2012.

---

21   For a detailed breakdown of spending per line of action foreseen in the Sahel action plan, see European External Action Service 2012. *Strategy for Security and Development in the Sahel: Implementation Progress Report*. Brussels, March.

22   See Gros-Verheyde, N. 2011. 4 ministres du Sahel à Bruxelles : Très discrètement. *Bruxelles2*, 8 December.

Numerous studies about the EU's Sahel Strategy have argued that its analysis is internally coherent but that persistent problems have plagued its implementation.[23] The first issue concerned the insufficient integration of the regional powers Algeria and Nigeria into the political framework. As many of the challenges the Sahel faces are regional in nature, effective regional cooperation including these influential states seems paramount – but this is an area where progress remained limited. In part, this reflects that EU Member States have different views on how to engage Algeria, which has strong but diverse bilateral ties to a handful of European capitals.[24] Secondly, the integration of different policy instruments remained challenging – in the sense that EU officials readily admit that major problems in terms of transparency and coherence persist. The third issue concerned the EU's unwillingness to incorporate military assistance into its foreign policy toolbox. Although options for military CSDP operations were discussed as early as 2009 – following the Malian request for assistance – several EU Member States were reticent to authorize any military engagement. Faced with such opposition (coming in particular from Germany), CSDP planners intentionally reframed the initial CSDP engagement in Niger as a civilian capacity-building mission, that is, as the proverbial thin end of the wedge for keeping the Sahel on the agenda. This illustrates that the effective implementation was severely constrained by disagreements amongst Member States about the appropriate policy tools as well as about the acceptable costs of an increased engagement.

The fourth and arguably most fundamental problem was the fact that the strategy's speed of implementation could not keep up with an acceleration of negative security trends on the terrain. In part, this was due to a sudden shock, namely the civil war and subsequent Western intervention in Libya. The downfall of the regime of Muammar Qadhafi in the summer of 2011 heralded the return of a significant number of well-trained mercenaries to northern Mali, the spread of heavy weapons from Libyan stocks into the illegal armaments circuit as well as the mass return of economic migrants and the associated loss of remittances.[25] Faced with these acute pressures, the already precarious situation in the Sahel went into a downward spiral that the EU's Sahel Strategy – in spite of its preventive ambitions – was unable to stop. Needless to say, the political disagreements amongst Member States did not benefit the EU's speed of response either. The resulting implosion

---

23   See Simon, Mattelaer and Hadfield, op. cit.; Bello, O. 2012. *Quick Fix or Quicksand? Implementing the EU Sahel Strategy.* Working Paper, no. 114, Madrid: FRIDE; and Rouppert, B. 2012. A state of play of the EU Strategy for the Sahel: One year later, disillusions and fears for the future in Mali. *Analysis Note*, Brussels: GRIP.

24   See Darbouche, H. and Dennison, S. 2011. *A 'Reset' with Algeria: The Russia to the EU's South.* London: European Council on Foreign Relations.

25   See United Nations 2012. *Report of the assessment mission on the impact of the Libyan crisis on the Sahel region (7 to 23 December 2011).* New York: UN Security Council (S/2012/42).

of the Malian state constituted the key event that catapulted the Sahel situation to the forefront of international attention.

The Implosion of the Malian State

At the start of 2012, an armed rebellion started in northern Mali. This led, in successive steps, to the partitioning of the country, a *coup d'état* in the rump state and a general political crisis that drew in the involvement of neighbouring states and the broader international community. This section discusses the different phases in the implosion of the Malian state: the gradual abandonment of the north, the *coup* in Bamako, the declaration of the (unrecognized) state of Azawad and the political limbo that followed. Ultimately, this led to a full-blown conflict in which France intervened on behalf of the Malian transitional government.

In the course of previous years, northern Mali had turned into the area in the Sahel in which governmental control had become the weakest. A precarious stability reigned since the previous Tuareg rebellion had come to an end in 2009. Yet the *Programme Spécial pour la Paix, la Sécurité et le Développement du Nord*, launched in 2010 by the fading regime of Malian President Amadou Toumani Touré and partially funded by the EU's IfS, was by some groups perceived as a drive towards militarization. Apart from stationing army garrisons in the north, hardly any governmental services were provided to the population. The situation started to unravel as Tuareg fighters who had become technically unemployed as a result of the downfall of Qadhafi returned to Mali. These former mercenaries possessed significant military expertise as well as heavy weapons and abundant financial resources. Tapping into a widespread perception that the Tuareg community was marginalized in Malian politics (contrary to the more inclusive government in Niger), a new instalment of the Tuareg rebellions ensued.

In mid-January 2012 a newly formed group called the *Mouvement National de Libération de l'Azawad* (MNLA) launched an insurgency offensive targeting military installations in the Gao region. By joining forces with *Ansar Dine*, another new group that was of Islamist inspiration, the MNLA was able to drive governmental forces out of northern Mali in the course of March. In early April the MNLA proclaimed the independence of what they called the state of Azawad, but failed to obtain international recognition.[26] In the ensuing months, however, the MNLA proved unable to assume territorial control. *Ansar Dine* and other Islamist groups such as AQIM and the *Mouvement pour l'Unicité et le Jihad en Afrique de l'Ouest* (MUJAO) made use of the resulting anarchy to install the rule of Islamic law in several cities. What began as a Tuareg revolt thus became ever more intertwined with various illicit trafficking and terrorist networks.

After suffering heavy losses in fighting the Tuaregs, Malian security forces abandoned their posts in the north. Disgruntled by the way the Malian government

---

26   *Financial Times* 2012. Mali rebels declare 'Azawad' independence, 6 April.

was handling the revolt (and in their perception had underinvested in the maintenance of appropriate military capabilities), a group of junior officers mounted a *coup* and installed a military junta on 21 March 2012.[27] This was immediately met by international condemnation, an economic embargo by ECOWAS and a freezing of all EU support apart from humanitarian aid.[28] A Framework Agreement signed on 6 April stipulated that the junta would hand power back to a transitional government led by President Diouncounda Traore. The state of Malian civil–military relations, however, remained precarious ever since.

It rapidly became clear that the Malian authorities would require significant external assistance to redress the situation. Within the framework of ECOWAS, preparations were undertaken with a view to restore the territorial integrity of Mali through an armed intervention (at the time known as the *Mission de la Cedeao au Mali* or MICEMA).[29] In September 2012, the Malian transitional authorities submitted a formal request for ECOWAS military assistance mandated by the UN Security Council under Chapter VII of the UN Charter. On 12 October, the Security Council adopted Resolution 2071, requesting the development of a concept of operations for an African-led international military force.[30] Three days later, the EU's Foreign Affairs Council tasked the EEAS to develop a Crisis Management Concept for a complementary EU training mission (EUTM Mali) for restructuring the Malian armed forces. This decision was accompanied by a major policy shift by Germany. At a policy speech in Strausberg on 22 October Chancellor Merkel – already under siege in several other European dossiers and therefore unwilling to rebuff France – announced that Germany was ready to commit the Bundeswehr to the training mission. An ECOWAS summit in November adopted the strategic concept of the African intervention plan.[31] In turn, the EU Foreign Ministers approved the EUTM Crisis Management Concept on 10 December 2012.[32] Ten days later, the UN Security Council adopted Resolution 2085, which mandated an Africa-led International Support Mission to Mali (AFISMA) and authorized the

---

27   See International Crisis Group 2012. *Putting Mali Back on the Constitutional Track*. Dakar/Brussels: International Crisis Group, 26 March.

28   See Council of the European Union 2012. *Foreign Affairs Council Conclusions*, doc 7849/12. Brussels, 23 March.

29   See Théroux-Bénoni, L.A. 2012. *From MICEMA to AFISMA: The Evolving Response of the International Community to the Situation in Mali*. Paper presented at the ETH conference 'International peacekeeping in Africa', Zürich, 23–4 November.

30   United Nations Security Council 2012. *Resolution 2071 (2012) adopted by the Security Council at its 6846th meeting, on 12 October 2012*, S/RES/2071 (2012). New York, 12 October.

31   *Jane's Intelligence Weekly* 2012. West African army chiefs conclude Mali intervention plan, 8 November.

32   Council of the European Union 2012. *Foreign Affairs Council Conclusions*, doc 17438/12. Brussels, 10 December.

use of force under Chapter VII.[33] These developments were the direct product of intense diplomatic efforts undertaken by the French representations in Brussels, New York and in various African countries.

Although many lamented the slow speed at which both the EU and the UN formulated a policy response to the de facto partitioning of Mali, it must be taken into account that several actors had open misgivings about this plan.[34] First and foremost Algeria showed a sceptical attitude. Keeping in line with the history of earlier Tuareg rebellions, Algiers attempted to mediate between the conflict parties. Algerian suspicions about French designs in the Sahel had to be overcome by an elaborate process of diplomatic courtship by France and the US – ultimately culminating in an official state visit by President Hollande in which he publicly acknowledged the suffering that French colonial rule had inflicted on the Algerian people.[35] Perhaps not uncoincidentally, the EU in the same time frame signed a financing agreement with Algeria for €58 million in grants for supporting the preservation of cultural heritage, the improvement of transport infrastructure and the addressing of youth unemployment.[36] Secondly, the Obama administration also harboured doubts of its own, which pertained above all to questions of military feasibility and scepticism of African abilities to take on such a mission.[37] American military advisers privately cautioned against relying on troops from countries such as Nigeria to take on the challenges posed by desert warfare. Yet, at the same time, French leadership in the Sahel was broadly welcomed as it fitted into the 'leading from behind' posture the US had already adopted in the Libyan conflict. Even within Mali, thirdly, opinions diverged about the prospect of intervention. Some within the remains of the Malian armed forces harboured grave doubts about the precise aims of the intervention: was it about re-conquering the north, re-establishing civilian rule in the south, or both? In December 2012 Prime Minister

---

33   United Nations Security Council 2012. *Resolution 2085 (2012) adopted by the Security Council at its 6898th meeting, on 20 December 2012*, S/RES/2085 (2012). New York, 20 December.

34   The government of Niger was particularly vocal in lamenting the slow and in its view inadequate response of the international community. See Rousselin, P. 2012. Mahamadou Issoufou : Il faut intervenir 'le plus vite possible'. *Le Figaro*, 12 November. Many observers also criticized the EU for its inability to act quickly – see, for example, Heisbourg, F. 2013. France to the rescue. *International Herald Tribune*, 16 January.

35   *Le Monde* 2012. Hollande reconnaît les 'souffrances' infligées à l'Algérie par la colonisation. 20 December. See also Dennison, S. 2012. *The EU, Algeria and the Northern Mali Question*. London: European Council on Foreign Relations.

36   European Union 2012. EU signs financing agreements with Algeria for €58 million of European grants. *Press Release*, doc A491/12. Brussels, 6 November.

37   Geneste, A. 2012. Multiplication d'obstacles pour une opération au Mali. *Le Monde*, 7 December.

Cheick Modibo Diarra was forced to resign under military pressure and replaced by Django Sissoko – again risking delays to the diplomatic process.[38]

The Islamist rebels in the northern part of Mali took advantage of this equivocating attitude of the international community by consolidating their positions. Early in 2013 they launched an offensive towards Bamako – threatening to make the implosion of Mali complete. They thereby forced the hand of France, which had been readying its own military assets for a possible intervention in Mali – even though French diplomats stressed that this was precisely the scenario they always strived to avoid.[39] The unilateral launch of the French *Operation Serval* on 11 January 2013 constituted the turning point at which diplomatic activities made way for action on the ground. The next section describes the multifaceted international response that followed.

Multiple Interventions in a European Master Framework

Although the outbreak of hostilities early in 2013 seemed to have caught many observers off guard, the logic of the French intervention was entirely in keeping with the broader French and European engagement in the region. In fact, *Operation Serval* was primarily aimed at preserving the broader plan for managing the Sahel crisis. Based on a carefully crafted division of labour between France, the EU and African partners, this plan consisted in supporting African forces in 'holding the fort' while the Malian military is being retrained, and at the same time mitigating regional risks by offering security assistance to other countries (in particular Niger and Libya). Given that the various rebel groups have effective ways of resisting this plan through insurgency tactics, it can be expected that these developments will take years to play out – and the precise implementation of the plan may well evolve along the way. This section sketches an overview of this campaign plan and highlights the central coordinating role played by the EU.

The rebel advance towards the towns of Douentza, Konna and Mopti – the geographical bottleneck between northern and southern Mali and therefore the logistical staging base for any intervention to retake the north – was met by French air strikes and the rapid mobilization of ground assets from various French bases in Africa. The first aim of *Operation Serval* was thus to prevent the rebel groups from derailing the intervention plan that had matured throughout 2012. Interestingly, France obtained from early on the permission for its aircraft to pass through Algerian airspace on their bombing runs to northern Mali.[40] As such,

---

38   Nossiter, A. 2012. Mali's Prime Minister Resigns After Arrest, Muddling Plans to Retake North. *New York Times*, 11 December.

39   See Adam, B. 2013. *Mali : de l'intervention militaire française à la reconstruction de l'état*. Brussels: GRIP, 12.

40   Oberlé, T. and Lasserre, I. 2013. Conflit au Mali : le soutien de l'Algérie sera crucial. *Le Figaro*, 15 January.

the Algerian government at least implicitly endorsed the French action. Several Western partners (including the US, the UK, Denmark, Belgium and others) offered bilateral assistance in the form of airlift capabilities or intelligence support.[41]

In a secondary phase, French, Malian and Chadian forces fought their way into the major population centres in the north. By the end of January 2013 the cities of Gao and Timbuktu were again in the hands of the Malian and French authorities and the secular MNLA was able to regain control over Kidal. Many of the Islamist rebels melted away into the mountainous countryside north of Kidal. In the following months, French forces engaged in counterinsurgency operations designed to weaken the rebels as much as possible before African forces would take over primary security responsibility. With Algeria attempting to secure its southern borders, the operational concept of this third phase seemed to exist in smashing the rebels between a French hammer and an Algerian anvil – with the obvious risk that rebels would scatter in different directions across Malian borders.

While *Operation Serval* ran its course, the dual plan of mobilizing African forces and European trainers gathered steam. On 15 January 2013, ECOWAS Chiefs of Defence met in Bamako to finalize the details of the AFISMA deployment, building on troops lifted in from Nigeria, Ivory Coast, Burkina Faso, Senegal and Chad. At an extraordinary meeting of the Foreign Affairs Council, EU Member States tasked the High Representative to provide financial and logistical support to AFISMA.[42] The EU Military Staff subsequently established a 'clearing house' support mechanism for assisting ECOWAS in a variety of ways (ranging from technical, material or advisory support to the provision of strategic airlift, planning and training).[43] In addition, at a donor conference held on 29 January the EU pledged €50 million from the African Peace Facility budget in order to finance AFISMA.[44] Soon afterwards, a proposal materialized for transforming AFISMA into a regular UN peacekeeping operation in order to secure sustainable long-term funding.[45] On 25 April 2013, the Security Council adopted Resolution 2100 and established the United Nations Multidimensional Integrated Stabilization Mission

---

41 See, for example, Codner, M. 2013. The British Military Contribution to Operations in Mali: Is This Mission Creep? *RUSI Analysis*, London, 30 January; and Gros-Verheyde, N. 2013. Renfort britannique pour l'opération au Mali. *Bruxelles2*, 13 January.

42 Council of the European Union 2013. *Foreign Affairs Council Conclusions*. Brussels, 17 January, doc. 5347/13.

43 European Union 2013. EEAS provides a 'clearing house' mechanism to support AFISMA mission in Mali. *Press Release*, doc A30/13. Brussels, 21 January. See also Gros-Verheyde, N. 2013. Au coeur de la clearing house : L'Etat-Major de l'UE à l'échelle euro-africaine. *Bruxelles2*, 25 February. According to military staffers, this boils down mostly to a brokering house for meeting African equipment requests.

44 European Commission 2013. Donor Conference on Mali: EU pledges €50 million to support an African-led peace operation (AFISMA). *Press Release*, doc IP/13/62. Brussels: European Commission, 29 January.

45 See the Letter dated 25 February 2013 from the Secretary-General addressed to the President of the Security Council. New York: UN Security Council (S/2013/112), §8; and

in Mali (MINUSMA). From July 2013 onwards, MINUSMA was mandated to stabilize key population centres and support the re-establishment of state authority. As such, the principal intent behind the AFISMA/MINUSMA operation was to generate a low-budget peacekeeping force able to temporarily fill the security vacuum that would emerges as the bulk of French forces are gradually withdrawn and while Malian forces are being rebuilt.

Parallel to the AFISMA/MINUSMA deployment, the EU accelerated the setting-up of its training mission EUTM Mali, which was formally established on 17 January 2013 with force generation conferences held on 29 January and 5 February. This mission (consisting of 200 military trainers, 200 logistical and medical personnel, a 150-men strong force protection element and 50-men command element) was officially launched on 18 February 2013, with trainings starting in April 2013 and common costs estimated at €12.3 million.[46] Commanded by Brigadier General François Lecointre, the objective of the mission was to provide advice and military training to approximately 3,000 of the Malian armed forces (that is about half of the total) across a range of issues but without physically accompanying Malian forces on combat operations (as was implied in the earlier Malian request). Particular attention was paid to recruitment and re-establishing the Malian command and control chain – seen as critical for ensuring operational effectiveness as well as disciplining troops to abide by international humanitarian law. At the same time, one can expect that EUTM Mali also served as an umbrella for engaging special operations forces for specific tasks under national command authority. Last but not least, the EU did not become directly engaged in re-equipping the (very poor) Malian armed forces, but here an indirect approach was pursued. The EU trust fund established for supporting AFISMA could also be used for equipping Mali itself and EU trainers stood ready to provide advice on equipment priorities.

These military activities were planned to go hand in hand with diplomatic initiatives. Security assistance was made conditional on the adoption of a political roadmap. Approved on 29 January, this roadmap foresaw the organization of early elections by the summer of 2013 and stressed the importance of civilian control over the armed forces. On 7 March, the Malian cabinet established a Commission of Dialogue and Reconciliation as a first step in meeting the demands of the international community before development cooperation would be resumed. In mid-February 2013, the EU already released €20 million through the IfS mechanism.[47] French forces also took care not to alienate the secular

---

Letter dated 27 February 2013 from the President of the Security Council to the Secretary-General. New York: UN Security Council (S/2013/129).

46   See Council of the European Union 2013. *Foreign Affairs Council Conclusions.* Brussels, 18 February, doc 6398/13. See Gros-Verheyde, N. 2013. La mission EUTM Mali : lancée ! *Bruxelles2,* 18 February.

47   European Union 2013. EU releases extra €20 million crisis response and stabilization support package for Mali. *Press Release,* doc A85/13. Brussels, 15 February.

Tuareg MNLA in order to prevent the Malian political class from thinking its opposition problems were resolved by third-party intervention.[48] In order to oversee the political process, High Representative Catherine Ashton proposed to nominate Michel Reveyrand de Menthon, a senior French diplomat, as EU Special Representative for the Sahel.[49]

Several other initiatives highlight the regional approach being taken by the EU. On the one hand, the Bamako liaison office of the (civilian) EUCAP Sahel mission was expanded with justice and police experts in an attempt to move beyond a military containment of the problem. Aimed at strengthening civilian law enforcement and judicial capacities under a joint umbrella, this mission is being looked at as the key instrument for addressing the long-term challenges of installing the effective rule of law. First established in Niger in the summer of 2012, the EUCAP Sahel mission was developed as a preventive measure to help the Sahelian states develop resilience in coping with terrorism and organized crime. The mission was also expected to provide a flexible mechanism for inserting security experts into the EU Delegations in the region, in order to ensure proper follow-up of EU-funded projects. On the other hand, the EU also made headway in planning for a border assistance mission to be set up in Libya, the Crisis Management Concept of which was approved on 31 January 2013.[50] Amongst other considerations, this border management effort plays to the idea that Libya's southern Fezzan region is key to controlling trans-Saharan movement. Such regional security initiatives are of course not the prerogative of the EU. Early in 2013, for example, the US African Command developed plans to set up a base for unmanned aircraft in Niger so as to be able to garner a better intelligence picture of the region.[51]

The importance of these regional dimensions is underscored by the multiple opportunities available to the Islamist rebels to resist Western designs. During the hijacking of the In-Amenas gas installation in south-eastern Algeria in January 2013, the perpetrators demanded that France would halt its operations in Mali. Kidnappings in Nigeria in 2013 constitute another example that Islamists groups can migrate throughout the broader Sahara region and attack Western interests wherever they are most vulnerable.[52] Given that such security threats do not respect national boundaries, the international response must inevitably follow

---

48   See Le Drian, J-Y. 2013. La fin de 'Serval' doit coïncider avec la solution politique au Mali. *Le Monde*, 12 March.

49   Gros Verheyde, N. 2013. Le représentant spécial pour le Sahel est connu. *Le Club de Bruxelles2*, 11 March.

50   Council of the European Union 2013. *EU prepares support to border management in Libya*, doc 5823/13. Brussels, 31 January.

51   Schmitt, E. 2013. US plans drone base in Africa's northwest. *International Herald Tribune*, 29 January.

52   See Bey, M. and Tack, S. 2013. The Rise of a New Nigerian Militant Group. *Stratfor Security Weekly*, 21 February.

a similar approach towards transnational law enforcement. Even if the EU sometimes follows a compartmentalized approach with respect to its different policy instruments – particularly evident in the setting-up of multiple CSDP missions in the same region – it can still serve as the most promising framework for policy coordination.

In sum, the international response to the Malian crisis has been multifaceted. Multiple international organizations (EU, ECOWAS, AU and the UN) have engaged in a series of roughly complementary actions across the full spectrum of crisis management activities. In this sense, the response to the Mali crisis mirrors the one taken in recent years towards Somalia and the Horn of Africa, in which an African Union force leads the fight against extremists with various supporting actions undertaken by the EU and other actors.[53] While the presence of African forces on the front lines gives some credence to the idea of 'African solutions', the centrality of the EU as a major donor and as military coordination mechanism leaves little doubt that the European engagement runs both deep and wide.

Conclusions: Complex European Engagement in the Sahel

What can one make of this analysis of the EU's role in the Sahel region? Three major conclusions stand out. Firstly, the EU's growing engagement has recently acquired a strategic dimension: it is the subject of political debate at the highest level and concerns the use of multiple instruments of power. Secondly, this expanded role of the EU is rooted in geopolitical interests as much as in European values. While idealism is never absent in the EU's external relations, the present crisis in the Sahel made the consideration of hard-nosed energy and security interests unavoidable. Thirdly, this growing 'European' engagement relies on a complex puzzle in which EU institutions and individual Member States constantly compete, complement and interact with one another. In that sense, the changing role of the EU cannot be fully separated from an analysis of French Africa policy and intergovernmental bargaining amongst European capitals.

The EU's engagement in the Sahel has clearly been on the rise. Whereas its role was functionally limited to the provision of development assistance and humanitarian aid until a few years ago, it now extends into a whole new range of more sensitive policy areas. The Sahel dossier now features as one of the major dossiers on the CSDP agenda, which is otherwise quite empty apart from the 'pooling and sharing' debate. Counterterrorism cooperation, such as some of the projects financed by the IfS, constitutes another prominent example of this trend. Although the EU is still cautious in contemplating the use of military instruments, widespread diplomatic support for the French *Operation Serval* indicates that the broader 'European' engagement now encompasses the full spectrum of policy

---

53   On the Horn of Africa see Chapter 4 by Alex Vines and Ahmed Soliman in this volume.

instruments. At the same time, the debate over the EU's role in the region has been lifted from a technocratic to the highest political level – occasionally even rising to the attention of the Heads of State and Government.[54] For all of these reasons, it can be said that the EU's engagement in the Sahel has acquired a strategic dimension: not because it has adopted a policy document and called it a strategy, but because it wields power and influence in function of specific political objectives. It can of course be pointed out that the EU is not the only international actor that has shown growing interest in the region. Yet thanks to the early warning and lobbying efforts by a handful of Member States, the EU moved earlier in putting the Sahel dossier on the agenda and is ready to engage deeper than other actors.

What factors can explain this suddenly growing interest for the Sahel? From a European perspective, this concerns a region in crisis at the very doorstep of the European southern neighbourhood. While the problems and challenges the region faces have been long in the making, it is clear that the traditional instruments used for dealing with the Sahel will no longer serve to safeguard the manifold European interests in the region. Several EU Member States have strong economic and strategic interests in the Sahel. These range from energy security (such as French uranium supplies from Niger) over the challenges that illicit trafficking poses for all southern EU Member States to terrorist threats that concern the security of all EU nationals visiting or working in the region. It is clear that not all Member States experience the impact of instability in the Sahel equally: some have large expatriate communities and investments in the region whereas others do not. As such, the presence of various national interests can be said to cluster together into something of a common European interest, albeit with important caveats.

This fact does not dislodge the more traditional understanding of a value-based European foreign policy. Precisely because interests are being pursued through a common multilateral framework, there will be more constraints imposed on their pursuit. The EU and its Member States can still hold onto their vision of a prosperous Sahel region that is developing economically and in a politically democratic manner. Paradoxically, the fact that 'hard' interests are being threatened means that the willingness to invest the required resources will increase substantially above the level that would otherwise be possible. The Sahel crisis also obliges the EU to work together with critically important partners such as Algeria and Libya on key political dossiers of mutual strategic interest. Again, this is something that would have been unimaginable a few years ago.[55]

The critical caveat with respect to the above analysis is that the EU does not operate as a single, consolidated actor in the region. Although Europeans can agree on the broad analysis of what happens in the Sahel, the disparities between Member States in terms of their respective economic and strategic interests, domestic

---

54   See, for example, European Council 2012. *Conclusions*, doc EUCO 156/12. Brussels, 19 October; and European Council 2013. *Conclusions*, doc EUCO 3/13. Brussels, 8 February.

55   On the European Neighbourhood Policy see Chapter 10 by Michael Leigh in this volume.

constraints and historical legacies imply that the European policy response constitutes a strange mix of shared undertakings and national complementary efforts. In spite of the current rhetoric about EU solidarity vis-à-vis the crisis in Mali, there can be no mistake about the fact that intra-EU disagreements about the appropriateness of the military instrument contributed massively to the EU's inability to prevent a regional degeneration, which was the original ambition of its Sahel Strategy. Disagreements about what is the advisable course of action arise between individual Member States as well as between Member States and EU institutions. As a result, the policy output follows a 'lowest common denominator' pattern as far as EU initiatives are concerned, which are then complemented by national actions as deemed appropriate. *Operation Serval* illustrated this dynamic in the starkest possible terms.

This state of affairs arguably qualifies as a tangible manifestation of the fact that individual Member States have partly convergent but still asymmetric interests in the conduct of their respective foreign policies. This makes the rather convoluted crisis response – involving different international organizations and parallel bilateral cooperation initiatives – politically inevitable. In a crude sense, the European engagement in the Sahel therefore boils down to a partial Europeanization of French strategic designs, with various caveats and constraints inserted by the European sparring partners. At the same time, the emergence of political bargains amongst European capitals that mix the realms of European foreign and domestic policies suggests that there may be a bright future for such arrangements. Such complex architecture for making foreign policy cannot be called strategically efficient, but precisely because it reflects political compromise it may allow for progress in unexpected areas. Albeit frustratingly slow in emergence, the EU's engagement in the Sahel constitutes a case in point.

Bibliography

Adam, B. 2013. *Mali : de l'intervention militaire française à la reconstruction de l'état*. Brussels: GRIP.

Augé, B. 2005. Les nouveaux enjeux pétroliers de la zone saharienne. *Hérodote*, 142(3), 183–205.

Bello, O. 2012. *Quick Fix or Quicksand? Implementing the EU Sahel Strategy*. Working Paper, no. 114. Madrid: FRIDE.

Berghezan, G. 2013. *Côte d'Ivoire et Mali, au coeur des traffics d'armes en Afrique de l'Ouest*. Brussels: GRIP.

Bey, M. and Tack, S. 2013. The Rise of a New Nigerian Militant Group. *Stratfor Security Weekly*, 21 February.

Boukraa, L. 2010. Du Groupe Salafiste pour la Prédication et le Combat (GSPC) à Al-Qaida au Maghreb Islamique (AQIM). *African Journal on Terrorism Studies*, 1, 35–57.

Chena, S. 2011. Portée et limites de l'hégémonie algérienne dans l'aire sahélo-maghrébine. *Hérodote*, 142(3), 108–24.

Codner, M. 2013. The British Military Contribution to Operations in Mali: Is This Mission Creep? *RUSI Analysis*, London, 30 January.

Council of the European Union 2010. *Final Report on the Sahel Security and Development Initiative*. Brussels, 1 October, doc 14361/10.

Council of the European Union 2010. *Foreign Affairs Council Conclusions*. Brussels, 25 October, doc 15350/10.

Council of the European Union 2011. *Strategy for Security and Development in the Sahel*, Annex to the Council Conclusions on a European Union Strategy for Security and Development in the Sahel, Brussels, 21 March.

Council of the European Union 2012. *Foreign Affairs Council Conclusions*, doc 7849/12. Brussels, 23 March.

Council of the European Union 2012. *Foreign Affairs Council Conclusions*, doc 17438/12. Brussels, 10 December.

Council of the European Union 2013. *Foreign Affairs Council Conclusions*, doc. 5347/13. Brussels, 17 January.

Council of the European Union 2013. *EU prepares support to border management in Libya*, doc 5823/13. Brussels, 31 January.

Council of the European Union 2013. *Foreign Affairs Council Conclusions*, doc 6398/13. Brussels, 18 February.

Darbouche, H. and Dennison, S. 2011. *A 'Reset' with Algeria: The Russia to the EU's South*. London: European Council on Foreign Relations.

Deltenre, D. 2012. *Gestion des ressources minérales et conflits au Mali et au Niger*. *Note d'Analyse*, Brussels: GRIP.

Dennison, S. 2012. *The EU, Algeria and the Northern Mali Question*. London: European Council on Foreign Relations.

Ellis, S. 2004. Briefing: The Pan-Sahel Initiative. *African Affairs*, 103(412), 459–64.

European Council 2012. *Conclusions*, doc EUCO 156/12. Brussels, 19 October.

European Commission 2013. Donor Conference on Mali: EU pledges €50 million to support an African-led peace operation (AFISMA). *Press Release*, doc IP/13/62. Brussels, 29 January.

European Council 2013. *Conclusions*, doc EUCO 3/13. Brussels, 8 February.

European External Action Service 2012. *Strategy for Security and Development in the Sahel: Implementation Progress Report*, Brussels, March.

European Union 2012. EU signs financing agreements with Algeria for €58 million of European grants. *Press Release*, doc A491/12. Brussels, 6 November.

European Union 2013. EEAS provides a 'clearing house' mechanism to support AFISMA mission in Mali. *Press Release*, doc A30/13. Brussels, 21 January.

European Union 2013. EU releases extra €20 million crisis response and stabilization support package for Mali. *Press Release*, doc A85/13. Brussels, 15 February.

Financial Times 2012. Mali rebels declare 'Azawad' independence, 6 April.

Geneste, A. 2012. Multiplication d'obstacles pour une opération au Mali. *Le Monde*, 7 December.

Grégoire, E. 2011. Niger : Un État à forte teneur en Uranium. *Hérodote*, 142(3), 206–25.

Gros-Verheyde, N. 2010. Au Sahel, pas de mission PeSDC pour l'instant, mais une mission quand même. *Bruxelles2*, 22 October.

Gros-Verheyde, N. 2011. 4 ministres du Sahel à Bruxelles : Très discrètement. *Bruxelles2*, 8 December.

Gros-Verheyde, N. 2013. Renfort britannique pour l'opération au Mali. *Bruxelles2*, 13 January.

Gros-Verheyde, N. 2013. La mission EUTM Mali : lancée! *Bruxelles2*, 18 February.

Gros-Verheyde, N. 2013. Au coeur de la clearing house : L'Etat-Major de l'UE à l'échelle euro-africaine. *Bruxelles2*, 25 February.

Gros-Verheyde, N. 2013. Le représentant spécial pour le Sahel est connu. *Le Club de Bruxelles2*, 11 March.

Heisbourg, F. 2013. France to the rescue. *International Herald Tribune*, 16 January.

Human Development Report 2013. *The Rise of the South: Human Progress in a Diverse World*. New York: United Nations Development Programme.

International Crisis Group 2012. *Putting Mali Back on the Constitutional Track*. Dakar/Brussels: International Crisis Group, 26 March.

Jane's Intelligence Weekly 2012. West African army chiefs conclude Mali intervention plan, 8 November.

Julien, S. 2011. Le Sahel comme espace de transit des stupéfiants : Acteurs et conséquences politiques. *Hérodote*, 142(3), 12–41.

Kandji, T., Verchot, L. and Mackensen, J. 2006. *Climate Variability and Climate Change in the Sahel Region: Impacts and Adaptation Strategies in the Agricultural Sector*. Nairobi: United Nations Environment Programme and World Agroforestry Centre.

Lacher, W. 2012. *Organized Crime and Conflict in the Sahel-Sahara Region*. Carnegie Papers – Middle East. Washington, DC: Carnegie Endowment for International Peace.

Lacoste, Y. 2011. Sahara, perspectives et illusions géopolitiques. *Hérodote*, 142(3), 12–41.

Lecocq, B. 2010. *Disputed Desert: Decolonisation, Competing Nationalisms and Tuareg Rebellions in Northern Mali*. Leiden: Brill.

Le Drian, J-Y. 2013. La fin de 'Serval' doit coïncider avec la solution politique au Mali. *Le Monde*, 12 March.

Le Monde 2012. Hollande reconnaît les 'souffrances' infligées à l'Algérie par la colonisation. 20 December.

Lohmann, A. 2011. *Who Owns the Sahara? Old Conflicts, New Menaces: Mali and the Central Sahara between the Tuareg, Al Qaida and Organized Crime*. Friedrich Ebert Stiftung, Regional Office Abuja.

López Blanco, M. 2011. *A Strategy for Security and Development in the Sahel. Presentation at the Transatlantic Symposium on Dismantling Transnational Illicit Networks*, Lisbon, 18 May.

López Lucia, E. 2012. *The EU Foreign Policy after Lisbon: The Case of the European Strategy for Security and Development in the Sahel*, paper presented at the GR:EEN First Annual Conference 'The Nature of the EU as a Global Actor', Milan, 13–14 February.

Nossiter, A. 2012. Mali's Prime Minister Resigns after Arrest, Muddling Plans to Retake North. *New York Times*, 11 December.

Oberlé, T. and Lasserre, I. 2013. Conflit au Mali : le soutien de l'Algérie sera crucial. *Le Figaro*, 15 January.

Raffray, M. 2013. *Les rebellions touarègues au Sahel*. Cahier du RETEX. Paris: Centre de Doctrine d'Emploi des Forces.

Rouppert, B. 2012. A state of play of the EU Strategy for the Sahel: One year later, disillusions and fears for the future in Mali. *Analysis Note*. Brussels: GRIP.

Rousselin, P. 2012. Mahamadou Issoufou : Il faut intervenir 'le plus vite possible'. *Le Figaro*, 12 November.

Schmitt, E. 2013. US plans drone base in Africa's northwest. *International Herald Tribune*, 29 January.

Simon, L., Mattelaer, A. and Hadfield, A. 2012. *A Coherent EU Strategy for the Sahel*. Brussels: European Parliament (DG External Policies PE 433.778).

Théroux-Bénoni, L.A. 2012. *From MICEMA to AFISMA: The Evolving Response of the International Community to the Situation in Mali*. Paper presented at the ETH conference 'International peacekeeping in Africa', Zürich, 23–24 November.

Tisseron, A. 2011. Enchevêtrements géopolitiques autour de la lutte contre le terrorisme dans le Sahara. *Hérodote*, 142(3), 98–107.

United Nations 2012. *Report of the assessment mission on the impact of the Libyan crisis on the Sahel region (7 to 23 December 2011)*. New York: UN Security Council (S/2012/42).

United Nations 2013. *Letter dated 25 February 2013 from the Secretary-General addressed to the President of the Security Council*. New York: UN Security Council (S/2013/112).

United Nations 2013. *Letter dated 27 February 2013 from the President of the Security Council to the Secretary-General*. New York: UN Security Council (S/2013/129).

United Nations Security Council 2012. *Resolution 2071 (2012) adopted by the Security Council at its 6846th meeting, on 12 October 2012*, S/RES/2071 (2012). New York, 12 October.

United Nations Security Council 2012. *Resolution 2085 (2012) adopted by the Security Council at its 6898th meeting, on 20 December 2012*, S/RES/2085 (2012). New York, 20 December.

Chapter 4

The Horn of Africa: Transnational and Trans-Regional Dynamics in Europe's Broader Neighbourhood

Alex Vines and Ahmed Soliman

Introduction: The Horn of Africa's Challenges in Regional Terms[1]

Within Africa, the Horn of Africa stands out in terms of its political, developmental and security challenges.[2] Its experiences do not compare well to other parts of the continent, and resist conventional efforts to categorize and understand them. Regional dynamics also bear some similarities to those in the Middle East, with which the Horn of Africa shares some cultural affinities – unsurprising given the proximity of the Horn to the Gulf states, North Africa and the Levant. While comparisons with the Middle East also fall short, the events of the 'Arab Spring' have correctly focused minds on dynamics in the Horn that have the potential to fuel similar upheaval. Nevertheless, regimes in the region have proved resistant to change fuelled by socioeconomic pressures, which have fed into serious protests in Ethiopia, Uganda and Sudan.

The Horn of Africa is important to the European Union (EU) in terms of its geo-strategic significance; the scale of its humanitarian and developmental challenges; the negative impact of piracy off the coast of Somalia on international maritime security and regional and international economic activities; the effects of irregular migration out of the region, including into Europe, and the attendant significance of the region's diaspora communities in the EU; and the threat of terrorism, both in the region and through its linkages to Europe.

This chapter begins by providing an overview of the current political economy of the region. It moves on to describe some of the background leading up to the adoption of the EU's 'Strategic Framework for the Horn of Africa'. It examines

---

1 This chapter draws upon Soliman, A., Mosley, J. and Vines, A. 2012. *The EU Strategic Framework for the Horn of Africa: A Critical Assessment of Impact and Opportunities*. Brussels: European Parliament (DG External Policies PE 433.799).

2 The Horn of Africa is defined, for the purpose of this chapter and by the EU, as the countries belonging to the Inter-Governmental Authority on Development (IGAD): Djibouti, Eritrea, Ethiopia, Kenya, Somalia, South Sudan, Sudan and Uganda. See Map IV in the Annex.

how the approach is fairing since its adoption in 2011, and highlights some of the EU funding instruments used to implement policies in the region. Next, an analysis of the EU special envoy for the Horn of Africa's appointment, key challenges and relations is provided, followed by a look at the coherence of the EU's ongoing civilian and military missions. The chapter concludes by questioning the applicability of the EU's democracy and human rights agenda and conditionality toward development efforts with the region.

Political and Economic Realities that Persist in the Region

Effective, external engagement must take account of the political and economic realities that persist in the region. Some of these realities are tackled below.

Conflict

The region has experienced active conflict for decades – in Ethiopia this trend stretches back even further. Whereas conflicts in other parts of Africa have begun to cool following the turbulence of the post-Cold War 1990s, the Horn of Africa has resisted this trend. The last decade has seen two Ethiopian military interventions in Somalia; a Kenyan intervention in Somalia; a brief clash between Eritrea and Djibouti; clashes between newly independent South Sudan and Sudan; and continuing insurgencies in Sudan, South Sudan, Ethiopia and Somalia. Ethiopian airstrikes on Eritrean territory in March 2012 served as a reminder that while open hostilities have been largely absent since the two countries' 1998–2000 war, unresolved tensions related to the conflict remain and are a key factor in the regional security picture. The political crisis in South Sudan that erupted in December 2013 has already claimed thousands of casualties and caused half a million people to be displaced.

Violence has long been an important element of identity formation across the region, including through indigenous imperialist projects and processes of state formation and consolidation, as well as through the attendant resistance to and attempts to escape from the states in the region. These dynamics predate the colonial presence in the Horn, and have continued afterwards – especially in Ethiopia, Eritrea and Sudan. The current ruling parties in South Sudan, Uganda, Ethiopia and Eritrea have their roots in resistance movements which spawned insurgencies and overthrew the pre-existing regime (or in the case of South Sudan secured the right to secession).

Insecurity in one country is frequently linked to another.[3] States in the region have intervened in their neighbours' conflicts for decades. Many state borders cut through economic or social zones, providing avenues for the transmission of

---

3   Healy, S. 2008. *Lost Opportunities in the Horn of Africa*. Africa Programme Report. London: Chatham House.

instability from one to the other. Arid and semi-arid regions in Somalia, eastern Ethiopia and northern Kenya form one such region – with trade, linguistic and religious ties providing linkages across borders. Similarly, Ethiopia's south-western and western frontiers have linkages into Sudan, South Sudan and Kenya. Relatively porous borders allow for population movement, in terms of displacement by conflict or food insecurity; or of military deployments or militia movements, who might use poorly policed border regions as a zone of operation. Even localized conflicts in such regions – for example over access to land or water – can spill across borders, making them difficult to contain.

Governance

Insecurity has fed into the generally poor track record of governance in the region, reinforcing and exacerbating its impacts. Changes of government/regime have rarely been achieved by other than violent means: the 2010 elections in Somaliland and the 2002 elections in Kenya both saw the presidency transferred to an opposition political party, but remain rare exceptions. With Mwai Kibaki unable to stand for a third term, the 2013 Kenyan elections resulted in a relatively peaceful transfer of power to a new political dispensation. Under the Jubilee Coalition, Uhuru Kenyatta – a member of Kenya's political elite – was declared president. Even the political transition in Ethiopia following the death of Prime Minister Meles Zenawi did not represent a transfer of power outside the ruling party.

In Eritrea, Ethiopia, Somaliland, Uganda, South Sudan and Sudan, the current political dispensation was introduced violently, either through civil war or a *coup d'état*. With the exception of Somaliland, Ethiopia and Somalia, all those states are still led by former insurgents or *coup* leaders. Governments in Ethiopia, Eritrea, South Sudan, Sudan and Uganda still define themselves in large part in national security terms. Somalia is struggling to re-introduce state institutions after more than 20 years of civil war. In South Sudan, political rivalry between the president and the former vice-president has escalated into full-scale civil conflict. Even Kenya's relative stability has been punctuated by election-related violence since the re-introduction of multiparty politics in the 1990s. Djibouti, while stable if not democratic, hosts French and US military bases, and is a key logistics centre for anti-piracy missions in the Gulf of Aden and off the east coast of Somalia.[4] In such a context, it is perhaps unsurprising that regional governments are perceived by many citizens in the region less as service providers and more as a threat to be evaded – particularly by those at the margins of society or the frontiers of states.

Growth

In spite of the security conditions, Kenya, Ethiopia and Uganda have managed to significantly boost economic growth rates in the last decade. With the exception of

---

4   See Map IV in the Annex.

Kenya, states in the region are building on a very low economic base and remain dependent on the export of primary commodities. Growth is thus also highly vulnerable to shocks, external or internal. Sudan's and Eritrea's economies only picked up once oil (Sudan) and mining (Eritrea) operations came on stream. But Sudan's economy, as well as South Sudan's, has been hugely and detrimentally affected by instability following the July 2011 spilt, especially as a result of the halt in oil exports from South Sudan in 2012, the threat by Sudan in 2013 to do the same and the internal crisis now enveloping the south. Kenya's economy is relatively more diversified, and the country serves as an important financial and investment hub for East Africa. Kenya's growth trajectory has not yet recovered to its pre-2008 trend, holding steady around 5 per cent.[5] The effects of the global downturn exacerbated the impacts of the early 2008 post-election violence on Kenya's economy, denting its recovery prospects.

Nevertheless, continued growth in most countries of the region has helped to transform perceptions of the region from being dominated by famine or violence towards increasingly attractive investment destinations. Slow growth and limited financial returns in the more developed markets of Europe and the United States have also helped to drive interest in riskier emerging regions such as East Africa – and Kenya and Ethiopia in particular. A significant element of risk remains, in part linked to the threat of insecurity. Another factor is inflation; most countries in the region have experienced double-digit inflation along with higher growth rates in the last five years, although for different reasons. All countries are to a greater or lesser extent sensitive to fluctuations in global commodity prices, which have been rising again following a brief pause during the global economic downturn. However, Ethiopia's inflation is also fuelled by monetary policy, including intentional devaluation of the birr, but also heavy government borrowing. Sudan and South Sudan's recent inflationary pressures have been influenced strongly by monetary policy in the wake of disruptions to oil exports, which has seen government revenues in both countries plunge. Lacklustre monetary policy in Kenya also fed strong inflation during 2011.[6]

As such, while the growth story is an important element of the Horn of Africa's regional trajectory, these recent economic gains remain fragile. In the case of Sudan, the economy has actually contracted in the last two years, and is projected to do so again. High prices also have the capacity to feed into social unrest, or to exacerbate the vulnerability of certain populations – especially those already affected by food insecurity.

Another important aspect of the economic story has been the improvement of essential infrastructure – especially in terms of transportation and power. These improvements have had regional impacts, reflecting potential and actual linkages and dependencies between neighbours. For example, Ethiopia has remained

---

5   World Bank 2013. *Kenya: Country Results Profile*, November, http://go.worldbank. org/GI5VJ50Z70 [accessed: 30 December 2013].

6   Soliman, Mosley and Vines, op. cit., 12.

dependent on Djibouti's ports for the vast majority of its external trade for more than a decade, after its border with Eritrea was closed by the war. Ethiopia, meanwhile, is developing a number of hydroelectric dams – boosting its generation capacity to the point where it will be able to export power to its neighbours. Projects to develop transmission infrastructure are underway, connecting Djibouti, Kenya and Sudan to Ethiopian supplies. Kenya remains the main '*entrepôt*' for trade into Eastern Africa, via existing port facilities at Mombasa. Ground has been broken on a Kenyan project to develop a new deep-water port at Lamu, with the aim of providing a new logistics hub and transport corridor serving not only Kenya but also Ethiopia, South Sudan and Uganda.

Some of these projects are some way off from completion, but they point to the economic interconnections between the countries of the region – linkages and dependencies – which feed into and are reinforced or undermined by the region's security dynamics.[7] Eritrea's economy would naturally be dominated by trade and investment links with Ethiopia, to both countries' benefit, were it not for the severing of relations. Insecurity in Somalia prevents its ports from challenging Djibouti or Kenya as a regional hub, despite its long coastline. South Sudan's disputes with Sudan have pushed it towards expanding trade routes via Kenya, while trade through existing and more logical links from Port Sudan is undermined. Meanwhile, the proposed port at Lamu and the rail/road/pipeline corridor connecting it with South Sudan have received a boost, helping Kenya to continue to bolster its role as a regional gateway – but potentially intensifying concerns in Uganda and Tanzania that Kenya's businesses and services will undermine their own offerings. Although the East African Community (EAC) is making tangible progress on economic integration, forward momentum faces the prospect of interruptions due to political factors.

Cooperation

Although the region's interconnectedness and dependencies are manifold, cooperation between states remains lukewarm.[8] This is reflected in the relative weakness of the regional bloc, the Inter-Governmental Authority on Development (IGAD). Although IGAD has served as an important forum – most notably providing the auspices for the peace negotiations that led to transitional arrangements in Sudan (2005–11) and Somalia (2004–12) – it remains largely subservient to the agendas of its members. Conflicts between members have undermined its coherence. Eritrea's membership has been suspended since it withdrew in protest over Ethiopia's December 2006 intervention in Somalia – a fundamental split in the bloc which has continued to dominate its agenda since then. Uganda, Kenya,

---

7 Love, R. 2009. *Economic Drivers of Conflict and Cooperation in the Horn of Africa*. Africa Programme Briefing Paper 2009/01. London: Chatham House.

8 Healy, S. 2011. *Hostage to Conflict: Prospects for Building Regional Economic Cooperation in the Horn of Africa*. Africa Programme Report. London: Chatham House.

Djibouti and Ethiopia all have troops in Somalia at present. Ethiopia and Kenya in particular have an interest in Somalia's future federal arrangements, given the establishment of regional administrations alongside their common borders. Sudan and Uganda have a long history of mutual interference in the other's security, which has fuelled insurgencies in both countries. These dynamics, and the intervention of Ugandan troops in South Sudan at the request of President Kiir, pose problems for the ongoing IGAD negotiations aimed at ending the conflict and for finding a regionally brokered political solution moving forward. Perceptions of Eritrea as a regional spoiler, undermining the security of its neighbours (especially Somalia), must be tempered with the understanding that foreign policy in the Horn of Africa is driven in large part by the logic of 'the enemy of my enemy is my friend'; if Asmara interferes, its interference is not so different from that of its neighbours – its main characteristic is that it punches above its weight, in terms of the size of its population and economy.

In light of these tangled dynamics, it is essential to view the Horn of Africa through a regional lens – in addition to maintaining bilateral relations – in order for the EU's engagement to be coherent, and to support the body's goals.

Utility of a Regional Approach

As a pillar of the African Union's (AU) regional integration framework, IGAD has the potential to benefit from broader regional institutional improvements. In practice, it has largely failed to keep pace with other regional blocs, and even on less politically sensitive issues such as trade, IGAD has not played a leading role – its members are part of more functional regional trade blocs including the EAC and the Common Market for Eastern and Southern Africa (COMESA). In terms of the AU regional security agenda, IGAD was unable to provide the framework for a regional stand-by brigade, which instead is being developed in common with the members of the EAC as an East African Stand-by Force (ESF).

States of the region have demonstrated a track record of resisting external influence. In Ethiopia and Eritrea, in particular, independence and self-reliance form an essential part of the national identity – in Ethiopia grounded in the 1896 defeat of Italian forces at the Battle of Adwa, and in Eritrea in the 30-year liberation struggle from Ethiopia, ultimately achieved without external support (and in the face of significant external assistance to its foe in Addis Ababa). In Sudan, a protracted Western policy of isolation – most visibly embodied by the International Criminal Court's (ICC) issue of an arrest warrant for President Omar Hassan al-Bashir – has left Khartoum reluctant to engage in dialogue. Ethiopia and Uganda have been adept at maintaining important security relationships with Western powers, which has proved useful in limiting external criticism of governance shortcomings in both countries.

The EU Strategic Framework for the Horn of Africa

The EU and its Member States are the largest providers of development and humanitarian assistance to the Horn of Africa, as well as being key partners of the AU and IGAD. The United Kingdom, Italy and France have strong historical ties to the region and Europe hosts the largest concentrations of diasporas from the region, all meaning that the EU is in a position to be an important driver for change.[9]

EU concern for the Horn of Africa came to the fore in 2006 with the European Commission Communication 'Strategy for Africa: An EU regional political partnership for peace, security and development in the Horn of Africa'.[10] Under the Swedish Presidency in December 2009 a more comprehensive 'EU Policy on the Horn of Africa' was adopted.[11] These two documents were the building blocks for the current comprehensive strategy for the region.

The EU adopted a 'Strategic Framework for the Horn of Africa' in November 2011.[12] It marked a significant shift in the EU's approach to the region – coordinating action across Member States, and providing a more coherent voice in the region through the appointment of a European Union Special Representative (EUSR). The creation of this position was recommended in the 2009 policy. Italy had lobbied strongly for the role and for it to be filled by a former Italian politician and other European candidates were also short-listed. The post was filled in early 2012 by a Greek national, Alexander Rondos (see below).

Drafted by the Horn of Africa Division of the European External Action Service (EEAS), under the leadership of the Director for Africa Nick Westcott, the Strategic Framework guides EU action for greater peace, stability and prosperity in the region. It sets out five areas for EU action, proposing how to pursue its approach in partnership with the region and key partners.[13]

---

9 Hagström Frisell, E., Tham Lindell, M. and Skeppström. E. 2012. Land in Sight? The EU Comprehensive Approach towards Somalia. *FOI – Swedish Defence Research Agency*, FOI-R 3462, Stockholm, June.

10 The Communication built on two existing strategies: The European Consensus for Development and the EU Strategy for Africa, both initiated in 2005. European Commission 2006. *Strategy for Africa: An EU Regional Political Partnership for Peace, Security and Development in the Horn of Africa*. Brussels, 20 October.

11 Council of the European Union 2009. *An EU Policy on the Horn of Africa – Towards a Comprehensive EU Strategy*, Brussels, 10 December.

12 Council of the European Union 2011. *Strategic Framework for the Horn of Africa*, Council Conclusion, Brussels, 16858/11, 14 November.

13 The five areas are: building robust and accountable political structures; contributing to conflict resolution and prevention; mitigating security threats emanating from the region; promoting economic growth; and supporting regional economic cooperation. As well as areas for action, specific sub-strategies and action plans are subject to agreement by the Commission, Council and Member States. The High Representative/Vice President, EU

How is the Strategic Framework Faring in Practice?

The adoption of the Strategic Framework for the Horn of Africa should open new opportunities for successful engagement in the region. The EU and its Member States undertake a wide range of activities, from humanitarian operations to capacity building of regional institutions, anti-piracy missions and military training. By providing an overarching set of principles for European engagement, the Strategic Framework offers the potential for the combined impact of Member States and EU institutions to be harnessed to push for the EU's goals in the region.

The prospect of more coherent action offers the opportunity for the EU to be recognized in the region as an actor in its own right, and with the influence that the scale of EU investment should bring. Through the appointment of the EUSR for the Horn of Africa, the EU has the potential to speak more clearly with one voice in the region. Doing so would allow the EU to exploit more fully its comparative advantage as one of the most significant sources of assistance and investment into the region and an important trade partner.

One early sign of a cost-benefit with the Strategic Framework is that where before there was a sense that the EU was undertaking separate actions and policies in the region that were not linked, the document has given the EU a set of common objectives and aims in its approach to the Horn of Africa. However, its instruments still form a mosaic of intervention in the region; two years after the Strategic Framework's inception it remains difficult to assess whether there has been a significant improvement in the coherence of approach.

In late 2012 the EEAS was preparing a review of the Strategic Framework to present to the Council. This draft review was stuck for much of 2013 in internal EU consultations, including with the Commission's Directorate-General Development Cooperation (DG DevCo) which was concerned that the EEAS was proposing a new Strategic Framework for the Horn of Africa rather than updating the current one to accommodate changes in the region. However, a 2013 Council Working document on an 'Integrated EU Approach to Security and Rule of Law in Somalia', prepared by the EEAS in cooperation with the Commission, EUSR and EU Delegation, claimed to build on the Horn of Africa Strategic Framework by considering 'coherence and synergies between EU instruments'.[14]

In addition, a thorough report on the Strategy was adopted by the European Parliament's Committee on Foreign Affairs in January 2013.[15] Also, Catherine

---

Delegations in the region, Commission and Member States work together to implement this Strategic Framework. Ibid.

14 European Commission and High Representative 2013. *Joint Staff Working Document on an 'Integrated EU Approach to Security and Rule of Law in Somalia'*, SWD(2013) 277 final, Brussels, 12 July.

15 European Parliament 2012. *Report: EU Strategy for the Horn of Africa*, Committee on Foreign Affairs, (2012/2026(INI)), Rapporteur: Charles Tannock, Brussels, 10 December.

Ashton, the EU's High Representative of the Union for Foreign Affairs and Security Policy and Vice-President of the European Commission (HR/VP), presented an implementation review of the Horn of Africa Strategic Framework to the Council in January 2013, commenting that 'the political and security situation has developed favourably'.[16]

This monitoring is commendable and the Strategic Framework should be reviewed annually in order to highlight implementation gaps and opportunities to improve coordination in such a shifting region. Cooperation with the region will be enhanced if the Parliament ensures its findings from this, and subsequent studies on the region are sent to the Pan-African Parliament, the IGAD secretariat and national parliaments of the region.

EU Funding for the Horn of Africa

The EU implements its policies in the Horn of Africa through geographical and thematic financial instruments. It draws on an array of means to implement action, including: development cooperation through the European Development Fund (EDF) and Member States' bilateral programmes, joint programming between the EU and its Member States in the regions' countries where appropriate, relevant EU budget lines, trade instruments, conflict prevention and crisis response, including the Common Security and Defence Policy (CSDP), diplomacy, EUSRs, cooperation and dialogue through the Cotonou Partnership Agreement of 2000. The EU also provides humanitarian assistance to the most vulnerable populations in accordance with humanitarian principles.

A new generation of financial instruments and country and regional strategies will be implemented under the Multiannual Financial Framework 2014–20. The need to start programming for the EU's new budget presents an opportunity to set aside internal EU struggles over the division of responsibilities and to put cooperation with partner countries at centre stage. The 'Strategic Framework for the Horn of Africa' should provide coherence in the next cycle of programming, making it easier to determine priorities for each of the countries as well as areas of regional support.[17] Three of the financial instruments relevant to the Horn of Africa are outlined below.

---

16 Council of the European Union 2013. *Implementation Review of the Horn of Africa Strategic Framework Presented by the HR/VP*, Political and Security Committee, 11 January, https://www.gov.uk/government/uploads/system/uploads/attachment-data/file/224337/evidence-eeas-hoa-strategic-framework-review.pdf [accessed: 30 November 2013].

17 Interview with an EU official, Brussels, August 2012.

The European Development Fund

The EDF is the geographical instrument for the group of African, Caribbean and Pacific countries (ACP).[18] Under the 10th EDF (2007–13), €17.7 billion out of a total of €22.7 billion was given to support National and Regional Indicative Programmes (NIPs and RIPs).[19] Of that figure, countries in the Horn of Africa received €2 billion. Sudan and South Sudan were ineligible[20] and Ethiopia alone received €644 million in development assistance. In the same period, the EU also allocated €645 million to the four Regional Economic Communities (RECs) of the Eastern and Southern Africa and Indian Ocean (ESAIO) region: IGAD, COMESA, EAC, and the Indian Ocean Commission (IOC). In 2010, the EU signed project financing agreements totalling €118 million to support diverse regional economic integration and development projects in the region as well as the RECs regional cooperation and global economic integration.[21]

The European Community Humanitarian Office (ECHO)

The EU is the world's biggest donor of humanitarian aid working mostly in the areas of food crises, catastrophes, and risk reduction.[22] From 2011 to 2012 the European Commission allocated €313 million of humanitarian aid to the Horn of Africa in the form of food assistance, nutrition, water and sanitation.[23] Because of the need to remain independent, DG ECHO is also not included in the EU Delegations on the ground.[24] Despite its independence, DG ECHO cooperates

---

18   The EDF is currently funded outside the EU budget based on national contributions. Some EU Member States and the Commission are pushing for it to be included in the EU budget, to increase public control of this aid, as well as transparency and effectiveness. See European Commission 2011. Communication from the Commission to the European Parliament, the Council, the European Economic and Social Committee and the Committee of the Regions, *A Budget for Europe 2020 – Part I*, COM(2011) 500/I final, Brussels, 26 June.

19   The EDF for 2014–20 amounts to €34 billion, aimed at financing poverty reduction in cooperation with developing countries.

20   Due to Sudan not having ratified the revised Cotonou Agreement, which provides the legal framework for relations between the EU and the ACP.

21   The overall objective of the 10th EDF ESAIO Regional Strategy Paper (RSP) is to contribute to the eradication of poverty in member countries and assist them in attaining the Millennium Development Goals (MDG) as enshrined in the Cotonou Partnership Agreement by supporting economic growth and developing trade.

22   ECHO has an annual budget averaging €1 billion, which is not reliant on emergency contributions from Member States in order to avoid the risk of politicizing aid.

23   European Commission 2012. Disaster resilience in the Horn of Africa to be strengthened further with new aid injection from the European Commission. *Press Release*, IP/12/864, Brussels, 31 July.

24   Aid is directed first and foremost at the people. This is one of the reasons why ECHO is not a direct part of EU crisis management and has not been integrated into the

with DG DevCo, the EEAS and the EU Delegations in the field. There are ECHO field offices in Djibouti, Eritrea, Ethiopia, Uganda, and a regional desk in Nairobi in charge of Somalia.

The Instrument for Stability (IfS)

Launched in 2007, the IfS has intensified the Commission's work in the area of conflict prevention, crisis management and peace-building. The instrument should react 'swiftly' to unforeseen crises, working alongside humanitarian aid and the EU's other external assistance. Over a quarter of funds, the largest share, is given to projects in Africa.[25] In the Horn of Africa the IfS has assisted on several issues: early recovery programmes in Ethiopia after the Horn of Africa drought, as part of other humanitarian relief efforts (€13.75 million); support to stability in post-referendum Sudan (€18 million); and continued assistance to countries engaged with piracy trials linked to the EU's CSDP Atalanta counter-piracy naval operation.[26]

Deployment, which can take up to six months, is still an issue of capacity that requires improvement.[27] Most funds are used in response to short-term crises (less than two years), but where valuable IfS programmes should lay the basis for continued EU action under long-term instruments or risk being significantly undermined.

---

structures of the EEAS. It can only be an integral part of a comprehensive approach if these principles are respected. See European Union 2013. *Instrument for Aid*, http://europa.eu/legislation-summaries/humanitarian-aid/r10001-en.htm [accessed: 4 October 2013].

25   The IfS supports activities in situations when timely financial help cannot be provided from other EU sources. The EEAS and the Service for Foreign Policy Instruments (FPI), in cooperation with DG DevCo and the EU Delegations, are responsible for the planning and implementation of this instrument's activities. The IfS had a budget of €2 billion for 2007–13, increasing to around €2.8 billion between 2014 and 2020. Crisis response projects under the IfS focus on a wide range of issues, such as support to mediation, confidence building, interim administrations, strengthening rule of law, transitional justice or the role of natural resources in conflict. See European Union 2013. *Instrument for Stability*, http://ec.europa.eu/europeaid/how/finance/ifs-en.htm [accessed: 4 October 2013].

26   The EU has signed prisoner transfer agreements with the Seychelles (2009) and Mauritius (2011) and is negotiating one with Tanzania. Transfers to Kenya are possible on a case-by-case basis but Kenya has shown reluctance to try and detain transferred piracy suspects as the judicial system is not fully prepared to cope with the additional complexities and workload. See European External Action Service 2012. *The EU fight against piracy in the Horn of Africa*. Factsheet, June, http://eeas.europa.eu/agenda/2012/200212-factsheet-piracy.pdf [accessed: 4 October 2013].

27   Interview with an EU Delegation official, August 2012.

The EU Special Representative for the Horn of Africa

Alexander Rondos brings considerable experience of the region to his role as EUSR from the world of development and emergency relief as well as politics. Initially appointed for six months in January 2012, his mandate is now extended annually on a rolling basis subsequent to review,[28] 'encompassing all strands of EU action, with, in the first instance, a focus on Somalia and piracy'.[29]

There were 11 EUSRs working to promote the EU's policies and interests in different areas of the world until October 2013.[30] Four of them worked on Africa and of those, three had a presence in the Horn of Africa. Alexander Rondos' mandate is supposed to see him coordinate closely with the EUSR for Sudan and South Sudan, Rosalind Marsden, as well as Gary Quince, the EUSR to the AU, based in Addis Ababa. He also works with Stavros Lambrinidis, the EUSR for Human Rights, whose mandate includes work affecting the region.

Rosalind Marsden's mandate as a Special Representative of the EU was not extended beyond October 2013, with Alexander Rondos' portfolio now expanded to include the Sudans. Increasing the mandate of the EUSR for the Horn of Africa was envisaged as part of a streamlining of EUSRs. It enables Rondos to have a much broader regional focus, however, it also leaves the EUSR increasingly overstretched, having to prioritize when responding to developing crises. Given recent events in South Sudan, this decision has proved ill-timed. Motions on Sudan and South Sudan were tabled at the European Parliament in October 2013 and January 2014 respectively, with both calling for an extension of the mandate of the Special Representative for Sudan and South Sudan.[31] This decision has undoubtedly weakened the EU's position at a time of real crisis and during a

---

28   Alexander Rondos' mandate, which expired on 31 October 2013, has been extended 12 months to 31 October 2014.

29   To enhance the coherence, quality, impact and visibility of the EU's multifaceted action in the region, an EUSR, in close consultation with the EUSR for Sudan and South Sudan, will contribute to the EU's regional approach to the interrelated challenges facing the Horn. See Council of the European Union, *Strategic Framework for the Horn of Africa*, op. cit.

30   On EUSRs see Grevi, G. 2007. *Pioneering Foreign Policy: The EU Special Representatives. Chaillot Paper*, no. 106, Paris: EUISS, October. See also Middleton, R., Melly, P. and Vines, A. 2011. *Implementing the EU concept on mediation: learning from the cases of Sudan and the Great Lakes*. Ad hoc study for the European Parliament's Committee on Foreign Affairs. Brussels: European Parliament (DG External Policies PE 433.473 EN).

31   European Parliament 2014. *Joint motion for a resolution on the situation in South Sudan* (2014/2512(RSP)), 14 January, http://www.europarl.europa.eu/sides/getDoc.do?type=MOTION&reference=P7-RC-2014-0018&format=XML&language=EN [accessed: 4 February 2014]; and European Parliament 2013. *European Parliament resolution on clashes in Sudan and subsequent media censorship* (2013/2873(RSP)), B7-0448/2013, 8 October, http://www.europarl.europa.eu/sides/getDoc.do?type=MOTION&reference=B7-2013-0448&language=EN [accessed: 4 February 2014].

critical period, with elections currently on the horizon in Sudan in 2015 and the potential for further instability as a result.

As the EU's political envoy for the Horn of Africa, Alexander Rondos spends at least half of his time in the region. He has met all the region's leaders, including Eritrea's Isaias Afewerki, and has been present during IGAD's South Sudan mediations in early 2014. He was also in Somalia during the lead up to and after the September 2012 Presidential elections, which saw the establishment of Somalia's first permanent government in over 20 years. The EUSR has the freedom to travel between EU Delegations in the region and has established a small representative office in Mogadishu. His insistence on 'flying the flag' in Somalia, facilitated by the improved security situation in the capital, indicates the EU understands the need to shift the centre of its policy engagement to the Somali capital.

The other half of the EUSR's time is spent in Europe reporting progress and lobbying to ensure continued Member State engagement, support and endorsement for the EU's activities in the region.[32] Although not in charge of the EU's interventions in the region, nor able to take a position on finances, he can make recommendations and his role helps to federate the different strands of EU action (including DG DevCo and the EEAS).

There seems to be consensus among EU Member States and officials on the need for an EUSR, to play an important coordinating role and as a political face for the EU's instruments and action in the region. The appointment of an EUSR for the Horn of Africa strengthens the Strategic Framework. The EU must ensure that the personal nature of the EUSR and his desire for autonomy is balanced with the need to ensure that he contributes to developing an effective approach to the region that is in the interest of all stakeholders, while helping to minimize the risk of overlapping and confused policies and instruments.

Other International Actors

The EUSR's presence in Somalia improves his ability to establish and enhance coordination between Somalia's international partners, particularly non-traditional partners such as Turkey, Saudi Arabia, Qatar and Iran, as well as multilateral fora such as the Arab League and the Organization of Islamic Cooperation (OIC). It is important that the EUSR is not constrained by the immediate geography of the region and that he interacts with neighbouring countries such as Egypt, a member of the European Neighbourhood Policy (ENP), and Yemen. Alexander Rondos

---

32   Rondos has good relations with the EEAS in Brussels where he has an office in the Africa Managing Directorate, next to the Horn of Africa section. The EUSR for the Horn of Africa's reports directly to the HR/VP, Catherine Ashton, and also maintains close relations with the Political and Security Committee (PSC). See House of Lords 2012. Interview with Alexander Rondos, before House of Lords Select Committee on the European Union, External Affairs (Sub-Committee C), *Inquiry on Combating Somali Piracy: The EU's Naval Operation Atalanta*, Thursday 21 June.

has been engaged in discussions with the United Arab Emirates on regional interests including counter-piracy, with the possibility of joint action on maritime capacity building. Lobbying key international actors at the right level is critical to enhancing the coherence, quality, impact and visibility of the EU's actions on the Horn of Africa.

Africa's geopolitical importance is growing, as indicated by the interest of emerging powers such as Brazil, India and China on the continent. The economic crisis in Europe might reduce Member States' capacities for influence in the region, which makes collective representation, 'speaking with one voice,' under the EU more important. This is especially true in the Horn of Africa, where relations are based on strong bilateral associations with European countries.[33]

One of the EUSR's main focuses is to address the underlying challenges of the region, making complementary use of the EU's instruments, while reinforcing their political coordination. Rondos's team is able to do this by fleshing out the Strategic Framework with specific sub-strategies and annual action plans for the region.[34] In 2012, the Supporting Horn of Africa Resilience (SHARE) initiative was launched jointly by DG ECHO and DG DevCo to support drought and food resilience.[35] In January 2013, the EU Counter-terrorism Action Plan for the Horn of Africa and Yemen was launched. It is supposed to help build regional capacities to tackle the threat of terrorism, supporting regional law enforcement cooperation and countering violent extremism. EUSR Rondos hopes this can be the beginning of work towards framing regional security architecture that prevents conflict between countries in Horn of Africa.[36]

Launched by the Commission in 2012, SHARE is an example of the Strategic Framework's role in guiding action and promoting good coordination between DG ECHO and DG DevCo. The instrument links short-term humanitarian aid with development coordination mechanisms 'to bridge solid links between relief, recovery and long-term development that aims to break the vicious cycle of crises in the region'.[37] The main idea is to link relief, rehabilitation and development (LRRD). The Commission is investing more than €270 million in SHARE to support recovery from the 2011 drought and work to strengthen the population's resistance to future crises.[38]

---

33   Despite the EU's contribution to development and humanitarian assistance in the region, alliance with US anti-terror policies has fostered the perception of a lack of credibility.

34   These are subject to subsequent decisions by the Commission, Council and Member States.

35   The other Action Plans are on counter-terrorism and piracy. Interview with an EU official, Brussels, August 2012.

36   House of Lords, op. cit.

37   The EU's humanitarian aid to the region adheres to the fundamental humanitarian principles of impartiality, neutrality and non-discrimination as laid out in Art. 214 TFEU.

38   See European Commission 2012. *Horn of Africa – SHARE*, http://ec.europa.eu/echo/policies/resilience/share-en.htm [accessed: 4 October 2013].

These plans, as well as those which are in the pipeline, are important. Efforts towards diplomatic progress are not always visible. A patient approach is required where the EU is engaged in mediation and social reconstruction, such as Sudan, South Sudan and Somalia.

The conflict between Ethiopia and Eritrea is the most important fault line in the region. Tensions stretch back decades, and the stand-off which has held for the past 10 years has fed directly into instability in Somalia, Sudan and Djibouti. Moreover, the closure of the border to economic activity has had and continues to have significant negative consequences for both countries. The conflict is also holding up any meaningful chance of regional integration with the wider Horn of Africa. Although these factors appear to be well understood, the Strategic Framework is remarkably quiet on this issue. A more clear and unified effort from the EU, with the EUSR as an interlocutor to push both sides towards engagement, could yield some important progress on this stalemate.

EU Common Foreign and Security Policy (CFSP) in the Horn of Africa

The stability of the Horn of Africa is of major strategic importance to the EU, as cross-border dynamics in particular (for example, illegal migration and refugee flows, trafficking in arms and drugs, and terrorism) can reach far beyond the immediate neighbourhood and can even pose a threat to European security. The EU places more and more emphasis on engagement by military means, directly and indirectly, including through the African Peace Facility (APF). The APF is an instrument under the EDF that supports the African Peace and Security Agenda/ Architecture (APSA). Over €740 million has been channelled through it since 2004, providing €600 million to African-led Peace Support Operations (PSOs).[39]

The APF's financial support to the African Union Mission in Somalia (AMISOM) is an integral part of the EU's comprehensive and long-term approach to support security and development efforts of the AU in Somalia.[40] On top of its country allocation of €212 million to Somalia for the 10th EDF, the EU contributed €325 million to AMISOM through the APF,[41] providing over €15 million per

---

39   Also €100 million to strengthening African institutional capacities in peace and security at continental and regional level, and €15 million to a number of mediation activities. The facility is a major financing instrument of the Joint Africa-EU Strategy (JAES), and the partnership on peace and security, adopted in 2007. At the time of writing, the next phase of the APF is currently being developed under the 11th EDF (2014–20).

40   The EU is the biggest donor to Somalia, having committed €315.4 million since 2008 for governance, security, and economic growth and an additional €200 million for 2011–2013. See European External Action Service 2013. *The Way Out: Stabilisation in Somalia through assistance and dialogue*, http://www.eeas.europa.eu/piracy/stabilisation-en.htm [accessed: 4 October 2013].

41   Covering allowances, operational running costs, transportation, medical expenses, housing, fuel, and communication equipment.

month in financial support.[42] The AFP also contributed towards resolving the conflict in Darfur by supporting the African Union Mission in Sudan (AMIS) with €305 million between 2006 and 2007.[43] Mediation actions supported by the APF include the African Union High Level Implementation Panel (AUHIP) on Sudan, which includes support for civil society engagement in the negotiations.[44]

While recognizing the regional interconnectedness of most conflicts in the Horn, the EU has emphasized the Somali crisis in its operations. With the Strategic Framework, the EU aims to bring coherence to the different CFSP missions, and the EUSR is charged with bringing unity to the EU's security responses, especially on piracy, which has its root causes in the instability of Somalia. The EU institutions are still learning comprehensiveness 'by doing'[45] and have had to cope with the institutional instability caused by the creation and setting up of the EEAS. The cohesion of CSDP actions on Somalia is even more of a challenge given that the complexity of the security issues in the country stretches beyond piracy, and especially as counter-piracy policies do not only concern the EU.

The EU is currently conducting three CSDP operations targeting the Somali region: the European Union Naval Force Somalia (EU NAVFOR) – Operation Atalanta, which fights piracy off the Somali coast; the European Union Training Mission Somalia (EUTM), which contributes to the training of Somali security forces; and the European Union Maritime Capacity Building Mission in the Horn of Africa (EUCAP Nestor), launched in July 2012 to strengthen maritime capacity building in the region (RMCB).[46] A brief analysis of each of these missions is provided below.

EU NAVFOR – Operation Atalanta

EU NAVFOR was launched as a response to the increasing challenge of piracy off the coast of Somalia in 2008, particularly because of its negative effects on humanitarian efforts and maritime traffic in the region.[47] Contributing Member

---

42   Interview with an EU official, Brussels, August 2012.

43   Until AMIS handed over to the African Union/United Nations Hybrid Operation in Darfur (UNAMID).

44   The EU offered technical assistance and expertise in drawing up the tabled oil deal, as well as border demarcation and management and is ready to act as a guarantor in the signing of these agreements. The EUSR, Rosalind Marsden, and other international envoys from the US, the UK and China are present at mediations and have regular engagement with the panel and both parties.

45   Interview with EU Delegation official, August 2012.

46   The EU also recently launched the European Union Aviation Mission in South Sudan (EUAVSEC), a civilian CSDP mission to strengthen the capacity of Juba International Airport.

47   The mission is funded via the Athena mechanism with a budget of €14.9 million from 2013 to 2014 covering the costs for the operational and force headquarters, as well as medical services and transport. Mission costs were €8.6 million for 2012, €8.05

States bear the cost of the resources they deploy themselves.[48] These costs are not public, but one report puts combined EU Member States costs for EU NAVFOR at €1.5 billion per year.[49] The current mandate was renewed in 2012 until December 2014, and the area of operation extended to include Somali coastal areas as well as internal and territorial waters, in order to disrupt pirate logistic dumps on Somali shores.[50]

Figures from the International Maritime Bureau (IMB) show that recent pirate activity emanating from Somalia's coastline has fallen dramatically. In 2011 there were 199 incidents of attempted hijacking; in 2012 this figure dropped by almost two thirds to 70 and in 2013 only 13 incidents had been reported.[51] This reduction includes successful hijackings and also the number of attempts made, demonstrating that piracy has become a less attractive and rewarding means of revenue generation for many young Somalis.

Piracy is a symptom of political instability in Somalia, not a cause. Only by improving stability, security and governance structures in the country will a solution to the problem be found. There is compliance, but little traction politically among Horn of Africa states on piracy; it is not a priority concern. Understanding the need to introduce on-land initiatives in order to more permanently curb piracy is generally accepted, while the international community is gradually delivering on the comprehensive approach promised after the 2012 and 2013 London Conferences on Somalia.

The EU should continue to assist Atalanta through direct measures that dissuade piracy. This could be done by working towards stopping the current catch and release practice, putting more emphasis on supporting the judicial and detention capacities of local administrations, and disabling pirates' capacities on-shore. More needs to be done to track financial flows and prosecuting investors in Somalia and elsewhere. In addition, the EU should actively address concerns of

---

million for 2011 and €8.4 million for 2010. Operation Headquarters are in Northwood, United Kingdom.

48   In the case of Germany this amounted to €59.1 million in 2009 and €65 million in 2010. See Deutscher Bundestag 2011. *Antwort der Bundesregierung auf die kleine Anfrage von Abgeordneten und der Fraktion der SPD*, Drucksache 17/6715, Berlin, 1 August, 12.

49   Also noted was the fact that piracy attacks had not been successful on ships that followed the guidelines on how to avoid piracy. See Holzer, G. and Jürgenliemk, H. 2012. The Somali Crisis and the EU: Moving onshore and committing to Somalia. *GGI Analysis Paper*, no. 5, Brussels: Global Governance Institute.

50   Typically, EU NAVFOR consists of four to seven surface combat vessels, one or two auxiliary ships and two or three Military Patrol and Reconnaissance Aircraft. These are deployed in the area of operation that covers about the size of the EU. The area comprises the South of the Red Sea, the Gulf of Aden and the Western Indian Ocean, including the Seychelles. See also Map IV in the Annex.

51   IMB Piracy Reporting Centre 2013. *Piracy & Armed Robbery News & Figures*, November, http://www.icc-ccs.org/piracy-reporting-centre/piracynewsafigures [accessed: 4 October 2013].

Somali coastal communities with regard to illegal fishing and waste dumping, and react towards their fears that their livelihoods are being endangered.

European Union Training Mission Somalia

EUTM has contributed to the reform of the Somali security sector through training and support for Somali forces in Uganda since 2010.[52] By the end of the final intake of soldiers in Uganda in December 2013, almost 3,600 officers had been trained. The impact this has had on the Somali National Army (SNA) is still minimal, although properly trained officers are boosting command and control structures. These soldiers account for 25 per cent of the SNA and are now fully involved in joint operations with AMISOM in Somalia, contributing to the improvement of the security in Mogadishu and its surrounding areas.[53] The EU recently modified and extended the EUTM mandate until 2015 and the improving security situation will enable the gradual relocation of all activities to Mogadishu in 2014.

The mission is part of a wider international effort consisting of the vetting of trainees, training and monitoring of the forces once back in Somalia, as well as the funding and payment of salaries. It is executed in close coordination with the Somali government, Uganda, the AU, the UN and the US.[54] The US adds financial assistance, logistical and technical support and supports the recruitment process of the government in Mogadishu. AMISOM soldiers carry the responsibility for reintegrating soldiers into the SNA over a period of three months. EUTM eases AMISOM's training burden, freeing resources for its counter-insurgency efforts.[55] As part of the new mandate, EUTM personnel in Mogadishu provide political and strategic advice to the Somali Ministry of Defence and the Chief of the Defence forces, advice on security sector development as well as specialized military training and mentoring in the training domain.

EUTM has been successful in integrating the efforts of a diverse set of actors to efficiently train the forces of the Somali government. There have been problems with EUTM, none more so than its initial deployment in Uganda and not Somalia. Additionally, the EU had no means of validating the integration of trained soldiers

---

52   Its original operational budget of €4.8 million lasted 15 months, from August 2011 until 31 October 2012. The budget was extended to €11.6 million from February 2013 to March 2015. Council of the European Union 2012. *EUTM Factsheet*, 26 March, http://www.consilium.europa.eu/uedocs/cms-data/docs/missionPress/files/Fact%20sheet%20EUTM%20-%20EN-March%202012.pdf [accessed: 4 February 2012].

53   Official troop figures are about 10,000 but in reality there are far less.

54   And previously the Transitional Federal Government (TFG). Uganda provides basic training and European instructors teach special skills such as infantry techniques (Ireland), urban warfare (Portugal), and communications (Germany). The training also covers international humanitarian law and human rights, as well as the protection of civilians, including specific protection needs of women and children.

55   International Crisis Group 2011. *Somalia: the Transitional Government on Life Support*. Nairobi/Brussels: International Crisis Group, 15.

back into the SNA. Significant efforts have gone into the selection of candidates from across the clans, as well as the integration of female soldiers. Defections to *al Shabaab* were an issue of contention, linked to the lack of regular and sufficient payment of soldiers and the difficulty of monitoring the integration of trainees back into the SNA. This is combined with resentment at AMISOM troop's far larger wages.

The permanent Somali Federal Government has provided impetus for the nationalization of trainees. In the medium-to-long term, building a national army that is loyal to Somalia above individual leaders or regional governments is important for the security of the country and the region. Although EUTM has been partly symbolic until now, it is a step in the right direction and directly supports the capacity building of the Somali security sector. It is promising that the EU and its partners continue to expand support for the development of SNA inside Somalia.

EUCAP Nestor

EUCAP Nestor could potentially become the instrument which gives cohesion to the security operations in the region. It aims to enhance the maritime capacities of several countries in the Horn of Africa and the Western Indian Ocean, strengthening their capability to effectively govern their territorial waters and reinforcing their ability to fight piracy.[56] The mission seeks to strengthen the seagoing maritime capacities and rule of law sector, initially in the Somali regions of Puntland, Galmudug and Somaliland, notably by supporting the development of a Coastal Police Force. EUCAP Nestor is a civilian mission of 175 people augmented with military expertise. Training takes place both in the Djibouti Regional Training Centre as well as in the countries concerned.[57]

Ultimately, EUCAP Nestor is supposed to offer an exit strategy for operation Atalanta through the gradual take-over of the responsibilities for maritime security by regional states themselves. This is important, as political willingness for EU NAVFOR to remain a 'playground for unemployed navies' will not last in the current austere financial climate.[58] However, capacity building also requires time and political will. Given the enduring nature of piracy, it will take much longer to develop than the two-year mandate provided. It will also require more than the €22 million funding currently allocated and will need support from other international partners interested in regional maritime security, such as the UAE.[59] Building the capacity of five countries (that require ships) to do the job of the best navies in

---

56 Djibouti, Kenya, Seychelles and Somalia, with plans to extend into Tanzania.

57 Activities include expert advice on legal, policy and operational matters concerning maritime security, coast guard training to develop the ability to enforce law on the sea, and procurement of the necessary equipment.

58 Helly, D. 2011. *Lessons from Atalanta and EU counter-piracy policies*. Seminar Report. Paris: EUISS, March.

59 House of Lords, op. cit.

the world seems overly ambitious, especially given that countries in the Horn of Africa do not prioritize anti-piracy as highly as EU Member States do.

The resources spent by the EU patrolling the coast of the Horn of Africa are 'ten times the amount spent on development and humanitarian aid'.[60] And it is the efforts being made at sea – by international navies and the shipping industry – which have thus far had the biggest success in curtailing pirate activity emanating from Somalia. These gains should be celebrated, but their limited nature must also be acknowledged. Long-term solutions can only be found by ensuring security for Somalis as well as focusing on socioeconomic development. The chance of earning up to $6,000 for a few weeks' work as a pirate in a country where the average annual income is $600 will continue to be attractive to some until significant change occurs within Somalia. The availability of realistic employment opportunities and alternative livelihoods for many in Somalia's coastal communities requires increased security on-land, winning the trust of investors in new business and at sea, and allowing Somalia's domestic fishing industry to flourish again.

Coherence between CSDP Operations

There was very little complementarity between these CSDP activities until 2012. The launch of EUCAP Nestor marks a shift of resources away from military-centric strategies towards more strategic long-term planning in the region. In addition, an EU Operations Centre for the Horn of Africa was activated in March 2012 to coordinate and increase synergies between the three CSDP actions in the Horn of Africa. The centre provides direct support to the operations commander for the planning and conduct of the RMCB mission, and facilitates coordination between EUTM and EU NAVFOR and their interaction with Brussels-based structures.

In the past, CSDP missions have suffered from being disconnected from other EU political and financial actions. The actions described above, as well as the gradual embedding of the EU's military component within the EEAS, will ensure that CSDP engagement in the region falls closer in line with existing activities. EUCAP Nestor is unlikely to be the instrument that pulls together the EU's security operations in the region, given the limited achievements towards enhancing regional maritime capacities in the last two years. However, if the purpose of EU engagement is to build peace and improve lives, it is essential that military activities continue to be firmly linked to other activities supporting the security sector and development. In this regard, the increase in coordination of CSDP missions, facilitated partly by the political leadership of the new EUSR for the region, should result in better feedback to the political structures in Brussels and thus enable improved strategic planning for CSDP missions and operations in the Horn of Africa. In future, the Strategic Framework will hopefully influence the planning process and development of operational plans.

---

60   Holzer and Jürgenliemk, op. cit.

EU Engagement with the Inter-Governmental Authority on Development

The EU actively supports the AU in its national and regional engagements on the Horn of Africa and provides funding for the RECs in the region,[61] of which IGAD, headquartered in Djibouti, most fully represents the countries of the Horn of Africa. The EU and the AU work on the assumption that the best structures for regional engagement in Africa are the RECs. Publicly, both the AU and IGAD have welcomed the EU's stepped up engagement in the region. Political dialogue between the EU and its Horn of Africa partners is the key to a successful implementation of the Strategic Framework. Such a dialogue must rely on mutual interests in order to foster ownership of the strategy by those Member States.

IGAD remains an under-developed instrument for the enhancement of regional cooperation, integration and security, having lagged behind real political processes in the region, as well as being reliant on the shifting alliances between leaders in the Horn of Africa.[62] Without a more effective regional organization, there is little prospect of meaningful and durable improvements in terms of either security or integration. The future prosperity and development of the Horn of Africa hinge on improvements on both counts. As such, despite the challenges IGAD faces it has a potentially important role to play in the region.

On balance with other commitments the capacity-building element of support for IGAD remains weak. The EU and Alexander Rondos have already signalled the need to help IGAD with improving its own institutional and operational capacity.[63] Further resources should be devoted to such actions, because of the €645 million allocated to the four RECs in the ESAIO under the 10th EDF, including IGAD, only 5 per cent (€32 million) was earmarked to assist the region in knowledge development and institutional capacity building.[64] The majority of funding for the APF supports PSOs: under the 9th EDF, 90 per cent of resources were devoted to PSOs (with AMIS getting the majority), with only 10 per cent (€34 million) allocated to capacity building. This increased to €65 million[65] in the 10th EDF, but it is clear that the lessons learnt have not been fully integrated into current financial planning. Capacity should be reinforced through improved dialogue and increased long-term funding based on requirements in human resources, material resources, expertise and institutional organization.

---

61   Under the 10th EDF (2008–13) €645 million has been allocated to the four RECs of the ESAIO region. In 2010, the EU signed project financing agreements totalling €118 million to support regional economic integration and development projects.

62   Healy, S. 2011. Seeking Peace and Security in the Horn of Africa: the contribution of the Inter-Governmental Authority on Development. *International Affairs*, 87(1), 105–20.

63   House of Lords, op. cit.

64   See EC-ESAIO RSP and RIP (2008–13): http://ec.europa.eu/development/icenter/repository/Signed-RSP-PIR-ESA-2007-2013.pdf [accessed: 4 October 2013].

65   Mainly used to finance African training centres and develop strategic transport capabilities within the AU.

The opportunity to push for IGAD's independence and to build its capacity cannot be achieved without buy-in from its own members, pointing to a long, slow process. However, if the EU is able to take advantage of the coherence offered by the Strategic Framework, if the role of the EUSR can be used to push this agenda with each EU Member State, and if the EU can be the catalyst for other international partners providing more long-term funding for IGAD's capacity building, then there is the possibility of improvement.

The EU's Promotion of Democracy and Human Rights

The EU has fully embraced the promotion of human rights, democratic principles and good governance as a tool to foster the growth of its relationships with African states (see, for example, Art. 21 TEU). As the relationship between the two continents has expanded from a primarily economic one to one that addresses political issues, this has become one of the sharpest debates.[66] The European Commission's new development approach, an 'Agenda for Change', approved by the Council in 2012,[67] refocuses EU development assistance on fewer sectors supporting democracy, human rights and good governance and creating inclusive and sustainable growth. These issues are intended to feature more prominently in political dialogue with recipient countries and are associated with stricter conditionality.[68]

There is a question as to whether the human rights and democracy framework makes sense for engagement with the Horn of Africa, where political space remains restricted, and de facto one-party states are led by African 'strong men'.[69]

---

66   In terms of the ACP-EU relationship, Article 9 of the Cotonou Partnership Agreement defines as 'essential' respect for human rights, adherence to democratic principles and the rule of law. They are also acknowledged as common value for the vision of development echoed in the JAES, with these issues integrated into Country Strategy Papers (CSP), dialogues and all relevant external assistance instruments. Council of the European Union 2007. *Lisbon Declaration, EU-Africa Summit (Lisbon, 8–9 December 2007)*. 16343/07 (Presse 290), Lisbon, 9 December; European Commission 2007. Communication from the Commission to the European Parliament and the Council. *From Cairo to Lisbon: The EU-Africa Strategic Partnership*, COM(2007) 375 final, Brussels, 27 June.

67   Building on commitments made in the 2005 European Consensus on Development. European Commission 2011. *Increasing the Impact of EU Development Policy: An Agenda for Change*. Brussels, 13 October.

68   Priority is given to sub-Saharan Africa, including countries in the Horn of Africa. Under the 'differentiation' principle, the EU will allocate a greater proportion of funds where aid can have the highest impact: in the regions and countries that are most in need, including in fragile states. The implication is that countries that fall outside those regions, or that fail to meet the new criteria, will receive less aid. Ibid.

69   In Eritrea, Ethiopia, Sudan, South Sudan and Uganda there exist clear institutional barriers and limits to what can be achieved by promoting locally driven democratization processes.

Previous to the death of Meles Zenawi, this could be attributed to five of the eight IGAD Member States, outside of which Somalia has seen civil war since 1991 and Kenya experienced violently disputed elections in 2008. Crackdowns on the political opposition, the media and civil society are common place in the region, as are violent attempts to prevent citizens from exercising their legitimate right to vote during elections.

The EU's policy of 'more for more' – one of the pillars of the ENP – is based on positive conditionality: if partner countries introduce more reforms then they stand to receive further integration and funds.[70] Attempts to use aid to incentivize states to reform their institutions and policies are tested in the Horn of Africa.[71] Democratic and human rights reform conditions attached to assistance are resisted by authoritarian regimes. In addition, non-traditional (that is, non-Western) donors such as China, Qatar and Turkey challenge the EU's model with their respect for a sovereignty or 'no strings attached' approach to development. This weakens EU conditionality and threats of aid suspension. If the EU is to be credible in its promotion of democracy and human rights, it must 'be exemplary in ensuring respect for human rights' in its own affairs.[72] Governments in the Horn of Africa are quick to point out double standards, further undermining cooperation with the region.

The EU has inconsistently applied conditionality in the region, turning a blind eye to deteriorating governance and human rights violations where these issues are trumped by strategic interests – such as security, trade and poverty reduction.[73] These values compete with other EU and Member State goals, making conditionality less effective. The example of Ethiopia demonstrates this dilemma. Ethiopia is one of the EU's largest recipients of EDF funding.[74] The EU Joint

---

70   European Commission and High Representative 2013. Joint Communication of the European Parliament, the Council, the European Economic and Social Committee and the Committee of the Regions. *European Neighbourhood Policy: Working towards a Stronger Partnership.* JOIN(2013) 4 final, Brussels, 20 March.

71   If African states fail to adhere to democratic principles, the EU has the power to suspend aid after an enquiry. Breaches of Article 9 of the Cotonou Agreement can lead to the suspension of aid under Articles 96 and 97. The Articles define 'cases of flagrant violation' and 'appropriate measures' which must be taken proportional to violations. The main reasons for sanctions under Article 96 are *coups d'état*, flawed or non-transparent electoral processes and violations of democratic principles; under Article 97 it is cases related to serious corruption.

72   Zimelis, A. 2011. Conditionality and the EU-ACP Partnership: A Misguided Approach to Development? *Australian Journal of Political Science*, 46(3), 404.

73   Del Biondo, K. 2011. EU Aid Conditionality in ACP Countries: Explaining Inconsistency in EU Sanctions Practice. *Journal of Contemporary European Research*, 7(3), 381.

74   The largest in the Horn of Africa with €644 million under the 10th EDF (2008–13). Current EDF bilateral support allocates €49 million towards strengthening democratic governance: including €29 million for capacity building in key institutions, and €10 million

Cooperation Strategy, started in 2011, lays out the development challenges and priorities for the 'EU+' group (EU institutions, Member States and Norway) in support of the Ethiopian government's Growth and Transformation Plan, from 2011 to 2015.[75] The EU relationship with Ethiopia goes beyond development assistance. Ethiopia is an important regional power and has a strong partnership with the EU based on commercial links and state support. Addis Ababa is also the home of the AU and the EU's main Delegation in the region.

Political space in the country has been restricted since a crackdown on the political opposition following heavily contested elections in 2005.[76] In the 2010 elections, opposition parties saw their representation reduced to just 3 of 547 parliamentary seats. The EU Election Observation Mission noted that there was a lack of transparency in the process, a lack of a level playing field and a narrowing of political space.[77] Although successive elections were flawed, the EU only suspended budget support for one year in 2005. Support has since increased despite further restrictions on the media and NGOs.[78] This is because the EU and its international partners rely on Ethiopia as a strategic ally in the securitization of the region, on issues such as counter-terrorism and peace and security in Somalia. Additionally, Ethiopia's economic growth and its performance towards the MDGs are impressive. Donors continue their programmes despite restrictions because they are well run and suspending them would have worse consequences for human rights and marginalized communities.[79] These factors make it difficult to see the EU enforcing conditionality, or anything other than quiet diplomacy, in attempts to encourage Ethiopia to further human rights or democratization.

The human rights and democratization agenda will continue to gain very little traction in the Horn of Africa. It is suggestive that Somalia and South Sudan,

---

for developing the dialogue between state and non-state actors with a view to creating an open, democratic and participatory society. €10 million are also provided for promoting gender equality and women's empowerment and rights. See European Commission 2007. *Ethiopia-EC Country Strategy Paper and National Indicative Programme for the period 2008–2013*, 9 December, http://ec.europa.eu/development/icenter/repository/scanned-et-csp10-en.pdf [accessed: 4 October 2013].

75   Galeazzi, G., Helly, D. and Kräte, F. 2013. All for One or Free-for-All? Early Exeriences in Joint-EU Programming. *European Centre for Development Policy Management*. Briefing Note, no. 50, Maastricht: ECDPM, May, 4.

76   Which the EU Election Observer Mission noted 'fell short of international principles for genuine democratic elections'. See European Union 2005. *Election Observer Mission to Ethiopia 2005*, http://www.eueom.eu/files/dmfile/FinalReport.pdf [accessed: 4 October 2013].

77   European Union 2010. *Election Observation Mission to Ethiopia 2010*, http://eeas.europa.eu/eueom/pdf/missions/eu-eom-ethiopia-preliminary-statement-25052010-en.pdf [accessed: 4 October 2013].

78   Del Biondo, op. cit., 384.

79   Human Rights Watch 2010. *One Hundred Ways of Putting Pressure*. New York: Human Rights Watch.

countries which have yet to emerge out of post-conflict scenarios, offer the most fertile ground for the EU's new policies and initiatives. Violations of citizen's rights in the region will continue, as will lip service towards democracy – and there is little doubt so will the EU's preference for engagement and influence over conditionality and sanctions.

Conclusion

Although bilateral engagement will continue to be essential, the EU's long-term aims cannot be promoted without a coherent regional framework. This is true both in terms of promoting regional stability, poverty reduction and development, and in terms of limiting the impacts of the region's insecurity on Europe itself, either through inflows of economic migrants and asylum seekers, by the added costs and insecurity for international shipping caused by Somali piracy or by the export of militant/terrorist ideologies.

The Strategic Framework represents a wider EU shift away from development towards security issues – this has at times caused a tug of war over the spine of the approach between the Commission's DG DevCo and the EEAS. With both the EEAS and DG DevCo leading on different steps, regular information exchange and good collaboration becomes vital and more complicated. Coherence and cooperation between the EEAS, DG DevCo and Member States is important for putting into action the guidelines that have been agreed upon. The creation of the EEAS and the Strategic Framework has enabled the EU to better put its collective resources into practice but the EU should continue working towards fine-tuning its internal institutional working relationships, as well as the instruments at its disposal, so that it is able to respond more flexibly and quickly to situations in the region.

It is important that when it comes to breathing life into the Strategic Framework, sufficient freedom is given to the EEAS, DG DevCo and the EUSR to guide the EU's approach to the region and Member States should work towards supporting the collective objectives set out in the document. Divergent approaches between EU institutions and Member States can impede the achievement of important goals. Speaking with one voice is difficult, yet reaching consensus on important areas of action is important if the EU's contribution to the region is to be valuable.

The EU has a strategic partnership with the AU. Therefore, considering joint-way-forward processes with key REC partners on the continent would demonstrate a willingness to work towards mutual aspirations. The EU and the AU could work towards enhancing the capacity and strengthening the mandate of IGAD. The EU could take leadership in the process of convincing the broad range of external states with active interests in the region (such as Turkey, Saudi Arabia, the UAE, India, Egypt and China), including those who subscribe to the ENP integration principles, to provide more long-term funding for IGAD's capacity building.

Improving its currently under-realized potential would enable the body to play a more robust role in promoting regional cooperation, integration and stabilization.

The Strategic Framework has evolved out of a series of strands, but the goal is that it becomes 'more than a sum of its parts', where there is medium-to-long-term strategic planning and an understanding of what the EU wants to achieve in the region. Ultimately, with the right level of buy-in from all stakeholders, the Strategic Framework will enable the EU to achieve a comprehensive understanding of the Horn of Africa's complexities and develop an approach that will be much greater than the current sum of its parts.

Bibliography

Council of the European Union 2007. *Lisbon Declaration, EU-Africa Summit (Lisbon, 8–9 December 2007)*. 16343/07 (Presse 290), Lisbon, 9 December.

Council of the European Union 2009. *An EU Policy on the Horn of Africa – Towards a Comprehensive EU Strategy*, Brussels, 10 December.

Council of the European Union 2011. *Strategic Framework for the Horn of Africa*, Council Conclusion, Brussels, 16858/11, 14 November.

Council of the European Union 2012. *EUTM Factsheet*, 26 March, http://www.consilium.europa.eu/uedocs/cms_data/docs/missionPress/files/Fact%20 sheet%20EUTM%20-%20EN_March%202012.pdf [accessed: 4 February 2012].

Council of the European Union 2013. *Implementation Review of the Horn of Africa Strategic Framework Presented by the HR/VP*, Political and Security Committee, 11 January, https://www.gov.uk/government/uploads/system/uploads/attachment_data/file/224337/evidence-eeas-hoa-strategic-framework-review.pdf [accessed: 30 November 2013.

Del Biondo, K. 2011. EU Aid Conditionality in ACP Countries: Explaining Inconsistency in EU Sanctions Practice. *Journal of Contemporary European Research*, 7(3), 380–95.

Deutscher Bundestag 2011. *Antwort der Bundesregierung auf die Kleine Anfrage von Abgeordneten und der Fraktion der SPD*, Drucksache 17/6715, Berlin, 1 August.

European Commission 2006. *Strategy for Africa: An EU regional political partnership for peace, security and development in the Horn of Africa*, COM(2006) 601 final, Brussels, 20 October.

European Commission 2007. Communication from the Commission to the European Parliament and the Council. *From Cairo to Lisbon: The EU-Africa Strategic Partnership*, COM(2007) 375 final, Brussels, 27 June.

European Commission 2007. *Ethiopia-EC Country Strategy Paper and National Indicative Programme for the period 2008–2013*, 9 December, http://ec.europa.eu/development/icenter/repository/ scanned_et_csp10_en.pdf [accessed: 4 October 2013].

European Commission 2011. Communication from the Commission to the European Parliament, the Council, the European Economic and Social Committee and the Committee of the Regions. *A Budget for Europe 2020 – Part I,* COM(2011) 500/I final, Brussels, 26 June.

European Commission 2011. *Increasing the Impact of EU Development Policy: An Agenda for Change.* Brussels, 13 October.

European Commission 2012. Disaster resilience in the Horn of Africa to be strengthened further with new aid injection from the European Commission. *Press Release,* IP/12/864, Brussels, 31 July.

European Commission 2012. *Horn of Africa – SHARE,* http://ec.europa.eu/echo/policies/resilience/share_en.htm [accessed: 4 October 2013].

European Commission and High Representative 2013. Joint Communication of the European Parliament, the Council, the European Economic and Social Committee and the Committee of the Regions. *European Neighbourhood Policy: Working towards a Stronger Partnership.* JOIN(2013) 4 final, Brussels, 20 March.

European Commission and High Representative 2013. *Joint Staff Working Document on an 'Integrated EU approach to Security and Rule of Law in Somalia',* SWD(2013) 277 final, Brussels, 12 July.

European External Action Service 2012. *The EU fight against piracy in the Horn of Africa.* Factsheet, June, http://eeas.europa.eu/agenda/2012/200212_factsheet_piracy.pdf [accessed: 4 October 2013].

European External Action Service 2013. *The way out: Stabilisation in Somalia through assistance and dialogue,* http://www.eeas.europa.eu/piracy/stabilisation_en.htm [accessed: 4 October 2013].

European Parliament 2012. *Report: EU Strategy for the Horn of Africa,* Committee on Foreign Affairs (2012/2026(INI)), Rapporteur: Charles Tannock, Brussels, 10 December.

European Parliament 2013. *European Parliament resolution on clashes in Sudan and subsequent media censorship (2013/2873(RSP)),* B7-0448/2013, 8 October, http://www.europarl.europa.eu/sides/getDoc.do?type=MOTION&reference=B7-2013-0448&language=EN [accessed: 4 February 2014].

European Parliament 2014. *Joint motion for a resolution on the situation in South Sudan (2014/2512(RSP)),* 14 January, http://www.europarl.europa.eu/sides/getDoc.do?type=MOTION&reference=P7-RC-2014-0018&format=XML&language=EN [accessed: 4 February 2014].

European Union 2005. *Election Observer Mission to Ethiopia 2005,* http://www.eueom.eu/ files/dmfile/FinalReport.pdf [accessed: 4 October 2013].

European Union 2010. *Election Observation Mission to Ethiopia 2010,* http://eeas.europa.eu/ eueom/pdf/missions/eu-eom-ethiopia-preliminary-statement-25052010-en.pdf [accessed: 4 October 2013].

European Union 2013. *Instrument for Aid,* http://europa.eu/legislation-summaries/humanitarian-aid/r10001-en.htm [accessed: 4 October 2013].

Galeazzi, G., Helly, D. and Kräte, F. 2013. All for One or Free-for-All? Early
    Exeriences in Joint-EU Programming, *European Centre for Development
    Policy Management*. Briefing Note, no. 50, May.
Grevi, G. 2007. *Pioneering Foreign Policy: The EU Special Representatives.
    Chaillot Paper*, no. 106, Paris: EUISS, October.
Hagström Frisell, E., Tham Lindell, M. and Skeppström, E. 2012. Land in Sight?
    The EU Comprehensive Approach towards Somalia. *FOI – Swedish Defence
    Research Agency*, FOI-R 3462, Stockholm, June.
Healy, S. 2008. *Lost Opportunities in the Horn of Africa*. Africa Programme
    Report. London: Chatham House.
Healy, S. 2011. *Hostage to Conflict: Prospects for Building Regional Economic
    Cooperation in the Horn of Africa*. Africa Programme Report. London:
    Chatham House.
Healy, S. 2011. Seeking Peace and Security in the Horn of Africa: The contribution
    of the Inter-Governmental Authority on Development. *International Affairs*,
    87(1), 105–20.
Helly, D. 2011. *Lessons from Atalanta and EU Counter-piracy Policies*. Seminar
    Report. Paris: EUISS, March.
Holzer, G. and Jürgenliemk, H. 2012. The Somali Crisis and the EU: Moving
    onshore and committing to Somalia. *GGI Analysis Paper*, no. 5, Brussels:
    Global Governance Institute.
House of Lords 2012. Interview with Alexander Rondos, before House of Lords
    Select Committee on the European Union, External Affairs (Sub-Committee
    C), *Inquiry on Combating Somali Piracy: The EU's Naval Operation Atalanta*,
    Thursday 21 June.
Human Rights Watch 2010. *One Hundred Ways of Putting Pressure*. New York:
    Human Rights Watch.
IMB Piracy Reporting Centre 2013. *Piracy & Armed Robbery News & Figures*,
    November, http://www.icc-ccs.org/piracy-reporting-centre/piracynewsafigures
    [accessed: 4 October 2013].
International Crisis Group 2011. *Somalia: The Transitional Government on Life
    Support*. Nairobi/Brussels: International Crisis Group.
Love, R. 2009. *Economic Drivers of Conflict and Cooperation in the Horn of
    Africa*. Africa Programme Briefing Paper 2009/01. Chatham House: London.
Middleton, R., Melly, P. and Vines, A. 2011. *Implementing the EU concept on
    mediation: Learning from the cases of Sudan and the Great Lakes*. Ad hoc
    study for the European Parliament's Committee on Foreign Affairs. Brussels:
    European Parliament (DG External Policies PE 433.473 EN).
Pirozzi, N. 2009. *EU Support to African Security architecture: Funding and
    Training Components. Occasional Paper*, no. 76, Paris: EUISS, February.
Rondos, Alexander 2012. Interview before House of Lords Select Committee
    on the European Union, External Affairs (Sub-Committee C) *Inquiry on
    Combating Somali Piracy: The EU's Naval Operation Atalanta*, 21 June 2012.

Soliman, A., Mosley, J. and Vines, A. 2012. *The EU Strategic Framework for the Horn of Africa: A Critical Assessment of Impact and Opportunities*. Brussels: European Parliament (DG External Policies PE 433.799).

World Bank 2013. *Kenya: Country Results Profile*, November, http://go.worldbank. org/GI5VJ50Z70 [accessed: 30 December 2013].

Zimelis, A. 2011. Conditionality and the EU-ACP Partnership: A Misguided Approach to Development? *Australian Journal of Political Science*, 46(3), 389–406.

PART II
Geopolitical Dimensions beyond the ENP's East: Arabian Peninsula, Iraq and Iran

Chapter 5

State of Play: The EU, the Arabian Peninsula, Iraq, Iran and the ENP

Andrew Bower and Raphaël Metais

The European Union (EU), like its Member States, strongly believes in the relevance of its neighbouring region in the making of its foreign policy and its 'existing commitment to its relationship with the countries of the Mediterranean and the Middle East and its long standing engagement with the challenges confronting them'.[1] Keen to maintain a stable and secure neighbourhood vital to Europe's own stability, the European Commission has also stressed the need to go a step further to 'look beyond the Union's immediate neighbourhood' to the many neighbours of its own neighbourhood, to identify the various regional challenges and opportunities therein and the potential for further regional cooperation.[2]

Despite their regional proximity, the countries of the Arabian Peninsula (Bahrain, Kuwait, Oman, Qatar, Saudi Arabia, the United Arab Emirates and Yemen), Iraq and Iran present important differences both in terms of their relations with the EU and of their geopolitical specificities.[3] This chapter will address why the EU should look to the neighbours of its own neighbours in the Mediterranean and Middle East in the context of its European Neighbourhood Policy (ENP), sustaining the argument that many political, strategic and socioeconomic characteristics of the Arabian Peninsula, Iraq and Iran are relevant to and may determine the future of the EU's relations with its southern neighbourhood. This chapter will therefore present the main features of the Arabian Peninsula, Iraq and Iran's relations with the EU, will put forward the challenges and opportunities that lie ahead in these relations and will suggest possibilities for the EU to develop a more comprehensive approach towards these 'neighbours of the neighbours'. The chapter will first look at the state of play of European relations with the Arabian

---

1 European Council 2004. *Final Report: EU Strategic Partnership with the Mediterranean and the Middle East*, June, 1, http://consilium.europa.eu/uedocs/cmsUpload/ Partnership%20Mediterranean%20and%20Middle%20East.pdf [accessed: 11 November 2012].

2 European Commission 2006. *Communication from the Commission to the Council and the European Parliament on Strengthening the European Neighbourhood Policy*, COM(2006)726 final, Brussels, 4 December, 11.

3 See also Chapter 6 by Silvia Colombo and Chapter 7 by Clément Therme in this volume.

Peninsula. It will then focus on the EU's relations with Iraq and Iran, before drawing some tentative conclusions.

The EU and the Arabian Peninsula

For its geographical proximity, as well as its political, strategic and socioeconomic presence in the Mediterranean and the Middle East region, understanding the Arabian Peninsula and its relations with the EU is key in addressing the relevance of the neighbours of the EU's neighbours to the ENP. Countries of the Mediterranean and the Middle East are increasingly interconnected. Greater involvement of Gulf states in the EU's southern neighbourhood in recent years is bringing about developments of relevance to the ENP. In an evolving regional context, the EU's relations with its neighbourhood and the countries of the Arabian Peninsula will face new challenges and opportunities. In order to understand the nature of these relations and the reality of European engagement in the region and the potential for future relations, an insight into the existing agreements and frameworks for cooperation between the EU and the countries of the Peninsula will be presented. This section will then move on to identifying a number of challenges of the current geopolitical dimension of EU's relations in the Peninsula in the context of a changing environment.

Historically, the Arabian Peninsula has been a regional bastion for foreign actors engaged in the Mediterranean and Middle Eastern region. The European presence in the Gulf dates back to the years of the British Empire, which had developed in the Peninsula a transit region for the imperial trading routes of its East India Company. The discovery of the Peninsula's vast energy resources and the gradual fall of the British Empire throughout the early twentieth century drew to the region unprecedented attention of new Western actors, on which the United States capitalized to remain until today the dominant foreign power in the region.[4] Prior to the Arab oil embargo of 1973, the United Kingdom remained the only European power to have developed substantive ties with the countries of the Peninsula as a result of its colonial heritage. The European Community, for its part, did not in its early years aspire to any form of engagement.[5] The oil embargo, which brought the countries of the Gulf to the forefront of international affairs, triggered to a great extent the Community's own engagement in the region.

The European Community's first steps towards the Arabian Peninsula in the 1970s stemmed from the emergence of European foreign policy ambitions and the objectives following the oil crisis. The Euro-Arab Dialogue, created in 1973, was to be the first significant framework for relations with countries of

---

4   Holden, D. 1971. The Persian Gulf: After the British Raj. *Foreign Affairs*, 49(4), 721–2.

5   Khader, B. 2005. Is there a role for Europe in Gulf security? *GCC-EU Research Bulletin*, no. 3, 10.

the Middle East, one in which the oil-rich countries of the Arabian Peninsula were to hold a central role. However, the Dialogue's inability to gain momentum and its inevitable collapse in 1989 did not provide for the expected furthering of European relations with the countries of the Middle East and the Arabian Peninsula in particular.[6]

Notwithstanding the predominance of bilateral relations at inter-state level, the European Community has increasingly engaged with the countries of the Arabian Peninsula since the 1980s. Four main themes have traditionally dominated these relations: energy, trade, security, and human rights. As the Arabian Peninsula holds the largest reserves of oil worldwide,[7] energy has been the backbone of the EU's relations with the region and is likely to remain so for years to come. As a result of the prosperity of the energy sector, the Arabian Peninsula has gradually developed into a relevant trading partner of the EU. While the Gulf is the EU's fifth largest export market,[8] the EU's internal market has been a leading destination for Gulf exports in a number of sectors.[9] In terms of security matters, the impact of 9/11 on the Arabian Peninsula and its relations with Western actors, including the EU, has been unprecedented. Since 2001, the EU has cooperated with countries such as Saudi Arabia in international counter-terrorism matters as well as calling upon them, and Yemen in particular, to address the threat of jihadist al-Qaeda groups present in the region since the early 1990s and the creation in 2009 of the militant Islamist group 'Al-Qaeda in the Arabian Peninsula' (AQAP) regrouping Saudi and Yemeni al-Qaeda branches.[10] Finally, divergences over human rights policies and recurrent violations of human rights in the countries of the Peninsula are a challenge to deepening relations with the EU and are, in fact, partly responsible for the deadlocked negotiations over an inter-regional trade agreement between the EU and the GCC.[11]

---

6   Nonneman, G. 2006. EU-GCC Relations: Dynamics, Patterns and Perspectives. *The International Spectator: Italian Journal of International Affairs*, 41(3), 59–60.

7   With estimated oil reserves of approximately 500 thousand million barrels by the end of 2012, the Arabian Peninsula holds 30 per cent of total world reserves; and with estimated natural gas reserves of approximately 43 trillion cubic metres 23 per cent of total world reserves. See British Petroleum 2013. *BP Statistical Review of World Energy*, http://www.bp.com/content/dam/bp/pdf/statistical-review/statistical-review-of-world-energy-2013.pdf [accessed: 18 December 2013].

8   The share of EU trade with the GCC represents only 4.2 per cent of total EU trade for 2012. European Commission 2013. *European Union, Trade with GCC*, http://trade.ec.europa.eu/doclib/docs/2006/september/tradoc-113482.pdf [accessed: 13 December 2013].

9   Ibid. The share of the Gulf's trade with the EU of total Gulf trade is 12.8 per cent for 2012.

10   Masters, J. and Laub, Z. 2013. Al-Qaeda in the Arabian Peninsula (AQAP). *Council on Foreign Relations*, 22 August, http://www.cfr.org/yemen/al-qaeda-arabian-peninsula-aqap/p9369 [accessed: 18 December 2013].

11   Nonneman, op. cit., 59–65.

These main themes are all translated in the existing frameworks developed by the EU with the countries of the region. Indeed, alongside the development of various frameworks in the Mediterranean region (multilateral Barcelona Process, bilateral Cooperation and Association Agreements with, at that time, Turkey, Malta, Cyprus and Greece), the European Economic Community (EEC) concluded a Cooperation Agreement with the Gulf Cooperation Council (GCC),[12] a regional integration project created in 1981 regrouping Bahrain, Kuwait, Oman, Qatar, Saudi Arabia, and the United Arab Emirates, in 1989 and with Yemen in 1998.[13]

EU-GCC Relations in a Changing Neighbourhood

Economic relations are the spearhead of the EU's interaction with the countries of the Gulf Cooperation Council. Overall trade between the EU and the GCC in 2012 reached €144.6 billion making the GCC the fifth largest market for EU exports.[14] The EU is the GCC's biggest trading partner.[15] The bulk of EU exports to the GCC are machinery and transport materials (46.5 per cent), while EU imports from the GCC are mainly fuels and derivatives (81.9 per cent).[16] An EU-GCC Joint Action Programme 2010–13 was adopted to pursue cooperation in the areas of financial, economic and monetary affairs. Under its multi-annual financial frameworks, EU expenditure targeting GCC countries fall under the Financing Instrument with Industrialized and other High-Income Countries and Territories

---

12   The Cooperation Agreement between the GCC and the European Economic Community, still in place today, aims to establish a 'contractual cooperation between equal partners on mutually advantageous terms in all spheres between the two regions and further their economic development, taking into consideration the differences in levels of development of the parties'. See Council of the European Union 1989. *Cooperation Agreement between the European Economic Community, of the one part, and the countries parties of the Charter of the Cooperation Council for the Arab States of the Gulf (the State of the United Arab Emirates, the State of Bahrain, the Kingdom of Saudi Arabia, the Sultanate of Oman, the State of Qatar and the State of Kuwait) of the other part.* OJ L54/3, 25 February, 3–4.

13   Echagüe, A. 2010. The Gulf Cooperation Council: The Challenges of Security, in Youngs, R. (ed.), *The European Union and Democracy Promotion: A Critical Global Assessment.* Baltimore, MD: John Hopkins University Press, 136.

14   The four Member States with the highest investments in GCC countries were, in 2012: The United Kingdom (€19 billion); France (€7.4 billion); Italy (€5.7 billion); and the Netherlands (€5.1 billion). See Bossdorf, M., Engels, C. and Weiler, S. 2013. *EU-GCC Invest Report 2013,* http://www.eu-gccinvest.eu/file/EU%20GCC%20Invest%20 Report%202013.pdf [accessed: 18 December 2013].

15   European Commission 2013, op. cit.

16   European Commission 2012. *Countries and Regions: Gulf Region,* http:// ec.europa.eu/trade/creating-opportunities/bilateral-relations/regions/gulf-region [accessed: 12 November 2012].

(ICI)[17] (2007–13) and the succeeding Partnership Instrument (PI)[18] (2014–20). GCC countries have also enjoyed preferential access to the EU's internal market under the Generalized System of Preferences (GSP); this situation changed, however, with the implementation of a revised GSP in 2014 seeing the exclusion of Gulf countries since they are classified as high-income countries.[19]

Political relations between the EU and the GCC have also emerged from the Cooperation Agreement of 1989. Joint Councils and Ministerial Meetings (Art.12) are held annually, offering an annual platform (Art.14) for both Contracting Parties to pursue the cooperation objectives outlined in the agreement and formulate any resolution, recommendation or opinion.[20] The annual Joint Councils between the EU and GCC have in recent years striven to strengthen strategic and dynamic ties in areas such as the fight against terrorism, economic growth, climate change, ongoing crises in the region, etc.[21] Stronger regional relations have, however, failed to materialize as a result of successive failed attempts to complete a regional free trade agreement.[22]

In the context of the 'Arab Spring' in the Mediterranean and Middle East, a new geopolitical environment is shaping new challenges and opportunities for EU-GCC relations. While also home to popular discontent,[23] the Gulf countries have demonstrated their ambitions to engage more actively in their own Arab neighbourhood. The EU, for its part, overcame initial internal stuttering to offer an inclusive and advanced policy framework through its revised ENP 'A New Response to a Changing Neighbourhood'.[24]

---

17   Council of the European Union 2006. *Council Regulation (EC) No 1934/2006 of 21 December 2006 establishing a financing instrument for cooperation with industrialised and other high-income countries and territories.* OJ L405/41, 30 December.

18   European Parliament and Council of the European Union 2014. *Regulation (EU) No 234/2014 of 11 March 2014 of the European Parliament and of the Council establishing a Partnership Instrument for cooperation with third countries.* OJ L77/77, 15 March.

19   European Commission 2012. *EU publishes revised preferential import scheme for developing countries,* 31 October, http://trade.ec.europa.eu/doclib/press/index.cfm?id=840 [accessed: 13 November 2012].

20   As laid out by Article 15 of the Cooperation Agreement, a Joint Cooperation Committee will assist the Joint Council in carrying out its duties: Council of the European Union 1989, op. cit., 6.

21   The 23rd EU-GCC Joint Council was held in Manama, Bahrain. See European Union 2013. *Remarks by High Representative Catherine Ashton following the 23rd EU-GCC Joint Council and Ministerial Meeting, Manama.* A 362/13, Brussels, 30 June.

22   Youngs, R. 2009. Impasse on Euro-Gulf Relations. *FRIDE Working Paper,* no. 80, Madrid: FRIDE, 2.

23   Coates Ulrichsen, K. 2011. Repositioning the GCC States in the Changing Global Order. *Journal of Arabian Studies,* 1(2), 243.

24   European Commission and High Representative 2011. Joint Communication to the European Parliament, the Council, the European Economic and Social Committee and

With steadily increasing oil prices and huge oil revenues, the countries of the Gulf have sought to maximize the returns of these opportunities through oil and oil-derivative exports as well as extensive foreign investment across many sectors (real estate, finance, tourism, etc.), averaging $140 billion between 2004 and 2007.[25] Through important government-led investment vehicles, so-called Sovereign Wealth Funds,[26] as well as private channels, the Gulf countries have strengthened and expanded their presence on international markets by moving away from their domestic 'comfort zone'. With the tightening of Western markets, Gulf investors have increased their presence in other Arab countries with which relationships have been strengthened in the current post-'Arab Spring' period.[27] Morocco provides a fitting example as a country traditionally turned towards Europe that has recently showed signs of interest in developing ties with other regional actors, arguably as a result of economic difficulties in the EU and instability in neighbouring countries of the Maghreb (Libya, Tunisia).[28] The Mediterranean and Middle East region is the biggest recipient of Gulf humanitarian and development aid assistance, having received 62 per cent of total Gulf aid assistance between 1970 and 2008 (compared to 21 per cent for Asia and 15 per cent for Africa).[29]

Beyond the economic sphere, the countries of the Gulf have also been playing active political roles in the region, such as in the mediation of crises in the case of Syria for example or through the provision of funding as seen with Saudi financial support to the *coup* that overthrew Egyptian president Hosni Mubarak.[30] Through unilateral action of GCC member countries, at best under the informal clout of the GCC itself, the region has witnessed greater engagement of the Gulf in the political developments in countries such as Egypt and Syria. Qatar's assertion of independent foreign policy objectives in the region offers an interesting example

---

the Committee of Regions. *A New Response to a Changing Neighbourhood*, COM(2011) 303, Brussels, 25 May.

25   Raphaeli, N. and Gersten, B. 2008. Sovereign Wealth Funds: Investment Vehicles for the Persian Gulf Countries. *Middle East Quarterly*, 15(2), 46.

26   Bazoobandi, S. 2013. *Political Economy of the Gulf Sovereign Wealth Funds: A Case Study of Iran, Kuwait, Saudi Arabia and the United Arab Emirates.* New York: Routledge, 1.

27   Baabood, A. 2009. The Growing Economic Presence of Gulf Countries in the Mediterranean Region, in *IEMED Mediterranean Yearbook.* Barcelona: IEMED/CIDOB, 206.

28   Rawi, A., Ayesha, K. and Tarun, K. 2008. Where Oil-Rich Nations Are Placing Their Bets. *Harvard Business Review*, 86(9), 122.

29   Momani, B. and Ennis, C.A. 2013. Between Caution and Controversy: Lessons from the Gulf Arab States as (Re-)Emerging Donors. *Cambridge Review of International Affairs*, 25(4), 613.

30   Hearst, D. 2013. Why Saudi Arabia is taking a risk by backing the Egyptian coup. *The Guardian*, 20 August, http://www.theguardian.com/commentisfree/2013/aug/20/saudi-arabia-coup-egypt [accessed: 20 December 2013].

of an evolving regional balance of power in which Gulf monarchies are carving out their role as regional mediators, frequently upstaging traditional Western actors.[31]

Gulf investments and aid donations can be interpreted as a means to promote particular interests in the Mediterranean and Middle East as well as an outcome of the 'race to power' in the region in which Saudi Arabia and Qatar are engaged.[32] Nonetheless, scholars such as Bessma Momani and Crystal Ennis argue that shared religious ties along with cultural Islamic charitable tradition – *zakat* – may constitute factors underpinning the important Arab solidarity observed through Gulf aid assistance to other Muslim countries in the Mediterranean and the Middle East.[33] Religious and cultural ties with Muslim Arab countries also provide the Gulf countries with a degree of political credibility when addressing domestic political affairs, particularly since the beginning of the 'Arab Spring'.[34] The argument can thus be made that 'the "Islam factor" and a pragmatic approach aimed at creating better prospects for business emerge as the two main drivers of GCC foreign policies in the Mediterranean'.[35]

The member countries of the GCC have become increasingly present in the Mediterranean and Middle East, driven by a range of economic, political and confessional ambitions. Across the Mediterranean, the EU has also reacted strongly to recent developments in the region, showing strong collective will to revise its ENP in line with new political and societal contexts in its neighbourhood. While motivations of the EU and GCC to engage may diverge substantially, both set of actors have seen their level of engagement increase in the region creating a new set of opportunities and challenges.

Yemen: A Case Apart in the Peninsula

Yemen is the only country of the Arabian Peninsula which is not a member of the GCC. It shares an important border with Saudi Arabia, but its internal situation is a stark contrast to its Saudi neighbour. Since the unification of North and South Yemen in 1990, the country has faced grave security, socioeconomic and political challenges, 'the scale of the problems facing the country evok[ing] alarmist fears

---

31   Heard-Bey, F. 2006. Conflict Resolution and Regional Cooperation: The Role of the Gulf Cooperation Council 1970–2002. *Middle Eastern Studies*, 42(2), 209. The case of the Qatari campaign in Libya is a good example. See Coates Ulrichsen, Repositioning the GCC States in the Changing Global Order, op. cit., 242.

32   Schumacher, T. and Fernandez Molina, I. 2013. EU and GCC Countries' Foreign Policies and the Mediterranean Neighbourhood – Towards Synergetic Cooperation? *Gulf Research Center Paper*, 11. http://eu-gcc.kcorp.net/common/publicationfile/35.pdf [accessed: 20 December 2013].

33   Momani and Ennis, op. cit., 612.

34   Tocci, N. et al. 2012. Ideational and Material Power in the Mediterranean: The Role of Turkey and the Gulf Cooperation Council. *The German Marshall Fund Mediterranean Paper Series*, Washington, DC, June, 4.

35   Ibid., 1.

about its potential to "fail" as a state'.[36] It is in the extremely fragile context following Yemeni unification that the Cooperation Agreement was concluded with the European Community in 1998, following an initial Development Cooperation Agreement signed with North Yemen in 1984, which was in 1995 extended to the entire country following reunification in 1990. The agreement signed in 1998 provides for long-term contractual commitments between both parties on a range of commercial, development, cultural and economic issues. It also encourages greater cooperation between Yemen and its neighbours. In this context, the agreement promotes enhanced coordination with existing cooperation programmes between the EU and countries of the GCC and in the Mediterranean and Middle East region (Art. 9).[37]

Alongside the creation of an EU Delegation in Sana'a in 2004, EU relations with Yemen were reinforced with the launch of a political dialogue between both parties in the context of the EU's Strategic Partnership with the Mediterranean and the Middle East (SPMME). The political dialogue focuses on the need to promote democratization and the respect of human rights, as well as to counter threats of terrorism and the proliferation of weapons of mass destruction.[38] The EU's 2007–10 Country Strategy Paper for Yemen, prepared in the framework of the Cooperation Agreement of 1998 and the SPMME of 2004, accompanied by an aid package of €60 million, focuses on two main objectives: assisting Yemeni authorities in the promotion of good governance and strengthening the authorities' capacities to combat poverty in line with the first Millennium Development Goal.[39]

EU-funded assistance to Yemen was initially carried under the budget lines for assistance to Asian and Latin American countries.[40] Since its unification in 1990, Yemen has received €300 million in EU assistance funds, primarily targeting food aid and security and economic development.[41] Under the 2007–13 Multi-Annual Indicative Programme, the EU provided €160 million in financial assistance to Yemen through the Development Cooperation Instrument (DCI). The DCI covers geographical programmes providing support for cooperation with 47 developing countries, including Yemen, across a range of areas,[42] as well

---

36   Durac, V. 2010. The European Union in Yemen: The Triumph of Pragmatism over Normativity? *European Foreign Affairs Review*, 15(5), 645–6.

37   Council of the European Union 1998. *Cooperation Agreement between the European Community and the Republic of Yemen*. OJ L72/18, 11 March.

38   Council of the European Union 2004. *Joint Declaration on Political Dialogue between the European Union and the Republic of Yemen*, 10763/04, Brussels, 6 July, 2.

39   European Commission 2006. *Yemen-European Community Strategy Paper for the Period 2007–2013*, 6, http://eeas.europa.eu/yemen/csp/07-13-en.pdf [accessed: 14 November 2012].

40   European Commission 2012. *EuropAid in the Gulf Region*, http://ec.europa.eu/europeaid/where/gulf-region/overview/index-en.htm [accessed: 18 December 2013].

41   Ibid.

42   Areas of cooperation include poverty eradication; fulfilment of MDGs; population needs; social cohesion; governance, democracy and human rights; trade and

as thematic programmes across all developing countries (migration and asylum; food security; 'Investing in People'; the European Instrument for Democracy and Human Rights; and non-state actors in development).[43] Under this 2007–13 financial framework, Yemen has also benefited from a range of European financial instruments such as the Stability Instrument (financial, economic and technical assistance in addressing political insecurity and crises; civil security; technological and nuclear threats) and the European Instrument for Democracy and Human Rights.[44] Financial support through the DCI is maintained under the 2014–20 multi-annual financial framework, with increased attention on human rights, democracy and good governance and targeting Least Developed Countries such as Yemen as a key priority.[45] Under the 2014–20 financial framework, the thematic programmes covered by the DCI focus, inter alia, on environment and climate change, sustainable energy, migration and asylum, and civil society organizations and local authorities.[46] In addition, as a least developed country, Yemen also benefits from trade incentives under the EU's 'Everything but Arms' initiative. Carried out under the GSP, this initiative grants Yemen duty-free and quota-free access to the EU market for all its exports.[47]

Since the unification of Yemen, observers have recurrently warned of a state on the brink of collapse. The country has remained politically and economically fragile, increasingly fractured since the ousting of President Saleh in February 2012 and the inefficiency of its public institutions, marked by high unemployment and poverty.[48] The fragility of Yemen and the porosity of its borders have created an environment for AQAP and other terrorist cells to exploit. Terrorist operative movements in Yemen and neighbouring Somalia, originating from Saudi Arabia,

---

regional integration; sustainable development; water resource management; infrastructure development; sustainable rural development; and assistance in post-crisis situations and fragile states.

43   European Parliament and Council of the European Union 2006. *Regulation (EC) No 1905/2006 of the European Parliament and of the Council of 18 December 2006 establishing a financing instrument for development cooperation.* OJ L378/41, 27 December.

44   European Commission 2006. *Yemen-European Community Strategy Paper*, op. cit., 8.

45   European Parliament and Council of the European Union 2014. *Regulation (EU) No 233/2014 of the European Parliament and of the Council of 11 March 2014 establishing a financing instrument for development cooperation for the period 2014–2020.* OJ L 77/44, 15 March.

46   Ibid.

47   Council of the European Union 2001. *Council Regulation (EC) No 2501/2001 of 10 December 2001 applying a scheme of generalized tariff preferences for the period from 1 January 2002 to 31 December 2004.* OJ L346/1, 31 December.

48   Sharp, J.M. 2010. Yemen: Background and U.S. Relations. *Congressional Research Service Report for Congress*, 2, http://www.fas.org/sgp/crs/mideast/RL34170.pdf [accessed: 20 December 2013].

Afghanistan and Pakistan represent a security threat to the region as a whole.[49] Security and counter-terrorism are thus central aspects of foreign actors' relations with Yemen, such as for neighbouring countries in the Gulf. The United States has also intensified its security and counter-terrorism attention towards Yemen, following attacks on the US Embassy in Sana'a in 2008 and the failed bomb attack on the Northwest Airlines Flight 253 in 2009.[50] The EU concentrates on the need to target security, stability and good governance through a focus on development cooperation, which it looks to address in the context of its Strategic Partnership with the Mediterranean and the Middle East.[51] Additionally to development assistance, the EU has sought to enhance the counter-terrorism capabilities of a number of target countries. The EU is focusing particular attention on Yemen and Somalia to counter the important terrorist threats in the region.[52] In its response to the 'Arab Spring', the EU has supported the transition following the stepping down of President Saleh in 2012, has played an outreach role to all parties and factions in the ensuing elections and has provided assistance in support of the political transition process.[53] The EU supports the implementation of further reforms in a 'peaceful and orderly transition', for 'inclusive, credible and transparent elections' in 2014 and remains particularly concerned with the humanitarian situation which continues to worsen in Yemen.[54]

By the very nature of its relations with the EU and by the extent of its presence in the Mediterranean and Middle East region, Yemen differs greatly from its GCC neighbours. Confusion under which '*chapeau*' of EU foreign policy Yemen should be categorized has been an impossible exercise. Yemen is the only country of the Arabian Peninsula which is not a member of the GCC; its level of development does not compare to its Gulf neighbours; furthermore, it is not clearly included in the EU's dealings with the Mediterranean and Middle Eastern region; and it does not fit under the ENP. There is, indeed, a 'real problem with where to fit Yemen'.[55]

Increasingly, however, Yemen has been developing into a 'buffer state' between the Peninsula and the Horn of Africa, two regional entities within the ring of neighbours of the EU's neighbours.[56] Albeit its geographical proximity to

---

49   Ibid., 4.

50   Ibid., 3.

51   European Commission, *Yemen-European Community Strategy Paper*, op. cit., 7.

52   Bures, O. 2011. *EU Counterterrorism Policy: A Paper Tiger?* Farnham: Ashgate, 237.

53   European Commission 2013. *EU's Response to the 'Arab Spring': The State-of-Play after Two Years*, 8 February, http://europa.eu/rapid/press-release-MEMO-13-81-en.htm [accessed: 20 December 2013].

54   Council of the European Union 2013. Council Conclusions on Yemen. *Foreign Affairs Council Meeting, Luxembourg, 24 June*, 2.

55   Durac, op. cit., 657.

56   Hill, G. 2010. Yemen: Fear of Failure. *MENAP Briefing Paper 2010/01*. London: Chatham House, 3, http://www.nrc.ch/8025708F004CE90B/(httpDocuments)/E39C81E7 8847A37FC12576F500684B52/$file/CHATHAM-Yemen-FearOfFailure-January2010.pdf

the GCC countries, its historical attachment to Saudi Arabia, and its close regional cooperation with the GCC, the Republic of Yemen also 'enjoys close relations' with countries of the Horn of Africa, predominantly focused on security issues.[57] The fragility of Yemen 'could expand a lawless zone stretching from northern Kenya, through Somalia and the Gulf of Aden, to Saudi Arabia'.[58] The precarious domestic situations of these countries are prone to the presence of terrorist cells and risks of maritime piracy, which have amplified concerns of an expanding 'zone of instability spanning the Gulf of Aden'.[59]

So far, the attention of international actors with regard to Yemen has remained restricted to the geographical boundaries of the Peninsula and its internal issues like the threat of terrorist groups such as AQAP (in 2009 in particular), overlooking the 'interconnected socio-political, economic and transnational challenges confronting Yemen, Somalia and their regional environs'.[60] If the EU is to address relations with Yemen adequately and in line with its political objectives, it is vital to build on the 'strategic significance of Yemen in a region as important as the Gulf'.[61]

This section has shown the extent to which relations between the EU and the countries of the Arabian Peninsula – GCC members and Yemen – have been driven since the 1990s by trade and energy and, increasingly so since 2001, by security and counter-terrorism priorities in the Mediterranean and Middle East region. Building on these observations, this chapter will now focus on the EU's interaction with Iraq and Iran and the challenges and opportunities ahead for greater EU engagement in the region.

The EU's Involvement in Iraq and the Prospects for its Future Regional Engagement

Since 2008, Iraq has entered the phase of development of its political institutions. This represents both a challenge and an opportunity for the EU. On the one hand, it is a challenge as the situation calls for a greater and more coherent involvement in a region which is still extremely volatile, not least since the Syrian crisis erupted in 2011. On the other hand, the situation also offers an opportunity for the EU as Iraq represents a country where the EU can still considerably develop its relations.

[accessed: 15 April 2013]. See also Chapter 4 by Alex Vines and Ahmed Soliman in this volume.

57   European Commission 2006, *Yemen-European Community Strategy Paper*, op. cit., 14.

58   Hill, op. cit., 11.

59   Mantzikos, I. 2011. Somalia and Yemen: The Links between Terrorism and State Failure. *Digest of Middle East Studies*, 20(2), 244.

60   Coates Ulrichsen, K. 2011. The Geopolitics of Insecurity in the Horn of Africa and the Arabian Peninsula. *Middle East Policy*, 18(2), 120–21.

61   Durac, op. cit., 655.

The main challenges that lie ahead for Iraq are the security situation between Shias and Sunnis, the nature of the federal structure of the country and the relationship between Baghdad and the provinces, good governance and the rule of law, the development of the oil sector and the lack of services to Iraqis, notably the supply of electricity.

Development of EU–Iraq Relations

In the 1980s, the relations between the European Economic Community and Iraq have been characterized by the ambiguities of dealing with a dictatorship that was perceived as representing a counterweight to the Iranian threat. Saddam Hussein, after having acted as vice-president since 1968, became president in 1979, the year of the Iranian Islamic revolution. He was considered an important bulwark against the propagation of the Iranian influence in the region. Therefore, despite his despotic regime and the blatant human rights violations, he benefited from European support during the Iran–Iraq war of 1980–88. The next decade started with the first Gulf War (1990–91) following the Iraqi invasion of Kuwait. An international coalition led by the US and supported by the UK and France swiftly defeated the Iraqi army while Saddam Hussein and his regime remained in place. A decade of UN sanctions and US military strikes (such as the 1998 *Desert Fox* operation, launched with the UK) against Iraq's belligerent intentions followed before the 2003 war was launched by the US.

In the EU and its Members States, the 2003 Iraq war is remembered as a rather painful moment. The EU's inability to respond in a coordinated manner to the war launched by the US has left profound wounds. In particular, the letter published by eight Member States, led by Spain and the UK, in support of the Americans in the *Wall Street Journal* ('Letter of 8') in January 2003 represented a severe breach of unity (there was an EU-15 common position on the role of the UN to solve the crisis). It was also a breach of the most fundamental principles of European foreign policy cooperation, namely consultations between partners before announcing diverging positions.[62] Nevertheless, the EU and its Member States were rather quick to act collectively towards Iraq once the division was overcome. One reason for that is that the EU represented a channel for countries such as France and Germany that refrained from dealing directly with the newly established Iraqi government but nevertheless did not want to be marginalized from this important policy issue.[63]

---

[62] Lewis, J. 2009. EU Policy on Iraq: The collapse and reconstruction of consensus-based foreign policy. *International Politics*, 46(4), 436–7.

[63] Burke, E. 2010. Iraq, a new European engagement, in R. Youngs (ed.), *The EU and Democracy Promotion, A Ccritical Global Assessment*. Baltimore, MD: John Hopkins University Press, 159.

The EU and Iraq: A Multifaceted European Involvement

The most visible dimension of the EU's involvement in Iraq is the EU Common Security and Defence Policy (CSDP) civilian mission EUJUST LEX.[64] The mission was launched in 2005 with the aim of training Iraqi officials in the fields of rule of law and human rights. Since its inception, the mission has trained more than 2,000 Iraqi officials (mainly policemen, magistrates and penitentiary staff as well as forensic officials) most of the time in EU Member States (as a consequence of the volatile security situation).[65] Despite some criticisms (notably on the lack of in-country training), the mission has generally been praised for its successes and its mandate has been extended by the Council to the end of December 2013, when the mission is set to end.[66] Therefore, addressing the issues of the neighbours of the EU's neighbours requires to look in detail at the different medium-and-long-term political frameworks through which the EU's action is channelled.

In terms of development cooperation, the EU has been active in Iraq since 2003. Between 2003 and 2009, the financial support on institution building in the fields of governance, rule of law and basic services was allocated on an annual basis (around €114 million per year on average).[67] In 2009–13, the European Commission adopted integrated assistance package programmes. The European Commission's action is guided by a Joint Strategy Paper which represents combined efforts of the European Commission, Sweden and Italy.[68] This Joint Strategy Paper and National Indicative Programme under the Development and Cooperation Instrument replaces the Commission's previous annual programming cycles and foresees an allocation of €95 million. It focuses on good governance, socioeconomic recovery through education and strengthening institutional capacity, water management and agriculture. The Strategy also mainstreams cross-cutting issues like human rights, gender and protection of vulnerable groups.[69]

---

64   European External Action Service 2013. *EU Integrated Rule of Law Mission for Iraq Factsheet*, http://www.eeas.europa.eu/csdp/missions-and-operations/eujust-lex-iraq/pdf/facsheet-eujust-lex-iraq-en.pdf [accessed: 3 January 2014].

65   Korski, D. 2009. The integrated rule of law mission for Iraq (EUJUST LEX), in G. Grevi, D. Helly, Damien and D. Keohane (eds), *European Security and Defense Policy, the First 10 Years (1999–2009)*. Paris: EUISS, 235.

66   European External Action Service 2013, op. cit.

67   European Commission 2012. *Country Cooperation: Iraq*, http://ec.europa.eu/europeaid/where/gulf-region/country-cooperation/iraq/iraq-en.htm [accessed: 10 November 2012].

68   European Commission 2011. *Cooperation between the EU and Iraq, Joint Strategy Paper 2011–2013*, http://eeas.europa.eu/iraq/docs/2011-2013-jsp-nip-en.pdf [accessed: 3 January 2014].

69   Ibid.

In the field of energy, a memorandum of understanding was signed in 2010 which creates a 'Strategic Energy Partnership' between the EU and Iraq.[70] Iraq has indeed become an increasingly important player in the field of energy and thanks to the development of resources in the northern part of the country, the International Energy Agency believes that, if political stability is guaranteed and investments in the supply chain are made, Iraq's fossil exports will match those of Saudi Arabia by 2035.[71] The EU's interest is therefore to help Iraq develop strong structures in order to satisfy the domestic energy needs (many Iraqis are still not connected to a reliable electricity network) and to ensure regular and reliable energy exports through the southern corridor.

In May 2012, the EU and the Iraqi government signed a Partnership and Cooperation Agreement (PCA)[72] which will constitute, once ratified,[73] the legal basis for further EU–Iraq cooperation. Besides providing the appropriate framework for political dialogue with regular meetings between ministers and officials, article 2 of the PCA constitutes the legal basis from which values such as human rights can be promoted.[74] On the economic side, it provides the basis for trade and investment promotion. Provisions on energy are also part of the Agreement.

Iraq and its Regional Environment: The Need for a Comprehensive Approach

When looking at EU–Iraq relations for the future, it seems important to try to understand how countries in the Middle Eastern region perceive the EU's involvement. Despite the profound differences between Arab countries themselves, the members of the Arab League have often complained about the EU approach leading to a 'Balkanization' of the Arab world.[75] In other words, the EU's action in

---

70   European Commission 2010. *Memorandum of Understanding between the Government of Iraq and the EU on Strategic Partnership on Energy*, Baghdad, 18 January, http://ec.europa.eu/energy/international/bilateral-cooperation/doc/iraq/2010-01-18-iraq-mou-en.pdf [accessed: 3 January 2014].

71   Birol, F. 2012. Conference for the presentation of the Iraq Energy Outlook of the International Energy Agency, Brussels, 18 October.

72   Council of the European Union 2012. *Partnership and Cooperation Agreement between the European Union and its Member States and the Republic of Iraq*. OJ L204/20, 31 July.

73   As of January 2014, 8 countries have ratified the Agreement. See ratification details at Council of the European Union 2014. *Agreement Details*, http://www.consilium. europa.eu/policies/agreements/search-the-agreements-database?command=details&lang=f r&aid=2011007&doclang=EN [accessed: 3 January 2014].

74   'Respect for democratic principles and human rights, as laid down in the Universal Declaration of Human Rights and other relevant international human rights instruments, as well as for the principle of the rule of law, underpins the internal and international policies of both Parties and constitutes an essential element of this Agreement'.

75   Lannon, E. 2008. The EU's Strategic Partnership with the Mediterranean and the Middle-East: A new geopolitical dimension of the EU's proximity strategy, in Dashwood,

the region is a factor of disunity: ENP countries (Mediterranean Arab states), the Arab states that are part of the ACP framework (Comoros, Djibouti, Mauritania, Somalia, Sudan), the Gulf Cooperation Council, Iraq and Yemen. From the EU's perspective, this might be problematic as most of the challenges (such as migration, energy, political stability, weapons of mass destruction, organized crime) have a clear regional dimension. This view had already been taken into account in the EU's Strategic Partnership with the Mediterranean and the Middle East of 2004. The final report, attached to the 2004 European Council Conclusions, outlined an 'East of Jordan Track' embracing the six Gulf Cooperation Council countries, Yemen, Iran and Iraq.[76] Whereas the bilateral contractual relations with Iraq have moved forward with the PCA, the strategic regional approach has not been further developed. If the EU is to strengthen its approach towards Iraq in the future, it needs to think of possible ways in which Iraq could be further included in existing cooperation frameworks and instruments. A regional approach should also include Iraq's main neighbour, Iran.

EU–Iran: Bilateral Challenges and the Regional Context

The inclusion of Iran in the EU's Strategic Partnership with the Mediterranean and the Middle East in 2004 followed a period of warming up in EU–Iranian relations between 1997 and 2002. Today, however, the normalization of the economic and political relations 'depends on progress in resolving the outstanding issues in connection with the Iranian nuclear programme'.[77] There is currently no EU Delegation in Tehran and practical cooperation is reduced to the lowest level: a few actions have been undertaken in the fields of student exchanges, drug control, humanitarian aid and refugees.[78]

Disrupted Attempts to Build a Lasting Relationship: A Short History

Following the Iran–Iraq war (1980–88) during which most of the European countries sided with Saddam Hussein's Iraq, the European Union embarked onto a more favourable policy towards Iran as it seemed increasingly difficult to neglect a key actor in the Middle Eastern region, both in geopolitical and economic

---

A. and Maresceau, M. (eds), *Law and Practice of EU External Relations.* Cambridge: Cambridge University Press, 360.

76   Ibid.

77   European External Action Service 2012. *Brief history of relations between EU and Iran*, http://eeas.europa.eu/iran/relations-en.htm [accessed: 11 November 2012].

78   European External Action Service 2012. *EU and Iran cooperation*, http://eeas. europa.eu/iran/cooperation-en.htm [accessed: 14 November 2012].

terms.[79] Shortly after having agreed upon the creation of a new Common Foreign and Security Policy (CFSP) in Maastricht, the European Council decided at the Edinburgh Summit in December 1992 to 'break the diplomatic ice' and start formal relations with Tehran.[80] This was made possible by President Rasfandjani's need to bring about post-revolutionary normality and post-war stability to Iran. Given the tumultuous relations since the 1979 Iranian revolution, however, the EU's offer consisted of a 'Critical Dialogue' rather than of a trade agreement, whereby all the problematic issues, including the question of human rights, would be addressed in priority. Despite heavy pressure from the US and Israel and criticism in Europe, relations with Iran were maintained and the EU did not follow the US sanctions enacted against Iran through the 1996 d'Amato-Kennedy Act.[81]

The first attempt to re-establish relations with Iran failed after a German court decision in April 1997[82] infuriated the Iranian leadership and led EU Member States to call back their ambassadors from Tehran. The diplomatic crisis was overcome by the election of the reformist Khatami to the presidency in 1997, which boded well for the future of the dialogue. The new 'Comprehensive Dialogue' allowed for regular meetings at the level of under-secretary of state, while working groups were established to deal with sectoral issues. On the basis of a Communication, the EU offered negotiations on a Trade and Cooperation Agreement combined with progress in the Political Dialogue while a Human Rights Dialogue was also set up.[83] Consequently, the years until 2002 were marked by hopes on the European side that under the leadership of Iranian reformists, dialogue and negotiations could yield progress both at economic and political levels. The discovery of an Iranian nuclear site in 2002, however, broke this dynamics. Since then, the nuclear issue has taken precedence over all the other issues and represents one of the main challenges in EU–Iranian relations.

Key Challenges in EU–Iranian Relations

Following the rejection by the Iranian authorities of a report by the International Atomic Energy Agency (IAEA) in June 2003, the Foreign Ministers of the EU's

---

79   Historical developments are taken from Posch, W. 2013. The EU and Iran, in Biscop, S. and. Whitman, R.G. (eds), *The Routledge Handbook of European Security*. London: Routledge, 179–81.

80   European Council 1992. *Conclusions of the Presidency, Edinburgh, 11–12December*,   http://www.european-council.europa.eu/council-meetings/conclusions/archives-1992–1975 [accessed: 4 January 2014].

81   Dufays, N. 2012. Les relations de l'UE avec la République islamique d'Iran: enjeux, perspectives et perceptions, in M. Makinsky (ed.), *L'Iran et les grands acteurs régionaux et globaux*. Paris: L'Harmattan, 421.

82   In the so-called 'Mykonos affair', Iranian officials were accused of terrorist activities in Berlin in the 1980s and sentenced to prison.

83   Commission of the European Communities 2001. *Communication on EU Relations with the Islamic Republic of Iran*, COM(2001) 71 final, Brussels, 7 February.

'big three' (France, United Kingdom, Germany) went to Tehran to try to convince the Iranians to comply with the Agency's requests. Soon after, the EU's High Representative for the CFSP, Javier Solana, was added to the team and the 'EU3' became the main framework for negotiations between the international community and Iran. In February 2006, the Iranian nuclear file was transmitted to the UN Security Council after another negative report by the IAEA. The new negotiation format was broadened to include the three other permanent members of the UN Security Council, the US, Russia and China, thus becoming the 'P5+1'. The group continued to be chaired by the EU High Representative, but in 2006 it adopted an approach largely shaped by the US policy of 'carrots and sticks', consisting of sanctions and incentives aimed at pushing the Iranians to negotiations.[84]

Despite the challenge of adopting a common position on such a sensitive issue, the EU's role in the negotiation process allowed to keep a coherent approach within the 'P5+1'. This approach has given an increasing importance to sanctions.[85] It has nevertheless been questioned by rising powers such as Turkey and Brazil, who managed to reach an agreement with the Iranian authorities in 2010 on the exchange of low enriched uranium against 20 per cent enriched fuel.[86]

Regarding human rights promotion, the EU's action towards Iran has been very limited, mainly consisting of declarations on the death penalty, including by the European Parliament.[87] The Human Rights Dialogue has been suspended since June 2004 due to the nuclear crisis.[88] The overall priority given to the nuclear file and the EU's coercive approach has also had a potentially negative impact on the promotion of human rights: adopting a tougher stance on the nuclear issue and implementing sanctions against the country actually provided the regime with excuses to commit human rights abuses such as arbitrary detention and even execution in the name of national security.[89] According to this view, a way forward would be to further take into account existing democratic movements of various roots (Islamic philosophy, women, students, and so forth) based on the specifically Iranian historical and political context. Another important aspect, however, is that due to the complex historical relations between the EU and Iran, Iranian organizations supported by Western funds are often suspected of being biased against the regime. Therefore, if the EU is to develop a strategic thinking for its 'broader neighbourhood', including Iran, it might be useful to look at the

---

84   Posch, op. cit., 184.

85   Another round of sanctions has been adopted by the EU on 15 October 2012.

86   *Joint Declaration by Iran, Turkey and Brazil*. New York, 17 May 2010, http://www.fas.org/nuke/guide/iran/joint-decl.pdf [accessed: 4 January 2014].

87   See, for instance, European Parliament 2011. *Buzek on the execution of Sahra Bahrami in Iran*, 30 January, http://www.europarl.europa.eu/document/activities/cont/2011 04/20110404ATT16874/20110404ATT16874EN.pdf [accessed: 4 January 2014].

88   Dufays, op. cit., 432.

89   Holliday, S.J. 2011. Democratization in Iran: A Role for the EU?, in Pace, M. (ed.), *Europe, the USA and Political Islam*. Houndmills: Palgrave Macmillan, 63.

possibilities to further include partners such as Turkey, who have adopted EU standards in the field of human rights and parts of the EU *acquis*.

Iran's relationships with its neighbours who are also embedded in the EU's policies represent another challenge for the EU. Iranian diplomacy in the broader region of the Middle East is characterized by a tension between, on the one hand, a sense of importance towards other Islamic nations derived from 'its perceived world-historical revolution' and, on the other hand, a sense of insecurity, strategic loneliness and the aspiration 'for more' which stems from its distinctive non-Arab identity.[90] This mixed feeling help explain the ambiguous relations that Iran has with its neighbours:[91] Iran plays a key role for many countries and retains a strong potential destabilizing power. In Iraq, the special relations that Iran developed with the Iraqi Shia politicians (such as the current Prime Minister Nouri Al-Maliki) or armed groups (for instance the Sadr militia) are of crucial importance in a context where the Iraqi government is struggling to establish strong institutions. Relations with Saudi Arabia and other GCC countries are extremely tense as the 'Arab Spring', which was supported by the Sunni regional powers and Shia Iran, has led to religious confrontations in Bahrain and Syria, thus creating the conditions of a Shia/Sunni 'Cold War' in the Middle East.

These three main challenges for EU–Iranian relations show paradoxically that Iran is at the centre of a potential conceptualization of the EU's engagement in the whole region but that many possible developments are currently blocked as a consequence of the rift over the nuclear programme. The deal reached between the 'P5+1' and Iran in Geneva on 23 November 2013 bodes, however, well for the future.[92] The deal satisfies both sides: while the US and the three EU Member States obtained that the enrichment programme is frozen, Iran interprets the agreement as recognizing its right to civil enrichment of uranium. The interim agreement that was successfully negotiated by the EU High Representative for Foreign Affairs and Security Policy will nevertheless need to be confirmed after May 2014, as it is only a first step with six months validity.[93]

---

90   Fahri, F. and Lotfian, S. 2012. Iran's Post-Revolution Foreign Policy Puzzle, in Nau, H.R. and Ollapally, D.M. (eds), *Worldviews of Aspiring Powers*. Oxford: Oxford University Press, 120.

91   Iran's geopolitical scope of action ranges from Lebanon and Palestine (through the Hezbollah and the Hamas) to Pakistan and Afghanistan via Syria, Iraq and the GCC countries.

92   Gordon, M.R. 2013. Accord Reached With Iran to Halt Nuclear Program. *The New York Times*, 23 November, http://www.nytimes.com/2013/11/24/world/middleeast/talks-with-iran-on-nuclear-deal-hang-in-balance.html?pagewanted=1&-r=0 [accessed: 4 January 2014].

93   European External Action Service 2013. *Joint Statement by EU High Representative Catherine Ashton and Iran Foreign Minister Zarif*, http://www.eeas.europa.eu/statements/docs/2013/131124-02-en.pdf [accessed: 4 January 2014].

Conclusions

This chapter asked why the EU should look to the neighbours of its own neighbours in the Mediterranean and Middle East in the context of its European Neighbourhood Policy. Taking a geopolitical approach, the chapter argued that many political, strategic and socioeconomic characteristics of the Arabian Peninsula, Iraq and Iran are relevant to the EU's relations with its southern neighbourhood. The chapter also shed light on the challenges and opportunities that lie ahead in these relations and suggested possibilities for the EU to develop a more comprehensive approach towards the 'neighbours of its neighbours'.

The EU's interaction with the countries of the Arabian Peninsula, Iraq and Iran is driven by the different economic, political and security contexts across the region, and is embodied in the variety of existing instruments and the policy priorities identified by the EU. While all of the EU's current contractual ties with the region have been developed in parallel and independently of the European Neighbourhood Policy, all underline the relevance of these neighbours of the EU's neighbours for the ENP for a number of reasons: oil-rich monarchies have proven their commitment to consolidate their presence and influence in the Mediterranean and Middle East region; the case of Yemen demonstrates the existence of overlaps with neighbouring regions beyond the boundaries of the Mediterranean and Middle East in the Horn of Africa and around the Gulf of Aden; Iraq's relevance to its regional environment deserves greater attention; the existing challenges of EU–Iranian relations, namely the Iranian nuclear programme, the situation of human rights, regional relations are central in addressing the reconceptualization of EU engagement in the region.

The EU's 'Balkanization' of the Mediterranean and Middle East region has prevented it from adapting to the realities of changing regional trends, in which boundaries between the EU's immediate and broader neighbourhood become increasingly blurred.[94] A geopolitical rethinking of EU policies in its neighbouring Mediterranean and the Middle Eastern region and in its ensuing relations with the Gulf thus seems necessary.

Timid EU efforts have seen the light, such as the adoption of an EU Strategic Partnership with the Mediterranean and the Middle East in 2004 or its 'East of Jordan Track' in 2006. Nonetheless, as ensuing chapters will show, greater EU attention towards geopolitical trends in the region appear necessary to focus efficiently on the countries of the Mediterranean and Middle East region, 'including the countries of the GCC, Yemen, Iraq and Iran'.[95]

---

94   Lannon, op. cit., 360.
95   European Council 2004, op. cit.

Bibliography

Baabood, A. 2009. The growing economic presence of Gulf countries in the Mediterranean region, in *IEMED Mediterranean Yearbook*. Barcelona: IEMED/ CIDOB.

Bazoobandi, S. 2013. *Political Economy of the Gulf Sovereign Wealth Funds: A Case Study of Iran, Kuwait, Saudi Arabia and the United Arab Emirates*. New York: Routledge.

Birol, F. 2012. Conference for the presentation of the Iraq Energy Outlook of the International Energy Agency, Brussels, 18 October.

Bossdorf, M. Engels, C. and Weiler, S. 2013. *EU-GCC Invest Report 2013*, http:// www.eu-gccinvest.eu/file/EU%20GCC%20Invest%20Report%202013.pdf [accessed: 18 December 2013].

Bourcier, N. 2012. Le Brésil, la Turquie et la Suède veulent peser plus dans le dossier iranien. *Le Monde*, 28 septembre, http://www.lemonde.fr/international/ article/2012/09/27/bresil-turquie-et-suede-veulent-peser-dans-le-dossier-du-nucleaire-iranien-1766696–3210.html [accessed: 14 November 2012].

British Petroleum 2013. *Statistical Review of World Energy*, http://www. bp.com/content/dam/bp/pdf/statistical-review/statistical_review_of_world_ energy_2013.pdf [accessed: 18 December 2013].

Bures, O. 2011. *EU Counterterrorism Policy: A Paper Tiger?* Farnham: Ashgate.

Burke, E. 2010. Iraq, a new European engagement, in R. Youngs (ed.), *The EU and Democracy Promotion: A Critical Global Assessment*. Baltimore, MD: Johns Hopkins University Press.

Coates Ulrichsen, K. 2011. Repositioning the GCC States in the Changing Global Order. *Journal of Arabian Studies*, 1(2), 231–47.

Coates Ulrichsen, K. 2011. The Geopolitics of Insecurity in the Horn of Africa and the Arabian Peninsula. *Middle East Policy*, 18(2), 120–35.

Commission of the European Communities 2001. *Communication on EU relations with the Islamic Republic of Iran*, COM(2001) 71 final, Brussels, 7 February.

Council of the European Union 1989. *Cooperation Agreement between the European Economic Community, of the one part, and the countries parties of the Charter of the Cooperation Council for the Arab States of the Gulf (the State of the United Arab Emirates, the State of Bahrain, the Kingdom of Saudi Arabia, the Sultanate of Oman, the State of Qatar and the State of Kuwait) of the other part*. OJ L54/3, 25 February.

Council of the European Union 1998. *Cooperation Agreement between the European Community and the Republic of Yemen*. OJ L72/18, 11 March.

Council of the European Union 2001. *Council Regulation (EC) No 2501/2001 of 10 December 2001 applying a scheme of generalized tariff preferences for the period from 1 January 2002 to 31 December 2004*. OJ L346/1, 31 December.

Council of the European Union 2004. *Joint Declaration on Political Dialogue between the European Union and the Republic of Yemen*, 10763/04, Brussels, 6 July.

Council of the European Union 2006. *Council Regulation (EC) No 1934/2006 of 21 December 2006 establishing a financing instrument for cooperation with industrialised and other high-income countries and territories.* OJ L405/41, 30 December.

Council of the European Union 2012. *Partnership and Cooperation Agreement between the European Union and its Member States and the Republic of Iraq.* OJ L204/20, 31 July.

Council of the European Union 2013. *Council Conclusions on Yemen.* Foreign Affairs Council Meeting, Luxembourg, 24 June.

Council of the European Union 2014. *Agreement Details*, http://www.consilium. europa.eu/policies/agreements/search-the-agreements-database?command=de tails&lang=fr&aid=2011007&doclang=EN [accessed: 3 January 2014].

Dufays, N. 2012. Les relations de l'UE avec la République islamique d'Iran: enjeux, perspectives et perceptions, in M. Makinsky (ed.), *L'Iran et les grands acteurs régionaux et globaux*. Paris: L'Harmattan.

Durac, V. 2010. The European Union in Yemen: The Triumph of Pragmatism over Normativity? *European Foreign Affairs Review*, 15(5), 645–61.

Echagüe, A. 2010. The Gulf Cooperation Council: The Challenges of security, in R. Youngs (ed.), *The European Union and Democracy Promotion: A Critical Global Assessment*. Baltimore, MD: Johns Hopkins University Press.

European Commission 2006. *Yemen-European Community Strategy Paper for the Period 2007–2013*, http://eeas.europa.eu/yemen/ csp/07_13_en.pdf [accessed: 14 November 2012].

European Commission 2006. *Communication from the Commission to the Council and the European Parliament on Strengthening the European Neighbourhood Policy*, COM(2006)726 final, Brussels, 4 December.

European Commission 2010. *Memorandum of Understanding between the Government of Iraq and the EU on Strategic Partnership on Energy*, Baghdad, 18 January, http://ec.europa.eu/energy/international/bilateral_cooperation/ doc/iraq/2010_01_18_iraq_mou_en.pdf [accessed: 3 January 2014].

European Commission 2011. *Cooperation between the EU and Iraq, Joint Strategy Paper 2011–2013*, http://eeas.europa.eu/iraq/docs/2011_2013_jsp_nip_en.pdf [accessed: 3 January 2014].

European Commission 2012. *EU Publishes revised preferential import scheme for developing countries*, 31 October, http://trade.ec.europa.eu/doclib/press/index. cfm?id=840 [accessed: 13 November 2012].

European Commission 2012. *Country Cooperation: Iraq*, http://ec.europa.eu/ europeaid/where/gulf-region/country-cooperation/iraq/iraq-en.htm [accessed: 10 November 2012].

European Commission 2012. *EuropAid in the Gulf Region*, http://ec.europa. eu/europeaid/where/gulf-region/overview/index_-en.htm [accessed: 18 December 2013].

European Commission 2012. *Countries and Regions: Gulf Region*, http:// ec.europa.eu/trade/creating-opportunities/bilateral-relations/regions/gulf-region [accessed: 12 November 2012].

European Commission 2013. *European Union, Trade with GCC*, http://trade. ec.europa.eu/doclib/docs/2006/september/tradoc_113482.pdf [accessed: 13 December 2013].

European Commission 2013. *EU's Response to the 'Arab Spring': The State-of-Play after Two Years*, 8 February, http://europa.eu/rapid/press-release_MEMO-13-81_en.htm [accessed: 20 December 2013].

European Commission and High Representative 2011. Joint Communication to the European Parliament, the Council, the European Economic and Social Committee and the Committee of Regions. *A New Response to a Changing Neighbourhood*, COM(2011) 303, Brussels, 25 May.

European Council 1992. *Conclusions of the Presidency*, http://www.european-council.europa.eu/council-meetings/conclusions/archives-1992–1975 [accessed: 4 January 2014].

European Council 2004. *Final Report: EU Strategic Partnership with the Mediterranean and the Middle East*, June, http://consilium.europa.eu/uedocs/ cmsUpload/Partnership%20Mediterranean%20and%20Middle%20East.pdf [accessed: 11 November 2012].

European External Action Service 2012. *Brief history of relations between EU and Iran*, http://eeas.europa.eu/iran/relations_en.htm [accessed: 11 November 2012].

European External Action Service 2012. *EU and Iran cooperation*, http://eeas. europa.eu/iran/cooperation_en.htm [accessed: 14 November 2012].

European External Action Service 2013. *EU Integrated Rule of Law Mission for Iraq Factsheet*, http://www.eeas.europa.eu/csdp/missions-and-operations/eujust-lex-iraq/pdf/ facsheet_eujust-lex_iraq_en.pdf [accessed: 3 January 2014].

European External Action Service 2013. *Joint Statement by EU High Representative Catherine Ashton and Iran Foreign Minister Zarif*, http://www.eeas.europa.eu/ statements/docs/2013/131124_02_en.pdf [accessed: 4 January 2014].

European Parliament 2011. *Buzek on the execution of Sahra Bahrami in Iran*, 30 January, http://www.europarl.europa.eu/document/activities/cont/201104/201 10404ATT16874/20110404ATT16874EN.pdf [accessed: 4 January 2014].

European Parliament and Council of the European Union 2006. *Regulation (EC) No 1905/2006 of the European Parliament and of the Council of 18 December 2006 establishing a financing instrument for development cooperation*. OJ L378/41, 27 December.

European Parliament and Council of the European Union 2014. *Regulation (EU) No 233/2014 of the European Parliament and of the Council of 11 March 2014 establishing a financing instrument for development cooperation for the period 2014–2020*. OJ L 77/44, 15 March.

European Parliament and Council of the European Union 2014. *Regulation (EU) No 234/2014 of 11 March 2014 of the European Parliament and of the Council establishing a Partnership Instrument for cooperation with third countries.* OJ L77/77, 15 March.

European Union 2013. *Remarks by High Representative Catherine Ashton following the 23rd EU-GCC Joint Council and Ministerial Meeting, Manama.* A 362/13, *Brussels*, 30 June.

Fahri, F. and Lotfian, S. 2012. Iran's Post-Revolution Foreign Policy Puzzle, in Nau, H.R. and Ollapally, D.M (eds), *Worldviews of Aspiring Powers.* Oxford: Oxford University Press.

Gordon, M.R. 2013. Accord Reached With Iran to Halt Nuclear Program. *The New York Times,* 23 November, http://www.nytimes.com/2013/11/24/world/middleeast/talks-with-iran-on-nuclear-deal-hang-in-balance.html?pagewanted=1&_r=0 [accessed: 4 January 2014].

Heard-Bey, F. 2006. Conflict Resolution and Regional Cooperation: The Role of the Gulf Cooperation Council 1970–2002. *Middle Eastern Studies,* 42(2), 199–222.

Hearst, D. 2013. Why Saudi Arabia is taking a risk by backing the Egyptian coup. *The Guardian,* 20 August, http://www.theguardian.com/commentisfree/2013/aug/20/saudi-arabia-coup-egypt [accessed: 20 December 2013].

Hill, G. 2010. Yemen: Fear of Failure. *MENAP Briefing Paper 2010/01.* London: Chatham House, http://www.nrc.ch/8025708F004CE90B/(httpDocuments)/E39C81E78847A37FC12576F500684B52/$file/CHATHAM_Yemen_FearOfFailure_January2010.pdf [accessed: 15 April 2013].

Holden, D. 1971. The Persian Gulf: After the British Raj. *Foreign Affairs,* 49(4), 721–35.

Holliday, S.J. 2011. Democratization in Iran: A Role for the EU?, in Pace, M. (ed.), *Europe, the USA and Political Islam.* Houndmills: Palgrave Macmillan.

Joint Declaration by Iran, Turkey and Brazil 2010. New York, 17 May, http://www.fas.org/nuke/guide/iran/joint-decl.pdf [accessed: 4 January 2014].

Khader, B. 2005. Is there a role for Europe in Gulf security? *GCC-EU Research Bulletin,* no. 3, 10–12.

Korski, D. 2009. The integrated rule of law mission for Iraq (EUJUST LEX), in Grevi, G., Helly, D. and Keohane, D. (eds), *European Security and Defense Policy, the First 10 Years (1999–2009).* Paris: EUISS.

Lannon, E. 2008. The EU's Strategic Partnership with the Mediterranean and the Middle-East: A new geopolitical dimension of the EU's proximity strategy, in Dashwood, A. and Maresceau, M. (eds), *Law and Practice of EU External Relations.* Cambridge: Cambridge University Press, 360–75.

Lewis, J. 2009. EU Policy on Iraq: The collapse and reconstruction of consensus-based foreign policy. *International Politics,* 46(4), 432–50.

Mantzikos, I. 2011. Somalia and Yemen: The Links between Terrorism and State Failure. *Digest of Middle East Studies,* 20(2), 242–60.

Masters, J. and Laub, Z. 2013. Al-Qaeda in the Arabian Peninsula (AQAP). *Council on Foreign Relations,* http://www.cfr.org/yemen/al-qaeda-arabian-peninsula-aqap/p9369 [accessed: 18 December 2013].

Momani, B. and Ennis, C.A. 2013. Between Caution and Controversy: Lessons from the Gulf Arab States as (Re-)Emerging Donors. *Cambridge Review of International Affairs*, 25(4), 605–27.

Nonneman, G. 2006. EU-GCC Relations: Dynamics, Patterns and Perspectives. *The International Spectator: Italian Journal of International Affairs*, 41(3), 59–74.

Posch, W. 2013. The EU and Iran, in Biscop, S. and Whitman, R.G. (eds), *The Routledge Handbook of European Security*. London: Routledge, 179–88.

Raphaeli, N. and Gersten, B. 2008. Sovereign Wealth Funds: Investment Vehicles for the Persian Gulf Countries. *Middle East Quarterly*, 15(2), 45–53.

Rawi, A. Ayesha, K. and Tarun, K. 2008. Where Oil-Rich Nations Are Placing Their Bets. *Harvard Business Review*, 86(9), 119–28.

Sharp, J.M. 2010. Yemen: Background and U.S. Relations. *Congressional Research Service Report for Congress*, http://www.fas.org/sgp/crs/mideast/RL34170.pdf [accessed: 20 December 2013].

Schumacher, T. and Fernandez Molina, I. 2013. EU and GCC Countries' Foreign Policies and the Mediterranean Neighbourhood – Towards Synergetic Cooperation? *Gulf Research Center Paper*, http://eu-gcc.kcorp.net/common/publicationfile/35.pdf [accessed: 20 December 2013].

Tocci, N. et al. 2012. Ideational and Material Power in the Mediterranean: The Role of Turkey and the Gulf Cooperation Council. *The German Marshall Fund Mediterranean Paper Series*. Washington, DC, June.

Youngs, R. 2009. Impasse on Euro-Gulf Relations. *FRIDE Working Paper*, no. 80, Madrid: FRIDE.

Chapter 6

The Gulf and the EU: Partners or Competitors?

Silvia Colombo

Introduction

Important changes have been ongoing in the broader Middle Eastern region since the 1980s with the first Gulf War (1980–88), the invasion of Kuwait by the Iraqi regime of Saddam Hussein (1990–91), the 2003 US-led invasion to topple the Iraqi dictator and, since 2011, the 'Arab Spring' revolutions. While the European Union (EU) has since the 1990s cultivated important and comprehensive relations with the Western part of the Arab world, it has at the same time somehow neglected the potential of its relations with the countries of the Arabian Peninsula. In other words, the EU has drawn an imaginary line between the southern and eastern Mediterranean, that is, its own strategic neighbourhood, and the other Arab (and non-Arab) countries lying further to the East. As a result of the transformative events that go under the name of the 'Arab Spring', the EU has started to understand that this line should be erased and that a renewed engagement with the Arab/Islamic world needs to bring the Gulf back into the Mediterranean.

This chapter deals with a specific portion of the Arab world that has been cut off from the EU's Mediterranean policy, that is, the countries of the Gulf Cooperation Council (GCC). It aims at shedding some light on the past, present and future of EU-GCC relations. As such it comes at a timely moment in which relations are at an all-time low and need to be revamped and rebuilt on new, more solid foundations. By tracing the evolution of the EU-GCC relationship, the chapter pinpoints the divergences as well as the convergences of interests and principles that have shaped this partnership. It argues that until recently the EU and the GCC have behaved more as competitors than as partners due to the underdeveloped character of their mutual engagement and the persistence of mistrust. While this situation has become more acute with the outbreak of the 'Arab Spring', the current changes in the common neighbourhood could pave the way for a more strategic relationship between Europe and the Gulf.

The first section of this contribution contextualizes the current state of EU-GCC relations in the framework of the history of cooperation between the two regions as well as with regard to the country-specific and regional economic and political dynamics. It then assesses the strengths and weaknesses embedded in EU-GCC relations by dwelling on both the structural and content-related obstacles that have so far hampered this relationship. In the conclusions, it reflects on the impact of the changing regional and international context on EU-GCC relations, also suggesting concrete ideas to foster mutual cooperation.

EU-GCC Relations: Historical Trajectory and the Current State of Affairs

The six GCC countries are today only loosely integrated despite the attempts to create a regional bloc. Inter-state rivalries, a lack of effective institutions and insufficient political will among the Member States have impeded GCC integration. To these factors, the smaller states' fear that any form of Gulf integration would mean sacrificing their sovereignty to Saudi Arabia's pre-eminence should be added. This has meant that bilateral relations with external powers, including the EU, have been a more attractive prospect for GCC Member States in the past three decades.

The GCC: A Mosaic of Regimes Facing a Changing Region

The Gulf Cooperation Council is a regional grouping bringing together Bahrain, Kuwait, Oman, Qatar, Saudi Arabia and the United Arab Emirates (UAE). Home to a population of 43 million people, the region exhibits high heterogeneity in the level of socioeconomic development with per capita incomes ranging between €54,000 and €12,000 in 2012.[1] The GCC region is well known for its hydrocarbon endowments, but since their discovery and the beginning of oil exploitation in the 1970s, reserves have decreased substantially in most countries, pushing governments to engage in economic diversification policies. The rapid socioeconomic growth experienced by the GCC countries over the past couple of decades has led to higher local demand for energy, thus making the GCC countries large consumers of fossil fuels. The rising local energy demand is stimulated by several factors, including the population increase, higher urbanization rates, the industrialization of the economies, changes in transportation modes and water scarcity. Today, the GCC countries are looking at several technologies, among which are nuclear power and renewable energy, in order to be able to supply part of the extra capacity needed.[2]

Security motives have been the driving force behind the GCC creation. In the aftermath of the first Gulf War between Iran and Iraq, the countries of the Arabian Peninsula decided to initiate a move towards regional integration with a view to dealing with possible security threats. After the GCC's creation on 25 May 1981,

---

1   World Bank 2013. *World Development Indicators*, http://data.worldbank.org/data-catalog/world-development-indicators [accessed: 20 August 2013].

2   Al-Shalabi, A., Cottret, N. and Menichetti, E. 2013. EU-GCC Cooperation on Energy. Technical Report, *Sharaka Technical Report*, no. 3, http://www.sharaka.eu/wp-content/uploads/2013/07/Sharaka-RP-03.pdf [accessed: 19 August 2013].

plans were laid out to enhance the regional integration in a way similar to that of the EU, with the stated goals of creating a customs union and adopting a single currency.[3] Despite these ambitious plans, progress has been slow and uneven. The GCC customs union was only established in 2003, but the full functioning of the project has been delayed by disagreements over a formula on how to divide customs revenues between the governments. Bahrain and Oman signed a free trade agreement (FTA) with the United States in 2004 and 2006 respectively, and, after numerous postponements, talks for the creation of the common currency have been frozen after Oman and the United Arab Emirates decided to opt out in 2006 and 2009 respectively.[4] Other GCC projects have also run into headwinds. For several years, the Gulf countries have been considering whether to introduce a Value Added Tax, perhaps at a unified rate of 5 per cent, in order to mitigate their reliance on oil income. However, in light of the current buoyancy in the oil sector, there is little immediate need for governments to raise more revenues.[5]

Several factors can be put forward to explain the slow progress in regional integration, including bureaucratic and administrative inefficiencies, as well as old rivalries and a desire among smaller Gulf states to retain their autonomy. Furthermore, as oil and hydrocarbon producers, the GCC countries have a similar economic structure, which restricts trade promotion and integration among them. This similarity in production structures translates into very low rates of intra-regional trade but, in recent years, trade volumes have been on the rise. Compared to 1980, when intra-GCC trade flows amounted to $8 billion only, by 2008, that figure had risen to $67 billion, amounting to about 6 per cent of the GCC's total world trade.[6] Bahrain and Oman have more diversified economies and larger intra-GCC trade orientations. In 2008, their intra-GCC import-export trade flows amounted to 18.34 per cent and 20.1 per cent, respectively, while Saudi Arabia had

---

3   Legrenzi, M. 2011. *The GCC and the International Relations of the Gulf: Diplomacy, Security and Economic Coordination in a Changing Middle East.* London-New York: I.B. Tauris.

4   Legrenzi, M. 2008. Did the GCC Make a Difference? Institutional Realities and (Un)Intended Consequences, in Harders, C. and Legrenzi, M. (ed.), *Beyond Regionalism? Regional Cooperation, Regionalism and Regionalization in the Middle East.* Aldershot: Ashgate, 107–24.

5   Colombo, S. and Committeri, C. 2013. Need to Rethink the EU-GCC Strategic Relation. *Sharaka Conceptual Paper*, no. 1, http://www.sharaka.eu/wp-content/uploads/2013/02/Sharaka-RP-01.pdf [accessed: 19 August 2013].

6   Nuruzzaman, M. 2013. Politics, Economics and Saudi Military Intervention in Bahrain. *Journal of Contemporary Asia*, 43(2), 368. If confronted with the intra-EU trade figure of 63 per cent between 1995 and 2011, it appears that intra-regional trade integration among the GCC countries still has a long way to go. See Ayadi, R. and Gadi, S. 2013. EU-GCC trade and investment relations: What prospects for an FTA between the two regions? *Sharaka Technical Report*, no. 5, http://www.sharaka.eu/wp-content/uploads/2013/10/Sharaka-RP-05.pdf [accessed: 7 November 2013].

a share of only 3.8 per cent.[7] Another feature of the GCC economies in addition to their weak regional integration is that they appear to be very state dominated, with governments holding important shares in the industrial and services sectors. In addition to structural economic factors rendering regional integration difficult, geopolitical factors, such as a degree of competition among the ruling families, help explain why the GCC countries fail to behave as a united bloc, despite their many common institutional characteristics.

In terms of political systems, countries in the region share many similarities, including the monarchical rule, no political parties and scarce avenues for popular political participation and dissent. These commonalities notwithstanding, some important differences exist. For example, Kuwait has a somewhat more open political system with parliamentary elections and a written constitution. The political development of Kuwait towards a fully democratic system is, however, hampered by the serious political crisis the country has been living since 2006, which has led to the fall of an incredible number of governments due to the conflicts existing between the elected National Assembly and the government, which is appointed by the Emir.[8] At the same time, this unstable situation has paralysed the economic and social development of the country since the early 1990s.

Also Bahrain has been in a state of deep crisis since 2011 although this crisis is of a different nature compared to the situation in Kuwait. The violent protests of March 2011, often but not always of a sectarian nature, are part of the wave of popular awakening that started in Tunisia and the demand for more rights. These events have caused a political paralysis in the country, despite the attempts to find a solution through a national dialogue process, as well as triggered the military intervention of the GCC arm – the Peninsula Shield Force – led by Saudi Arabia.

Compared to Kuwait and Bahrain, Saudi Arabia and Oman are relatively stable countries. The former has been able to build its stability on the enormous rents deriving from oil and displays many features of the rentier state mentality. The latter has so far successfully crafted its role as an autonomous foreign policy player in the region by maintaining good relations with the United States, its fellow GCC states and Iran. Nevertheless, in the long run problems may start to arise in both countries as a result of the delicate succession issue.[9] Both Saudi Arabia and Oman are struggling with an aging leadership and uncertainty surrounding the question of the succession, which will likely spur conflicts within the royal family and between it and the population.

To conclude this brief look at the political systems of the GCC countries, the cases of Qatar and the UAE tell the story of relatively stable countries with high

---

7   Nuruzzaman, op. cit., 368.

8   Coates Ulrichsen, K. 2012. Kuwait's Uncertain Path. *Foreign Policy*, 26 September, http://mideast.foreignpolicy.com/posts/2012/09/26/kuwait-s-uncertain-path [accessed: 20 August 2013].

9   Al-Rasheed, M. 2007. *Contesting the Saudi State: Islamic Voices from a New Generation*. Cambridge: Cambridge University Press.

rates of growth and the ability to attract foreign direct investments (FDI) well above those of the other GCC countries. At the same time, Qatar and the UAE seem to be immune from any form of domestic reform that could advance these political systems along the path of growing power sharing with the population. The case of the UAE is particularly worrying in the light of the repressive measures adopted in the aftermath of the Arab uprisings, namely against the Muslim Brotherhood.[10] This is accompanied by an increasingly strong dependence on foreign labour, largely coming from Asia, which helped kick-start the country's economic recovery after the 2009 crisis thanks to the development of the services sector, mainly logistics and tourism.

The GCC region has not been left untouched by the tremendous transformations triggered by the 'Arab Spring'. On the external front, the GCC states' responses to the changes taking place in countries like Tunisia, Egypt, Libya, Yemen and Syria have led to a growing and more visible involvement in their western neighbourhood, which corresponds to the southern neighbourhood of the EU. To this end, both material and ideational means have been deployed to foster the GCC countries' influence in a changing North African and Middle Eastern region.[11] At the political and religious level, Qatar has tried to capitalize on the coming to power of the Islamist parties in the region by making extensive use of its 'soft power' through *Al-Jazeera*.[12] At the economic level, some countries in the region have resorted to their enormous wealth to make generous financial assistance packages available to the cash-strapped 'Arab Spring' countries.

The debate about the revolutionary or counter-revolutionary nature of the GCC countries' engagement with North Africa and the Middle East notwithstanding,[13] the 'Arab Spring' is not only a regional development taking place in some distant part of the Arab world. It has instead important potential ramifications on the domestic front of each and every country of the Gulf.[14] Against this backdrop, all the GCC countries have attempted to contain the transnational wave of political

10   *Reuters* 2012. Dubai Police Chief Warns of Muslim Brotherhood, Iran Threat, 26   July,   http://www.reuters.com/article/2012/07/26/us-emirates-police-brotherhood-idUSBRE86P0EG20120726 [accessed: 22 August 2013].

11   Tocci, N., Maestri, E., Özel, S. and Güvenç, S. 2012. Ideational and Material Power in the Mediterranean: The Role of Turkey and the Gulf Cooperation Council. *Mediterranean Papers Series*. Washington, DC: German Marshall Fund of the United States–IAI, http://www.gmfus.org/wp-content/blogs.dir/1/files-mf/1339768226TocciEtAl-Turkey-GCC-Jun12-web.pdf [accessed: 23 August 2013].

12   Khatib, L. 2013. Qatar's Foreign Policy: The Limits of Pragmatism. *International Affairs*, 89(2), 417–31.

13   Jones, T.C. 2011. Counterrevolution in the Gulf. *Peace Brief*, no. 89, Washington, DC: United Institute of Peace, 15 April 2011, http://www.usip.org/publications/counterrevolution-in-the-gulf [accessed: 25 August 2013].

14   Schumacher, T. and Fernàndez Molina, I. 2013. EU and GCC Countries' Foreign Policies and the Mediterranean Neighborhood – Towards Synergetic Cooperation? *GRC Gulf Papers*, Gulf Research Center, 13, http://www.grc.net/index.

change to ensure the survival of the incumbent rulers through both military and patronage measures. Next to the military intervention in Bahrain to quell the Shia-led rebellion against the Sunni Al-Khalifa establishment, all countries have implemented welfare measures to buy social peace, with Saudi Arabia announcing in May 2011 a benefit package of $130 billion (€100 billion), roughly equivalent to the GCC's total exports to the BRIC countries in 2010, in addition to the construction of 500,000 new houses and the creation of 60,000 jobs in the public sector for Saudi nationals.[15]

One of the measures proposed by the Saudi King to foster integration within the GCC as a way to protect the regimes' stability was the initiative of the 'Gulf Union'. However, after some rounds of discussion all the GCC countries, excluding Saudi Arabia and Bahrain, have signalled their strong opposition to the plan, which seems to have been put aside. This in itself could be a sign of the fragility of the GCC as a regional organization, although according to some accounts the current flexible, non-centralized nature of the GCC is the only form in which it can exist, also in light of the diverging trajectories among its Member States identified above.[16] Despite all the shortcomings of the attempts to adopt an integration model based on the European experience, in December 2012 the Secretary-General of the GCC announced that its members had agreed on the creation of a unified military.[17] This decision was ratified by the six GCC countries in 2013. While having historically relied on bilateral security guarantees with the US, security and military cooperation could be the first step to develop a more integrated alliance among the six countries by enhancing interoperability and joint command and control.

The EU and the GCC: A Long History of Cooperation

The GCC region's resource endowments, the weaknesses in its regional economic integration and its growing importance in the Arab world have resulted in the development of important commercial and political links with other countries. While the GCC has privileged the United States as an international partner thanks to its engagement in the region since hydrocarbons were discovered, the region

---

php?frm-module=contents&frm-action=detail-book&pub-type=16&sec=Contents&frm-title=&book-id=81273&op-lang=en [accessed: 25 August 2013].

15   Hertog, S. 2011. The cost of counter-revolution in the GCC. *Foreign Policy*, 31 May, http://mideast.foreignpolicy.com/posts/2011/05/31/the-costs-of-counter-revolution-in-the-gcc [accessed: 13 March 2012].

16   Koch, C. 2012. A Union in Danger: Where the GCC is Headed is Increasingly Questionable. *GRC Analysis*. Gulf Research Center, http://www.grc.net/?frm-action=view-newsletter-web&sec-code=grcanalysis&frm-module=contents&show-web-list-link=1&int-content-id=79778 [accessed: 26 August 2013].

17   *Al-Arabiya* 2012. Gulf leaders agree on unified military command at Bahrain summit, 25 December, http://www.alarabiya.net/articles/2012/12/25/257017.html [accessed: 27 August 2013].

has attracted the attention of EU policymakers since the 1970s due to a mix of geopolitical and commercial interests. The first initiative structuring relations between the EU and the GCC countries dates back to 1974, when France pushed for the creation of the Euro-Arab Dialogue, following the Arab-Israeli War of 1973 and the first oil shock. The initiative, which was preceded by intense bilateral relations based on historical and colonial ties, did not target the GCC countries exclusively, but sought to establish a permanent dialogue between the European countries and the members of the Arab League. However, the initiative collapsed in 1989 without any significant achievement in terms of deepened cooperation.

A second, more successful attempt was made at the beginning of the 1980s as a direct consequence of the creation of the GCC in 1981. Over the 1980s, time was ripe to launch a European initiative targeted at the GCC. A Cooperation Agreement with the European Economic Community (EEC) was concluded in 1988 and entered into force in 1989. It was a fairly general document providing for the institutional framework to 'promote overall co-operation between equal partners on mutually advantageous terms in all spheres between the two regions and further their economic development, taking into consideration the differences in development of the parties'.[18] The main goals were to improve economic relations between the two regions, intensify trade and investment exchanges, strengthen inter-regional interdependence and initiate loose political dialogue. It was also intended to encourage GCC regional integration, contribute to strengthening stability in a region of strategic importance to the European Union, secure EU energy supplies and strengthen the process of economic development and diversification of the GCC economies. Thus, when it was concluded, the Cooperation Agreement had both an economic and a political dimension. From the economic perspective, the motivations of the EU countries were quite straightforward: the GCC countries were important suppliers of hydrocarbons and a growing export market for the European economies. Turning to the minor political dimension, the EU saw the GCC grouping as an important player to promote stability in the region. To achieve this goal, the Joint Cooperation Council comprising representatives of both sides and meeting once a year was created. The Council's aim was to reach the objectives set out in the Cooperation Agreement and to ensure its smooth operation. In practice, the annual meeting and the subsequent communiqués of the Joint Cooperation Council have simply become empty political statements on issues such as international stability and terrorism on which both parties tend to share the same views.

Beyond the Cooperation Agreement, the Gulf countries have not been included in the EU's external cooperation programmes until 2007, when the Council adopted

---

18 Council of the European Union 1989. *Cooperation Agreement between the European Economic Community, of the one part, and the countries parties of the Charter of the Cooperation Council for the Arab States of the Gulf (the State of the United Arab Emirates, the State of Bahrain, the Kingdom of Saudi Arabia, the Sultanate of Oman, the State of Qatar and the State of Kuwait) of the other part.* OJ L54/3, 25 February.

Regulation EC/1934/2006 establishing a Financing Instrument for Cooperation with Industrialized and other high-income Countries and territories (ICI) for the years 2007–13.[19] The instrument is allocated a small envelope of €172 million and targets, besides the GCC countries, other industrialized nations such as Australia, Canada, Japan and the United States. The fields of intervention of the ICI are broadly the same as those envisaged in the Cooperation Agreement. In 2014–20, this programme will be replaced by the Partnership Instrument (PI).

The inclusion of the GCC in the EU's external cooperation programmes came very late and was insufficient to fill the gap in EU-GCC relations after 20 years since the signing of the Cooperation Agreement. In addition to the shortcomings of the Agreement per se and its overly ambitious goals, the fact that the GCC countries have been disregarded when the EU structured its relations vis-à-vis the other Arab countries of North Africa and the Middle East can be viewed as a huge mistake. Relations with the southern and eastern Mediterranean countries have been one of the main pillars of the EU's foreign and security policy since the early 1990s, leading to the creation of the Euro-Mediterranean Partnership (EMP) in 1995 and later on to the establishment of the European Neighbourhood Policy (ENP) in 2003. The exclusion of the GCC countries from these policy frameworks has contributed to drawing a dividing line in the Arab world and its relations with the EU, despite the commonalities and strong relations existing between the Mediterranean area and the Gulf region. Furthermore, the structural imbalance between the EEC-GCC Cooperation Agreement, on the one hand, and the EMP and the ENP, on the other hand – all their limitations notwithstanding[20] – has jeopardized the EU's leverage in the Gulf region and has contributed to keeping the inter-regional relationship at a low strategic level. The failed attempts to conclude the FTA so far have further diminished the EU's influence in the region. All in all, a number of factors can be mentioned to explain the low strategic level of EU-GCC relations to date, among which the tendency to prioritize economic relations to the detriment of a broader set of issues is a key element.

The EU-GCC Cooperation between Strategic Interests and Structural Obstacles

Technical cooperation between the EU and the GCC as envisaged by the Cooperation Agreement was to be achieved in a number of fields, including

---

19   Council of the European Union 2006. *Council Regulation (EC) No 1934/2006 of 21 December 2006 establishing a financing instrument for cooperation with industrialised and other high-income countries and territories*. OJ L405/41, 30 December.

20   Aliboni, R. 2009. The ENP in the Mediterranean: Evaluating the political and strategic dimension, in Comelli, M., Eralp, A. and Üstün, Ç. (eds), *The European Neighbourhood Policy and the Southern Mediterranean*. Ankara: Middle East Technical University Press, 13–29.

economy and trade, agriculture and fisheries, industry, energy, science and technology, investment and environment. In spite of this comprehensive list of ambitious goals, EU-GCC relations have been largely confined to trade and economic issues for many years. This has prevented the development of a fully fledged multilateral relationship also taking into account other policy issues.

A Relationship Dominated by Economic Interests

Since its inception, the relationship between the European Union and the GCC has been dominated by trade and investment dynamics. This focus, and in particular the strong emphasis on the EU-GCC FTA, has interfered with political and governance issues, while neither track of cooperation has actually reached the desired results. Although a certain mismatch between political and economic goals exists in any relationship, in the Gulf such tensions have proven especially difficult to reconcile. The lack of flexibility with regard to economic policies has been an obstacle to political objectives, while short-term thinking on strategic challenges has failed to advance economic cooperation.

In economic terms, EU-GCC trade and investment relations have flourished driven by high oil prices and the Gulf countries' development imperatives. Trade patterns between the two regions are stable and show that the GCC exports to the EU are mainly oil, gas and related petrochemical products, while the region imports chiefly manufactured products and transport equipment from the EU. GCC imports from the EU, 70 per cent of which come from France, Germany and the UK, have a high value added and technological content.[21]

Competition from the so-called BRICs, and chiefly China, is growing also in knowledge-intensive manufactured products. This has led to a narrowing of the GCC region's trade balance with the EU, which in 2012 amounted to €22 billion in favour of Europe from €35 billion in 2009.[22] In recent years, trade between the GCC countries and China has soared, driven by Beijing's need for hydrocarbon resources and an increase in its exports' added value. Despite this rise, the EU still remains an important partner for the GCC but looking to the future, Chinese exports are likely to compete increasingly with those from the EU in the region. The figures of EU-GCC trade notwithstanding, from a European perspective, Gulf countries are minor trading partners. Between 2000 and 2011, their share of total EU exports amounted to approximately 3 per cent and their share of total imports averaged 2 per cent. Also, reflecting the diversification of the EU's hydrocarbon supplies, the GCC countries' share of total hydrocarbon imports averaged 8 per cent in the same period.[23]

---

21 Ayadi and Gadi, op. cit.

22 European Union 2013. *European Union, Trade in Goods with GCC*, 7 November, http://trade.ec.europa.eu/doclib/docs/2006/september/tradoc-113482.pdf [accessed: 31 December 2013].

23 Ayadi and Gadi, op. cit.

Investment relations between the EU and the GCC are dominated by Foreign Direct Investment flows. Between 1995 and 2011, GCC countries attracted a negligible share of the world's inward FDI flows (a mere 1.7 per cent compared to 26 per cent for the EU).[24] This modest performance is partly due to the role of the public sector in the hydrocarbon industry in most GCC countries and the limitations restricting the entry of foreign investors. These obstacles notwithstanding, the creation of the customs union in 2003 seems to have had a positive impact on the region's ability to attract FDI thanks to the abolition of tariffs among the GCC economies. In addition, the rise in foreign capital inflows observed in the early 2000s appears to have been influenced by the privatization measures pursued by countries such as Saudi Arabia, particularly in the hydrocarbon sector. With regard to the GCC region's outward direct investments, once again the performance of the region was modest over the period 1995 to 2011, with Saudi Arabia and the United Arab Emirates representing the most significant exporters of capital in the region.[25] Outward FDI from the GCC region is the result of several motivations, chiefly the need for economic diversification. As major hydrocarbon producers and exporters, GCC countries need to protect themselves from the 'Dutch disease' syndrome by diversifying their sources of income, which can be accomplished through the acquisition of foreign assets. EU Member States are among the most profitable destinations for the GCC countries' FDI, although they represent a minor share of direct investment inflows. However, this picture could be misleading as the levels of the GCC countries' FDI do not take the Sovereign Wealth Funds (SWFs) adequately into account. The establishment of SWFs in the GCC countries is not a new phenomenon, as some were set up as early as the 1970s. However, the majority were created at the beginning of the 2000s as oil prices and subsequent foreign exchange reserves increased, and governments in the region created funds to invest in assets overseas and to diversify the region's sources of income beyond hydrocarbons.[26] EU Member States have been important destinations for overseas investment of the GCC region's SWFs, although it is virtually impossible to quantify their investment due to the high level of secrecy surrounding them and their lack of transparency.[27]

------

24   Considering the share of inward direct investment relative to their size, however, the GCC countries significantly outperformed the EU and other economies (17 per cent of GDP in the GCC countries compared to 2 per cent for the EU). Ibid.

25   UNCTAD Statistics, http://unctad.org/en/Pages/Statistics.aspx [accessed: 22 August 2013].

26   Bahgat, G. 2011. Sovereign Wealth Funds in the Gulf: An Assessment. *Global Governance Paper*, no. 16, Kuwait Programme on Development, Governance and Globalization in the Gulf States. London: London School of Economics and Political Science, http://eprints.lse.ac.uk/55015/1/-Libfile-repository-Content-Kuwait%20Programme-Bahgat-2011.pdf [accessed: 30 August 2013].

27   For more details about the concerns raised by EU Member States with regard to the GCC SWFs becoming one of the largest foreign stakeholders in Europe and the bilateral and multilateral measures adopted to protect national strategic assets, see Hertog, S. 2007.

Any assessment of EU-GCC relations would not be complete without a reference to the FTA. The agreement was aimed at fostering the integration between the EU and the GCC by going beyond shallow integration and tariff dismantlement to address issues such as trade in services liberalization, investment regulations and government procurement rules. As stated before, negotiations for the creation of the FTA with the GCC countries were launched as part of a wider effort aimed at reinforcing the EU's engagement with the Arab world. Geopolitical considerations going beyond strictly economic motivations, such as the Gulf's importance as a hydrocarbon supplier as well as its economic and political influence in the region, seem to have played a prominent role. As for the GCC, instead, economic drivers rank high in explaining the motivations for an FTA with the EU. Within the scope of the FTA, the GCC countries would benefit from enhanced market access for their petrochemical industries. In turn, better market access for European goods and some degree of opening up in the services sectors of the GCC economies could generate spill-over and technology transfers supporting their diversification objective. Studies conducted to assess the impact of an FTA between the two regions tend to agree that the GCC countries would be the main beneficiaries from trade liberalization with the EU.[28]

The actual negotiations for the FTA and their failure provide useful insights about the development of EU-GCC relations. Although FTA talks were initiated in 1990, immediately after the signing of the Cooperation Agreement, the prospects of a region-to-region FTA only became realistic in 2003, when the GCC became a customs union.[29] The pace of negotiations accelerated in 2007 and there were high expectations that a conclusion would be reached in 2008 in light of the prevailing enthusiasm for the potentially positive repercussions on political and security cooperation between the two regions. However, this did not happen and negotiations were unilaterally interrupted by the GCC in December 2008, although informal contacts between the negotiators continue to take place.

Two reasons can be put forward to explain the failure to conclude the FTA after 20 years of negotiations. First, the EU's petrochemical lobby forcefully fought against trade liberalization, resulting in some EU Member State governments blocking duty-free access for petrochemicals from the Gulf.[30] Second, the human rights and illegal migration clauses embedded in the FTA – a standard

---

EU-GCC Relations in the Era of the Second Oil Boom. *Center for Applied Policy Research Working Paper*. Munich: CAP, http://www.cap.lmu.de/download/2007/2007-hertog.pdf [accessed: 30 August 2013]; and Bahgat, op. cit.

28 These studies are quoted extensively in Ayadi and Gadi, op. cit.

29 Koch, C. 2014. Constructing a Viable EU-GCC Partnership. *Global Governance Paper*, no. 34. Kuwait Programme on Development, Governance and Globalization in the Gulf States. London: London School of Economics and Political Science.

30 Khader, B. 2008. EU-GCC Relations: A Concise Balance Sheet of 25 Years (1981–2006), in Koch, C. (ed.), *Fostering EU-Italy GCC Cooperation: The Political, Economic and Energy Dimensions*. Dubai: Gulf Research Center, 17–49.

procedure in the EU's contractual foreign relations – were regarded by the GCC as an unwarranted attempt to interfere with the domestic development of these countries and thus rejected. On the one hand, the rejection by the GCC to abide by the EU's conditionality on the grounds that these issues have nothing to do with economic cooperation and dialogue has dampened the prospects for achieving the FTA and with it the progress in EU-GCC relations.[31] On the other hand, the EU's view is that to some extent the GCC countries' apparent aversion to the human rights clause disguises a more deep-rooted opposition to genuine liberalization, including in the services and investment sectors, and to the reduction of subsidies in their economies.[32]

The FTA negotiations have taken EU-GCC relations hostage for a long time, mostly due to disagreement over substantial issues. As a result, the political and security dialogue has remained outside the EU-GCC framework and any cooperation has been limited to political declarations or to bilateral arrangements between individual members of each group.[33] While the GCC has never hidden the fact that it sees the signing of the FTA as a prerequisite for deepened political cooperation, this aspiration has always been turned down by the EU, which has dealt with the GCC, in particular with Saudi Arabia and Qatar, merely as energy suppliers rather than as important geostrategic actors in the broader Mediterranean and Middle Eastern region. In recent years, the GCC countries have scaled up their presence in the North African and Middle Eastern economies, targeting primarily the tourism, real estate, energy, industry, transportation and telecommunications sectors.[34] It is worth noting that this increased engagement with the Arab neighbours preceded the eruption of the Arab uprisings in significant ways. In 2006, for the first time ever, the GCC countries overtook EU Member States as the leading investors in North Africa and the Middle East.[35]

The Tension between Multilateral and Bilateral Cooperation

The slow progress in the EU-GCC cooperation is mainly the result of structural deficiencies, including the fact that multilateral relations have suffered from the

31   Echagüe, A. 2007. The European Union and the Gulf Cooperation Council. *FRIDE Working Paper*, no. 39, Madrid: FRIDE, http://www.fride.org/download/WP39-EU-Persian-Gulf-EN-may07.pdf [accessed: 2 September 2013].

32   Youngs, R. 2009. Impasse in Euro-Gulf Relations. *FRIDE Working Paper*, no. 80, Madrid: FRIDE, http://www.fride.org/download/WP80-Impassse-in-euro-ENG-abr09.pdf [accessed: 2 September 2013].

33   Koch, op. cit.

34   Schumacher and Fernàndez Molina, op. cit.

35   De Saint-Laurent, B. et al. 2010. Investment from the GCC and Development in the Mediterranean. The Outlook for EU-GCC Financial and Economic Cooperation in the Mediterranean, in Aliboni, R. (ed.), *The Mediterranean: Opportunities to Develop EU-GCC Relations?* Rome: IAI Quaderni English Series, no. 18, http://www.iai.it/content. asp?langid=1&contentid=570 [accessed: 30 December 2013].

resilience of bilateral relations between individual EU Member States and the Gulf countries. Institutional deficiencies inside the GCC are partially responsible for this situation. While economic and financial regional integration is not yet complete, also decision-making on strategic issues such as foreign policy is still taking place at the individual state level rather than within the framework of the multilateral GCC. This is also reflected in the competition and rivalries that sometimes emerge in the positions of the six GCC states in relation to some strategic decisions regarding both domestic and external domains. Evidence for diverging positions within the GCC is, for example, the increased competition among regional actors in the wake of the 'Arab Spring'. Opposing national interests have arguably prevailed with regard to the preferred course of action vis-à-vis the complex Arab transitions. Against this backdrop, the most significant fault line is the one dividing Qatar, on the one hand, and Saudi Arabia and the UAE, on the other. More in general, Qatar's hyperactive foreign policy is seen by some analysts as a renewed attempt to preserve its autonomy – particularly from the regional 'big brother', that is, Saudi Arabia – and security by diversifying and balancing potentially conflicting alliances.[36]

The difficulties encountered in EU-GCC relations cannot be blamed on the Gulf partners alone. EU Member States have often developed an independent foreign policy, thus retaining as much freedom of manoeuvre as possible in terms of their bilateral relations with the GCC countries. This is the case, for example, of the United Kingdom, France and Germany, each of which has tried to cultivate a privileged relationship with individual GCC countries.[37] The mismatch between the EU Member States' bilateral foreign policies towards the Gulf and the multilateral EU-GCC cooperation framework has often left the EU institutions in the uneasy position to advocate for the application of conditionality in EU-GCC relations, while the EU Member States have continued to pursue their interests even going against the EU's policies. This is quite evident from the European Parliament resolution on the human rights situation in the UAE passed on 26 October 2013 and harshly criticized by the Emirati authorities.[38] The signing of numerous and important bilateral trade and defence contracts involving individual EU Member States signal to the GCC countries that it is possible to continue with business as usual in terms of their undemocratic, anti-rule of law practices and that it is

---

36   Roberts, D.B. 2012. Understanding Qatar's Foreign Policy Objectives. *Mediterranean Politics*, 17(2), 233–9; and Khatib, op. cit.

37   Baabood, A. and Edwards, G. 2007. Reinforcing Ambivalence: The Interaction of Gulf States and the European Union. *European Foreign Affairs Review*, 12(4), 537–54.

38   European Parliament 2012. *European Parliament resolution of 26 October 2012 on the human rights situation in the United Arab Emirates (2012/2842(RSP))*, http://www.europarl.europa.eu/document/activities/cont/201211/20121119ATT55902/20121119ATT5 5902EN.pdf [accessed: 30 August 2013]; *The National* 2012. FNC shocked by 'baseless' European human rights report, 29 October, http://www.thenational.ae/news/uae-news/fnc-shocked-by-baseless-european-human-rights-report [accessed: 30 August 2013].

not worth taking the EU seriously. This has more broadly to do with the ongoing structural difficulties of EU foreign and security policy, even after the entry into force of the Lisbon Treaty in December 2009.

After more than 20 years since the 1988 EEC-GCC Cooperation Agreement and many rounds of meetings, cooperation between the two sides remains dismally limited and does not live up to the potential and aspirations of both sides. In 2010, the EU and the GCC agreed on a Joint Action Programme for 2010–13 for the implementation of the Cooperation Agreement of 1988 as an attempt to relaunch multilateral relations after the breaking down of the FTA negotiations. The programme, which was supposed to be followed in 2014 by a new document on which, however, an agreement was not reached during the EU-GCC Joint Council and Ministerial Meeting held in Manama on 30 June 2013,[39] is once again a detailed but scarcely operational list of areas of cooperation ranging from trade and energy to culture and mutual understanding and higher education and scientific research. The Joint Action Programme has arguably not contributed to resurrecting and putting the EU-GCC cooperation on a new track; relations need to be recast by trimming the number of areas, in order to avoid an all-encompassing list that risks diluting the cooperation. It is also of utmost importance to consider the constraints and opportunities provided by the new regional and international context, which have increased the urgency to rethink the EU-GCC relationship by addressing the lack of political cooperation.

EU-GCC Relations: The Way Forward

Profound changes have taken place at the level of the European Union and of the GCC since 1988. While the world grapples with the impacts of two major processes and events, that is, the global financial and economic crisis and the 'Arab Spring', further reflection is needed about how to relaunch the relationship between the EU and the GCC in the most effective way in light of the changing environment.

Alternative Frameworks

Both the global financial and economic crisis and the 'Arab Spring' have provided new constraints and opportunities to the relationship between the EU and the GCC. With regard to the financial and economic crisis, it is not a coincidence that the negotiations for the FTA were unilaterally suspended by the GCC at the end of 2008. This was the moment in which the financial crisis started to grip the EU, thus altering, at least for the time being, the balance of power in favour of the GCC. While

---

39   EU-GCC Joint Council and Ministerial Meeting 2013. *Co-Chairs' Statement 23rd GCC-EU Joint Council and Ministerial Meeting, Manama – 30 June 2013*, http://www.consilium.europa.eu/uedocs/cms-Data/docs/pressdata/EN/foraff/137671.pdf [accessed: 15 July 2013].

the European Union has been significantly weakened by the crisis, the Gulf has acquired a more assertive role and is now in a stronger position to negotiate better terms in its relations with the EU. At the same time, Brussels has had to reassess the rationale of its relations with the GCC. The Gulf, once seen solely as a key provider of energy and a market for EU goods, has emerged as a valuable source of investment capital for distressed EU banks and institutions. In particular, the crisis dampened EU Member States' concerns about the penetration of GCC funds into their economies. For example, in 2008 the Abu Dhabi Investment Authority, an Emirati SWF, invested $6 billion in the British Barclays Bank. In 2011, Qatari Prime Minister Hamad bin Jassim bin Jaber bin Muhammad Al Thani announced his country's SWFs stood ready to invest $300 million in the troubled Spanish savings banks (*cajas de ahorros*). In November 2012, Italy and the Qatar Holding Company LLC, a subsidiary of the Qatar Investment Authority, announced the creation of a jointly owned fund – with a capital that could reach over $2 billion – mandated with investing in the Italian luxury and tourism industries.

Overall, changes in the global political economy have also increased the EU's appetite for a free trade deal with the GCC. As the balance of economic power is increasingly shifting towards Asia, the Gulf region appears to be extremely well positioned to act as a bridge between European and Asian markets. Furthermore, despite a certain degree of asymmetry in EU-GCC relations, the Gulf region continues to look at the EU as one of the most important strategic partners as well as a sort of model for its own internal evolution in the direction of increased regional integration. Having said that, time may not be ripe to conclude trade negotiations between the two blocs. From a purely economic point of view, domestic instabilities spilling from the unrest in the Southern Mediterranean compromise the ability of the Gulf countries to achieve their diversification objectives. Public spending has been diverted towards large-scale benefits packages, thus negatively impacting on the incentives to conclude the FTA with the EU. To this it should be added that the EU's standard clauses on the respect of human rights, democracy and the rule of law will likely continue to be rejected by the GCC countries, especially in the context of uncertainty prevailing in the region.

The 'Arab Spring', the second major transformation that has affected the region starting from 2011, has also had a major impact on the list of priorities of the EU and the GCC and on their cooperation. The increasingly assertive role of the GCC countries, and in particular of Saudi Arabia and Qatar, in relation to the events that have taken place in the Arab world has increased the premium associated with a more structured and strategic EU engagement with this region. It is indeed safe to argue that today much of the GCC's relevance in the EU's eyes derives from the former's active involvement in the latter's neighbourhood, that is, in the southern and eastern Mediterranean.

Against this backdrop, the outbreak of the 'Arab Spring' may provide an opportunity for increased cooperation between the EU and the GCC. Foreign policy initiatives aimed at the countries of the southern and eastern Mediterranean could be an interesting arena to implement confidence-building measures between the

EU and the GCC with a view to unblocking their political and security cooperation in the near future. As discussed, the political dialogue between the two regions has so far mostly remained declaratory and inconsequential on critical foreign policy issues. The EU-GCC Joint Council and Ministerial Meeting of 30 June 2013 has 'underlined the importance of further strengthening these ties, to serve as a solid and effective foundation for regional security and stability'.[40] Indeed, the EU and the GCC have always shared quite similar points of view on all the main regional issues, from Iraq and Afghanistan to Iran's nuclear programme. They also have a common interest to counter piracy in the Indian Ocean and the Gulf of Aden[41] and to prevent the collapse of the Syrian state. By capitalizing on their common views on a number of regional issues, the EU and the GCC could start a more frequent and effective exchange of opinions with a view to initiating burden sharing at the economic and financial level as well at the political and diplomatic level or developing a proactive joint response to the different situations created by the 'Arab Spring'.

While an EU-GCC multilateral initiative for the Mediterranean could be a welcome development, in the short-to-medium term it may be difficult to achieve given the current inward-looking approach of the EU Member States as a result of the economic crisis and the poorly integrated reality in the Gulf. In this light, it would still be possible to make use of the existing mechanisms and instruments to target transition and conflict-afflicted states with the involvement of selected (groups of) EU and Gulf states. While the need to collaborate with other external actors is mentioned indirectly in the 25 May 2011 document outlining the EU's revised European Neighbourhood Policy entitled 'A New Response to a Changing Neighbourhood',[42] one of the mechanisms available for such an EU-GCC joint cooperation targeting Arab Mediterranean countries is the Union for the Mediterranean launched in 2008. It establishes an intergovernmental framework to enhance cooperation in the Mediterranean through a number of concrete projects. The involvement of the GCC countries has so far been extremely modest, also taking into account that the whole project has suffered from the lack of a clear mission in the post-'Arab Spring' regional environment. Another potential instrument through which an EU-Gulf synergetic cooperation in the Arab Mediterranean could be initiated are the bilateral task forces like the one on Tunisia inaugurated by the EU in late 2011.[43] The aim of this instrument is to ensure effective coordination of the support provided in different sectors (labour

---

40   Ibid.

41   See Map IV in the Annex.

42   European Commission and High Representative 2011. Joint Communication to the European Parliament, the Council, the European Economic and Social Committee and the Committee of Regions. *A New Response to a Changing Neighbourhood.* COM(2011) 303, Brussels, 25 May.

43   On the EU Taskforces see http://ec.europa.eu/commission-2010-2014/ashton/topics/20130305-3-en.htm [accessed: 30 December 2013].

market, small and medium-sized enterprises, investment) by a range of actors and stakeholders, including individual European and Arab countries, the international financial institutions, civil society organizations and the private sector.

With regard to the scope of these joint cooperation initiatives, concrete projects targeting renewable energies, infrastructure and water management come to mind. In all these sectors, in addition to the general reconstruction of the Arab Mediterranean countries and the macro-stabilization of their economies, the GCC countries could make financial support available, while the EU Member States, companies and institutions could complement with their technical expertise as well as with their focus on good governance, institution building and the rule of law. In this way, the process of bridging the literal 'gulf' existing between the EU and the GCC could start, with positive repercussions both on the effectiveness of their engagement with the North African and Middle Eastern countries and on the future of the bloc-to-bloc relationship.

Conclusions

This chapter has assessed the history and the state of affairs of the relationship between the EU and the GCC with a view to advancing a number of concrete proposals as to how to revamp the two blocs' mutual engagement and to turn their cooperation into a truly strategic relationship beyond ad hoc convergence or competition. A new era in EU-GCC relations has not started yet and serious adjustments need to be made to this relationship with a view to making it truly strategic for both sides. On the one hand, the EU seems to have understood that it cannot fail to develop its relations with this important partner and it is thus trying to engage more with the GCC. Strengthening cooperation between the EU and the GCC at this point would be highly symbolic for the GCC, a sign of acknowledgement of its renewed and more assertive role on the global scene. On the other hand, the GCC countries have felt emboldened by their resilience in the face of the tremendous changes sweeping in the region and are capitalizing on their economic, financial and foreign policy activism to gain a stronger footing in the Mediterranean region.

Any reassessment of EU-GCC relations should start from the awareness of the differences existing among the GCC countries. The GCC does not constitute a single bloc and disregarding these differences could negatively impinge on EU-GCC relations. Nowadays, the rationale for having close relations between the European and the GCC countries is different and perhaps stronger, as trade and investment relations have grown in light of the region's housing of the biggest sovereign investment vehicles. Foreign policy contacts and coordination have become necessary to tackle the difficult situation in the southern and eastern Mediterranean and, at the same time, competition from the Asian players is on the rise.

More recently, the events of the 'Arab Spring' have highlighted the little leverage enjoyed by the EU in the Gulf region and the lack of instruments in the field of foreign policy cooperation. The fact that the EU has not engaged the GCC in its initiatives directed towards the Mediterranean and the Middle East tells a lot about the short-sightedness of the EU in relation to the GCC. The risk is that the new political and socioeconomic regional developments will further dilute the European presence and influence in the Gulf region. The new regional context, characterized by the North African transitions, continuous instability in Syria and the confrontation with Iran on its nuclear programme, call for a more concerted effort by the EU and the GCC to turn their cooperation into a progressive force with regard to these issues. A number of initiatives targeted at the tremendous socioeconomic challenges facing the 'Arab Spring' countries could be an avenue of cooperation between the GCC and the EU. Not only would these initiatives benefit the cash-strapped Mediterranean economies thanks to the substantial surpluses enjoyed by the GCC that could be mobilized, but the Gulf countries could also benefit from partnering with the EU in light of the potential transfer of European know-how and technical knowledge to the GCC countries. Such a cooperation could help bridge the gap existing in foreign policy and political relations between the two blocs. It is, however, likely that obstacles might arise in the way of such a cooperation due to the largely still authoritarian and fragile nature of the political systems of the Gulf region. Domestic political reforms still represent a taboo in many if not all the GCC countries. In this domain, the EU also suffers from a tremendous lack of legitimacy and leverage in this part of the world, something that is the result of the many wrongdoings in other regions, including the Mediterranean, and that does not bode well for the success of the conditionality instruments the European Union makes use of to promote human rights, the rule of law and democracy. Still, the EU is faced with a dilemma about its role in promoting political reforms in the region: whether to push for change via the limited mechanisms it has at its disposal or to cooperate with the GCC countries' regimes, while closing an eye on human rights abuses, women's marginalization and the sheer lack of democratic practices.

Cooperation at the foreign policy level could distinctly benefit from any progress in the removal of the roadblocks to the conclusion of the FTA. As previously stressed, in many respects the GCC countries have tended to regard the FTA as a litmus test of the EU's seriousness in developing stronger relations between the two blocs. It is obvious that the FTA would represent an important step in the right direction as it would free up resources, rationalize economic relations, provide new incentives for the diversification of the GCC economies and allow political ties to be enhanced to a new level of engagement. To achieve this goal, a great deal of suspicion towards both sides' intentions needs to be dispelled and major efforts need to be made by both parties to lay the ground for such an achievement. To complement such efforts, it is of utmost importance to increase the contacts not only between the officials of both organizations or high-ranking figures from the political and economic establishment of individual states, but also between people, workers and students. The youth on both sides should be particularly targeted, for instance, by addressing the obstacles that keep the rate of participation of GCC students and faculty in EU higher education programmes extremely low. Increasing the EU's – so far ridiculously underdeveloped – institutional representation in the GCC countries could be a first step in this direction. Further cooperation in this sector could be facilitated by the liberalization of visa requirements on both sides. Reciprocal knowledge deriving from movements of people and exchanges is the necessary precondition underpinning any attempt at relaunching EU-GCC relations to confront the challenges of the new century.

Bibliography

Al-Arabiya 2012. Gulf leaders agree on unified military command at Bahrain summit, 25 December, http://www.alarabiya.net/articles/2012/12/25/257017. html [accessed: 27 August 2013].

Aliboni, R. 2009. The ENP in the Mediterranean: Evaluating the political and strategic dimension, in Comelli, M., Eralp, A. and Üstün, Ç. (eds), *The European Neighbourhood Policy and the Southern Mediterranean*. Ankara: Middle East Technical University Press, 13–29.

Al-Rasheed, M. 2007. *Contesting the Saudi State: Islamic Voices from a New Generation*. Cambridge: Cambridge University Press.

Al-Shalabi, A., Cottret, N. and Menichetti, E. 2013. EU-GCC Cooperation on Energy. Technical Report, *Sharaka Technical Report*, no. 3, http://www. sharaka.eu/wp-content/uploads/2013/07/Sharaka-RP-03.pdf [accessed: 19 August 2013].

Ayadi, R. and Gadi, S. 2013. EU-GCC trade and investment relations: What prospects for an FTA between the two regions? *Sharaka Technical Report*, no. 5, http:// www.sharaka.eu/wp-content/uploads/2013/10/Sharaka_RP_05.pdf [accessed: 7 November 2013].

Baabood, A. and Edwards, G. 2007. Reinforcing Ambivalence: The Interaction of Gulf States and the European Union. *European Foreign Affairs Review*, 12(4), 537–54.

Bahgat, G. 2011. Sovereign Wealth Funds in the Gulf: An Assessment. *Global Governance Paper*, no. 16, Kuwait Programme on Development, Governance and Globalization in the Gulf States. London: London School of Economics and Political Science, http://eprints.lse.ac.uk/55015/1/__Libfile_repository_ Content_Kuwait%20Programme_Bahgat_2011.pdf [accessed: 30 August 2013] [accessed: 30 August 2013].

Coates Ulrichsen, K. 2012. Kuwait's Uncertain Path. *Foreign Policy*, 26 September, http://mideast.foreignpolicy.com/posts/2012/09/26/kuwait_s_uncertain_path [accessed: 20 August 2013].

Colombo, S. and Committeri, C. 2013. Need to Rethink the EU-GCC Strategic Relation. *Sharaka Conceptual Paper*, http://www.sharaka.eu/wp-content/uploads/2013/02/Sharaka_RP_01.pdf [accessed: 19 August 2013].

Council of the European Union 1989. *Cooperation Agreement between the European Economic Community, of the one part, and the countries parties of the Charter of the Cooperation Council for the Arab States of the Gulf (the State of the United Arab Emirates, the State of Bahrain, the Kingdom of Saudi Arabia, the Sultanate of Oman, the State of Qatar and the State of Kuwait) of the other part.* OJ L54/3, 25 February.

Council of the European Union 2006. *Council Regulation (EC) No 1934/2006 of 21 December 2006 establishing a financing instrument for cooperation with industrialised and other high-income countries and territories.* OJ L405/41, 30 December.

De Saint-Laurent, B. et al. 2010. Investment from the GCC and Development in the Mediterranean. The Outlook for EU-GCC Financial and Economic Cooperation in the Mediterranean, in Aliboni, R. (ed.), *The Mediterranean: Opportunities to Develop EU-GCC Relations?* Rome: IAI Quaderni English Series, no. 18, http://www.iai.it/content.asp?langid=1&contentid=570 [accessed: 30 December 2013].

Echagüe, A. 2007. The European Union and the Gulf Cooperation Council. *FRIDE Working Paper*, no. 39, Madrid: FRIDE, http://www.fride.org/download/WP39_EU_Persian_Gulf_EN_may07.pdf [accessed: 2 September 2013].

European Commission and High Representative 2011. Joint Communication to the European Parliament, the Council, the European Economic and Social Committee and the Committee of Regions. *A New Response to a Changing Neighbourhood.* COM(2011) 303, Brussels, 25 May.

European Parliament 2012. *European Parliament resolution of 26 October 2012 on the human rights situation in the United Arab Emirates (2012/2842(RSP))*, http://www.europarl.europa.eu/document/activities/cont/201211/20121119AT T55902/20121119ATT55902EN.pdf [accessed: 30 August 2013].

European Union 2013. *European Union, Trade in Goods with GCC*, 7 November, http://trade.ec.europa.eu/doclib/docs/2006/september/tradoc_113482.pdf [accessed: 31 December 2013].

EU-GCC Joint Council and Ministerial Meeting 2013. *Co-Chairs' Statement 23rd GCC-EU Joint Council and Ministerial Meeting, Manama – 30 June 2013,* http://www.consilium.europa.eu/uedocs/cms-Data/docs/pressdata/EN/foraff/137671.pdf [accessed: 15 July 2013].

Hertog, S. 2007. EU-GCC Relations in the Era of the Second Oil Boom. *Center for Applied Policy Research Working Paper*, Munich: CAP, http://www.cap.lmu.de/download/2007/2007_hertog.pdf [accessed: 30 August 2013].

Hertog, S. 2011. The cost of counter-revolution in the GCC. *Foreign Policy*, 31 May, http://mideast.foreignpolicy.com/posts/2011/05/31/the-costs-of-counter-revolution-in-the-gcc [accessed: 13 March 2012].

Jones, T.C. 2011. Counterrevolution in the Gulf. *Peace Brief*, no. 89, Washington, DC: United Institute of Peace, 15 April, http://www.usip.org/publications/counterrevolution-in-the-gulf [accessed: 25 August 2013].

Khader, B. 2008. EU-GCC Relations: A Concise Balance Sheet of 25 Years (1981–2006), in Koch, C. (ed.), *Fostering EU-Italy GCC Cooperation: The Political, Economic and Energy Dimensions*. Dubai: Gulf Research Center, 17–49.

Khatib, L. 2013. Qatar's Foreign Policy: The Limits of Pragmatism. *International Affairs*, 89(2), 417–31.

Koch, C. 2012. A Union in Danger: Where the GCC is Headed is Increasingly Questionable. *GRC Analysis*. Gulf Research Center, http://www.grc.net/?frm_action=view_newsletter_web&sec_code=grcanalysis&frm_module=contents&show_web_list_link=1&int_content_id=79778 [accessed: 26 August 2013].

Koch, C. 2014. Constructing a Viable EU-GCC Partnership. *Global Governance Paper*, no. 34. Kuwait Programme on Development, Governance and Globalization in the Gulf States. London: London School of Economics and Political Science.

Legrenzi, M. 2008. Did the GCC Make a Difference? Institutional Realities and (Un)Intended Consequences, in Harders, C. and Legrenzi, M. (eds), *Beyond Regionalism? Regional Cooperation, Regionalism and Regionalization in the Middle East*. Aldershot: Ashgate, 107–24.

Legrenzi, M. 2011. *The GCC and the International Relations of the Gulf. Diplomacy, Security and Economic Coordination in a Changing Middle East*. London-New York: I.B. Tauris.

Nuruzzaman, M. 2013. Politics, Economics and Saudi Military Intervention in Bahrain. *Journal of Contemporary Asia*, 43(2), 363–78.

Reuters 2012. Dubai Police Chief Warns of Muslim Brotherhood, Iran Threat, 26 July, http://www.reuters.com/article/2012/07/26/us-emirates-police-brotherhood-idUSBRE86P0EG20120726 [accessed: 22 August 2013].

Roberts, D.B. 2012. Understanding Qatar's Foreign Policy Objectives. *Mediterranean Politics*, 17(2), 233–9.

Schumacher, T. and Fernàndez Molina, I. 2013. EU and GCC Countries' Foreign Policies and the Mediterranean Neighborhood – Towards Synergetic Cooperation? *GRC Gulf Papers*, Gulf Research Center, no. 13, http://www.grc.net/index.php?frm_module=contents&frm_action=detail_book&pub_type=16&sec=Contents&frm_title=&book_id=81273&op_lang=en [accessed: 25 August 2013].

The National 2012. FNC shocked by 'baseless' European human rights report, 29 October, http://www.thenational.ae/news/uae-news/fnc-shocked-by-baseless-european-human-rights-report [accessed: 30 August 2013].

Tocci, N., Maestri, E., Özel, S. and Güvenç, S. 2012. Ideational and Material Power in the Mediterranean: The Role of Turkey and the Gulf Cooperation Council. *Mediterranean Papers Series*. Washington, DC: German Marshall

Fund of the United States–IAI, http://www.gmfus.org/wp-content/blogs.dir/1/
    files_mf/1339768226TocciEtAl_Turkey_GCC_Jun12_web.pdf [accessed: 23
    August 2013].

UNCTAD. 2013. Statistics, http://unctad.org/en/Pages/Statistics.aspx [accessed:
    22 August 2013].

World Bank 2013. *World Development Indicators*, http://data.worldbank.org/data-
    catalog/world-development-indicators [accessed: 20 August 2013].

Youngs, R. 2009. Impasse in Euro-Gulf Relations. *FRIDE Working Paper*, no. 80,
    Madrid: FRIDE http://www.fride.org/download/WP80_Impassse_in_euro_
    ENG_abr09.pdf [accessed: 2 September 2013].

Chapter 7

Iran and Iraq: Between Reconstruction and Containment

Clément Therme

Introduction

'Why do we forget that every state defines its policy according to its geography and that we do not have the same as our friends?'[1] The French intellectual Régis Debray outlines this common sense thinking regarding states' foreign policy in order to oppose the French reintegration into the military command of the North Atlantic Treaty Organization (NATO). In the same article, he also notes that if the European Union (EU) wished to follow its own destiny, it had to change its international posturing which kept the European regional organization at the same level of independence on the international stage as a dominion state of the United States (US).[2] This criticism is noteworthy because the international security agenda, as defined in Washington, is not always fully in line with EU interests. This is true in general, but it is even more accurate in the case of European Union's policies towards Iraq and Iran after 2003. Therefore, this chapter will shed some light on the policies of the EU and its Member States regarding the reconstruction of Iraq and the containment of Iran as well as their compatibilities (or incompatibilities) with US policy in the region. It will show that the EU's relations with these two regional powers in the Middle East face very different challenges which have led to different strategies and policy frameworks.

At the latest since the 2003 US military intervention in Iraq, the EU Member States have been unable to define a common strategy despite sharing the same values such as the universal defence of human rights and the need to support democratization in the Middle East. Their divisions can best be explained by both internal and external factors. Regarding the external factors, the Middle Eastern strategy of the Bush junior administration divided EU Member States in 'old' and

---

1 'Pourquoi oublier que tout Etat a la politique de sa géographie et que nous n'avons pas la même que celle de nos amis?'. Debray, R. 2013. Lettre ouverte à M. Hubert Védrine. La France doit quitter l'OTAN, *Le Monde Diplomatique*, March, 7, http://www.monde-diplomatique.fr/2013/03/DEBRAY/48843 [accessed: 13 May 2013] [author's translation].

2 Ibid.

'new' Europe.[3] The rise of emerging powers like China and Russia and their energy interests also contribute to limit the EU's possibilities to challenge US policy objectives regarding the oil and gas sectors of these two countries. Finally, the *sui generis* legal status of the EU complicates its international actions as a unified political actor. Indeed, the EU is not a classical political entity aiming at ensuring the security of its citizens towards external threats. For instance, Iranian diplomats prefer to negotiate directly with the US given the uncertain nature of EU external action and the perceived EU subservience to US and Israeli policy objectives.

Among the internal factors are the opposite interests of EU Member States and of oil and gas companies with regard to both Iraq and Iran. This competition constitutes a hurdle to building a constructive partnership and to resisting Washington's pressure to redirect European investments from the Iranian oil and gas sectors to Iraq despite the limited opportunities in a failed state such as Iraq after 2003. Another internal factor is the political divergence inside the EU. On the one hand, the East European Member States and the United Kingdom prefer to build an exclusive alliance with the US rather than a more independent EU Common Foreign and Security Policy (CFSP). On the other hand, the rest of the EU Member States is trying to balance the geopolitical alliance with Washington with strategic partnerships with Russia and China. These two conflicting views cohabit inside the EU and affect its decision-making process vis-à-vis both Iran and Iraq. Finally, the EU has since 2012 shown more ability to define a negative agenda in terms of sanctioning Iran, including an oil and gas embargo, rather than a capacity to propose a diplomatic solution to the Iranian nuclear crisis or a political solution to the civil war in Iraq.

This chapter will first analyse the challenges that the European Union is facing in Iran and Iraq since the 1990s. Then, it will focus on the strategies and the EU's frameworks of cooperation in both countries. Finally, Iran–Iraq relations and their relations with neighbours will be examined.

What Are the Challenges that the EU Faces in Iran and Iraq?

Given their geopolitical weight as re-emerging regional powers, studying the case of these two 'neighbours of the neighbours' of the European Union is particularly relevant. There are contradictory dynamics in the relations, on the one hand, between the EU and Iran and, on the other hand, between the EU and Iraq.

The Iranian Case

Since July 2012, the oil embargo implemented by the EU has shown the failure of both the 'Critical Dialogue' and the 'Comprehensive Dialogue' with Iran.

---

3   *BBC News* 2003. Outrage at 'old Europe' remarks. 23 January, http://news.bbc.co.uk/2/hi/europe/2687403.stm [accessed: 13 May 2013].

The 'Critical Dialogue' was established in December 1992 at the EU Summit in Edinburgh.[4] This dialogue was 'critical' because of EU concerns regarding Iran's support of international terrorism and due to the *fatwa* edict by Ayatollah Khomeini against the British writer Salman Rushdie.[5] The 'Critical Dialogue' became 'comprehensive' one year after Khatami's rise to the presidency in 1997 and European hopes that the Islamic Republic of Iran would evolve from an Islamist theocracy to a democratic Islamic Republic. Eventually, these hopes turned out to be wishful thinking and the political nature of the Iranian regime still remains the main hurdle to a thaw in EU–Iranian relations. This political dimension has to be taken into consideration when analysing the rapprochement between the European Union and Iran during the 1990s. Nevertheless, at that time, the basis of the new dynamics between Brussels and Tehran was the Iranian need of cooperation to realize an ambitious policy of economic reconstruction and development of its energy sector. Given the hostile Iranian–American relationship, Europe became not only the main source of technologies but also the main trading partner for the Islamic Republic of Iran.

The current confrontational course of relations between Iran and the EU could be defined as economic warfare and ideological confrontation because of the rhetorical challenge of the Islamic Republic of Iran vis-à-vis 'European values' such as human rights and democracy. Moreover, relations worsened in the 2000s after the failure of cooperation in the oil and gas sectors. Iran has been excluded as a gas supplier of the Nabucco pipeline project although the Azerbaijani gas production was not able to provide a sufficient quantity of gas for this pipeline project. To involve Iran in a gas relationship, it would have been necessary to invest in the Iranian gas sector in order to increase the gas production – Iran is still a net importer of gas. For ideological reasons and because of the ongoing strategic confrontation regarding the nuclear issue, diplomatic dialogue between the EU and Iran looks like the last resort to avoid the transformation of economic warfare into open military conflict.

Mahmoud Ahmadinejad's rise to power in 2005 also complicated the EU stance regarding the nuclear issue. Indeed, during the Rafsanjani and Khatami presidencies (1989–2005) the main slogan of Iranian diplomacy was dialogue and *détente*. After 2005, the 'principalists' (*osulgarayan*) implemented an aggressive diplomacy which has contributed to an alignment of EU Member States to US foreign policy.[6] The question of sanctioning Iran to avoid an Israeli military

---

4   European Council 1992. *European Council in Edinburgh, 11–12 December 1992, Conclusions of the Presidency*, para 15, http://www.european-council.europa.eu/media/854346/1992-december-edinburgh-eng-.pdf [accessed: 13 May 2013].

5   Posch, W. 2006. The EU and Iran: A tangle web of negotiations, in Posch, W. (ed.), *Iranian Challenges*, *EUISS Chaillot Paper*, no. 89, Paris: EUISS, 100.

6   The 'principalists' are a political faction organized against the reformists during the presidential campaign of 2005. Their main ideological tenets are based on the 1979 revolutionary ideals: cultural rejection of the West, 'anti-imperialism' and messianism.

intervention against Iranian nuclear facilities became the *leitmotif* of the countries at the forefront of the 'international community' to stop the Iranian nuclear programme. This rhetoric of threatening Iran with the adoption of increased EU sanctions outside the United Nation Security Council came to the fore of the EU Member States' diplomatic agenda after the rise of a conservative government in Germany in 2005, when Angela Merkel became chancellor, and the rise of the so-called French neo-conservatives during the Sarkozy presidency (2007–12).

The new diplomatic approach of the 'EU3' (Germany, France, United Kingdom) was reinforced by the June 2009 presidential election and the repression of the Iranian 'Green' opposition.[7] The paradox of this new European stance was that reinforced EU sanctions were targeting the most Westernized part of society because the severing of banking relations was most damaging to Iran's tiny private sector. In doing so, the EU was in a process of creating so many juridical hurdles that it became difficult to determine what was still legal in trading with Iran. The peculiarity of EU sanctions regarding Iran is linked to their double nature: there are both prolonging and accentuating sanctions of the United Nations Security Council (UNSC).[8] For instance, the EU list includes about 350 targets beyond the UN list, aiming more specifically at the Islamic Revolutionary Guard Corps (IRGC) and the Islamic Republic of Iran Shipping Lines (IRISL).[9]

In 2012, the implementation of an EU oil embargo marked the climactic moment of the EU's unilateral sanctioning policy. This strategy was the result of tighter British sanctions against the Iranian Central Bank and the severing of oil relations with the Islamic Republic. The deterioration of Iranian-British relations provoked a break of bilateral diplomatic ties after an assault against the British diplomatic mission based in Tehran. Following this Iranian–British diplomatic conflict, France declared its solidarity with its British ally and reduced its diplomatic presence in Tehran to the minimum, anticipating what Paris believed to be an imminent Iranian assault against the French diplomatic presence. The report of the International Atomic Energy Agency (IAEA) published in November 2011 also contributed to the EU's confrontational behaviour regarding the Iranian

---

For a critical analysis of the management of the nuclear dossier during the Ahmadinejad presidency, see Zibakalam, S. 2013. Rais jomhur ayande ba parvande-ye hastei tshe mikonad? (Iran's Next President and the Nuclear Dossier), *irdiplomacy.ir*, 2 ordibehesht 1392 [accessed: 22 April 2013].

7   Khosrokhavar, F. 2009. La crise en Iran révèle la tumultueuse naissance d'une société libre, *Le Monde*, 27 juin; Khosrokhavar, F. 2010. Djombech-e sabz: harekat novin demokratik dar iran (The Green movement: Harbinger of a new democracy). *Iran Nameh. A Persian Journal of Iranian Studies*, XXV(4), 487–503; and Parsi, R. 2011. Iran in the shadow of the 2009 presidential election. *EUISS Occasional Paper*, no. 90, Paris: EUISS, 15–21.

8   For the historical background regarding EU sanctions policy, see Beaucillon, C. 2012. Comment choisir ses mesures restrictives ? Guide pratique des sanctions de l'UE. *EUISS Occasional Paper*, no. 100, Paris: EUISS, 13–14.

9   Giumelli, F. 2013. How EU sanctions work: A new narrative. *EUISS Chaillot Paper*, no. 129, Paris: EUISS, 28.

nuclear 'intentions'.[10] Indeed, for the first time, an IAEA report evoked 'possible military dimensions' of the Iranian nuclear programme, but still, there was no 'smoking gun' and the definitive proof of an Iranian military nuclear programme was not on the table.[11]

Beyond these political tensions, in January 2012, the EU approved a new set of sanctions targeting the Iranian oil and gas sectors. This was an 'unexpected' move for the Iranian decision-makers who believed that the EU was not able to take such a collective decision.[12] This de facto oil embargo was highly encouraged by the US and the Israeli authorities which had been lobbying the EU Member State governments to take such a political step since the emergence of the Iranian nuclear dossier on the international agenda in 2002. The resilience of European international energy companies was overcome by the US commitment to favour the participation of big EU oil and gas companies in the reconstruction of the Iraqi oil and gas sectors through the transfer of Iranian investment projects to Iraq.

The Iraqi Case

In sharp contrast to its stance towards Iranian oil and gas resources, the EU has been a staunch supporter of Iraqi reconstruction since the fall of Saddam Hussein. Iraq has taken on a significant geopolitical position in the region since the regime change in 2003. Nevertheless, an ambiguity has remained unsolved: 'whether the new Iraq is an ally of the United States, as President Barack Obama's administration claims, or a client state of Iran, as many of its neighbours fear'.[13]

During the 1990s, the US dual-containment policy towards Iraq and Iran was not fully implemented by the EU. At this time, the EU diplomatic approach distinguished the Iraqi case from the Iranian one. The American decision to target Iran had been taken in 1993 and was first announced by Martin Indyk, a former US Assistant Secretary of State for Near East Affairs.[14] During the 1990s

---

10   Report by the Director General 2011. Implementation of the NPT Safeguards Agreement and relevant provisions of Security Council resolutions in the Islamic Republic of Iran, IAEA, Boards of Governors, GOV/2011/65, 8 November, 7, http://www.iaea.org/Publications/Documents/Board/2011/gov2011-65.pdf [accessed: 12 May 2013].

11   A parallel can be drawn with the Iraqi situation just before the 2003 war. Hans Blix presented the justification provided by the Bush administration in the absence of a 'smoking gun': 'Protesting that smoking guns were unnecessary, the US administration asserted that Iraq had not taken the necessary strategic decision to disarm'. Blix, H. 2004. *Disarming Iraq: The search of weapons of mass destruction.* London: Bloomsbury, 240.

12   Bassiri Tabrizi, A. and Hanau Santini, R. 2012. EU sanctions against Iran: New wine in old bottles? *ISPI Analysis*, no. 97, Milano: ISPI, 2.

13   al-Sheikh, S. and Sky, E. 2012. Is Iraq an Iranian Proxy? *Foreign Affairs*, http://www.foreignpolicy.com/articles/2012/10/11/is-iraq-an-iranian-proxy   [accessed: 26 December 2013].

14   Nonneman, G. 2011. Europe, the US and the Gulf after the Cold War, in Möckli, D. and Mauer, V. (eds), *European-American Relations and the Middle East*. London:

the transatlantic divide deepened regarding both Iraq and Iran. The divergence regarding these two countries was grounded on both economic and political differences which were nevertheless much more salient towards Iran than towards Iraq. As underlined by Gerd Nonneman:

> The gradual and partial divergence over Iraq in the 1990s paled in comparison with the sharp difference concerning policy on Iran that emerged in the period from 1993. 'Dual containment' came as a shock to Iran ... It also irritated European diplomats and policy-makers, who argued that Iran, as a largely status-quo power and one that had been helpful over the Kuwait crisis, should be engaged with, even if critically.[15]

Beyond this geopolitical context, the economic factor also explains the EU's rejection of the 1996 US 'Iran Libya Sanction Act' to uphold a 'Critical' and 'Comprehensive Dialogue' with Iran. Indeed, the interests of European oil and gas companies were at stake: if the EU followed the US sanction policy, energy cooperation between Iran and the EU would have been threatened. Regarding Iraq, transatlantic tensions focused on the humanitarian consequences of the sanction regime. After the 'Iraq Liberation Act' of 1998, the US stated that the sanction regime would remain in place beyond the completion of Iraqi disarmament until the removal of Saddam Hussein's regime. At this time, France was the most critical EU Member State concerning the reach of sanctions and their objectives. Former French diplomat François Nicoullaud outlined the main transatlantic divergence regarding the Iraqi sanction regime:

> Over the years, the toll inflicted by the embargo on Iraqis' health and welfare raised growing questions in the international opinion. Humanitarian NGOs started producing reports detailing how sanctions were entailing hundreds of thousands deaths, especially among children. In 1997, the French president, Jacques Chirac, declared at an international Summit in Hanoi: 'Our goal is to convince, not to compel. I have never seen a policy of sanctions producing anything positive.' ... By December, 1998, the United States inflicted on the country a wave of targeted strikes, in principle to degrade its suspected WMD [weapons of mass destruction] capacities, more likely to help topple Saddam Hussein's regime. But the Regime held on, and a new war had to be launched in 2003 to finally bring it down.[16]

In other words, the goal of the international sanction regime was first to reach the objective of disarmament and then to promote regime change. Overcoming

---

Routledge, 208.

  15   Ibid., 209.

  16   Nicoullaud, F. 2013. *Iraq, Iran: The lesson of sanctions*. Paris: CERI, http://www.sciencespo.fr/ceri/en/content/iraq-iran-lesson-sanctions [accessed: 9 May 2013].

the division between 'old' and 'new' Europe, the EU in 2004 decided 'to strive towards establishing a regular cooperation framework with Iraq in all spheres'.[17] In 2006, the EU started to negotiate a Partnership and Cooperation Agreement (PCA) with Iraq which aims to:

> [f]acilitate Iraq's engagement with the international community and with the EU in particular, to the benefit of the internal and regional stabilisation process. Stimulate and anchor ongoing institutional and socio-economic reforms. Contribute to the socio-economic development of Iraq and to the improvement of living conditions in the country. Promote bilateral trade relations in accordance with WTO principles. Ensure a minimum level of predictability, transparency and legal certainty for economic operators. Improve the trade arrangements between Iraq and the EU.[18]

This set of objectives represents the European liberal values not only in political terms but they also follow an agenda of economic liberalization. However, the economic and political situation in Iraq undermines the EU's high ambitions of building a constructive and stable partnership. Indeed, the civil war and the inability of the Iraqi state to control the whole territory – given the de facto secession of the Iraqi Kurdistan province – are realities that directly challenge the European official discourse regarding 'state building' in Iraq. Also the difficult business environment is an obstacle to European investment in the country with the notable exception of the Kurdistan province. According to the 2013 'Doing Business' report of the World Bank, Iraq ranked 165th out of 185 countries and, except for Djibouti, the Iraqi economy had the worst ranking in the Middle East and North Africa (MENA) region.[19] In the same report, the Islamic Republic of Iran ranked 145th (20 ranks ahead of Iraq) despite the international and the Western sanction regimes.[20]

Moreover, the opening of an EU Delegation to the Republic of Iraq[21] has to be compared with the failure of establishing an EU Delegation to the neighbouring Islamic Republic of Iran, despite many discussions in this regard during the first Ahmadinejad presidential term (2005–09). The EU's political will to enhance its

---

17   European External Action Service 2013. *Cooperation between the European Union and Iraq. Joint Strategy Paper 2011–2013*, http://eeas.europa.eu/iraq/docs/2011-2013-jsp-nip-en.pdf [accessed: 26 December 2013].

18   European External Action Service 2013. *Partnership and Cooperation Agreement (PCA) with Iraq*, http://eeas.europa.eu/iraq/tca-en.htm [accessed: 26 December 2013].

19   World Bank 2013. *Doing Business 2013. Middle East and North Africa (MENA)*. Washington, DC: The World Bank, 6, http://www.doingbusiness.org/~/media/GIAWB/Doing%20Business/Documents/Profiles/Regional/DB2013/DB13-Middle-East-North-Africa.pdf [accessed: 11 May 2013].

20   Ibid.

21   See the official EEAS website: http://eeas.europa.eu/delegations/iraq/press-corner/all-news/index-en.htm [accessed: 11 May 2013].

economic relations with Iraq is not grounded on a rational analysis of political and economic realities. It is rather based on the political agenda of fighting 'nuclear proliferation' in the MENA region and based on a political assessment determining, from a Western perspective, who is potentially democratic and who is not. In the case of Iraq, the EU has started to more openly criticize the human rights situation (in particular on the issue of death penalty) after the intensification of the civil war during the spring 2013. Beyond this rhetorical approach and humanitarian assistance, it is clear that the European voice is not really heard in Iraq given the lack of credibility of the West regarding democratization in the Middle East. Indeed, the United States' 'democratization' of Iraq since 2003 and the establishment of a 'democratic' Islamic Republic in Afghanistan since 2001 demonstrate the ideological failure of the neo-conservative political project. In addition to this, the absence of EU unity regarding the Syrian crisis since 2011 weakened the EU as a political actor in the new Middle East which is emerging in the wake of the so-called 'Arab Spring'.

In April 2013, the rise of sectarian tensions in the Sunni provinces of Iraq underlined the state of civil war in the country. The Iraqi state has to confront sectarians' demands supported by regional powers such as Turkey, Saudi Arabia and Iran. This so-called 'Sunni Intifada' raises questions regarding the linkage between Syria and the unstable situation in Iraq. Nevertheless, the diversity of both the Iraqi Sunni and Shia communities must be stressed, and one must resist the temptation to oversimplify the factors explaining the failure of the Iraqi reconstruction considering only the religious aspects.[22] In this regard, Prime Minister Nouri Al-Maliki tries to enhance his personal authority beyond the Shia community through co-optation of Iraqi Sunni political personalities.

What are the EU's Strategies and Frameworks of Cooperation in Iran and Iraq?

There are different models of cooperation with the two neighbours of the EU's neighbours. Nevertheless, in both cases, the model is built upon a set of non-proliferation objectives and the promotion of European values such as human rights or cultural and religious tolerance.

EU Attitudes towards the Islamic Republic of Iran: From Containment to Hostility?

In the Iranian case, the EU framework is based on a confrontational approach rather than cooperation. Despite the existence of a few areas of cooperation (such

---

22   Regarding the critical analysis of the explanation of Middle Eastern tensions limited to the religious factors in general and the Sunni-Shia divide in particular, see Corm, G. 2012. *Pour une lecture profane des conflits. Sur le retour du religieux dans les conflits contemporains du Moyen-Orient.* Paris: La Découverte.

as drug trafficking, fighting al-Qaeda, stabilizing Iraq and Afghanistan), the nuclear issue has since the transfer of the Iranian dossier from the IAEA Board of Governors to the UN Security Council in 2006 become the main determinant of EU–Iran relations. Nevertheless, the coercive measures have led to catastrophic economic consequences for the Iranian deprived and middle classes.

Consequently, the International Crisis Group advised the United States and the European Union to 'provide clear guidelines to financial institutions indicating that humanitarian trade is permissible and will not be punished' and to 'consider allowing an international agency to play the role of intermediary for procuring specialised medicine for Iran'.[23] As Rouzbeh Parsi explained, there is 'a full range of policy options beyond sanctions, and even containment'.[24] He proposed that the EU, drawing on more than 30 years of diplomatic exchanges with Iran, mediate the crisis through acknowledging the status of the Islamic Republic of Iran as an essential political actor in the region in general and in Afghanistan and Iraq in particular.[25] Indeed, one has to consider that the Western containment policy regarding the Iranian nuclear programme is directly linked to Iran's role in its regional context. It is clearly not an easy task to pressure Iran regarding its nuclear programme and, at the same time, to engage the country in the search for a political solution in Afghanistan and Iraq.

Despite regular meetings of EU diplomats and the adoption of coercive measures, many divergences have remained as a result of conflicting economic interests between major European companies and states. The big European oil and gas companies have tried to resist the EU Member States' objective of severing economic ties with Iran. Until the last moment, the European energy sector tried to buy Iranian oil. The containment strategy against the Iranian energy sector is costly not only for the Iranian oil industry but also for the European oil and gas business.[26] Furthermore, given the high level of mistrust between the two sides, it will take a long time to rebuild an energy partnership between Iran and the EU. Despite the centrality of the sanctions in the evolution of the relationship, it is important to mention the persistence of cooperation on drug trafficking as well as the fight against al-Qaeda in Iraq (the Islamic Emirate of Iraq) and in Afghanistan (Taliban).[27]

---

23   International Crisis Group 2013. Spider Web: The Making and Unmaking of Iran Sanctions. *Middle East Report*, no. 13825, http://www.crisisgroup.org/en/regions/middle-east-north-africa/iraq-iran-gulf/iran/138-spider-web-the-making-and-unmaking-of-iran-sanctions.aspx?utm-source=iran-email-sm&utm-medium=1&utm-campaign=email-sm [accessed: 13 March 2013].

24   Parsi, R. 2012. Introduction: Iran at a critical juncture, in Parsi, R. (ed.), *Iran: A revolutionary republic in transition*, *EUISS Chaillot Paper*, no. 128, Paris: EUIIS, 21.

25   Ibid.

26   Blackden, R. 2013. Shell owes Iran $2.3bn for oil. *The Telegraph*, 21 March.

27   See Djalili, M-R. and Therme, C. 2008. Le flanc Est de l'Iran : opportunités et vulnérabilités. *Politique étrangère*, Autumn 2008/3, 601–12.

Following the rise of tensions between Iran and the West after Ahmadinejad's contested re-election as president in June 2009, the EU Member States decided to launch a new version of the TV channel Euronews in Farsi.[28] This decision is fully in line with the EU policy of supporting human rights and democracy inside Iran and to offer an alternative to the Iranian state media narrative and to enhance media pluralism in the Persian language. In addition, the EU Member States have been supporting Persian-language media based in the EU such as Rooz Online, BBC Persian or Radio Zamaneh. On the one hand, Iranian authorities have been accusing Iranian journalists working for these media in exile of being 'counter-revolutionary' (*zed-e enqelab*). On the other hand, the diffusion of Iranian state channels in the West were banned in response to the prohibition of Persian-language TV channels broadcast from the West in Iran.[29]

The Iraqi Case: EU Political Support to the New Regime

After the removal of Saddam Hussein, EU Member States established diplomatic ties with the new regime, and the EU has been coherently and permanently providing support to the political and economic reconstruction in Iraq. The EU looked forward to 'the transfer of sovereignty in Iraq to a transitional government at the end of June [2004] and to future national elections, with a vital and growing role for the UN endorsed by the United Nations Security Council'.[30] This EU position regarding the Iraqi post-war regime is defined on the basis of the US democratization project. Despite the rise of violence and terrorist acts inside Iraq since 2003, Brussels always presented a position based on democratic values and the defence of human rights. This rhetorical aspect is also reinforced by a more realist diplomatic stance regarding the necessity of a regional approach in solving the Iraqi permanent political crisis. Indeed, the EU's goal is to use the 'dialogue with Iraq's neighbours to encourage positive engagement and regional support for the political and reconstruction process in Iraq'.[31]

The EU provided since the fall of Saddam Hussein's regime financial and personnel support for the preparation of every election in close coordination with

---

28   See the official website of the Euronews Persian Channel: http://persian.euronews. com.

29   There is a debate on whether this ban is the consequence of a European Commission decision or a decision of the companies Eutelsat and Arqiva. See *Press TV* 2012. EU denies ordering satellite companies to take Iran channels off air, 17 October, http://www.presstv. com/detail/2012/10/17/267243/eu-denies-ordering-iran-channels-ban [accessed: 12 May 2013]; and *Press TV* 2012. *EU bans broadcast of Iranian TV channels on Hot Bird*, 15 October, http://www.presstv.com/detail/2012/10/15/266831/eu-bans-broadcast-of-iranian-channels [accessed: 12 May 2013].

30   Council of the European Union 2004. *Council Conclusions – Iraq 2004–2008*, Brussels, 17 May, http://eeas.europa.eu/iraq/docs/iraq-council-2004-08-en.pdf [accessed: 12 May 2013].

31   Ibid.

the UN. The EU is one of the most important donors in support of the Iraqi political and electoral process.[32] From 2005 to 2013 the EU carried out an integrated rule of law mission, EUJUST LEX Iraq, a civilian crisis management mission.[33] The EU is also concerned with the situation of refugees from Iraq and internally displaced persons.

The EU has condemned every attempt of terrorist groups in Iraq to destabilize the electoral process. In April 2013, during the campaign for provincial council elections, for instance, Catherine Ashton declared that '[e]lectoral violence is unacceptable. The High Representative remains confident that the Iraqi people will remain steadfast in their continued rejection of attempts to undermine Iraq's transition to democracy and lasting stability'.[34] This statement represents the essence of post-war Iraqi policy of the EU which supports the Iraqi transition to democracy. It is telling that Brussels has not been taking into consideration the 10 years of Iraqi civil war as an element demonstrating the inability of the West to export 'democracy' from outside and that an electoral process is yet necessary to establish a democratic regime but not sufficient. Moreover, despite the official EU support to the territorial integrity of Iraq, the de facto independence of the Kurdish province is from a long-term perspective a direct challenge to the political transition. It is also a hurdle to the establishment of a democratic regime. Indeed, secessionist claims could justify, from Baghdad's point of view, the instauration of an autocratic political system aiming to recover the territorial loss of the central state.

In 2010, the European Union signed a Memorandum of Understanding (MoU) on energy cooperation with the Republic of Iraq.[35] Beyond the general objectives, the MoU focused on gas cooperation projects such as the Arab gas pipeline, clearly indicating a reverse long-term strategy in reducing EU gas dependence vis-à-vis Russia.[36] Energy is the main area of cooperation between the EU and Iraq, in spite of political and legal hurdles slowing the reconstruction of the oil and gas sectors. The Iraqi state remains unable to control its entire territory. Energy companies have to deal with two political authorities: the central government of Iraq and the Kurdish

---

32   See European External Action Service 2013. *EU Assistance to Iraq*, http://eeas. europa.eu/iraq/assistance-en.htm [accessed: 26 December 2013].

33   Council of the European Union 2005. *Council Joint Action 2005/190/CFSP of 7 March 2005 on the European Union Integrated Rule of Law Mission for Iraq, EUJUST LEX*. OJ L62/37, 9 March.

34   European Union 2013. *Statement by the Spokesperson of the High Representative Catherine Ashton on the latest wave of attacks in Iraq*, A 206/13, Brussels, 16 April, http://www.consilium.europa.eu/uedocs/cms-Data/docs/pressdata/EN/foraff/136779.pdf [accessed: 12 May 2013].

35   European Commission 2010. *Memorandum of Understanding between the Government of Iraq and the EU on Strategic Partnership on Energy*, Baghdad, 18 January, http://ec.europa.eu/energy/international/bilateral-cooperation/doc/iraq/2010-01-18-iraq-mou-en.pdf [accessed: 11 May 2013].

36   On Iran as an alternative to Russian gas supplies to Europe, see Therme, C. 2008. *L'Iran: exportateur de gaz? Note de l'Ifri*. Paris: Ifri.

authorities. Despite these hurdles, the strengthening of energy ties has led to an increase of Iraqi oil production. In August 2012, Iraq became the second largest oil exporting country of the Organization of the Petroleum Exporting Countries (OPEC) with 3.2 million barrels per day (bpd) ahead of Iran with 2.7 million bpd. The Iraqi oil boom attracted not only EU oil and gas companies but also Chinese ones. Iraq produced over 3 million bpd of oil in March 2013 and is now regarded as the world's largest source of new oil.[37] At the same time, the decrease of US oil imports pushed Baghdad closer to Beijing. As a result, energy experts are speculating over the emergence of an energy partnership between Iraq and China, and '[t]he International Energy Agency (IEA) has projected that up to 80 percent of Iraqi oil will eventually be exported to Asia in general and China in particular'.[38]

The expected rise of Chinese influence in the Iraqi oil and gas sectors is a direct challenge to European plans following the US 'advice' of withdrawing from Iranian oil and gas sectors in order to invest in Iraq. At the same time, the concomitant Western containment against the Iranian energy sector and massive investment in the Iraqi sector could destabilize the friendly relations between Baghdad and Tehran.

Iran–Iraq Relations and their Neighbours

The bilateral relationship between Iran and Iraq is decisive in order to solve the Iraqi state-building crisis following the 2003 US military intervention. Ten years later, there is a risk of a deepening competitive dimension in Iran–Iraq relations due to the Iraqi objective of a becoming one of the main oil producers in the Middle East, whereas Iran is suffering from a Western embargo on its oil and gas sectors. According to the International Energy Agency, Iraq will be the main additional oil supplier for the international market in the next decades.[39] This perspective is a direct threat to the development of the oil and gas sectors in Iran. Indeed, in 2011, Iraq received $9 billion of international investment in its energy sector while Iran was trying to develop its oil and gas resources mainly based on national investment.[40] The EU has to balance its relations between Iran and

---

37   On the Iraqi oil and gas long-term development perspective, see International Energy Agency 2012. *Iraq Energy Outlook*. Paris: OECD/IEA.

38   Zambelis, C., 2013. China's Iraq Oil Strategy Comes into Sharper Focus. *China Brief*, 13(10), 9 May, http://www.jamestown.org/programs/chinabrief/single /?tx-ttnews%5Btt-news%5D=40861&cHash=20da431f.e2272ad34a6ace632cdecb96 [accessed: 11 May 2013].

39   International Energy Agency 2012. *Iraq Energy Outlook*. Paris: OECD/IEA.

40   On the issue of internal networks financing the Iranian oil industry, see Yong, W. 2013. *NIOC and the State – Commercialization, Contestation and Consolidation in the Islamic Republic of Iran*, MEP 5, Oxford Institute for Energy Studies, http://www. oxfordenergy.org/wpcms/wp-content/uploads/2013/05/MEP-5.pdf [accessed: 11 May 2013].

Iraq carefully in order to limit the potentially negative consequences of its tilt towards Iraq since the fall of Saddam Hussein's regime in 2003. The ability of EU countries to elaborate new comprehensive strategies aimed at stabilizing and developing the Union's broader neighbourhood regarding Iraq and Iran has been limited although in the case of Iraq EU Member States share a common interest in its re-emergence as one of the main oil suppliers on the international market.

The US military intervention contradicted the Islamic Republic of Iran's official vision of international relations based on anti-Americanism and anti-Zionism. Nevertheless, Tehran acted as a pragmatic regional power attempting to strengthen its regional position through the removal of the Saddam Hussein's regime, one of its more dangerous regional enemies. Officially, Tehran was against a unilateral US military intervention in Iraq. Yet, this opposition was limited to the identical Russian analysis considering the war against Iraq as 'a serious political mistake'.[41] On the one hand, Tehran feared the US military intervention because of the risk of military encirclement by US military forces. On the other hand, the removal of Saddam Hussein was also a victory for the Islamic Republic which tried to reach this very same objective during the first Gulf War (1980–88).

Beyond this a posteriori symbolic victory of the Islamic Republic of Iran, the US military occupation of Iraq meant the beginning of the end of the United States' position as a 'hyper-power'. First, Tehran became a more indispensable Middle Eastern power following the emergence of a friendly post-Saddam Iraqi regime. The position of its weakened neighbour removed one of Iran's main strategic vulnerabilities. Since then, any political solution to the Iraqi crisis has to be found in cooperation with Tehran. The failure of the Iraqi democratization project, as defined by the Bush administration, has provoked a significant rise of anti-Americanism in the Middle East instead of the so-called 'domino effect' that was supposed to generate a new democratization wave all over the region. Iraq faced 10 years of insecurity, and the anarchical situation in many provinces of Iraq reinforced Iran's dominant perception which equates democracy with the absence of state order. This perception is particularly relevant from the Iranian neighbouring province of Iraq, where a significant part of the population has a negative view of the US war against Iraq. Indeed, insecurity in Iraq has been contributing to the rise of instability on the Iranian side of the border.[42] Second, following the 2003 war, the structural evolution of American power on the international stage opened new opportunities for Iranian foreign policy in particular in its objective of resisting the Western unilateral sanction policy. The strategy consisted not only in overcoming EU and US sanctions through the search of partnerships with non-Western powers such as Russia and China but also in circumventing sanctions through friendly relationships with neighbouring countries, notably Iraq. For instance, to circumvent the EU oil embargo, Iran has been exporting part of its oil

---

41   Declaration quoted in Mendras, M. 2003. Les ambiguïtés de la Russie. *Esprit*, 35.

42   Personal interviews with Iranian citizens, Khuzestan, February 2008.

through the Iraqi Kurdistan province and Iranian oil dealers are using fake Iraqi documents to hide the Iranian origin of exports.[43]

However, there is still the trauma of Iraq's invasion of Iran in 1980. Consequently, Iran's first policy objective remains to anticipate and to limit the re-emergence of an Iraqi threat, and in order to do so, Tehran aims 'to keep Iraq in a dependent relationship'.[44] Iranian influence in Iraq is first and foremost political due to the ties between the new Iraqi political elite and the Islamic Republic of Iran. The fact that Iraqi political personalities spent many years of exile in Iran has contributed to the establishment of strong personal networks between the two countries. Iranian-Iraqi relations are also religious through the transnational networks of Shia clerics and the annual visits of Iranian pilgrims to the main Shia holy city in Iraq. Nevertheless, this influence is not a one-way relationship; Iraqi religious influence seeps through the border thanks to the Najaf theological school in general and the *marjaiyya* of Ayatollah Ali Sistani in particular. He is commonly considered as the most popular *marja* (imitating source) amongst the Iranian believers. Nevertheless, this Iraqi religious sphere of influence in Iran is not defined as a challenge to the official religious doctrine of the founder of the Islamic Republic of Iran, Ayatollah Khomeini, and its successor the current Supreme Leader, Ali Khamenei. According to a representative of the office of Ayatollah Sistani in Qom, there is no rivalry between grand Ayatollahs and their schools.[45]

Transnational networks between Iran and Iraq exist beyond traditional clerical family ties.[46] Between 2003 and 2006, the number of Iraqi refugees in Iran has been decreasing because of the fall of the Saddam Hussein regime and despite the persistent insecurity.[47] To solve the Iraqi political crisis, EU and US diplomacy have been engaging Iran on the shared goal of stabilizing the Iraqi territory and to restore the state order. There is indeed a shared view between Iran and the West regarding the necessity to reinforce the central Iraqi state and to enable a full control of its territory.

Moreover, the economic dimension has to be taken into consideration: in 2012, Iraq was the first market for Iranian non-oil exports worldwide, Iranian sales reaching an amount of almost $6 billion.[48] Finally, from the Iranian point of view,

---

43   *The Economist* 2013. Dodging sanctions in Iran. Around the block. How Iranian companies manage to keep trading with foreigners, 30 March.

44   Dodge, T. 2012. *Iraq: From War to a New Authoritarianism*. London: The International Institute for Strategic Studies, 186.

45   Personal interview with Rabbani Mahdi, one of the representatives of the office (*daftar*) of Ayatollah Ali Sistani in Iran, Qom, June 2006.

46   Chehabi, H.E. 2012. Iran and Iraq. Intersocietal linkages and secular nationalisms, in Amanat, A. and Vejdani, F. (eds), *Iran Facing Others Identity Boundaries in a Historical Perspective*. New York: Palgrave Macmillan, 191–218.

47   Ibid.

48   Coville, T. 2013. Les sanctions, facteurs de crise ou choc salutaire pour l'économie iranienne ? Paris: CERI, http://www.sciencespo.fr/ceri/en/content/les-sanctions-facteurs-de-crise-ou-choc-salutaire-pour-leconomie-iranienne [accessed: 11 May 2013].

the relationship with Iraq is also a political gateway to construct a comprehensive regional policy. The post-2003 geopolitical configuration was the first disruption of the regional equilibrium. The Syrian civil war since 2011 has been a second regional and international question. During the first period of the civil war, there was a rapprochement between the status quo powers such as the Syrian state, Russia, China, the Lebanese Hezbollah and Iran.[49] Iran perceives the question of Syria through the Khomeinist view of confronting the West worldwide and the 'Zionist regime' in the Middle East. According to the diplomatic adviser of the Supreme Leader, Ali Akbar Velayati, the Western diplomatic offensive against Bashar al-Assad is based on the anti-Zionist nature of the 'axis of resistance'.[50]

The Syrian crisis also resulted in a deterioration of Iran's diplomatic relations with Turkey. In the long term, Tehran hopes to spread its regional influence through a friendly Iraqi neighbour. This goal is a priority in the context of the civil war devastating the state infrastructure of Syria, Tehran's main state ally in the Middle East. From the EU's perspective, Iran's role as a regional power is difficult to integrate in a political vision in view of the priority to contain the rise of a nuclear Iran. Nevertheless, if the EU wants to be an actor in any political solution to the Syrian civil war, it is a requirement to build a trustful diplomatic relationship with the Islamic Republic of Iran. Consequently, to enable Brussels to mediate the crisis in Syria which entered, since 2012, in an internationalization process, Brussels could use the diplomatic channel with the Lebanese Hezbollah, one of the main actors to engage for reaching a political solution. As in the case of the Iranian nuclear programme during the 2000s, the EU is now under pressure to align its diplomatic position following Washington's and Tel Aviv's objectives.[51]

In June 2013, the election of a moderate Iranian President provoked a new willingness of EU energy companies to invest in Iran. In November 2013, the Geneva agreement was signed under the leadership of Russia and the US.[52] The EU representative played only a secondary role mainly due to an internal division of the EU regarding the Iranian nuclear issue. France was at the forefront of the Western efforts to delay a deal. This was fully in line with the rise of the French neo-conservatives since Sarkozy's presidency.

Inside the EU, the private sector is keen to invest in Iran. Nevertheless, given the legal framework, the establishment of contacts between European investors

---

49   Concerning Syria's role in Russian Middle Eastern policy, see Kreutz, A. 2010. Syria: Russia's Best Asset in the Middle East. *Russie.Nei.Visions*, no. 55, 12–13.

50   Quoted in the newspaper of the Iranian presidency, *Iran*, 25 February 2012.

51   *United Press International* 2013. EU under pressure to blacklist Hezbollah, 1 April, http://www.upi.com/Top-News/Special/2013/04/01/EU-under-pressure-to-blacklist-Hezbollah/UPI-98541364842526 [accessed: 12 May 2013].

52   European External Action Service 2013. *Joint Plan of Action*, Geneva, 24 November. http://eeas.europa.eu/statements/docs/2013/131124-03-en.pdf [accessed: 29 November 2013].

and Iranian officials remains at the informal level.[53] The Iranian officials at the Oil Ministry were nominated by President Rouhani in order to attract foreign investment and solve the problems of the Iranian oil and gas sectors.[54] According to Iranian officials, Iran is planning to offer international companies more lucrative contracts to attract at least $100 billion worth of investment in its oilfields over the next three years.[55] Iranian officials are using two main incentives to attract European energy companies: firstly, the threat of signing contracts with US oil and gas companies worth of $50 billion according to Iranian sources;[56] secondly, the prospects of joint ventures for onshore and offshore projects instead of the less lucrative *buy back* contracts. The new Iranian policy has to be understood in light of the rise of tensions between Iran and the West and the decreasing Iranian oil and gas production during the last 34 years.

Conclusion

This chapter examined the policies of the EU and its Member States regarding the reconstruction of Iraq and the containment of Iran as compared to the respective US policy. It also showed the geopolitical links between the Iraqi crisis since 2003 and the 'E3/EU+3' Iran talks (between, on the one hand, the EU High Representative, the United Kingdom, France, Germany, the US, China and Russia and, on the other hand, Iran). As a result of the failure of the American intervention in Iraq, the international community has less leverage in dealing with the Iranian nuclear question. Indeed, the US intervention in Iraq provoked a loss of political credibility for all Western countries which supported this war based on the false pretext of the existence of WMDs in Iraq[57] and on the official diplomatic rhetoric of exporting democracy. Ten years after the US intervention, it appears that there were no WMDs in Iraq and that the democratic project failed. This inability to restore the Iraqi state came with a high cost for the Western discourse regarding human rights and democratization in the area.

The EU should rethink its current ad hoc policy based on reaction rather than a comprehensive set of principles that apply to the whole Middle East. First, the main EU objective should be to restore Middle Eastern stability instead of pursuing a selective policy to support democratization. The democratic discourse still follows a double standard approach. In the case of states perceived as hostile,

---

53   See, for instance, the visit of Total's vice-president for Middle Eastern affairs to the National Iranian Oil Co. in October 2013. Facon, B. 2013. Iranian Officials Say Some Western Companies Start Own Outreach to Tehran. *The Wall Street Journal*, 15 October.

54   See Yong, op. cit.

55   Malbrunot, G. 2013. L'Iran retire des posters anti-américains. *Le Figaro*, 28 October.

56   Ibid.

57   See Blix, op. cit.

such as Syria, the democratic objectives come first. On the contrary, concerning a friendly autocratic regime such as Bahrain, the EU diplomatic discourse is more than moderate and there is a lack of effective EU support to the popular uprising. Second, the linkage between the Syrian crisis and the Iranian nuclear question should be addressed in a way avoiding the *hiatus* created by, on the one hand, the EU unilateral sanction policy against the Islamic Republic of Iran and, on the other hand, the necessity to co-opt Tehran to find a political solution to the Syrian and Lebanese crises. Third, the EU should support the implementation of Israel's international legally binding obligations regarding the military occupation of the West Bank and Gaza. It is detrimental to EU 'soft power' to invoke international law while dealing with the Iranian nuclear programme and to offer an exemption to Tel Aviv's non-compliance with international law.

The main challenges facing the EU in a volatile Middle East is to overcome the dichotomy between a proactive policy regarding the Iraqi construction and a hostile attitude towards Iran. The risk of pursuing such a policy is to destabilize the Middle East area further through the weakening of the Iranian state. Indeed, the EU oil embargo could lead to an increase of tensions between Iran and the West. The new transatlantic convergence has paradoxically led the EU to be at the forefront of the 'international community' in confronting Iran's nuclear ambitions. This new role should not provoke a more radical policy of the EU Member States towards Iran than the Obama administration's relative moderation. It would be surprising to witness the rise of a new generation of EU neo-conservatives after their ideological failure in the US.

Bibliography

al-Sheikh, S. and Sky, E. 2012. Is Iraq an Iranian Proxy? *Foreign Affairs*, http://www.foreignpolicy.com/articles/2012/10/11/is_iraq_an_iranian_proxy [accessed: 26 December 2013].

Bassiri Tabrizi, A. and Hanau Santini, R. 2012. EU Sanctions against Iran: New Wine in Old Bottles? *ISPI Analysis*, no. 97, Milano: ISPI.

BBC News 2003. Outrage at 'old Europe' remarks. 23 January, http://news.bbc.co.uk/2/hi/europe/2687403.stm [accessed: 13 May 2013].

Beaucillon, C. 2012. Comment choisir ses mesures restrictives ? Guide pratique des sanctions de l'UE. *EUISS Occasional Paper*, no. 100, Paris: EUISS.

Blackden, R. 2013. Shell Owes Iran $2.3bn for Oil. *The Telegraph*, 21 March.

Blix, H. 2004. *Disarming Iraq: The Search of Weapons of Mass Destruction*. London: Bloomsbury.

Chehabi, H.E. 2012. Iran and Iraq. Intersocietal linkages and secular nationalisms, in Amanat, A. and Vejdani, F. (eds), *Iran Facing Others Identity Boundaries in a Historical Perspective*. New York: Palgrave Macmillan, 191–218.

Corm, G. 2012. *Pour une lecture profane des conflits. Sur le retour du religieux dans les conflits contemporains du Moyen-Orient*. Paris: La Découverte.

Council of the European Union 2005. Council Joint Action 2005/190/CFSP of 7 March 2005 on the European Union Integrated Rule of Law Mission for Iraq, EUJUST LEX. OJ L62/37, 9 March.

Council of the European Union 2004. *Council Conclusions – Iraq 2004–2008*, Brussels, 17 May, http://eeas.europa.eu/iraq/docs/iraq_council_2004-08_ en.pdf [accessed: 12 May 2013].

Coville, T. 2013. Les sanctions, facteurs de crise ou choc salutaire pour l'économie iranienne ? Paris: CERI, http://www.sciencespo.fr/ceri/en/content/ les-sanctions-facteurs-de-crise-ou-choc-salutaire-pour-leconomie-iranienne [accessed: 11 May 2013].

Debray, R. 2013. Lettre ouverte à M. Hubert Védrine. La France doit quitter l'OTAN, *Le Monde Diplomatique*, March, 7, http://www.monde-diplomatique. fr/2013/03/DEBRAY/48843 [accessed: 13 May 2013].

Director General 2011. Implementation of the NPT Safeguards Agreement and relevant provisions of Security Council resolutions in the Islamic Republic of Iran, IAEA, Boards of Governors, GOV/2011/65, 8 November, 7, http://www. iaea.org/ Publications/Documents/Board/2011/gov2011-65.pdf [accessed: 12 May 2013].

Djalili, M-R. and Therme, C. 2008. Le flanc Est de l'Iran : opportunités et vulnérabilités. *Politique étrangère*, 3, 601–12.

Dodge, T. 2012. *Iraq: From War to a New Authoritarianism*. London: The International Institute for Strategic Studies.

European Commission 2010. *Memorandum of Understanding between the Government of Iraq and the EU on Strategic Partnership on Energy*, Baghdad, 18 January, http://ec.europa.eu/energy/international/bilateral_cooperation/ doc/iraq/2010_01_18_iraq_mou_en.pdf [accessed: 11 May 2013].

European Council 1992. *European Council in Edinburgh, 11–12 December 1992, Conclusions of the Presidency*, http://www.european-council.europa. eu/media/854346/1992_december_-_edinburgh__eng_.pdf [accessed: 13 May 2013].

European External Action Service 2013. *Cooperation between the European Union and Iraq. Joint Strategy Paper 2011–2013*, http://eeas.europa.eu/iraq/ docs/2011_2013_jsp_nip_en.pdf [accessed: 26 December 2013].

European External Action Service 2013. *EU Assistance to Iraq*, http://eeas.europa. eu/iraq/assistance-en.htm [accessed: 26 December 2013].

European External Action Service 2013. *Partnership and Cooperation Agreement (PCA) with Iraq*, http://eeas.europa.eu/iraq/tca_en.htm [accessed: 26 December 2013].

European External Action Service 2013. *Joint Plan of Action*, Geneva, 24 November. http://eeas.europa.eu/statements/docs/2013/131124_03_en.pdf [accessed: 29 November 2013].

European Union 2013. *Statement by the Spokesperson of the High Representative Catherine Ashton on the latest wave of attacks in Iraq*, A 206/13, Brussels, 16

April, http://www.consilium.europa.eu/uedocs/cms_Data/docs/pressdata/EN/foraff/136779.pdf [accessed: 12 May 2013].

Facon, B. 2013. Iranian Officials Say Some Western Companies Start Own Outreach to Tehran. *The Wall Street Journal*, 15 October.

Giumelli, F. 2013. How EU sanctions work: A new narrative, *EUISS Chaillot Paper*, no. 129, Paris: EUISS.

International Crisis Group 2013. Spider Web: The Making and Unmaking of Iran Sanctions, *Middle East Report*, no. 13825, http://www.crisisgroup.org/en/regions/middle-east-north-africa/iraq-iran-gulf/iran/138-spider-web-the-making-and-unmaking-of-iran-sanctions.aspx?utm_source=iran-email-sm&utm_medium=1&utm_campaign=email-sm [accessed: 13 March 2013].

International Energy Agency 2012. *Iraq Energy Outlook*. Paris: OECD/IEA.

Khosrokhavar, F. 2009. La crise en Iran révèle la tumultueuse naissance d'une société libre, *Le Monde*, 27 juin.

Khosrokhavar, F. 2010. Djombech-e sabz: harekat novin demokratik dar iran (The Green movement: Harbinger of a new democracy). *Iran Nameh. A Persian Journal of Iranian Studies*, 25(4), 487–503.

Kreutz, A. 2010. Syria: Russia's Best Asset in the Middle East. *Russie.Nei.Visions*, no. 55.

Malbrunot, G. 2013. L'Iran retire des posters anti-américains. *Le Figaro*, 28 October.

Mendras, M. 2003. Les ambiguïtés de la Russie. *Esprit*, 35.

Nicoullaud, F. 2013. *Iraq, Iran: The lesson of sanctions*. Paris: CERI, http://www.sciencespo.fr/ceri/en/content/iraq-iran-lesson-sanctions [accessed: 9 May 2013].

Nonneman, G. 2011. Europe, the US and the Gulf after the Cold War, in Möckli, D. and Mauer, V. (eds), *European-American Relations and the Middle East*. London: Routledge, 203–19.

Parsi, R. 2011. Iran in the shadow of the 2009 presidential election. *EUISS Occasional Paper*, no. 90, Paris: EUISS.

Parsi, R. 2012. Introduction: Iran at a critical juncture, in Parsi, R. (ed.), *Iran: A Revolutionary Republic in Transition. EUISS Chaillot Paper*, no. 128, Paris: EUISS.

Posch, W. 2006. The EU and Iran: A tangle web of negotiations, in Posch, W. (ed.), *Iranian Challenges. EUISS Chaillot Paper*, no. 89, Paris: EUISS.

Press TV. 2012. EU bans broadcast of Iranian TV channels on Hot Bird, 15 October, http://www.presstv.com/detail/2012/10/15/266831/eu-bans-broadcast-of-iranian-channels [accessed: 12 May 2013].

Press TV. 2012. EU denies ordering satellite companies to take Iran channels off air, 17 October, http://www.presstv.com/detail/2012/10/17/267243/eu-denies-ordering-iran-channels-ban [accessed: 12 May 2013].

The Economist 2013. Dodging sanctions in Iran. Around the block. How Iranian companies manage to keep trading with foreigners, 30 March.

Therme, C. 2008. L'Iran: exportateur de gaz ? *Note de l'Ifri*. Paris: Ifri.

United Press International 2013. EU under pressure to blacklist Hezbollah, 1 April, http://www.upi.com/Top-News/Special/2013/04/01/EU-under-pressure-to-blacklist-Hezbollah/UPI-98541364842526 [accessed: 12 May 2013].

World Bank 2013. *Doing Business 2013. Middle East and North Africa (MENA)*. Washington, DC: The World Bank, h.ttp://www.doingbusiness.org/~/media/GIAWB/Doing%20Business/Documents/Profiles/Regional/DB2013/DB13-Middle-East-North-Africa.pdf [accessed: 11 May 2013].

Yong, W. 2013. *NIOC and the State – Commercialization, Contestation and Consolidation in the Islamic Republic of Iran*, MEP 5, Oxford Institute for Energy Studies, http://www.oxfordenergy.org/wpcms/wp-content/uploads/2013/05/MEP-5.pdf [accessed: 11 May 2013].

Zambelis, C., 2013. China's Iraq Oil Strategy Comes into Sharper Focus. *China Brief*, 13(10), 9 May, http://www.jamestown.org/programs/chinabrief/single/?tx_ttnews%5Btt_news%5D= 40861&cHash=20da431fe2272ad34a6ace632cdecb96 [accessed: 11 May 2013].

Zibakalam, S. 2013. Rais jomhur ayande ba parvande-ye hastei tshe mikonad? (Iran's Next President and the Nuclear Dossier), *irdiplomacy.ir*, 2 ordibehesht 1392 [accessed: 22 April 2013].

PART III
Geopolitical Dimensions beyond the ENP's East: Central Asia

Chapter 8

State of Play: The EU, Central Asia and the ENP

Francesca Fenton

The European Union (EU) has a relatively short-lived but highly developed relationship with Central Asia, which it defines to include five republics: Kazakhstan, Kyrgyzstan, Uzbekistan, Tajikistan and Turkmenistan.[1] This chapter explores how the EU's relationship with the Central Asian region has developed since its inception in the early 1990s to the present day. It also seeks to determine the extent to which the goals, methods and thinking behind the EU's strategy towards Central Asia are linked to the European Neighbourhood Policy (ENP). After an initial period of relative disinterest, the EU became increasingly preoccupied with the Central Asian republics towards the end of the twentieth century. This growing interest culminated in the publication of a Central Asia Strategy in 2007,[2] the goals of which are best examined in light of the wider geopolitical context. Borrowing from its ENP toolkit, the EU's policy towards Central Asia is similar to its neighbourhood policy. As is the case with the ENP, although some successful initiatives have been implemented, a great deal is left wanting.

The Central Asian Enigma

For the best part of the twentieth century Central Asia remained an enigma to Europe. Even though the 'Great Game' had been played out between Britain and Russia a century earlier, with the two countries fiercely competing for influence in the region, strategic rivalry during the 1900s remained limited. To a Western eye the five 'stans' – Kazakhstan, Uzbekistan, Turkmenistan, Kyrgyzstan and Tajikistan – were Soviet Republics, controlled by Moscow and firmly isolated by their Communist rule.[3]

---

1 Council of the European Union 2007. *European Union and Central Asia: Strategy for a New Partnership*, 10113/07, Brussels, May, 2.

2 Ibid.

3 Melvin, N.J. 2008. Introduction, in Melvin, N.J. (ed.), *Engaging Central Asia: The European Union's New Strategy in the Heart of Eurasia*. Brussels: Centre for European Policy Studies, 2.

When the Soviet Union collapsed in 1991, little changed. The European Communities were struggling to come to terms with political consolidation, frantically negotiating the Maastricht Treaty and considering what to do about the Central and Eastern European countries that were, after all, at their doorstep.[4] In the mid-1990s most EU Member States simply placed roving ambassadors in Ankara or Moscow to cover the region, with only France, the UK and Germany opening diplomatic representations in the majority of the Central Asian republics.[5]

Ties to the European Union were notably weak at this time. In 1994 an EU Delegation opened in Kazakhstan, which was also responsible for Tajikistan and Kyrgyzstan.[6] Generic EU programmes such as the 'Technical Assistance to the Commonwealth of Independent States' (TACIS), which had been designed to provide 'technical assistance in support of the economic reform progress' in the former Soviet states, 'aimed at bringing about transition to a market economy and reinforcing democracy' in the region.[7] This, coupled with various bilateral Partnership and Cooperation Agreements (PCAs) that were concluded with the Central Asian republics in 1996,[8] was supposed to signal a renewed interest on the part of the EU. Instead, however, engagement 'remained modest', lacking both the 'necessary resources' and a 'clear sense of political priorities' to have a real impact at this time.[9]

Renewed Interest – The Central Asia Strategy and its Relationship with the ENP

Towards the end of the 1990s, large hydrocarbon and gas reserves in Kazakhstan, Turkmenistan and Uzbekistan began to attract considerable Western attention.[10] Moreover, increasing demand for these resources, coupled with a need to diversify

---

4   Warkotsch, A. 2011. Introduction, in Warkotsch, A. (ed.), *The European Union and Central Asia*. Abingdon: Routledge, 4.

5   Melvin, op. cit., 2.

6   Ibid.

7   European Commission 1997. *Tacis Interim Evaluation Report*. Brussels, June, 11.

8   In 1996 the European Communities and their Member States concluded PCAs with Kazakhstan, Uzbekistan, Kyrgyzstan and Turkmenistan. The PCA with Turkmenistan is yet to be ratified, as both the European Parliament and various Member States have opposed it, reproaching the Turkmen authorities for prolonged human rights abuses in their country. Nevertheless, an interim trade agreement signed with Turkmenistan, was approved by the European Parliament in 2009. As a result of the civil war in Tajikistan in the 1990s, a PCA with this country was only signed in 2004. For more information, see European Union 2013. *Partnership and Cooperation Agreements (PCAs): Russia, Eastern Europe, the Southern Caucasus and Central Asia*, http://europa.eu/legislation_summaries/external_relations/relations_with_third_countries/eastern_europe_and_central_asia/r17002_en.htm [accessed: 11 November 2013].

9   Melvin, op. cit.

10   Warkotsch, op. cit.

supplies, meant that the 'safe export of Caspian energy' was rapidly becoming 'a policy priority' for the EU.[11] The Interstate Oil and Gas Pipeline Management (INOGATE) programme of 1995,[12] the 2000 Commission Green Paper on Energy and the 2004 Baku Initiative were introduced.[13] These signalled the first attempt at bringing together the EU's major supply and transit countries on its Eastern flank and all three initiatives included the Central Asian republics.[14]

A second catalyst for renewed EU interest in Central Asia was the spill-over effect of the 2001 'war on terror' in Afghanistan, as practically overnight the republics became crucial providers of military bases and over-flight rights for the Western allies.[15] While being helpful in this regard, however, the region was at the same time a growing source of concern: the global nature of terrorist and criminal operations meant that 'their activities in Central or South East Asia' posed a real 'threat to European countries or their citizens'.[16] A third catalyst was the 2004 and 2007 enlargements of the EU and the subsequent development of the European Neighbourhood Policy. These policies brought the EU closer to the Central Asian region, rendering it increasingly vulnerable to the fragile states located there.[17] Migration pressures, religious extremism and the spread of organized crime were all threats that the Union could only afford to ignore for so long.[18]

With the above in mind, the EU came up with a 'Strategy for a New Partnership' with Central Asia in 2007.[19] Referred to by some academics as a 'New Ostpolitik', the strategy was initiated by the German Council Presidency, which was keen to improve cooperation with the countries of the former Soviet Union.[20] Its overarching goal was to promote stability[21] through 'the development and

---

11   Ibid.

12   The INOGATE programme supports energy policy cooperation between the EU and the littoral states of the Black and Caspian Seas and their neighbouring countries. See http://ec.europa.eu/europeaid/what/energy/policies/eastern-neighbourhood/inogate_en.htm [accessed: 2 January 2014].

13   For more information on the 2000 Commission Green Paper on Energy and the 2004 Baku Initiative, see http://europa.eu/legislation_summaries/energy/external_dimension_enlargement/l27037_en.htm   and   http://ec.europa.eu/dgs/energy_transport/international/regional/caspian/energy_en.htm [accessed: 2 January 2014].

14   Denison, M. 2009. The EU and Central Asia: Commercialising the Energy Relationship. *EUCAM Working Paper*, no. 2, Brussels: EUCAM, July, 5.

15   Warkotsch, op. cit.

16   European Council 2003. *A Secure Europe in a Better World – The European Security Strategy*, Brussels, 12 December, 6.

17   Warkotsch, op. cit., 5.

18   Ibid.

19   Council of the European Union 2007, op. cit.

20   Warkotsch, op. cit., 1.

21   Schmitz, A. 2011. The Central Asia Strategy: An Exercise in EU Foreign Policy, in Warkotsch, A. (ed.), *The European Union and Central Asia*. Abingdon: Routledge, 12.

consolidation of stable, just and open societies'.[22] In order to realize this goal the EU developed seven priority areas where it would 'share experience' to promote change.[23] These included (1) good governance, the rule of law, human rights and democratization; (2) youth and education; (3) economic development, trade and investment; (4) energy and transport; (5) environmental policies; (6) combating common threats; and (7) intercultural dialogue.[24] Tied up with the overarching desire to promote stability, the Member States decided that a 'common response' was needed to tackle concerns surrounding border management; migration; organized crime; international terrorism and human, drugs and arms trafficking.[25] An increasingly engaged EU approach would also facilitate efforts in the energy sphere: by strengthening local energy markets, improving investment conditions and increasing energy production and efficiency in Central Asia, the EU sought to diversify energy supplies and their distribution in the region.[26]

In order to promote these diverse and wide-ranging priority areas, the EU Strategy introduced a number of concrete policy initiatives, a few of which were 'of special importance for the EU'.[27] These included setting up a regular regional political dialogue at Foreign Minister level, as well as an Energy Dialogue to promote energy security.[28] A Rule of Law Initiative was also established, together with a Human Rights Dialogue that was to take place regularly with each Central Asian state.[29] Finally, the EU introduced a European Education Initiative and an e-Silk Highway, with the aim of encouraging more people-to-people exchanges between Europe and Central Asia.[30] With all these priority areas and policy initiatives in mind, the EU Strategy endeavoured to strike a balance between a bilateral and regional approach.[31] On the one hand, cooperation had been designed in accordance with individual needs, requirements and performance; on the other hand, a strong focus was placed on region-wide projects that could tackle regional challenges.[32]

It is important to note that aside from the TACIS programme, as well as the Strategy just outlined, the EU has two other core tools in its toolkit for fostering relations with Central Asia. These include the European Instrument for Democracy and Human Rights (EIDHR), which is a worldwide programme designed to promote human rights and democracy, and the EU Special Representative (EUSR)

---

22 Council of the European Union 2003, op. cit., 2.
23 Ibid.
24 Council of the European Union 2007, op. cit.
25 Ibid., 3.
26 Ibid.
27 Schmitz, op. cit.
28 Council of the European Union 2007, op. cit.
29 Ibid.
30 Ibid.
31 Schmitz, op. cit.
32 Ibid.

for Central Asia.[33] The latter position was created in 2005 and has been occupied by three people: Jan Kubis of Slovakia, Pierre Morel of France and Patricia Flor of Germany.[34] The EUSRs in Central Asia have been tasked with promoting the EU's visibility, fostering cooperation, contributing to democratization and addressing key regional threats.[35]

Linking the Central Asia Strategy to the ENP

The extent to which the logic guiding the ENP, and most notably the Eastern Partnership,[36] resembles the EU's Central Asia Strategy, is striking. Both the Eastern Partnership and Central Asia Strategy start with a global approach, before differentiating between partners by advocating deeper bilateral engagement.[37] Although the Eastern Partnership is more ambitious than the Strategy through, for example, offering countries to sign Association Agreements with Deep and Comprehensive Free Trade Areas (DCFTAs), the logic guiding this bilateral engagement is similar. For example, fundamental to both approaches is deeper economic integration, both in terms of boosting EU trade with the region and of boosting intra-regional trade.[38] Moreover, just as accession to the World Trade Organization (WTO) is 'a specific precondition on the road towards the establishment of a DCFTA' for the Eastern partners,[39] the EU considers WTO accession as being key to ensuring necessary reforms in the Central Asian republics.[40] Another similarity arises over the issue of energy security: one of the main pillars of the Eastern Partnership's bilateral track is 'deeper cooperation to enhance the energy security of the partners of the EU',[41] which is similar to the Strategy – 'the EU and Central Asia share a paramount interest in enhancing energy security'.[42] The multilateral tracks of the EU approach to these regions

---

33   Urdze, S. 2011. The tool kit of EU-Central Asian Cooperation, in Warkotsch, A. (ed.), *The European Union and Central Asia*. Abingdon: Routledge, 27–8.

34   Council of the European Union 2012. *Council Conclusions on Central Asia*, 3179th Foreign Affairs Council meeting, Luxembourg, 25 June.

35   Urdze, op. cit.

36   There are six Eastern Partners – Ukraine, Moldova, Georgia, Belarus, Azerbaijan and Armenia. See European Commission 2008. Communication from the European Commission to the European Parliament and the Council, *'Eastern Partnership'*, COM(2008) 823, Brussels, 3 December.

37   Ibid., 11.

38   Ibid., 16.

39   Lannon E. and Van Elsuwege P. 2012. The Eastern Partnership, in Lannon, E. (ed.), *The European Neighbourhood Policy's Challenges/Les défis de la politique européenne de voisinage*. Brussels: P.I.E. Peter Lang, 294.

40   Council of the European Union 2007, op. cit., 16.

41   European Commission 2008, op. cit.

42   Council of the European Union 2007, op. cit., 18.

also address this issue, as the EU's long-term ambition in both regions is to create integrated regional energy markets.[43] More generally, the four thematic platforms outlined in the Eastern Partnership's multilateral dimension (democracy, good governance and the rule of law; economic integration; energy security and contacts between people),[44] are also 'priority areas' of the Central Asia Strategy.[45] It is clear that when elaborating its approach to Central Asia and Eastern Europe, the EU was once again recycling its toolkit.

With an understanding of the founding components of the EU's policy towards Central Asia the focus needs to be broadened now. The next section takes a geopolitical turn, to situate the EU's efforts in a global context.

The Bigger Picture – The 'New Great Game'

In what has become known as the 'New Great Game', the EU is competing with the US, Russia and China when executing policy in the Central Asian republics, which inevitably affects its ability to succeed.[46] This next section considers the foreign policy goals of Russia and China,[47] which are not always in harmony with EU objectives.[48]

Russia

In the years following the dissolution of the Soviet Union, Russia, like the EU, was relatively disinterested in Central Asia.[49] With the inauguration of Vladimir Putin as President in 2000, however, this attitude shifted significantly. The adoption of three important foreign policy documents – the National Security Concept, the Russian Military Doctrine and the Foreign Policy Concept – clearly demarcated an increased importance of the region to the Kremlin.[50] Fearing the evolving unipolar system with the United States at its helm, these documents highlighted how important the countries of the Commonwealth of Independent States (CIS) were to Russia and its

---

43   Ibid., 20; and Lannon and Van Elsuwege, op. cit., 298.

44   European Commission 2008, op. cit.

45   Council of the European Union 2007, op. cit.

46   Freire, M.R. and Kanet, R.E. 2010. *Key Players and Regional Dynamics in Eurasia: The Return of the 'Great Game'.* London: Palgrave Macmillan, 1–2.

47   Owing to space constraints, the current chapter does not take into account American foreign policy objectives with regards to Central Asia (which are broadly in line with those of the EU). For more information on US thinking, see ibid.

48   See also Chapter 9 by Alexander Warkotsch and Chapter 12 by Jonatan Thompson in this volume.

49   Peyrouse S., Boonstra J. and Laurelle M. 2012. Security and Development Approaches to Central Asia. The EU Compared to China and Russia. *EUCAM Working Paper*, no. 11, Brussels: EUCAM, May, 6.

50   Ibid.

attempts to create a balanced, multipolar world order.[51] As Freire and Kanet point out, the Russian rationale was reasonably straightforward: in a constant search for counter-balance and primacy, Putin was keen to boost ties with as many countries as possible.[52] The last word of this quotation – primacy – is particularly important. Attempting to rebuild 'Greater Russia', Putin sought to restore the Russian hegemony in the CIS region during the first decade of the twenty-first century.[53] Indeed, after the terrorist attacks of 11 September 2001 in the US, the newly inaugurated President became highly perturbed by the surging American and European interests in the region. From this point onwards, Central Asia was deemed part of Russia's 'geo-political and geo-economic ideational heritage'.[54]

In this quest for primacy, another key Russian goal has been to ensure that the country maintains significant influence over Central Asian energy resources, especially over their transit.[55] In line with the EU's logic, Russia has also been keen to protect itself from destabilizing factors emanating from the five Central Asian republics, such as military extremism and drug trafficking.[56] In preparation for a post-2014 Afghanistan, it is arguable that Russia now prioritizes this security logic.[57] Already in 2009 Laurelle noted that '[f]or the Kremlin, the region's growing strategic insecurity and the risks of destabilisation constitute the *first motif* of involvement'.[58] To summarize, Russia clearly has four principal foreign policy goals when it comes to Central Asia. These include ensuring that the Central Asian republics remain in Russia's sphere of influence, preventing regional instability, providing security, and controlling the development and transit of Central Asia's energy resources.[59]

China

The need to secure access to energy resources to satisfy a seemingly insatiable Chinese demand for energy is the main driver behind the policy of the People's Republic of China (PRC) towards Central Asia. According to forecasts of the International Energy Agency, the PRC is set to import over 80 per cent of its oil by 2035 and thus desperately needs to establish good relations with oil producing

---

51   Freire and Kanet, op. cit.

52   Ibid., 2.

53   Nygren, B. 2010. Russia and the CIS Region, in Freire, M.R. and Kanet, R.E. (eds), *Key Players and Regional Dynamics in Eurasia: The Return of the 'Great Game'*. London: Palgrave Macmillan, 15.

54   Ibid., 22.

55   Ibid., 23.

56   Peyrouse, Boonstra and Laurelle, op. cit., 7.

57   Ibid.

58   Laurelle, M. 2009. Russia in Central Asia: Old History, New Challenges?, *EUCAM Working Paper*, no. 3, Brussels: EUCAM, September, 4 [emphasis added].

59   Peyrouse, Boonstra and Laurelle, op. cit., 6.

countries.[60] Wanting to diversify sources and reduce its dependency on the Middle East, China is therefore actively pursuing Central Asian energy projects.[61]

As a major goal of China's foreign policy is to counter threats to the country's integrity, or to the stability of the PRC regime, China's intentions towards the Central Asian region are also tied up with the country's internal security agenda.[62] For decades now China has been trying to cope with a volatile situation in its Western Xinjiang province, where the Uyghur movement has been pushing for increased autonomy.[63] Calling for the uniting of the Uyghurs living in Kazakhstan, Kyrgyzstan and Tajikistan with those living in China, the movement seeks to create a new, independent 'East Turkistan' that would result in the breaking up of the Xinjiang province.[64] For obvious reasons, politicians in Beijing want to prevent such an outcome and, holding the firm belief that the Muslim minority movements of the Uyghur population in Xinjiang are destined to fail provided that they are not financially aided by foreign assistance, the Chinese actively seek to constrict the action of Western players in the region.[65] China is looking to shelter Xinjiang from foreign influence, be it from religious influences spilling over from Central Asia, or from 'ideological' influences regarding democratization and self-determination coming from the West.[66] This is especially worrying when considering that one of the EU's priorities is to promote democracy in the region. Indeed, there is a clear tension between the EU's foreign policy agenda and the Chinese vision of how the region should develop.

To summarize, Chinese foreign policy goals towards Central Asia are threefold: to secure much needed energy supplies, to prevent the rise of instability resulting from ethnic tensions emanating from the Uyghur movement and to temper mounting Western influence in the Central Asian republics. Although Russia and China are not the only powers fighting over Central Asian resources, one can clearly see how their diverging foreign policy goals could lead to geopolitical struggles for influence. How the EU has dealt with these geopolitical considerations will be the subject of the next section, which looks into its Central Asia Strategy today.

---

60   International Energy Agency 2010. *World Energy Outlook 2010*, Paris: International Energy Agency, 99.

61   Blank, S., 2010. *International Rivalries in Eurasia*, in Freire, M.R. and Kanet, R.E. (eds), *Key Players and Regional Dynamics in Eurasia: The Return of the 'Great Game'*. London: Palgrave Macmillan, 45.

62   Ibid., 40.

63   Dwivedi, R. 2006. China's Central Asia Policy in Recent Times. *China and Eurasia Forum Quarterly*, 4(4), 141.

64   Ibid.

65   Ibid.

66   Ibid.

The EU's Central Asia Strategy and the Eastern Partnership

With all of these competing foreign policy goals in mind, it is interesting to consider how the EU Central Asia Strategy has been implemented. In 2008 the Council published a Joint Progress Report,[67] which was unsurprisingly upbeat.[68] There had been a significant increase in the number of high-level meetings since the adoption of the Strategy and three important initiatives had been introduced promoting its original priorities at the regional level.[69] These included a Rule of Law initiative for Central Asia that was launched in 2008 during the French Presidency of the Council,[70] a European Education Initiative for Central Asia and an Environment and Water Initiative.[71] Kazakhstan was also singled out in the Joint Progress Report, which outlined the possibility of the country establishing an enhanced PCA with the EU.[72] It was thought that an enhanced PCA 'could become a model for future contractual relations with other Central Asian countries, depending notably on the pace of reforms'.[73] The last part of this sentence once again reinforces ties between the ENP and the Central Asia Strategy: this is a clear push for conditionality, in line with the EU's 'more for more' approach in the ENP.[74]

All of the initiatives mentioned above are additions to regional programmes that had already been developed through the TACIS instrument, and which continue to receive funding through both the EU's Development Cooperation Instrument (DCI)[75] and the European Neighbourhood Policy Instrument (ENPI).[76] Such

---

67   Council of the European Union 2008. *Joint Progress Report by the Council and the European Commission to the European Council on the implementation of the EU Strategy for Central Asia*, 11402/10, Brussels, 28 June.

68   Schmitz, op. cit., 14.

69   Ibid.

70   European Commission 2008. *European Rule of Law Initiative for Central Asia*, http://eeas.europa.eu/central_asia/docs/factsheet_law_en.pdf [accessed: 3 January 2014].

71   European Commission 2008. *European cooperation in education in Central Asia*, http://eeas.europa.eu/central_asia/docs/factsheet_education_en.pdf [accessed: 3 January 2014]; European Commission, 2008. *EU action on water resources in Central Asia as a key element of environmental protection*, http://eeas.europa.eu/central_asia/docs/factsheet_environment_en.pdf [accessed: 3 January 2014].

72   Council of the European Union 2008, op. cit., 28.

73   Ibid.

74   European Commission 2011. *A New Response to a Changing Neighbourhood*. Brussels, 25 May, http://ec.europa.eu/world/enp/pdf/com_11_303_en.pdf [accessed: 3 January 2014].

75   European Parliament and Council of the European Union 2006. *Regulation (EC) No 1905/2006 of the European Parliament and of the Council of 18 December 2006 establishing a financing instrument for development cooperation*. OJ L378/41, 27 December.

76   European Parliament and Council of the European Union 2006. *Regulation (EC) 1638/2006 laying down general provisions establishing a European Neighbourhood and*

programmes include INOGATE, the Transport Corridor Europe Caucasus Asia (TRACEA),[77] the Border Management Programme in Central Asia (BOMCA), and the Central Asia Drug Action Programme (CADAP).[78] This ENPI funding aspect is extremely important as it reinforces the idea that the Central Asian republics have become inextricably linked to the ENP in Eastern Europe and the Southern Caucasus. In its Regional Strategy Paper for Assistance to Central Asia for the period 2007–13, the Commission highlighted that the Strategy 'cannot be seen separately' from the ENP, and as such it would be necessary to 'anchor the Central Asian countries in broader EU policies promoted by the ENPI'.[79]

On the basis of Article 27 of the ENPI Regulation, the five republics could participate in regional assistance programmes with the EU's Eastern neighbours.[80] Furthermore, any regional cooperation for Central Asia would come to 'rely as much as possible on the enhanced regional co-operation initiatives and mechanisms under the ENPI Regional Strategy (East) 2007–2013'.[81] An example of a concrete initiative that the European Commission hoped to pursue was the integration of the transport markets of the Central Asian states with the ENPI Eastern countries.[82]

Despite this flurry of initiatives, progress on human rights promotion has been less forthcoming. Notwithstanding the fact that human rights issues are 'systematically raised in all relevant dialogue fora', the Central Asian states are 'not very receptive to the human rights agenda'.[83] Fierce competition with Russia and China has further dampened the EU's ability to voice human rights issues: these countries do not attach any conditionality to their regional investments, making it difficult for the EU to impose tough political demands. On the whole then there is wide agreement that the Strategy's 'policy of dialogue and engagement seems to have done almost nothing to affect the behaviour of the Central Asian governments'.[84] Moreover, it has been labelled an 'exclusive, elite-driven process' that has conflicting goals: democracy promotion, for example, may result in further regional instability, which would clash with the Strategy's core guiding principle.[85]

Partnership Instrument. OJ L 310/1, 9 November. As of 2014 the ENPI has become the ENI.

77   For more information on TRACEA, see http://ec.europa.eu/europeaid/where/asia/regional-cooperation-central-asia/transport/traceca_en.htm [accessed: 3 January 2014].

78   Urdze, op. cit., 24. For more information on BOMCA, see http://www.bomca.eu and on CADAP, see http://www.cadap.eu [accessed: 3 January 2014].

79   European Commission 2007. *European Community Regional Strategy Paper for Assistance to Central Asia for the Period 2007–2013*, Brussels, 7.

80   Ibid.

81   Ibid., 22.

82   Ibid., 13.

83   Melvin, N. 2012. The EU Needs a New Values-Based Realism for its Central Asia Strategy. *EUCAM Policy Brief*, no. 28, Brussels: EUCAM, October, 2.

84   Ibid.

85   Ibid.

With this arguably questionable progress in mind, it is interesting that in June 2012, the EU issued a Ministerial statement on the fifth anniversary of its Strategy, concluding that the latter has 'proven itself and remains valid'.[86] While the seven priority areas remained important, Ministers noted that one in particular – security promotion and Afghanistan – had taken centre stage.[87] Indeed, as 'security issues have come to fore in relations' between Central Asia and the EU, Ministers considered it necessary to introduce 'a regular High Level EU-Central Asia Security Dialogue, as part of the regional political dialogue'.[88] The inaugural round of this dialogue took place in June 2013.[89] At the time, Member States agreed to further advance the EU's border and counter-drug addiction programmes (BOMCA and CADAP), renew and update the EU-Central Asia Action Plan on Drugs, and foster improved connections between EU programmes in Central Asia and Afghanistan along the shared borders in the region.[90] Highlighting the importance of security concerns, a press communiqué issued after the inaugural session states that the dialogue will take place 'regularly': the next round will be held in Tajikistan in 2014.[91]

Conclusion

This chapter set out to outline the EU's evolving relationship with Central Asia and to determine the extent to which the EU's policy towards the Central Asian region mirrors the ENP. Immediately following the dissolution of the Soviet Union, the EU was relatively disinterested in Central Asia. Gradually, however, this disinterest faded, as energy security problems, 9/11 and the development of the European Neighbourhood Policy forced the Union and its Member States to take the region seriously.

In 2007 a Strategy was published, which had seven priorities and one overarching goal: the EU wanted to promote stability in a region that had, all of a sudden, come to neighbour its neighbours. One cannot fail to notice the striking similarities between the methodology underpinning the Central Asia Strategy and the ENP, highlighted by the fact that regional programmes designed for Central Asia have become inextricably linked to those introduced for the Eastern neighbours. In 2012 the EU undertook an internal assessment of both past and future engagement, and it will be interesting to examine how its approach to the Eastern Partners affects the Union's relations with the Central Asian republics. As security concerns come to the fore, the EU may have to rethink its cooperation

---

86   Council of the European Union 2012, op. cit.
87   Ibid.
88   Ibid.
89   European External Action Service 2013. *EU-Central Asia High Level Security Dialogue*, A 315/13, Brussels, 13 June.
90   Ibid.
91   Ibid.

with Russia and China, in support of a mutually beneficial and balanced approach to the security question. Doing this, while at the same time promoting democracy and human rights, however, remains a huge challenge. And it is a challenge that the EU will have to face if it is to remain a credible actor in the region.

Bibliography

Blank, S. 2010. International rivalries in Eurasia, in Freire, M.R. and Kanet R.E. (eds), *Key Players and Regional Dynamics in Eurasia: The Return of the 'Great Game'*. London: Palgrave Macmillan, 29–54.

Council of the European Union 2007. *European Union and Central Asia: Strategy for a New Partnership*, 10113/07, Brussels, May 2007.

Council of the European Union 2008. *Joint Progress Report by the Council and the European Commission to the European Council on the implementation of the EU Strategy for Central Asia*, 11402/10, Brussels, 28 June.

Council of the European Union 2012. *Council Conclusions on Central Asia*, 3179th Foreign Affairs Council meeting, Luxembourg, 25 June.

Denison, M. 2009. The EU and Central Asia: Commercialising the Energy Relationship. *EUCAM Working Paper*, no. 2, Brussels, July.

Dwivedi, R. 2006. China's Central Asia Policy in Recent Times. *China and Eurasia Forum Quarterly*, 4(4), 139–59.

European Commission 1997. *Tacis Interim Evaluation Report*. Brussels, June.

European Commission 2007. *European Community Regional Strategy Paper for Assistance to Central Asia for the Period 2007–2013*, Brussels.

European Commission 2008. Communication from the European Commission to the European Parliament and the Council, *Eastern Partnership*, COM(2008) 823, Brussels, 3 December.

European Commission 2008. *EU Action on Water Resources in Central Asia as a Key Element of Environmental Protection*, http://eeas.europa.eu/central_asia/docs/factsheet_environment_en.pdf [accessed 3 January 2014].

European Commission 2008. *European Cooperation in Education in Central Asia*, http://eeas.europa.eu/central_asia/docs/factsheet_education_en.pdf [accessed: 3 January 2014].

European Commission 2008. *European Rule of Law Initiative for Central Asia*, http://eeas.europa.eu/central_asia/docs/factsheet_law_en.pdf [accessed: 3 January 2014].

European Commission 2011. *A New Response to a Changing Neighbourhood*. Brussels, 25 May, http://ec.europa.eu/world/enp/pdf/com-11-303-en.pdf [accessed: 3 January 2014].European Council 2003. *A Secure Europe in a Better World – The European Security Strategy*, Brussels, 12 December.

European Council 2003. *A Secure Europe in a Better World – The European Security Strategy*, Brussels, 12 December.

European External Action Service 2013. *EU-Central Asia High Level Security Dialogue*, A 315/13, Brussels, 13 June.

European Parliament and Council of the European Union 2006. *Regulation (EC) 1638/2006 laying down general provisions establishing a European Neighbourhood and Partnership Instrument*. OJ L 310/1, 9 November.

European Parliament and Council of the European Union 2006. *Regulation (EC) No 1905/2006 of the European Parliament and of the Council of 18 December 2006 establishing a financing instrument for development cooperation*. OJ L378/41, 27 December.

European Union 2013. *Partnership and Cooperation Agreements (PCAs): Russia, Eastern Europe, the Southern Caucasus and Central Asia*, http://europa.eu/legislation_summaries/external_relations/relations_with_third_countries/eastern_europe_and_central_asia/r17002_en.htm [accessed: 11 November 2013].

Freire, M.R. and Kanet, R.E. 2010. *Key Players and Regional Dynamics in Eurasia: The Return of the 'Great Game'*. London: Palgrave Macmillan.

International Energy Agency 2010. *World Energy Outlook 2010*. Paris: International Energy Agency.

Lannon, E. and Van Elsuwege, P. 2012. The Eastern Partnership, in E. Lannon (ed.), *The European Neighbourhood Policy's Challenges/Les défis de la politique européenne de voisinage*. Brussels: P.I.E. Peter Lang, 285–322.

Laurelle, M. 2009. Russia in Central Asia: Old History, New Challenges?, *EUCAM Working Paper*, no. 3, Brussels: EUCAM, September.

Melvin, N.J. 2008. Introduction, in Melvin, N.J. (ed.), *Engaging Central Asia: The European Union's New Strategy in the Heart of Eurasia*. Brussels: Centre for European Policy Studies, 1–8.

Melvin, N.J., 2012. The EU Needs a New Values-Based Realism for its Central Asia Strategy, *EUCAM Policy Brief*, no. 28, Brussels, October.

Nygren, B. 2010. Russia and the CIS Region, in Freire, M.R. and Kanet R.E. (eds). *Key Players and Regional Dynamics in Eurasia: The Return of the 'Great Game'*. London: Palgrave Macmillan, 13–28.

Peyrouse, S., Boonstra J. and Laurelle M. 2012. Security and Development Approaches to Central Asia: The EU Compared to China and Russia. *EUCAM Working Paper*, no. 11, Brussels: EUCAM, May.

Schmitz, A. 2011. The Central Asia strategy: An exercise in EU Foreign Policy, in Warkotsch, A. (ed.), *The European Union and Central Asia*. Abingdon: Routledge, 11–21.

Urdze, S. 2011. The TOOL KIT of EU-Central Asian cooperation, in Warkotsch, A. (ed.), *The European Union and Central Asia*. Abingdon: Routledge, 22–32.

Warkotsch, A. 2011. Introduction, in Warkotsch, A. (ed.), *The European Union and Central Asia*. Abingdon: Routledge, 1–8.

Chapter 9

The Caspian Sea Region: The Struggle for Resources

Alexander Warkotsch

Introduction

Back in the nineteenth century when Imperial Russia threatened India, the jewel of the British crown, observers referred to this competition for influence and acquisition of territory as the 'Great Game'.[1] After the break-up of the Soviet Union, soon talk of a 'New Great Game' came up. The revival of the term, however, was not sparked by rivalry over the control of land. This time the term stood for the competition of international energy consortia for the region's huge oil and gas resources.[2] However, it did not take long before it began to symbolize the increasing rivalry among these companies' host countries, in particular Russia, China, Iran and the United States, and their largely conflicting geo-economic interests in Central Asia.

With the lingering debate about declining global oil and gas reserves and rising costs for satisfying the global energy demand, import-dependent countries like China and most of the European countries have become increasingly worried about their energy security. In light of these concerns they began to discover nearby Central Asia and the South Caucasus as an important additional source for energy. On the other side, energy exporting Russia has been eager not to lose grip on its traditional southern backyard. It has been pulling strings to secure control over the Caspian region's energy export infrastructure and resources in order to preserve its role as Europe's main energy supplier. At the same time, the United States has started in the 1990s to support and facilitate strategic pipeline constructions that would bypass Russia, trying to foster the region's independence from its old hegemonic power. In the context of this struggle, the Caspian region's[3] energy rich countries Azerbaijan,

---

1   Edwards, M. 2003. The New Great Game and the New Great Gamers: Disciples of Kipling and Mackinder. *Central Asian Survey*, 22(1), 83–102.

2   For a discussion of the term 'Great Game' in its current use, see ibid. See also Chapter 8 by Francesca Fenton in this volume.

3   The Caspian region includes the littoral countries of the Caspian Sea Russia, Azerbaijan, Iran, Turkmenistan, and Kazakhstan. If discussed in an energy context the Caspian region is often extended to the Central Asian country of Uzbekistan. While Azerbaijan is part of the European Neighbourhood Policy (ENP), the Central Asian

Kazakhstan, Turkmenistan and Uzbekistan have seen 'a meteoric rise ... to centre stage of world politics'.[4] A trend that has been reinforced in the aftermath of the events of 11 September 2001 when most of the neighbouring Central Asian regimes have agreed to become important logistical hubs for operations of the US and the North Atlantic Treaty Organization (NATO) in Afghanistan.

The aim of this chapter is twofold: first it analyses the attractiveness of Central Asia's energy reserves for contributing to the European Union's (EU) energy security. Second, it examines the chances of the EU to successfully secure itself a stake in the oil and gas resources of the region against the background of the interests of other external players (for example, Russia, China, and the US) in the region. For this purpose, this chapter is structured as follows: building on a short analysis of the EU's energy future in the context of available Caspian energy reserves, the first part outlines the EU's strategy in tapping Caspian, in particular Central Asian oil and gas resources. This is followed by the main part of the analysis which focuses on the interests and strategies of key players in the 'New Great Game'. A central concern here is the extent to which the interests of these players are compatible with those of the EU. The chapter closes by giving a brief outlook on the EU's chances and impediments to successfully secure itself a noteworthy stake in the region's oil and gas exports.

The Future of EU Energy Security and Central Asian Energy Resources

In 2011, the EU-27 imported about 83 per cent of its crude oil, 64 per cent of natural gas and 47 per cent of its coal demand.[5] Fossil fuel projections towards 2030 indicate that gas demand is most likely to rise while oil consumption will stagnate at the current high level.[6] So far, Russia is the EU's most important energy supplier. Russia's shares of EU gas, oil, and coal imports amount to 34 per cent, 33 per cent and 26.2 per cent respectively. For the sake of comparison, Norway and Libya, the EU's second and third largest supplier of oil, account for about 15 and 10 per cent of imports. In the field of gas, Norway and Algeria contribute 31 and 14 per cent to the EU's demand.[7] Though EU energy imports are likely

---

countries Kazakhstan, Turkmenistan and Uzbekistan are not. The latter are the focus of this chapter. See Map III in the Annex.

4   Manning, R.E. 2000. The Myth of the Caspian Great Game and the New Persian Gulf. *Survival*, 7(2), 15.

5   European Commission 2011. Directorate General for Energy, *Key figures*, 6, http://ec.europa.eu/energy/observatory/countries/doc/key_figures.pdf [accessed: 27 February 2013].

6   European Commission 2008. *Europe's energy position. Past and present*, http://ec.europa.eu/energy/publications/doc/2008_moe_maquette.pdf [accessed: 8 March 2013].

7   European Commission 2010. *EU Energy and Transport in Figures*. Statistical Pocketbook. Brussels: Publications Office of the European Union, 31; European Commission 2011, op. cit., 5–6.

to further diversify as a consequence of increasing liquefied natural gas (LNG) imports from Africa and the Middle East, additional political steps towards energy diversification are necessary. In particular the EU's strong dependency on Russian energy is more and more worrying European decision-makers. Such concerns have significantly increased after the two 'gas crises' of 2006 and 2009, when Russian-Ukrainian disputes over gas prices, debt and transit fees led to interruptions in gas flows to the EU. Similar energy disputes have at times threatened to disrupt the flow of Russian gas and oil through Belarus.[8]

In the late 1990s, strategists have started to think about Central Asian oil and gas resources as a supplementary energy supply for the EU, and the tapping of Caspian energy resources has since then found its way into various EU strategy papers and resolutions, including the Council's 2007 Central Asia Strategy.[9] Though Central Asia's energy potential has occasionally been overestimated, the region is nonetheless part of a 'strategic energy ellipse' reaching from the Persian Gulf to the Caspian Sea and Russia.[10] Three of the five Central Asian states have significant energy reserves:[11] Kazakhstan has by far the largest reserves: it ranks in the global 10 of countries for oil reserves and in the top 15 of countries for gas reserves. Turkmenistan has huge unexplored gas reserves that rank in the global five. Uzbekistan enjoys self-sufficiency in energy and is a significant gas producer but uses most of its resources for domestic demand. On the other side, the Kyrgyz Republic and Tajikistan have significant hydropower resources but desperately need oil and gas imports. Due to the Soviet legacy of rapid development of oil and gas fields in some parts of the region – most notably in Uzbekistan – energy resources are nearly exhausted, in other parts – mainly in Kazakhstan and Turkmenistan – they are partly yet unexplored or underdeveloped. Furthermore, a relatively low degree of energy efficiency, the excessive style of energy consumption and the low degree of renewable energy production are a heritage of Soviet times that causes high levels of domestic resource consumption.[12]

---

8   Petersen, A. and Barysch, K. 2012. *Russia, China and the Geopolitics of Energy in Central Asia*. London: Centre for European Reform, 8.

9   Götz, R. 2011. Energy cooperation: The Southern gas transport corridor, in Warkotsch, A. (ed.), *The European Union and Central Asia*. Abingdon: Routledge, 148; and Council of the European Union 2007. *European Union and Central Asia: Strategy for a New Partnership*, 10113/07, Brussels, May.

10   According to Kemp and Harkavy, energy-rich Caspian countries, Turkey, Iran, the Arabian Peninsula, and Iraq create a 'strategic energy ellipse' with more than 70 per cent of global proven oil reserves. Kemp, G. and Harkavy, R. 1997. *Strategic Geography and the Changing Middle East*. Washington, DC: Brookings Institution Press.

11   See US Energy Information Administration country pages for exact figures of energy reserves, http://www.eia.gov/countries [accessed: 27 December 2013]; and Kemp and Harkavy, op. cit.

12   Götz, op. cit., 149.

Regardless of these uncertainties, since the late 1990s Europe has started to think of Central Asia as a potential 'additional filling station'. Since EU gas demand is likely to increase more sharply than oil demand, Turkmenistan is of particular interest to Europe. Turkmenistan produces roughly 70 billion cubic metres of natural gas every year. This equals about 20–25 per cent of total EU gas imports.[13] So far, however, about two-thirds of Turkmenistan's gas exports are sold to Russia's Gazprom monopoly on the basis of mid-and-long-term supply agreements. Interesting to note is that Turkmenistan has made efforts to break out of Russia's hold on its exports. It has opened gas pipelines to China and Iran, and has agreed to supply energy for the EU-backed Nabucco gas pipeline.[14] Uzbekistan holds a similar significant amount of natural gas (*c.*65 billion cubic metres). Most of these resources, however, are used for domestic consumption and by the year 2030 Uzbekistan is estimated to lose self-sufficiency in domestic gas consumption, making it a net importer of natural gas. With a current volume of about 8 billion cubic metres, Kazakhstan is not yet a significant exporter of natural gas. However, its importance as a natural gas exporter – according to estimates of the International Energy Agency – is likely to rise to about 35 billion cubic metres by 2030.[15] Still, factoring in Kazakh long-term supply agreements with Russia, China, Iran and other parts of the Commonwealth of Independent States (CIS), the only likely Central Asian source for significant gas exports to Europe is Turkmenistan. With only Turkmenistan contributing significantly to any gas transport towards the EU, additional gas from Azerbaijan will most likely have to ensure the necessary capacity utilization and economies of scale in order to make the EU's tapping of Caspian resources economically viable.

The EU's Central Asia Strategy in the Energy Sector

Given the EU's stated interest in Caspian energy, the question of the Union's strategy in tapping these resources arises. Under the heading 'Strengthening energy and transport links' the EU's Central Asia Strategy mentions several key elements for fostering EU-Central Asian cooperation in the energy and transportation field.[16] The Strategy starts by stating that 'the EU and Central Asia share a paramount interest in enhancing Energy Security as an important aspect of global security. There is a common interest in diversifying export routes, demand and supply structures and energy sources'.[17] The Strategy continues by stating that 'the EU ... is ready to consider all options for the development and transportation of these

---

13   European Commission 2010, op. cit., 31.

14   Much of this Turkmen export diversification effort is owed to differences of opinion with Russia over gas export prices.

15   Götz, op. cit., 155.

16   Council of the European Union 2007, op. cit.

17   Ibid.

resources, in co-operation with other interested partners'.[18] Interesting to note here is the non-confrontational approach of the EU by emphasizing cooperation over unilateral action. It remains unclear, however, whether the EU would eventually be willing to cooperate with Russia in linking the Caspian with the EU, as 'other interested partners' is not further specified. However, the pipeline routing currently promoted by the EU indicates a preference for circumventing Russian territory. The Strategy continues by stating that the 'development of resources in oil and gas has significantly increased the role of Central Asian states as energy producers and transit countries' and that 'increasing oil and gas exploitation will contribute to better world market supplies' which in turn 'will be conducive to diversification'.[19] The Strategy continues that because 'gas deliveries from the region are of special importance to the EU' a long-term partnership 'based on common interests and reciprocity' should be established over the years to come'.[20] In order to implement this agenda suggestions for concrete action include conducting an enhanced regular Energy Dialogue with Central Asian states and 'support[ing] the exploration of new oil, gas and hydro-power resources and the upgrading of the existing energy infrastructure' as well as 'the development of additional pipeline routes and energy transportation networks'.[21] Furthermore, the Strategy announces that the EU 'will lend political support and assistance to Central Asian countries in developing a new Caspian Sea-Black Sea-EU energy transport corridor' and attract 'investment towards energy projects of common and regional interest'.[22] Following the publication of the EU's Central Asia Strategy the European Commission has signed Memoranda of Understanding (MoUs) with Kazakhstan, Uzbekistan and Turkmenistan in which the Strategy's energy goals have been mutually agreed on.[23]

Since November 2008 Kazakhstan has been transporting oil through the 2005 opened and US-backed Baku–Tbilisi–Ceyhan (BTC) pipeline that bypasses Russia on its way to Europe.[24] The Kazakh oil shipments from the Tengiz field have been the first significant step toward connecting Central Asia's oil resources to Western markets. According to Azeri BTC officials, Kazakhstan is showing interest in also transporting oil from the recently developed Kashagan field through the BTC

18   Ibid.
19   Ibid.
20   Ibid.
21   Ibid.
22   Ibid.
23   For the MoUs see the Commission's web page on energy relations with the Caucasus and Central Asia, http://ec.europa.eu/energy/international/caucasus_central_asia_en.htm [accessed: 25 March 2013].
24   *Oil and Gas Journal* 2008. BP to Flow Kazakh Oil Through BTC Pipeline, http://www.ogj.com/articles/print/volume-106/issue-39/general-interest/bp-to-flow-kazakh-oil-through-btc-pipeline.html [accessed: 26 March 2013].

pipeline.[25] However, so far, most of Kazakhstan's oil currently is still transported via the Caspian Pipeline Consortium (CPC) pipeline that goes through Russian territory, skirting the Caspian Sea's northern shores. Since August 2010 Turkmen oil is shipped to Baku by tanker and then transported through the BTC pipeline to the Turkish port of Ceyhan. The capacity of the BTC pipeline is about 1.2m barrels of oil per day, and Turkmen oil accounts for about 4–5 per cent of this volume.[26] Next to Kazakh and Turkmen oil, the BTC pipeline is also transporting oil from the Azeri–Chirag–Guneshli (ACG) oil fields as well as oil and gas condensate from the Shah Deniz field in the Azerbaijani sector of the Caspian.[27]

The transportation of Central Asian gas towards Europe is lacking behind the recent progress that was made in the oil sector. This is first and foremost because a BTC gas equivalent is missing so far. The EU is currently supporting what it calls a 'Southern Gas Corridor' stretching from Azerbaijan to Turkey into the EU. The corridor aims at opening up Azeri gas as well as gas from Central Asia and the Middle East for the EU market. As far as the Caspian is concerned, gas pipelines will reach from Azerbaijan to Georgia into Turkey and the EU. There has been a lot of political bickering and economic uncertainty about the Southern Gas Corridor. However, in late June 2012 Azerbaijan and Turkey agreed on building a Trans-Anatolian Pipeline (TANAP) – a pipeline that reaches from the Georgian–Turkish to the Turkish–Bulgarian border where the 'European leg' of the pipeline starts.[28] It remains unclear if the pipeline corridor from Turkey to Europe will stretch through South-Eastern Europe or if it will cross the Adriatic Sea into Italy.[29] Two pipeline options are discussed by the British Petrol (BP)-led Shah Deniz consortium: first, 'Nabucco West', stretching from Turkey, Bulgaria, Romania, to Austria and, second, the 'Trans-Adriatic Pipeline' from Turkey to Greece, Albania and Italy.[30] With British Petrol committing its Shah Deniz resources to the EU's Southern Gas Corridor 10 billion cubic metres of Azerbaijani gas will eventually find its way to Europe by 2018.[31] Economic feasibility, however, is still not fully guaranteed as

25   *Trend News Agency* 2012. *Minister: Kazakhstan Interested in Transporting Oil via BTC*, http://en.trend.az/capital/energy/2091089.html [accessed: 26 March 2013].

26   British Petrol 2010. *BP in Georgia*, RFE/RL 2010, http://www.bpgeorgia.ge/go/doc/1339/150562 [accessed: 2 January 2014].

27   *News Az* 2013. *BTC Transports Over 6m Tonnes of Turkmen Oil*, http://www.news.az/articles/economy/76507 [accessed: 25 March 2013].

28   Atlantic Council 2012. *European Energy Security: Southern Gas Corridor on the Move*, http://www.acus.org/new_atlanticist/european-energy-security-southern-gas-corridor-move [accessed: 14 March 2013].

29   Ibid.

30   *Bloomberg* 2012. Nabucco Outbids SEEP for Shah Deniz Gas, http://www.bloomberg.com/news/2012–06–27/nabucco-outbids-seep-for-shah-deniz-gas-nefte-compass-reports.html [accessed: 19 October 2012].

31   *Turkish Weekly* 2012. Turkmen Gas: Through Caspian Sea to Europe, http://www.turkishweekly.net/news/141507/turkmen-gas-through-caspian-sea-to-europe.html [accessed: 15 October 2012].

it remains unclear to what extent Turkmen and Kazakh gas could be used for the gas corridor.

Since Kazakh and Turkmen resources will be key for ensuring the necessary economics of scale of any EU-supported pipeline infrastructure the interesting question that arises at this point (next to technical and market issues) is if the EU will be able to successfully compete with other major powers (in particular Russia and China) over these resources.

The Geopolitics of Energy Relations in the Caspian Region

The following section sketches the energy interests of the United States, Russia, China, Turkey and Iran and the way they use energy and corresponding infrastructure projects as an instrument of exerting geopolitical power in the region.

The United States

US interests in Central Asia and, more broadly, in the Caspian region are geo-strategic. From an energy perspective, Central Asian is of only limited importance to the US. The US does not need Caspian gas for its domestic supply, especially after the US is about to achieve self-sufficiency following its shale gas revolution. As regards oil, Caspian resources are perceived as a valuable addition to global supply, notably with the Middle East facing increased political instability.[32]

This, however, hardly means that the US is not involved in pipeline politics in the Caspian. Given that energy is such an important revenue-generating source in Kazakhstan, Turkmenistan and Uzbekistan and, therefore, a crucial factor for the economic development of these key Central Asian countries, the Clinton administration soon realized that Central Asia will not gain true independence as long as they are still dependent on Russian infrastructure for their energy export. As a result, in the 1990s, major US oil companies like Chevron or Exxon Mobil have, with the support of the US government, started strategic pipeline constructions that bypass Russia. A major example of US-promoted transport infrastructure is the before mentioned Baku–Tbilisi–Ceyhan oil pipeline. Next to US-led infrastructure projects, the US is also politically supporting EU energy initiatives like Nabucco. Strategically, the US and the EU share the goal of breaking Russia's firm grip on Central Asian energy infrastructure. However, slight differences of opinion exist with regard to the alternative pipeline routing as Washington tends to favour core allies such as Georgia and Turkey as transit countries at the expense of options of better economic viability. Naturally, the US and EU Member States also compete for lucrative business deals for their respective oil companies.[33]

---

32 Petersen and Barysch, op. cit., 32.

33 Warkotsch, A. 2011. The EU and Central Asian Geopolitics, in Warkotsch, A. (ed.), *The European Union and Central Asia*. Abingdon: Routledge, 68.

Especially with the terrorist attacks of 11 September 2001 and the rising threat of radical Islamism, the focus of US policy in Central Asia shifted away from energy towards the fight against international terrorism. Since the late 1990s the US has viewed Central Asia as a potential victim of radical, Taliban-ruled Afghanistan – a fear that was fuelled by regular insurgencies of the militant, Taliban-supported 'Islamic Movement of Uzbekistan' (IMU) into the Fergana valley. As a result, in the years following 9/11, the US has provided significant assistance to the Central Asian regimes to build up anti-terrorism, intelligence and law enforcement capabilities.

While for most part of the 1990s the US considered Central Asian energy in the context of fostering independence from Moscow by securing alternative infrastructure linkage to Western markets, the issue of energy after 9/11 became important as a means of consolidating Central Asian regimes and shield them from domestic radical Islamism. According to Jaffe and Soligo:

> post-September-11 strategic considerations and concerns about the rise of terrorism and Islamic fundamentalism in the Caspian region have had serious implications for the importance of Caspian energy resources in US thinking. No longer just a means of diversification ... the Caspian energy resources became critical for the economic health (and thereby counter-terrorism potential) of the states of the region ... Thus, in one fell swoop, US interests in the resource development and export routes of Caspian Basin petroleum were linked to US strategic concerns about terrorism.[34]

Much assistance has been granted not only to fight terrorism but also to ensure cooperation of Central Asian rulers as their countries became a major logistic hub for US and NATO forces in Afghanistan.[35] Almost from the very beginning, the Kremlin had tried to undermine this cooperation. In 2009, for example, Russia attempted to convince Kyrgyzstan to close the US-run Manas airbase by offering the country hundreds of millions of dollars in grants and loans. Knowing that they have become essential for NATO operations and also being aware of Russia's dislike of having Western troops stationed in its own backyard, many Central

---

34   Jaffe, A.M. and Soligo, R. 2004. Re-evaluating US Strategic Priorities in the Caspian Region: Balancing Energy Resource Initiatives with Terrorism Containment. *Cambridge Review of International Affairs*, 17(2), 261.

35   Nichol, J. 2012. *Central Asia: Regional Developments and Implications for U.S. Interests*. Congressional Research Service Report (RL 33458), Washington, DC, 7, http://www.fas.org/sgp/crs/row/RL33458.pdf [accessed: 15 March 2013]. In fiscal year 2000 total US assistance for Central Asia was at $220 million. Since 9/11 budget allocations for the region have doubled. For example, the fiscal year 2010 has seen an allocation of $436 million (ibid., 62).

Asian regimes have started a 'cat-and-mouse' game, trying to play off the US and Russian governments against each other for their own benefit.[36]

Russia

From Russia's point of view, the Central Asian republics (and the Caspian region in general) should and would naturally fall in its own sphere of influence; a region in which Moscow has traditionally enjoyed considerable political and economic leverage over the past centuries. Russia has sought to maintain its influence by bilateral economic and security cooperation and through integrating Central Asia into various Russia-led regional organizations, in particular the CIS, the Collective Security Treaty Organization, and the Eurasian Customs Union. Central Asian regimes have responded to such initiatives with varying degrees of enthusiasm.[37] Mostly as a reaction to Russian hegemonic ambitions, many countries in the region pursue what they call a 'multi-vector' foreign policy, a strategy that seeks to further national interests by balancing Russian, Chinese and Western influence.

Energy has been an important part of Russia's effort to maintain political control over the region. Such control, however, is not only satisfying Russia's legacy as the dominant political power in the region, there are also important economic interests involved. First, Russia is eager to secure the Caspian as a source of cheap energy assets in order to keep its energy holdings internationally competitive. Second, when Russia signed the EU-Russian energy dialogue in October 2000, the EU was hoping for securing long-term access to Russian oil and gas.[38] In particular due to rising domestic consumption, Russia's energy consortia need Central Asian resources to satisfy the EU's energy needs. Third, and most importantly, Russia is eager to prevent Caspian producers from concluding contracts directly with European customers, thereby safeguarding Russia's dominant position on the EU's energy import market. For example, Russia is trying to undermine the construction of the Nabucco pipeline by supporting the financially less viable South Stream pipeline. It also obstructed the construction of the trans-Caspian gas link, which would have allowed Turkmen gas to flow

---

36 The West has, however, not only increased its funding. Many NATO members find themselves now also in the middle of difficult balancing acts between ensuring Central Asian cooperation while at the same time not turning two blind eyes on authoritarianism and human rights violations in the region.

37 Petersen and Barysch, op. cit., 27.

38 Grant, C. and Barysch K. 2003. The EU-Russian Energy Dialogue. *Centre for European Reform Briefing Note*, London: Centre for European Reform, 1, http://www.cer. org.uk/sites/default/files/publications/attachments/pdf/2011/briefing_eu_russia-3858.pdf [accessed: 15 December 2013].

directly into the Southern Gas Corridor.[39] Furthermore, in 2010 Russia offered to buy the entire gas output of Azerbaijan[40] – the most likely source of early gas for the EU-promoted Southern corridor – and promised Turkmenistan to buy up to 30 million cubic metres of gas annually. This is far in excess of what Russia could have absorbed in its own market environment. Many of these offers are therefore likely to have just been aimed at keeping European consortia away from Caspian resources and avoid the construction of further East–West pipeline infrastructures.[41] In this regard, Chow and Hendrix point out that '[t]he Russian attitude seems to be, if Central Asian gas is to be exported by a route other than Russia, it is better for the gas to go east than west, where it would compete against Russian gas in its primary European market'.[42] Building on this logic, a Gazprom subsidiary, for example, built the Turkmen stretch of the Central Asia-China gas pipeline which runs from Turkmenistan through Uzbekistan and Kazakhstan to China. This, however, should not obscure the fact that Russia is also concerned over China's growing economic and strategic importance and that there are fears to be marginalized by the rivalry between the two superpowers China and the US. The so far rather rudimentary energy cooperation between Russia and China will therefore hardly blossom in the near future as Russia fears to become an accessory of China's rise by supplying much needed raw materials to China's economy.[43]

China

After the dissolution of the Soviet Union, border demarcation was at the centre of Chinese-Central Asian relations. From the mid -1990s on attention then moved towards energy, containing separatist pressure in China's Muslim province Xinjiang, and global power considerations.[44] As regards energy relations, Chinese interests are twofold: first, it hopes to improve its energy security, thereby safeguarding essential economic growth. What makes Caspian energy especially attractive to China is that it helps reduce the geopolitical vulnerabilities of relying

---

39   *Asia Times Online* 2011. Moscow issues trans-Caspian project warning, 2 December [accessed: 11 October 2012].

40   *RIA Novosti* 2010. Russia's Gazprom ready to buy all Azerbaijan's gas, 19 June, http://en.rian.ru/exsoviet/20100619/159493755.html [accessed: 25 March 2013].

41   Petersen and Barysch, op. cit., 30.

42   Chow, E. and Leigh, H. 2010. *Central Asia's Pipelines: Fields of Dreams and Reality. NBR Special Report*, no. 25, 38, http://csis.org/files/publication/1009_EChow_LHendrix_CentralAsia.pdf [accessed: 25 March 2013].

43   Blank, S. 2006. *Russo-Chinese Energy Relations: Politics in Command.* IAGS Report, London; and Petersen and Barysch, op. cit., 14.

44   As far as great power rivalry is concerned, China is first and foremost concerned about US and NATO involvement in direct proximity to its western border. Interestingly enough, at the same time it also seems to worry about re-surging Islamist extremism in the Afghan–Central Asian region after NATO combat troops will have left post-2014.

on sea-borne energy imports across international waters dominated by the United States.[45] Second, China aims at turning its poverty-stricken province of Xinjiang into an important energy hub for the import and transit of Central Asian energy, thereby starving Uyghur separatists from new recruits by offering better living conditions for the region's impoverished population.

Interesting to note is that China's enormous demand for energy resources should have driven it into forging a strategic energy partnership with Russia. But Beijing is aware that Russian energy policy towards China is largely driven by geo-strategic considerations and therefore difficult to predict and build on.[46] Furthermore, from a Chinese perspective it may also be easier to deal with smaller, less powerful Central Asian states than with Russia that is still hooked on its former great power status.[47]

While the EU is following a 'market-based approach'[48] with only limited political involvement in actual pipeline and energy deals, China is favouring government-to-government contacts with its state-owned China National Petroleum Corporation (CNPC) acting as a key player in brokering energy deals in the region. So far, the CNPC has been quite successful in securing some important energy deals. Most importantly, the CNPC became the first foreign company to be allowed to exploit Turkmen onshore gas resources. China is also building the Central Asia–China Gas Pipeline (CAGP) that stretches over 1,800 kilometres from Turkmenistan through Uzbekistan and Kazakhstan to Western China. The CAGP has been the first and so far only big gas pipeline that broke up Russia's monopoly over Eurasian gas transport. The CAGP will be achieving a capacity of 40 billion cm per year which equals about one-third of China's total gas demand.[49] This, however, should not obscure the fact that the level of China's involvement in Caspian energy affairs significantly lacks behind Western companies. Estimates by the International Energy Agency are that in 2009 the share of Chinese companies in total Caspian oil and gas production was around only 7 per cent, compared to about 38 per cent for private international (mostly Western) companies.[50]

---

45   Peyrouse, S. 2009. Central Asia's Growing Partnership with Central Asia. *EUCAM Working Paper*, no. 4, Madrid: FRIDE, 8, http://www.fride.org/download/EUCAM_WP4_ Central_Asia.pdf [accessed: 26 March 2013].

46   Petersen and Barysch, op. cit., 40.

47   Ibid.

48   Council of the European Union 2007, op. cit., 22.

49   *Asia Times Online* 2011. China's Gas Imports Jump, 24 June, http://atimes. com/atimes/China-Business/MF24Cb01.html [accessed: 16 October 2012]; *China Daily* 2011. Natural Gas Consumption to Increase, 21 January, http://www.chinadaily.com.cn/ bizchina/2011–01/21/content_11893444.htm [accessed: 4 June 2011]; and Petersen and Barysch, op. cit., 40.

50   Petersen and Barysch, op. cit., 43.

Turkey

After the break-up of the Soviet Union, Turkey had high hopes for its relations with Central Asia. Building on the idea of pan-Turkism, Ankara envisioned something like a Turkish Commonwealth comprising Azerbaijan, Georgia and the five Central Asian republics with Turkey as the lead nation. The idea of pan-Turkism – which was encouraged by the United States to contain Russian and Iranian influence in the region – builds on the common cultural heritage between Turkey and the Caspian region (in particular ethnic, religious, historical and linguistic bonds). These ambitions, however, did not fall on fruitful ground in Central Asia. It quickly became obvious that Turkey lacked the financial and economic power to function as a centre of political and economic gravitation for the newly established republics. Moreover, the latter also quickly became sceptical of trading their old hegemon (Russia) for a potential new one (Turkey) whose model of market economy and democracy never became a very appealing option for the heavy-handed regimes of Central Asia.[51] By the mid-1990s Turkey slowly but steadily buried its high hopes for Central Asia and started to turn towards a more realistic policy approach. At the core of this new approach has been energy, in particular improving energy security and generating revenue from energy transit fees. The World Bank estimated Turkey's net energy imports in 2012 to be at 71 per cent.[52] Import dependency for gas is especially high and the International Energy Agency estimates it to be around 98 per cent of Turkey's gas needs.[53] Similar to the other external actors in the region, Turkey is therefore eager to increase Turkmen and Kazakh gas imports as a nearby source for domestic energy consumption.

Furthermore, Turkey is looking towards Caspian energy as a significant generator of transit fees. Turkey is already an important hub for exporting Caspian oil and gas. The International Finance Corporation, the private sector branch of the World Bank group, estimated in 2009 that Turkey received up to $1.5 billion in transit fees from the Baku–Tbilisi–Ceyhanoil pipeline.[54] With projects like 'Nabucco West' and the Trans-Adriatic Pipeline, income from transit fees will rise significantly. It is therefore hardly surprising that Turkey is heavily lobbying for its territory to function as the central hub for European energy imports from the Caspian basin. In this context it is interesting to note that with the realization of

---

51   Warkotsch 2011, op. cit., 68.

52   World Bank 2013. *Energy imports*, database, http://data.worldbank.org/indicator/EG.IMP.CONS.ZS [accessed: 14 March 2013].

53   International Energy Agency 2009. *Energy Policies of IEA Countries*, 67, http://www.iea.org/publications/freepublications/publication/turkey2009.pdf   [accessed: 15 March 2013].

54   International Finance Corporation 2009. *Baku-Tbilisi-Ceyhan Oil Pipeline Project* (Media Briefing), http://www.ifc.org/ifcext/btc.nsf/Content/MediaBriefing [accessed: 9 November 2009].

Nabucco and similar energy projects, Ankara might generate itself an important additional bargaining chip for its quest to eventually join the European Union.

Iran

During the 1990s Turkey and Iran shared a similar ambition towards the Central Asian region. Like Turkey, also Iran tried to establish itself as an important point of economic, political and cultural reference for Central Asian policy-makers. Soon after the break-up of the Soviet Union, Iran launched a comprehensive and religiously motivated effort of cultural diplomacy.[55] This included, for example, the opening of Persian language satellite stations to broadcast Iranian TV and radio throughout Central Asia, government-sponsored missionary activities of Shia Islam (including the opening of mosques and education programmes for mullahs in Iranian *madrasas*) as well as the opening of schools and teacher training programmes. Former Iranian Foreign Minister Abbas Maleki described this phase of Iranian–Central Asian relations as a period of 'initial euphoria'.[56] However, it soon became clear that Iran, like Turkey, did not possess the necessary means to successfully counter the still predominant Russian influence of that time. Next to the lack of necessary financial and economic power, Iran's Shia Islam suffered from the fact that Tehran's euphoria was not reciprocated by the mainly Sunni Central Asian republics.[57] By the mid-1990s Iran's objectives in Central Asia changed from a mainly religious focus to becoming exclusively secular in nature, concentrating on 'enhancing regional stability, discouraging unfriendly penetration, developing neighbourly relations and economic co-operation and maintaining good relations with Russia'.[58] The core of this set of objectives undoubtedly is targeted at containing US influence in the region – especially since 11 September 2001 when Tehran has started to increasingly feel encircled by the US military presence in Central Asia, Afghanistan and Iraq.[59]

---

55   Jalali, Ali A. 1999. Islam as a Political Force in Central Asia: Iranian Influence. *Central Asia Monitor*, 7(2), 1–7.

56   Maleki, A. 1993. *Teheran Times*, 22 February, 4.

57   A member of the Turkmen Foreign Office stated in that regard: 'The Turkmen have never really been strong Muslims. We are nomads. I do not think we will ever become like the Iranians ... We need Iran to get our goods to the sea and for trade ... But we certainly do not want to be an Islamic State'. Quoted in Menashri, D. 1998. Iran and Central Asia: Radical Regime, Pragmatic Politics, in Menashri, D. (ed.), *Central Asia Meets the Middle East*. London: Frank Cass, 90.

58   Herzig, E. 1995. *Iran and the Former Soviet South*. London: Royal Institute of International Affairs, 65.

59   Kozahnov, N. 2012. Iran Struggles Unsuccessfully for Influence in Central Asia. *Washington Institute Policy Watch*, no. 1976, http://www.washingtoninstitute.org/policy-analysis/view/iran-struggles-unsuccessfully-for-influence-in-central-asia [accessed: 8 March 2013].

The US-Iranian enmity is key to Iran's almost total isolation in Caspian energy deals. Aside from some recent small- and medium-scale Turkmen–Iranian gas pipeline projects that brought Turkmen annual gas deliveries to Iran to 20 billion cubic metres, Tehran does hardly play a noteworthy role in the Caspian energy game. Contrary to the US, the European Union has never been categorically at odds with the idea to use Iran as a possible energy export route for Caspian oil and gas.[60] With infrastructure programmes like TRACEA (Transport Corridor Europe Caucasus Asia) and INOGATE (Interstate Oil and Gas Transport to Europe), the EU has even actively been helping to facilitate inter-regional links between Central Asia and Iran. However, it goes without saying that political frictions revolving around Iran's nuclear ambitions and its anti-Western posture in Middle East politics make the EU refrain from pushing for a more prominent role for Iran in the export of Caspian energy.[61] Still, even Tehran's most outspoken critics would have to admit that Iran's geographical location makes it a natural energy bridge for the export of Caspian oil and gas. This is even more true if Iran's comparatively high degree of political stability, its huge potential of skilled labour and its significant experience in the oil and gas industry are factored in.

Conclusion: EU Policy and Institutional Handicaps in Securing Caspian Energy Resources

The aim of this chapter was to shed light on the chances of the EU to successfully secure itself a stake in the oil and gas resources of the Central Asian region against the background of the interests of other external players in the region. The analysis has shown that the EU faces three types of co-players in its struggle for Caspian energy resources: the first category is made of the second-tier powers Turkey and Iran. Both used to have greater political and economic ambitions towards the region during the 1990s. The lack of sufficient financial means and power projection capabilities, however, shattered those hopes. In comparison to major players like Russia, China or the United States, they almost exclusively draw influence from their (potential) importance as a transportation hub for Central Asian energy and other export goods. Given that the EU is already actively supporting current and future energy export infrastructure that uses Turkish territory as a main transit route, the EU and Turkey can undoubtedly be considered strategic partners in the 'New Great Game'. As regards Iran, the EU is at least – and contrary to the US – not fully at odds with the mid-and-long-term idea of using Iran as a further possible export route for Caspian energy. Furthermore, from Tehran's perspective, a more prominent role of the EU in Central Asia is likely to balance US power in

---

60   *BBC News* 2010. Turkmenistan opens new Iran gas pipeline, 6 January, http://news.bbc.co.uk/2/hi/asia-pacific/8443787.stm [accessed: 28 March 2013].

61   See also Chapter 7 by Clément Therme in this volume.

the region. It is therefore improbable that increased EU engagement in the energy sector will meet with opposition from in Iran.

As far as the United States as a global player are concerned, interests in the field of Central Asian energy export are also largely in line with those of the EU. Washington considers Caspian resources a valuable addition to global supply but has no interest in tapping specifically these resources for satisfying domestic energy demand. It is to be expected that the US and the EU Member States continue to compete for lucrative business deals for their respective oil companies. However, given that the EU is following its 'market based approach to investment and procurement and transparent',[62] major frictions over bidding decisions are unlikely.

The main obstacles regarding the EU's tapping of Caspian energy resources derive from the third category of co-players, the EU's geo-economic rivals Russia and China due to both countries having shown a history of heavy lobbying against EU-supported export infrastructure. In the case of Russia, this is first and foremost because preserving a monopoly over the region's oil and gas (export) infrastructure is an important means of also maintaining political control over its traditional southern backyard. For China energy security is desperately needed for sustaining the necessary economic growth to ensure social stability and, finally, regime legitimacy.

So far, the amount of Central Asian energy committed to the EU market is lacking the necessary volume to ensure the economic viability of EU-supported pipeline projects. The crucial question therefore is whether local leaders will be willing to withstand Russian and Chinese business proposals and instead conclude long-term supply agreements with European partners.

It is hard to foresee to what extent the further tying of Central Asian resources to the EU can be achieved. However, what can be said is that there are certain factors at work that both work in favour and against the EU. Among the factors that work in Brussels' favour are, first, the EU's lack of geopolitical ambitions. Russia still considers Central Asia as its natural sphere of influence and tends to use its military, political and economic power to preserve a pre-eminent position in the region, including muscling its way into energy development projects. Central Asia had for centuries been under the control of Tsarist and Soviet rulers. The appeal of substituting this control now with Russian hegemony is limited. Most of the region's regimes therefore favour what they call a 'multi-vector' foreign policy that is balancing off various foreign influences against each other. In contrast to Russia, the EU is following a civilian approach with policies that are targeted at fostering the region's independence instead of exerting hegemonic control. From a Central Asian perspective, the EU is therefore well-suited to function as an important agent for fostering Central Asian autonomy and may also function as a balancer to Russian (and Chinese) influence. Second, Russian and Chinese energy companies are state-owned. Doing business with these companies usually involves the political

---

62   Council of the European Union 2007, op. cit., 22.

meddling of Moscow and Beijing into energy deals. In the EU, however, where private companies are in the lead of energy procurement, the risk of facing similar 'political pressure' is comparatively low. On the other hand, the EU is also facing certain obstacles that might work against the EU and its chances of successfully tapping significant parts of the region's energy resources:[63] first, working procedures of the EU's multi-level system of governance are difficult to understand and often come along with cacophonic and lengthy decision-making.[64] From a Central Asian perspective, it may be less confusing to deal with (semi-)authoritarian nation states like Russia or China and their fast and single-voiced decision-making. Second, Western demands of compliance with democracy and human rights standards upset Central Asian governments and complicate business negotiations.[65] Due to the non-democratic nature of political systems in Russia and China, Central Asian rulers can be sure that similar demands will not be voiced in Moscow or Beijing. Third, energy agreements in the region often come along as package deals that involve cooperation in the field of security (for example, military training schemes, arms deliveries, intelligence sharing). This is something Central Asian regimes are – for reasons of regime stability – particularly interested in and which the EU, due to its nature of still being largely a civilian power,[66] is offering only to a small extent through its Border Management Programme (BOMCA).[67]

---

63   Müller-Brandeck-Bocquet, G. 2000. Die Mehrdimensionalität der EU-Außenbeziehungen, in: Schubert, K. and Müller-Brandeck-Bocquet, G. (eds), *Die Europäische Union als Akteur in der Weltpolitik.* Opladen: Leske und Budrich, 29–44; and Jünemann, A. 2000. Auswärtige Politikgestaltung im EU-Mehrebenensystem. Eine Analyse der strukturellen Probleme am Beispiel der Euro-Mediterranen Partnerschaft, in Schubert, K. and Müller-Brandeck-Bocquet, G. (eds), *Die Europäische Union als Akteur in der Weltpolitik.* Opladen: Leske und Budrich, 65–80.

64   The various players in the EU's system of governance often pursue different political emphases in their dealings with international partners. The European Parliament, for example, is mainly concerned about the promotion of democracy and human rights while the Council's agenda tends to be preoccupied with security concerns. The Commission in turn seems to be first and foremost interested in facilitating trade and investment. Köhler, M. 1998. La Politique Méditerranéenne: Suivi de la conférence de Barcelone. European Parliament Research Service (unpublished working paper), 24, quoted in Jünemann, op. cit., 78.

65   Bohr, A. 2010. Central Asia: Responding to the Multi-Vectoring Game, in Niblett, R. (ed.), *America and a Changed World: A Question of Leadership.* London: Wiley-Blackwell/Chatham House, 116.

66   Dûchene, F. 1973. The European Community and the Uncertainties of Interdependence, in Kohnstamm, M. and Hager, W. (eds), *A Nation Writ Large? Foreign Policy Problems before the European Community.* London: Macmillan, 1–21; and Whitman, R. 1998. *From Civilian Power to Superpower? The International Identity of the European Union.* Basingstoke: Palgrave.

67   MacFarlane, N. 2003. International organisations in central Asia: Understanding the limits. *Helsinki Monitor*, 14(3), 287–99; Warkotsch 2011, op. cit.; and Warkotsch, A. 2006. *Die Zentralasienpolitik der Europäischen Union.* Frankfurt: Peter Lang, 155, 177.

Bibliography

Asia Times Online 2011. Moscow Issues Trans-Caspian Project Warning, 2 December, http://www.atimes.com/atimes/Central_Asia/ML02Ag01.html [accessed: 11 October 2012].

Asia Times Online 2011. China's Gas Imports Jump, 24 June, http://atimes.com/atimes/China_Business/MF24Cb01.html [accessed: 16 October 2012].

Atlantic Council 2012. *European Energy Security: Southern Gas Corridor on the Move*, http://www.acus.org/new_atlanticist/european-energy-security-southern-gas-corridor-move [accessed: 14 March 2013].

BBC News 2010. Turkmenistan Opens New Iran Gas Pipeline, 6 January, http://news.bbc.co.uk/2/hi/asia-pacific/8443787.stm [accessed: 28 March 2013].

Blank, S. 2006. *Russo-Chinese Energy Relations: Politics in Command.* IAGS Report, London.

Bloomberg 2012. Nabucco Outbids SEEP for Shah Deniz Gas, http://www.bloomberg.com/news/2012–06–27/nabucco-outbids-seep-for-shah-deniz-gas-nefte-compass-reports.html [accessed: 19 October 2012].

Bohr, A. 2010. Central Asia: Responding to the Multi-Vectoring Game, in Niblett, R. (ed.), *America and a Changed World: A Question of Leadership.* London: Wiley-Blackwell/Chatham House, 109–24.

British Petrol 2010. *BP in Georgia*, RFE/RL 2010, http://www.bpgeorgia.ge/go/doc/1339/150562 [accessed: 2 January 2014].

China Daily 2011. Natural Gas Consumption to Increase, 21 January, http://www.chinadaily.com.cn/bizchina/2011-01/21/content_11893444.htm [accessed: 04 June 2011].

Chow, E. and Leigh, H. 2010. *Central Asia's Pipelines: Fields of Dreams and Reality. NBR Special Report*, no. 25, http://csis.org/files/publication/1009_EChow_LHendrix-CentralAsia.pdf [accessed: 25 March 2013].

Council of the European Union 2007. *European Union and Central Asia: Strategy for a New Partnership*, 10113/07, Brussels, May.

Dûchene, F. 1973. The European Community and the uncertainties of interdependence, in Kohnstamm, M. and Hager, W. (eds), *A Nation Writ Large? Foreign Policy Problems before the European Community.* London: Macmillan, 1–21.

Edwards, M. 2003. The New Great Game and the New Great Gamers: Disciples of Kipling and Mackinder. *Central Asian Survey*, 22(1), 83–102.

European Commission 2008. *Europe's energy position: Past and present*, http://ec.europa.eu/energy/publications/doc/2008_moe_maquette.pdf [accessed: 8 March 2013].

European Commission 2010. *EU Energy and Transport in Figures.* Statistical Pocketbook. Brussels: Publications Office of the European Union.

European Commission 2011. Directorate General for Energy, *Key figures*, http://ec.europa.eu/energy/observatory/countries/doc/key_figures.pdf [accessed: 27 February 2013].

Götz, R. 2011. Energy cooperation: The Southern gas transport corridor, in Warkotsch, A. (ed.), *The European Union and Central Asia*. Abingdon: Routledge, 148–62.

Grant, C. and Barysch K. 2003. The EU-Russian Energy Dialogue, *Centre for European Reform Briefing Note*, London: Centre for European Reform, http://www.cer.org.uk/sites/default/files/publications/attachments/pdf/2011/briefing-eu-russia-3858.pdf [accessed: 15 December 2013].

Herzig, E. 1995. *Iran and the Former Soviet South*. London: Royal Institute of International Affairs.

International Energy Agency 2009. *Energy Policies of IEA Countries*, http://www.iea.org/publications/freepublications/publication/turkey2009.pdf [accessed: 15 March 2013].

International Finance Corporation 2009. *Baku-Tbilisi-Ceyhan Oil Pipeline Project* (Media Briefing), http://www.ifc.org/ifcext/btc.nsf/Content/MediaBriefing [accessed: 9 November 2009].

Jaffe, A.M. and Soligo, R. 2004. Re-evaluating US Strategic Priorities in the Caspian Region: Balancing Energy Resource Initiatives with Terrorism Containment. *Cambridge Review of International Affairs*, 17(2), 255–68.

Jalali, Ali A. 1999. Islam as a Political Force in Central Asia: Iranian Influence. *Central Asia Monitor*, 7(2), 1–7.

Jünemann, A. 2000. Auswärtige Politikgestaltung im EU-Mehrebenensystem. Eine Analyse der strukturellen Probleme am Beispiel der Euro-Mediterranen Partnerschaft, in Schubert, K. and Müller-Brandeck-Bocquet, G. (eds), *Die Europäische Union als Akteur in der Weltpolitik*. Opladen: Leske und Budrich, 65–80.

Kemp, G. and Harkavy, R. 1997. *Strategic Geography and the Changing Middle East*. Washington, DC: Brookings Institution Press.

Kozahnov, N. 2012. Iran Struggles Unsuccessfully for Influence in Central Asia. *Washington Institute Policy Watch*, no 1976, http://www.washingtoninstitute.org/policy-analysis/view/iran-struggles-unsuccessfully-for-influence-in-central-asia [accessed: 8 March 2013].

MacFarlane, N. 2003. International Organisations in Central Asia: Understanding the Limits. *Helsinki Monitor*, 14(3), 287–99.

Maleki, A. 1993. *Teheran Times*, 22 February, 4.

Manning, R.E. 2000. The Myth of the Caspian Great Game and the New Persian Gulf. *Survival*, 7(2), 15–33.

Menashri, D. 1998. Iran and Central Asia: Radical Regime, Pragmatic Politics, in Menashri, D. (ed.), *Central Asia Meets the Middle East*. London: Frank Cass, 73–97.

Müller-Brandeck-Bocquet, G. 2000. Die Mehrdimensionalität der EU-Außenbeziehungen, in: Schubert, K. and Müller-Brandeck-Bocquet, G. (eds), *Die Europäische Union als Akteur in der Weltpolitik*. Opladen: Leske und Budrich, 29–44.

News Az 2013. *BTC Transports Over 6m Tonnes of Turkmen Oil*, http://www.news.az/articles/economy/76507 [accessed: 25 March 2013].

Nichol, J. 2012. *Central Asia: Regional Developments and Implications for U.S. Interests*. Congressional Research Service Report (RL 33458), Washington, DC, http://www.fas.org/sgp/crs/row/RL33458.pdf [accessed: 15 March 2013].

Oil and Gas Journal 2008. BP to Flow Kazakh Oil through BTC Pipeline, http://www.ogj.com/articles/print/volume-106/issue-39/general-interest/bp-to-flow-kazakh-oil-through-btc-pipeline.html [accessed: 26 March 2013].

Petersen, A. and Barysch, K. 2012. *Russia, China and the Geopolitics of Energy in Central Asia*. London: Centre for European Reform.

Peyrouse, S. 2009. Central Asia's Growing Partnership with Central Asia. *EUCAM Working Paper*, no. 4, Madrid: FRIDE, http://www.fride.org/download/EUCAM_WP4_Central_Asia.pdf [accessed: 26 March 2013].

RFE/RL. 2010. *Turkmen Oil Starts Flowing through BTC Pipeline*, http://www.rferl.org/content/Turkmen_Oil_Starts_Flowing_Through_BTC_Pipeline/2126224.html [accessed: 25 March 2013].

RIA Novosti 2010. Russia's Gazprom ready to buy all Azerbaijan's gas, 19 June, http://en.rian.ru/exsoviet/20100619/159493755.html [accessed: 25 March 2013].

Trend News Agency 2012. Minister: Kazakhstan Interested in Transporting Oil via BTC, http://en.trend.az/capital/energy/2091089.html [accessed: 26 March 2013].

Turkish Weekly 2012. Turkmen Gas: Through Caspian Sea to Europe, http://www.turkishweekly.net/news/141507/turkmen-gas-through-caspian-sea-to-europe.html [accessed: 15 October 2012].

Warkotsch, A. 2006. *Die Zentralasienpolitik der Europäischen Union*. Frankfurt: Peter Lang.

Warkotsch, A. 2011. The EU and Central Asian Geopolitics, in Warkotsch, A. (ed.), *The European Union and Central Asia*. Abingdon: Routledge, 63–73.

Whitman, R. 1998. *From Civilian Power to Superpower? The International Identity of the European Union*. Basingstoke: Palgrave.

World Bank 2013. *Energy imports*, database, http://data.worldbank.org/indicator/EG.IMP.CONS.ZS [accessed: 14 March 2013].

PART IV
Diplomatic Dimensions beyond the ENP: Lessons for EU Diplomacy

Chapter 10

The European Neighbourhood Policy:
A Suitable Case for Treatment

Michael Leigh

Introduction

Ten years ago the European Union (EU) launched its 'wider Europe' policy, which later became the European Neighbourhood Policy (ENP).[1] This chapter looks at the lessons that can be drawn from a decade's experience with these initiatives and their implications for the EU's relations with countries further afield. It examines the origins of the ENP and the extent to which it fulfilled its initial goals. It considers how recent political and economic developments in Eastern Europe, the Southern Caucasus, North Africa and the Levant affect the viability of the ENP. The chapter analyses the impact of events following the November 2013 Vilnius Summit on the ENP Eastern Partnership and its prospects. Finally, it draws some conclusions concerning the need for a lighter, more differentiated, more strategic approach to countries in the EU's immediate neighbourhood and beyond.

European Neighbourhood Policy Origins and Scope

The ENP was a response to the political changes which accompanied the fall of Communism and the EU's subsequent decision to extend membership to reforming countries in Central and Eastern Europe. The ENP expressed the EU's willingness to engage with countries in Eastern Europe, the Southern Caucasus, North Africa and the Eastern Mediterranean on the basis of close association rather than membership. Nonetheless, the proposed form of engagement drew heavily on the enlargement model, a type of 'enlargement-lite'. It is, therefore, worth recalling the main features of the enlargement experience which influenced the ENP.

EU enlargement has been widely seen as the EU's most effective external policy and one of the EU's main historical accomplishments. Indeed, it is both an external and an internal policy as it involves the extension of the EU's laws

---

1 European Commission 2003. Communication from the Commission to the Council and the European Parliament, *Wider Europe – Neighbourhood: A New Framework for Relations with our Eastern and Southern Neighbours*, COM(2003) 104 final, Brussels, 11 March.

and rules to a new set of countries and their eventual assumption of the rights and obligations of membership. The principal credit for the peaceful manner in which half the European continent shifted from autocracy and state control of the economy to democracy and market-based systems accrues to the peoples directly concerned and their leaders. The goal of EU membership encouraged them to accept far-reaching reforms, despite the heavy short-term costs, and provided a blueprint for the adoption of new political, economic and legal processes.

Accession preparations and accompanying aid programmes, surveillance and 'conditionality' steered the countries concerned towards the necessary reforms. Most of the countries which joined the EU in 2004 have done well in shifting to new standards in public life. But there has also been backsliding with respect to fundamental freedoms, as well as fall-out from the EU's economic and financial crisis. In several countries, the profound and lasting adoption of liberal democracy looks like the work of a generation.

With the 2004 enlargement of the EU from 15 to 25 members on the horizon, EU policy makers decided to send a strong message of continued engagement to countries bordering the enlarged European Union. There had been considerable local cross-border trade between Ukraine on the one side and Poland, Hungary and Slovakia on the other before their accession to the EU. There were fears in Ukraine and in Moldova that enlargement would bring down the barriers, trapping them on the wrong side of a newly impermeable frontier. Similar considerations applied to Belarus, which had close links with Lithuania and Poland. However, the overtly autocratic regime in Belarus precluded its effective inclusion in any new pan-European initiative.

Concerns about the response to enlargement in 'wider Europe' were not entirely altruistic. EU policy makers saw a risk of political and economic instability in Eastern Europe. This could spill over into the EU itself, bringing criminality, corruption, trafficking, smuggling, and even political subversion. Failed states or dysfunctional democracies in the EU's immediate hinterland would be vulnerable to Russian pressures to return to the fold. Ukraine's importance as a transit country for energy added to these concerns. Political leaders and diplomats from the new Member States in Central Europe saw Ukraine, especially, as a buffer zone keeping Russia at a safe distance.

In the rhetoric of the day, the general objective of the ENP was to create a ring of well-governed countries, or as often put, a 'ring of friends', around the enlarged EU.[2] The ENP's founding fathers envisaged a set of countries increasingly engaged with the EU and, therefore, less vulnerable to the different forms of instability mentioned above.

Another consideration prompting an EU initiative towards neighbouring countries was the possibility that they, too, might apply for membership. The EU treaties provide that any European country which shares the EU's values may

---

2   Council of the European Union 2003. *A Secure Europe in a Better World: European Security Strategy*, Brussels, 12 December, 7–8.

apply for membership. Leaders of most EU Member States had not prepared their citizens for the imminent accession of 10 new countries and 100 million new EU citizens. Many recoiled at the risk of another wave of applications from countries still further east. To stave off such a prospect, they seized upon the ENP as an alternative to membership.

This thinking echoed former European Commission President Jacques Delors's 1989 proposal to create a European Economic Space (later the European Economic Area – EEA) to deter European Free Trade Association (EFTA) countries from applying for EU membership.[3] In fact, Austria, Finland, Sweden and Norway did apply for membership and Switzerland rejected the EEA in a referendum. This left a rump EEA comprising the EU Member States, Iceland, Liechtenstein and Norway, following Norway's rejection of EU membership in a 1994 referendum. While circumstances and actors in the first decade of the twenty-first century were different, the EEA experience might have raised questions about the utility of proposing a 'second tier' category of participation in the internal market, as a deterrent to membership applications.

The ENP began as a modest initiative addressed mainly to Ukraine and Moldova but quickly morphed into a macro-framework covering practically all countries that bordered the EU to the east and the south. The ENP produced a new generation of Association Agreements, linked to Deep and Comprehensive Free Trade Areas (AA-DCFTA), which gave some traction to countries like Ukraine and Moldova in resisting absorption into a new post-Soviet bloc. This 'civilizational struggle' intensified in 2013, as Russian President Putin tried to bully Eastern European countries into joining a customs union with Russia, Belarus and Kazakhstan, the forerunner of the much wider 'Eurasian Union' which he envisaged for 2015. These developments are considered further below.

Eastern Europe did not figure prominently in the foreign policy preoccupations of Spain, Italy, Portugal, or Greece. A Spanish diplomat told the author that any mention of neighbours evoked 700 years of Al-Andalus for his countrymen. From a southern European perspective, a new neighbourhood policy had to include Morocco and other countries around the southern and eastern rim of the Mediterranean Sea.

The accession of Cyprus and Malta in 2004 projected the EU further into the Mediterranean and strengthened arguments for adding a southern dimension to the new neighbourhood policy. Risks related to political instability and terrorism as well as the trafficking of people, drugs and arms from North Africa and the Middle East matched or surpassed those coming from the east. The former colonial powers in southern Europe had strong traditional, political, energy and commercial ties with countries in North Africa and the Levant. Such considerations led the European Commission President of the time, the former Italian Prime Minister Romano Prodi, to advocate the inclusion of the southern and eastern rim of the

---

3   Delors, J. 1989. Statement on the Broad Lines of Commission Policy. *Bulletin of the European Communities*, Supplement no. 1, Strasbourg, 17 January, 5–19.

Mediterranean Sea in any new initiative. So the European Commission proposed a neighbourhood policy, the ENP, covering both Eastern Europe and the Southern and Eastern Mediterranean.[4] This reflected the EU's consensual approach to decision-making in which all Member States could find their interests reflected.

The ENP seemed to offer neighbouring countries an opportunity to embrace the European model of society, while stopping short of actual EU membership. However, many of these early hopes were disappointed because of failures to deliver by both sides and because of changed political circumstances. What had begun as an initiative designed to address specific challenges to the east, including the risk of premature membership applications, became a broader and more diffuse policy, covering countries that were not situated on the European continent and which, therefore, could not have an 'accession perspective'. Most of these countries had autocratic forms of government whose leaders showed no inclination to join the transition train.

To complicate matters further, three additional countries voiced their discontent at exclusion from the new initiative. Georgia, Armenia and Azerbaijan were not terrestrial neighbours of the enlarged EU. At a pinch, Georgia could be considered a maritime neighbour across the Black Sea, once Bulgaria and Romania joined the EU in 2007. Armenia would become a neighbour if Turkey, a candidate for membership since 1999, eventually joined the EU. Armenians and Georgians cherished their Christian heritage and considered themselves profoundly European. Georgia joined the Council of Europe in 1999; Armenia and Azerbaijan followed in 2001. The commitment of the regimes of these three countries to democracy, the rule of law and the protection of human rights was uneven, to say the least. The resulting diversity among ENP partner countries obscured the relatively clear objectives of the EU's original approach to 'wider Europe'.

Paradoxically, the Arab uprisings delivered the final blow to the ENP model in North Africa and the Levant. One EU Foreign Minister told the author in October 2013 that there was no chance that Mediterranean countries could implement AA-DCFTAs for decades. Dysfunctional democracy, state failure, persistent authoritarianism and civil war in North Africa and the Middle East called for a more robust response than the 'soft power' inherent in the ENP.

Thus the 'Eastern Partnership', introduced on the initiative of Poland and Sweden in 2008, effectively became the torch bearer of the ENP.[5] By a circuitous route, the ENP again came to focus in 2012–13 on countries like Ukraine, Georgia and Moldova, which were its original *raison d'être*.

The inspiration for the ENP was pragmatic, seeking to protect the interests of the EU and its Member States. But it also claimed to be based on 'shared values'. In fact, shared values were an aspiration rather than a reality in most partner

---

4 European Commission 2003, op. cit.

5 European Commission 2008. Communication from the Commission to the European Parliament and the Council, *Eastern Partnership*, COM(2008) 823/4, Brussels, 3 December.

countries. The gap between aspiration and reality proved to be one of the ENP's main deficiencies.

The Enlargement Method

The ways and means by which the ENP sought to achieve its objectives were inspired by the enlargement process. For each partner, the EU set out a series of reform objectives spanning democracy, the rule of law, human rights, economic liberalization, the adoption of certain EU laws and standards and 'capacity building' to ensure that the reforms were properly implemented. The EU undertook to monitor progress in implementing the reforms through annual progress reports, modelled on those for enlargement countries.

In exchange for progress registered, the EU promised to give the partner country a 'stake' in the EU's internal market, to bring it into various EU regulatory bodies, to step up financial assistance, provide better market access, and to facilitate travel to the EU. Various EU bodies were mobilized to provide training and technical assistance. Instruments like 'twinning', which had proved useful in preparing candidates for membership, were extended to countries in the neighbourhood. Under this initiative, experts from EU Member States were seconded as advisers to ministries, parliaments and regulatory bodies in partner countries.

This policy developed a certain momentum initially. Member States supported it because it filled a gap, promised greater stability in the EU's hinterland, and put paid to any notion that countries like Ukraine or Georgia could expect EU membership within the foreseeable future. There was considerable excitement on the side of partner countries, whose nightmares about 'fortress Europe' seemed to recede. Israeli officials and diplomats, in particular, saw considerable scope for an enhanced relationship with reciprocal benefits.[6] The Israeli government, among others, signed up to quite intrusive human rights conditionality, in exchange for what it perceived, for a time, as a break-through in consolidating relations with the EU. The Jordanian, Tunisian and Moroccan governments competed to acquire 'advanced status' in their association with the EU through the ENP.[7]

In a round of intense negotiations, Action Plans were agreed with most neighbouring countries. The Action Plans had a similar template, with variations adapted to each country's situation and capacities. At times Member States considered that the European Commission was running ahead too rapidly and insisted that they be consulted in advance on each Action Plan before giving their approval. If the negotiations were challenging, implementation, particularly of political reforms, proved even more problematic.

---

6 Author's interviews.

7 See, for example, European Commission 2010. The EU agrees to grant Jordan advanced status partnership. *Press Release*, IP/10/1388, Brussels, 26 October.

Rethinking the European Neighbourhood Policy

Despite the ENP's initial popularity, it quickly ran into criticisms from partner countries, Member States and the policy community. Some of these criticisms referred to the design of the ENP itself, others to a lack of political will on either side to act on the basis of the priorities set out in the Action Plans. Some joked that the ENP countries pretended to reform while the EU pretended to give them a 'stake' in the internal market.

The notion that the EU could project its values, standards and procedures onto countries that did not have the incentive of eventual membership came under increasing scrutiny. Disappointment at the results of the 'colour revolutions' in Georgia and Ukraine and of the Arab uprisings in 2011 and 2012 put into question some of the fundamental assumptions underlying the ENP. The European Neighbourhood Policy has been adjusted to take into account the difficulties which have arisen and the changed circumstances.[8] This is, however, fine tuning and a fundamental rethink of the approach has yet to be undertaken.

This is all the more necessary in light of the destabilization of Ukraine, heightened tension between the West and Russia, and abandonment of the notion of transition towards more open societies in much of North Africa and the Levant. Sectarianism, civil strife and armed conflict have largely put paid to the ENP's vision of a ring of well-governed states to the EU's south and south-east.

The European Commission's 2013 ENP progress report points out that insufficient 'progress was made on the key recommendations on the freedom of association, expression and assembly, a free press and media, the rule of law and an independent judiciary and the fight against corruption' in most countries, and it draws attention to 'backsliding of reforms' in some countries.[9] Despite this realistic assessment, and some further adjustments, the fundamental methodology of the ENP remains unchanged. The following sections examine key features of this approach, including its objectives and methodology.

End Goal

Whereas the enlargement process leads to membership, the ENP's goal remains unclear. A membership perspective will not be offered to neighbouring European countries for the foreseeable future. Any effective foreign policy needs an

---

8   See, in particular, European Commission and High Representative 2011. Joint Communication to the European Parliament, the Council, the European Economic and Social Committee and the Committee of the Regions. *A New Response to a Changing Neighbourhood*, COM(2011) 303, Brussels, 25 May.

9   European Commission and High Representative 2013. Joint Communication to the European Parliament, the Council, the European Economic and Social Committee and the Committee of the Regions. *European Neighbourhood Policy: Working towards a Stronger Partnership*, JOIN(2013) 4 final, Brussels, 20 March 2013, 3–4.

objective, so that a convincing narrative can be developed and instruments, as well as public opinion, mobilized to achieve the agreed goal. The absence of an end goal was partly remedied by the introduction of a new objective: the conclusion of Association Agreements incorporating Deep and Comprehensive Free Trade Areas initially with Ukraine, Moldova, Georgia and Armenia.

AA-DCFTAs were intended to give substance to the Eastern Partnership.[10] These agreements go far beyond traditional free trade agreements in goods. They also cover aspects of trade in services and call for considerable regulatory convergence. Their scope is wider than the original 'Europe Agreements' which were a stepping stone towards membership for countries in Central and Eastern Europe.

AA-DCFTAs for Eastern partners seemed to introduce a much needed degree of clarity and differentiation into the ENP. However, the picture was again clouded following the 'Arab Spring', beginning in Tunisia in December 2010. These uprisings were at first interpreted in Brussels as the start of a process resembling 'transition' in Central and Eastern Europe. For many, it was as if another Berlin wall had fallen. In devising a response, the European Commission and the High Representative now proposed AA-DCFTAs as the goal of the EU's partnership with Mediterranean countries too.[11] However, this was put forward as a quick response with little reflection as to its feasibility.

Proper implementation of ambitious and demanding AA-DCFTAs with these countries is not practicable in the short-to-medium term. Most North African leaders would prefer immediate improvements in their countries' access to EU markets for the relatively few goods they produce which enjoy comparative advantages. These often compete with similar, mostly agricultural products from the EU's Southern Member States, which are, themselves, in a prolonged state of crisis. Market openings that would bring immediate benefits are, therefore, particularly hard to obtain.

In any event, the first AA-DCFTA to be negotiated, the agreement with Ukraine, long remained unsigned because of the country's failure to meet the political conditions which had been set and, subsequently, because of the decision of the Ukrainian President, Viktor Yanukovych, not to conclude the agreement at the Vilnius Summit in November 2013.[12] In retrospect, the wisdom of cranking up the pressure on the President to make a 'civilizational choice' for his country on a specific date set by the EU, provided he released his main opponent, who had been

---

10 Ibid., 8–9; COM(2008) 823/4, op. cit.

11 European Commission and High Representative 2011. Joint Communication to the European Council, the European Parliament, the Council, the European Economic and Social Committee and the Committee of the Region. *A Partnership for Democracy and Shared Prosperity with the Southern Mediterranean*, COM(2011) 200 final, Brussels, 8 March.

12 European Commission 2013. *Implementation of the European Neighbourhood Policy in 2012 Regional Report: Eastern Partnership*, SWD(2013) 85 final, Brussels, 20 March, 2.

convicted in a court of law, can be questioned. The imminent prospect of default was uppermost on Yanukovych's mind as he prepared for the summit. The AA-DCFTA, and linked assistance, offered no solution to Ukraine's financial plight. Russia, however, offered to finance Ukraine's debt in exchange for abandonment of the AA-DCFTA. Russia also exerted strong counter pressure in favour of the customs union linking Russia, Kazakhstan and Belarus. In September 2013, Armenia ceded to this pressure, agreed to join the customs union and stepped back from plans to initial the DCFTA which had been negotiated. The political credibility and economic viability of the customs union depends largely on Ukraine's eventual participation. This, however, appears remote after Russia's annexation of Crimea and the destabilization of Eastern Ukraine by Russian supported 'separatists'.

In any event, AA-DCFTAs are incompatible with the customs union. Thus any country ceding to Russian pressure puts itself out of the running to conclude such an agreement with the EU. The de-escalation of tensions, the removal of mutual sanctions and a new form of engagement between Russia and the EU would be needed to break through this zero-sum situation.[13]

Multiple Policy Frameworks

The ENP has had difficulty achieving brand recognition as the main framework for EU relations with neighbouring countries because it overlaps with numerous earlier and later initiatives. Many observers, particularly in the US, now perceive the Eastern Partnership as the main framework for the EU's relations with Eastern European countries. The Eastern Partnership was welcomed in Washington as a response to the (now disappointing) 'colour revolutions'. Americans are perplexed by continued references to the more diffuse ENP as the umbrella for the EU's relations with these countries.

Looking south, the Euro-Mediterranean Partnership or 'Barcelona process' was launched in 1995 as the main framework for the EU's relations with countries in North Africa and the Levant. Since then it has won some brand recognition but is tarnished through the previous involvement of the *anciens régimes* in these countries. The 2008 Union for the Mediterranean, which, in a typical compromise, was annexed to the Euro-Mediterranean Partnership, added to the confusion.[14] Similar remarks apply to the EU's 2008 launch of the 'Black Sea Synergy' whose goals include the promotion of democracy, the rule of law and economic

---

13   The EU allowed Putin's narrative that it was forcing Ukraine to choose between Brussels and Moscow to gain general currency. In reality, the AA-DCFTA is compatible with the existing limited Free Trade Agreement between Ukraine and the Customs Union.

14   European Commission 2008. Communication from the Commission to the European Parliament and the Council. *Barcelona Process: Union for the Mediterranean*, COM(2008) 319, Brussels, 20 May.

development.[15] In 2011 the EU put forward a 'Partnership for Democracy and Shared Prosperity with the Southern Mediterranean' in response to the 'Arab Spring', largely inspired by the existing ENP of which it is said to form a part.[16]

While each of these frameworks has its own logic, rooted in particular political and economic circumstances, together they fail to deliver a clear message as to the EU's intentions. There is an inherent difficulty in formulating a coherent policy framework for such diverse countries. The EU's consensual approach to decision-making produces complex package deals with pay offs to different Member States. The result is a confusing accumulation of overlapping policy frameworks, with process more visible than concrete results. Instead, the EU needs to develop tailor-made forms of engagement with individual countries designed to respond to their particular needs and capacities. Impact and effectiveness should also be prized above fine-sounding policy frameworks in relations with countries further afield.

Political Conditionality

The EU stipulates that progress towards higher standards in public life is a condition for signing Association Agreements. This implies free and fair elections, the rule of law, including an independent and efficient justice system, and the respect for human rights. These general principles have been translated into specific commitments in the Action Plans and in the Association Agreements negotiated with Ukraine, Georgia and Moldova.[17] Such conditionality delayed signature of the agreement with Ukraine and, if applied rigorously, would for the moment preclude implementation of similar agreements with most other countries covered by the ENP. In its 2013 Progress Report the European Commission recognizes that there has been little progress in meeting core conditions in several countries.[18]

Experience over the past decade suggests that the EU, or indeed any other external actor, has a limited capacity to exercise political leverage in countries which are not themselves firmly committed to Western-oriented reforms. Candidates for EU membership do feel compelled to deliver on political reforms, as these form an integral part of accession negotiations and are conditions for membership. Even in this context there is a certain margin of appreciation as to what realistically can be expected of a candidate within a given time period. When membership is distant

---

15   Joint Statement of the Ministers of Foreign Affairs of the countries of the European Union and of the wider Black Sea area, Brussels, 14 February 2008; European Commission 2007. Communication from the Commission to the Council and the European Parliament. *Black Sea Synergy – A New Regional Cooperation Initiative*, COM(2007) 160 final, Brussels, 11 April.

16   COM(2011) 200 final, op. cit.

17   European Commission 2014. *The EU's Association Agreements with Georgia, the Republic of Moldova and Ukraine*, MEMO/14/430, Brussels, 23 June, http://europa.eu/rapid/press-release_MEMO-14-430_en.htm [accessed: 30 July 2014].

18   JOIN(2013) 4 final, op. cit., 4.

or uncertain, as in the case of Turkey, the EU's political leverage diminishes even further. This kind of leverage also slips once an accession treaty has been signed. There have been various examples of backsliding after accession, notably in Bulgaria, Hungary, Romania, and Croatia.

Even the promise of membership and incentives in the form of the abolition of visa requirements and financial assistance have only been partly successful in persuading countries in the Western Balkans to overcome the burden of the past and to improve standards in public life. Despite progress in Croatia, which joined the EU in July 2013, and Serbia, dysfunctional democracy and state failure, as well as bilateral conflicts, have proved recalcitrant in much of the Western Balkans.

If conditionality has its limits even in countries preparing to join the EU, it is much more difficult to exercise in countries that have not been given an accession perspective. Furthermore, it may be necessary for security, energy or commercial reasons to engage with countries like Egypt, Algeria or Azerbaijan, even when reforms are inadequate or there is a reassertion of authoritarian rule.

Despite these qualifications, pro-democracy advocates in the countries themselves often welcome conditionality as a means to keep up the pressure on refractory regimes. The EU needs to nudge governments towards better governance without allowing political conditionality to block closer relations. In countries further afield, where the EU has even less leverage, pragmatism, long the byword of Member States, also needs to inform policy making at EU level.

Mixed Messages

EU Member States regularly confirm that political conditionality and the promotion of democracy, the rule of law and the protection of human rights are the foundations for the EU's relations with third countries. On the whole, however, they prefer to delegate the promotion of such values to EU institutions while pursuing bilateral relations on the basis of security, commercial and energy interests. This results in mixed messages to partner countries, particularly in North Africa and the Levant, because of the strength of traditional ties, and also in Azerbaijan, because of its growing role in ensuring Europe's energy security.

The EU, in practice, followed this two-pronged approach in relations with Mediterranean countries for the two decades preceding the Arab uprisings. Member States pursued bilateral relations in a pragmatic fashion, establishing close diplomatic, commercial and personal ties with autocratic rulers. The Southern Member States, in particular, drew on links going back to colonial times to build a privileged position in terms of trade, investment, public procurement, and energy supply. The EU institutions, by contrast, were tasked with promoting regional cooperation, good governance, and the protection of human rights. The credibility of EU conditionality was often called into question by the interest-based approach of the Member States. The EU and its Member States manifestly did not speak with one voice.

The most notorious divergence occurred in 2003, the year the EU began its 'wider Europe' initiative. During a visit to Tunisia, French President Jacques Chirac stated: 'The first of human rights is to have food, medical care, education, and housing ... From this point of view, we have to recognize that Tunisia is well advanced compared to many countries'.[19] Such sentiments, couched in milder terms, were repeated by European leaders until the eve of Ben Ali's overthrow. Italy maintained good relations with Libya under both centre-left and centre-right governments. Egypt enjoyed close links with many Member States despite the continuing state of emergency and the persistence of repression. Spanish and French diplomats and business people gave particular priority to Morocco.

The EU itself has been somewhat inconsistent in the application of conditionality, working closely with the leaders of the *anciens régimes* in North Africa and the Middle East. Former President Hosni Mubarak of Egypt was, together with former French President Nicolas Sarkozy, Co-President of the Union for the Mediterranean until his overthrow in February 2011. To be sure, the EU urged such authoritarian leaders to show greater respect for fundamental rights and freedoms but the message was muted.

Mixed messages about political conditionality have weakened the EU's leverage with neighbouring countries. Similarly, with countries beyond the EU's immediate hinterland, the EU and its Member States must align their messages if their combined efforts are to produce results.

Incentives

In the absence of an offer of membership, the main incentives for reform proffered by the EU are better market access, more financial assistance, lighter procedures for visitors to the EU, and participation in EU technical agencies and other bodies. The EU's approach has been summed up in the phrase 'more for more', that is, the more a neighbouring country is ready to reform, the more benefits the EU is ready to provide. This approach is unexceptionable in itself and largely common sense. There is more scope for cooperation, and even integration, with a country which is a functioning democracy and has an open economy. There is less scope for engagement with authoritarian regimes and pre-modern societies.

The incentives offered, however, are insufficiently attractive to be game changers in countries which are resistant to democratic reform. Third countries, less subject to checks and balances, are able to provide much higher levels of financial support, when it suits their political or ideological agenda. EU financial support to Egypt, for example, is dwarfed by funds from Gulf states.

Political leaders in neighbouring countries would be more responsive to immediate, unilateral improvements in market access for the relatively few

---

19   Quoted in Garçon, J. 2003. Droits de l'homme en Tunisie: Chirac blanchit Ben Ali. *Libération*, 5 December.

products which they can produce at competitive prices, or to visa facilitation for business people, students and other frequent travellers to the EU. But a complex process of negotiation, leading to Deep and Comprehensive Free Trade Areas in the medium term, is not as compelling.

Indeed, questions have been asked in Ukraine and elsewhere about the balance of advantages under such agreements. They impose a heavy political, administrative, and financial burden before trade benefits start to be felt, despite the formally 'asymmetric' timing of trade openings. Negotiating membership in EU regulatory agencies and other bodies is an arduous task. In the absence of an offer of membership, such incentives are not sufficient to determine outcomes in countries where very different political forces and ideologies are contending for power. If the EU is to be welcome as a partner in countries facing profound internal challenges, it needs to provide support in forms which genuinely respond to local needs, and to be modest about its capacity to shift the balance between contending forces.

Shared Values

The ENP has often been said to rest on 'shared values'. The countries of Eastern Europe and the Southern Caucasus that are members of the Council of Europe in principle subscribe to the kind of values on which the EU itself is founded. The 'colour revolutions' brought initial hopes, later disappointed, that Georgia and Ukraine would move steadily forward along the path of political transition, as countries in Central and Eastern Europe had done a decade earlier.

In most post-Soviet countries, there are grievous shortcomings in the treatment of opposition figures, the exercise of fundamental freedoms, such as freedom of expression, the independence of the judiciary and other core democratic values and practices.[20] Even where electoral democracy has been established little progress has been made towards liberal democracy. This was recognized by Commissioner Štefan Füle in remarks on the 2013 ENP progress reports. 'Elections are important, but often only a first step towards democracy', he said. 'Political reforms to ensure respect for fundamental rights and freedoms of assembly, association, expression and the media are still incomplete'.[21]

Bruce Jackson has eloquently described what he calls the 'post-Soviet twilight' in an article published in 2013. 'Political liberty and dissent are constrained by secret police, tax police, libel laws, or bans on NGOs throughout the post-Soviet world. But this is what the "post-Soviet twilight" could be expected to look like:

---

20   The European Commission's Progress Report on Ukraine from 2013 remarks that '[c]onfidence in Ukraine's judiciary was undermined by trials ... which indicated a selective use of justice vis-à-vis leaders of the opposition'. European Commission 2013. *Implementation of the European Neighbourhood Policy in Ukraine Progress in 2012 and recommendations for action*, SWD(2013) 84 final, Brussels, 20 March, 5.

21   Füle, S. 2013. *Speech: Presentation of the European Neighbourhood Policy package*. European Parliament Foreign Affairs Committee, Brussels, 20 March 2013.

remnants of an autocratic political culture jutting like shards of glass upwards through the torn fabric of the Russian and Soviet empires'.[22]

The 2013 edition of Freedom House's annual survey of political rights and civil liberties comments: 'With Russia setting the tone, Eurasia (consisting of the countries of the former Soviet Union minus the Baltic States) now rivals the Middle East as one of the most repressive areas of the globe ... Ukraine suffered a decline for a second year due to the politically motivated imprisonment of opposition leaders, flawed legislative elections, and a new law favouring the Russian-speaking portion of the population.'[23] After the overthrow of President Yanukovych, the country's new rulers proved equally sectarian in trying to ban the use of Russian as an official language. While Freedom House registers progress in electoral democracy in Armenia and Georgia, there are many countervailing forces in these countries. Freedom House rates Azerbaijan as having one of the world's most repressive regimes.[24]

Under these circumstances, the very notion of 'transition' can be called into question. These countries may be involved in transition in the minimal sense of change or passage from one state to another. But 'political transition' today implies a transformation, with the progressive adoption of a different set of goals, objectives, values, commitments, and behaviour. In this sense, it is far from clear that the countries covered by the Eastern Partnership, including post-Maidan Ukraine, are, in fact, involved in a transition process towards Western-style societies.

In North Africa and the Levant, electoral democracy was established, to various degrees, following the overthrow of a number of tyrannical regimes. Other authoritarian regimes remain in place. Considerable time will be needed to ascertain the extent to which Western values will progressively permeate these societies and be safeguarded by institutions. There are signs that electoral democracy may be accompanied by an infusion of quite different values, often inspired by religion. These values may not be congruent with those prevailing in the European Union, especially regarding the rights of women, children and minorities, freedom of expression and a number of other fundamental freedoms. Violent repression, in the name of secularism, is equally alien to Western values.

The changes in North Africa have improved the enjoyment of political rights to a limited degree. There have also been serious setbacks and 'transition' in this region is not necessarily a linear process. In some cases, the transition appears to be from autocracy, to electoral democracy and back to authoritarian rule. In others dysfunctional democracy or state failure prevails. Values other than those widespread in the EU have also been liberated by the overthrow of authoritarian regimes. Third countries, notably in the Gulf, compete to propagate their own

---

22   Jackson, B.P. 2013. The Post-Soviet Twilight. *Hoover Institution Policy Review*, 177, 1 February.

23   Puddington, A. 2013. *Freedom in the World 2013: Democratic Breakthroughs in the Balance*. Washington, DC: Freedom House, 7.

24   Ibid.

values. A type of society may eventually emerge which combines improved governance and living standards with beliefs and practices that are inimical to political freedom and civil rights, as understood in the West.

Under these circumstances, the assumption underlying the ENP that the EU's partner countries to the east and south are committed to shared values needs to be re-examined. To be sure, it is important for Europeans and Americans to promote such values, through aid programmes, 'twinning', training and other policy instruments, to the extent that this is permitted by the host countries' authorities. Initiatives such as the European Endowment for Democracy are to be welcomed in this context, despite the modesty of the funds available.[25] Such support is helpful in efforts to promote moves towards liberal democracy and the strengthening of civil society. But, on the whole, shared values are an aspiration rather than a current reality. Any mechanical calibrating of the EU's degree of engagement with the manifestation of shared values is to be avoided. This lesson is particularly pertinent in more distant regions where 'shared values' appear even less plausible as the basis for bilateral relations.

More for More?

The 'more for more' approach implies that the EU's degree of engagement with a country is determined by the partner's implementation of an agreed programme of EU-inspired reforms. It is directly modelled on the enlargement process, without the incentive of eventual membership. It implies a ratcheting up of benefits when specific agreed reforms are carried out. The success of this approach depends on shared values, clear objectives, mutual political will to pursue these objectives, the credibility of incentives and the avoidance of mixed messages from the EU institutions and the Member States.

However, partner countries are subject to diverse influences, not all of which point in the direction of the progressive adoption of EU norms and values. Member States face multiple challenges, particularly given the persistent economic and financial crisis, and uncertainty over the EU's future architecture. This makes them cautious about trade 'concessions', the freer movement of persons and additional financial support. Indeed, small increments of financial aid from the EU, as a reward for better governance, pale into insignificance compared with financial support from Gulf countries.

'More for more' may be a useful policy prescription in the relatively few cases where elected leaders show an apparent inclination to embrace the European model as the focus for their own policies. Indeed, the EU should be quick off the mark in such cases, without waiting for complex policy frameworks to be agreed

---

25 The European Endowment for Democracy (EED) signed a €6.2 million grant contract with the European Commission. Several Member States together with Switzerland have pledged up to an additional €8 million for EED activities. The initial budget for the EED will be around €14 million.

or a clear consensus to emerge among the EU's members. In the first half of 2011 Tunisia appeared to offer the EU a golden opportunity to support political change. The EU should not hesitate to respond to demands for support from Tunisians who have an inclusive approach to democratic change.

'More for more' cannot always be the yardstick for calibrating the EU's degree of engagement with a neighbouring country, or a country further afield. There are many reasons for engaging with a country other than its desire to become more like ourselves.

More for Less?

Sometimes the EU or its Member States may well need to offer 'more for less'. As in the past, Europeans may be obliged to engage with regimes whose commitment to Western values is at best erratic, on the basis of security, commercial or energy interests. This is a normal occurrence in international relations and has to figure in formulating the EU's goals towards a country or region. A few examples will suffice to illustrate the point.

Egypt's 82 million people are a natural market for Greece and other struggling southern European countries. The purchasing power of Egyptian consumers has been cut back since the overthrow of the *ancien régime*. There are shortages of food and other basic commodities. Sound economic policies, including the elimination of fuel subsidies, are needed to strengthen the Egyptian economy. Support from the International Monetary Fund (IMF) and the EU is crucial in winning popular consent for such policies. The principal conditionality for such support is economic rather than political.

At the same time, Egypt's pivotal position in the Middle East and the size of the population mean that the European Union cannot allow it to fail. The consequences of outright economic collapse in Egypt would be incalculable. European countries, the EU, the US and international organizations may need to support Egypt economically, independently of the course of its political reforms. The withholding of assistance in the case of a major breach of democratic norms may sometimes be politically unavoidable. But others will step in to fill the gap and such decisions need to be carefully weighed.

In the political domain, Egypt can at times play a valuable role in containing tensions between Israel and Hamas in Gaza. This is of value to the parties themselves and to the international community as a whole, whatever the state of domestic reforms in Egypt. Egypt can block the smuggling of arms and other supplies into Gaza if it chooses to do so. The maintenance in force of Egypt's peace treaty with Israel is another factor supportive of regional stability.

Azerbaijan holds one of the keys to the energy security of Turkey and of Europe as a whole. Azerbaijan can contribute to the diversification of Europe's energy sources through investment in gas pipelines across Turkey and into Southern and Central Europe, reducing dependence on Russia. In the political domain, it is in the interest of the EU, Member States and Turkey to prevent the outbreak of hostilities between Azerbaijan and Armenia over Nagorno-Karabakh. These are objectives which should be pursued on their own merits, independently of political conditionality.

To be sure, Egypt and Azerbaijan might become more dependable partners with which the EU could develop a wider range of links if they embarked on a genuine transition process. This is to be encouraged through political contacts at all levels and through support for civil society, to the extent possible. But engagement to strengthen regional security, energy security, and trade cannot always be dependent on political reforms, however desirable these may be.

Jordan has for decades been a pillar of stability in a troubled region, despite profound internal tensions. The government's legitimacy is not founded on popular sovereignty as understood in Europe or the United States. Jordan's stability is in the interest of its own citizens as well as the people of Syria, Lebanon, Israel and, indeed, the EU and the US.

There is a major risk of spill-over of instability from Syria into Jordan. Jordan has received a large number of refugees with which it can hardly cope, since the outbreak of civil strife and violent repression in Syria. Jordan needs Western political, diplomatic and financial support more than ever in these circumstances. The EU should also support Israel's decision to sell natural gas to Jordan, to replace interrupted supplies from Egypt. An effective EU foreign and security policy would actively pursue such objectives, independently of the state of political reforms within Jordan. This does not preclude support for greater political liberty, civil society, and better governance, within the constraints of the fragile national and regional context.

European and wider Western interests are at stake in the spread of violence by extremist groups and rival clans in the Middle East, North Africa and adjoining regions. France sought over-flight rights across Algeria for its intervention to prevent violent extremists from tightening their control in Mali, despite Freedom House's rating of the country as 'not free'.[26] Similar remarks apply to Algeria's possible hosting of drone bases, cooperation on intelligence gathering and provision of gas to Europe.

The King of Morocco has been holding the line in his country against the rise of extremist violence seen elsewhere in North Africa. The country is extending its outreach throughout the wider Atlantic to diversify its external relations and commercial ties. This deserves encouragement and support, especially given Morocco's proximity to Portugal, Spain, France, Italy, Malta and the EU as such. To be sure, there are unresolved issues that need to be addressed in the Western Sahara and, indeed, in the sound management of Morocco's economy and the degree of freedom accorded to its people. Morocco's people aspire to higher living standards and suffer from wide income disparities. They often vote with their feet. For a multitude of reasons the EU needs to engage with Morocco.

An approach inspired by the enlargement experience does not necessarily offer the best policy mix for countries that are on different trajectories. In any event,

---

26   Puddington, op. cit.

insistence by Brussels on political conditionality lacks credibility when Member States pursue separate policies inspired by security, commercial or energy interests. National ministers become irritated if criticisms by EU officials of a neighbouring country's human rights record jeopardize ongoing bilateral negotiations.

Leaders in Eastern Europe, North Africa, the Levant and, still more, in countries further from Europe increasingly question the legal, moral or political grounds for EU insistence on respect for European values and standards. The EU's promotion of its own model is greeted with further scepticism because of persistent economic and financial problems in Europe since 2008.

Assessment

Overall, efforts to impose respect for democracy, the rule of law and the protection of human rights in neighbouring countries by applying political conditionality have failed. There are limits to the EU's capacity to influence putative transition processes without the inducement of membership. Post-Soviet and non-member Mediterranean countries are subject to a range of pressures, and of value systems, many of which diverge significantly from the principles on which the EU is based. Electoral democracy does not always lead to liberal democracy, in the short run at least. Relatively free and fair elections may produce 'winner-take-all' governments, as in Egypt or Ukraine, sparking new rounds of resistance and repression.

The EU aspires to a Common Foreign and Security Policy (CFSP). The EU's neighbourhood is the part of the world where such a policy could, potentially, have the most influence. To do so, however, it must take into account all relevant considerations, not just the degree to which a given country has embraced the EU's own values. Member States necessarily take security, geopolitics, trade and energy supply into account when shaping their foreign policies. Like its members, the EU itself may often need to engage with states whose values it does not share.

The EU enunciated the principle of 'more for more' following the Arab uprisings. This meant the more a country took concrete steps to reinforce democracy and the rule of law, the more the EU would be ready to engage with it. But this principle cannot always provide the right answer. Strategic considerations may sometimes require 'more' engagement even where there is 'less' reform. As we have seen, Azerbaijan and Algeria are important to the EU's energy and military security despite their lack of political reform. The EU must engage Libya on energy, refugee and asylum issues, despite its dysfunctional political system. State failure in Libya is not in the EU's interest. It poses numerous threats to European security in the broadest sense. The EU, therefore, must engage with Libya however poor its performance in terms of EU values and standards.

The EU needs a form of engagement with each partner, carefully calibrated to its own strategic interests, combining pragmatism with support for good governance and reform when there is a credible commitment to political change within a country itself. This conclusion is even more pertinent to countries further afield.

If a partner appears genuinely committed to improvements in governance and respect for fundamental rights, as appears to be the case, to some extent, in Moldova, Georgia and Tunisia, the EU should offer forms of encouragement which have real resonance with the population. Upgrades in 'status' or incremental increases in financial assistance, which are marginal in terms of gross national product (GNP) or by comparison with support from wealthy bilateral donors, have little impact. The EU has done well to identify visa facilitation and progress towards visa free travel as meaningful incentives. Scholarships, 'twinning' and other 'people-to-people' initiatives also resonate with the population.

At the outset, the EU invited Russia to become a partner in its new neighbourhood policy. Russia declined, preferring to develop a 'strategic partnership' with the EU, on a par with the EU's relationship with the US. Such a partnership between the EU and Russia has proved elusive, after years of fitful negotiations. Indeed, Russia mounted a major campaign to dissuade former Soviet states from concluding agreements with the EU under its neighbourhood policy. Instead, it has sought to draw them into its own customs union, with Belarus and Kazakhstan, as a forerunner of a more far-reaching Eurasian Economic Union announced for 2015. This Russian campaign transformed the ENP, in the eyes of some political leaders in Eastern Europe and the Southern Caucasus, into an alternative 'civilizational project', incompatible with closer ties with other former Soviet states. They felt obliged to choose between the EU and Russia.

Following blandishments from Moscow, the Armenian President chose the customs union with Russia, Belarus and Kazakhstan.[27] In November 2013, the Ukrainian President rejected, provisionally at least, the AA-DCFTA his government had negotiated with the EU, provoking popular demonstrations in the streets of Kiev and other Ukrainian cities. These demonstrations were as much a condemnation of crony capitalism and the kleptocratric regime as an embrace of the EU.

The decision of the Ukrainian President, Victor Yanukovich, to break off negotiations with the EU and to reject the AA-DCFTA in the days before the November 2013 Vilnius Eastern Partnership Summit arose from a number of considerations: the country's dire financial straits and the belief that Russia was more likely than the EU or the IMF to provide financial stop gaps without imposing tough conditions; Russian 'sticks and carrots'; disdain for the transparency and openness, for example in public purchasing, that adoption of EU standards would require; and fear of the consequences for himself and his clique of releasing Yulia Timoshenko from prison for medical treatment, though this demand could probably have been finessed if Yanukovich had not walked away from the table.

While the Ukrainian government might have proved recalcitrant under any circumstances, the EU made a number of mistakes which diminished the attractiveness of its offer. It was not wise to present Ukraine with an exceedingly

---

27   *Reuters* 2013. Armenia says will join Russia-led customs union, 3 September, http://www.reuters.com/article/2013/09/03/us-armenia-russia-customsunion-idUSBRE9820U520130903 [accessed: 4 January 2014].

demanding DCFTA that required it to adopt a large part of the EU's laws, rules and standards (the *acquis*) without the prospect of membership. The considerable costs of adjusting to the EU's regulatory regime (health, safety and environment) would kick in at an early stage. In practice, most trade benefits would flow only in the medium term, despite the 'asymmetric' scheduling of trade openings. The EU was ready to mobilize its existing panoply of aid instruments to help with adjustment. But these did not appear commensurate with the costs of adopting EU standards and no visible new form of assistance was offered.

The EU should have put forward a much lighter form of engagement, emphasizing support for political transition and offering real benefits to the population (visa facilitation, scholarships, etc.). The EU should have crafted an agreement that did not give the appearance of forcing Ukraine to choose between Russia and the EU. In reality the DCFTA would have been compatible with Ukraine's 1993 free trade agreement with Russia and similar agreements with other former Soviet states. But this fact was not communicated clearly to the Ukrainian people. The DCFTA is, indeed, incompatible with the 2010 customs union concluded by Russia, Belarus and Kazakhstan (an arrangement which is itself in violation of several of Russia's WTO commitments). Finally, making signature of the agreement hang on the fate of a single person, however emblematic, was the *coup de grace*.

Russia's pressure on Ukraine, Moldova, Armenia and Georgia, taken together with the situation in most Arab countries around the Mediterranean, marked the end of a 10-year effort to put into place a comprehensive neighbourhood policy that would deliver a ring of well-governed neighbours This policy, and its various declinations, was too closely modelled on the enlargement process (but without the incentive of actual membership), and too little differentiated; the ENP provided too few benefits in exchange for political reforms which many partner governments, anyway, had little intention of carrying out.

A radical revamp of the ENP should be the top priority of the new High Representative/Commission Vice President, appointed following the European Parliament elections in May 2014. The lessons drawn from 10 years' experience with the ENP will also be important for the EU's relations with countries further afield. The assumptions underlying the ENP have significantly influenced the EU's approach to countries around the world, *mutatis mutandis*.

For reasons linked to the notion of European identity, the EU as such gives prominence to governance and human rights issues in its embryonic foreign policy. This leaves Member States free to pursue policies based on their own particular interests. The EU will never have a convincing foreign and security policy as long as such incoherence persists. Instead of delegating issues of principle to the EU, while pursuing their own business as usual, the Member States, on the initiative of the new High Representative, should seek to craft a balanced, effective and realistic CFSP, making use of all EU instruments. The rise and fall of the ENP will be highly instructive in this exercise.

Towards a Renewed European Neighbourhood Policy

The European or, indeed, Western model is not necessarily the main source of inspiration for leaders in regions beyond the EU's own frontiers.[28] Most countries to the EU's east have entered a kind of 'post-Soviet twilight' while to the south a hybrid form of governance with Islamic characteristics is taking shape, influenced by donors and trading partners in the Middle East and the Persian Gulf.[29]

Under these circumstances, the EU should consider a more pragmatic, selective case-by-case approach, inspired by classic foreign policy rather than the enlargement experience. The EU is trying to build up a Common Foreign and Security Policy, with the instruments put in place by the Lisbon Treaty (Art. 21–46 TEU). The region of the world where the EU can expect to exercise most influence is its own neighbourhood. To exercise such influence, the EU needs to take a pragmatic approach, combining support for progressive change with the pursuit of security, energy and commercial interests. There is no reason to be squeamish about this. In reality, it has been the approach of the Member States throughout the ENP experiment.

The EU should encourage respect for democratic norms and practices as well as market-oriented economic reforms. This means supporting civil society and institution building, when invited to do so, with a degree of modesty about the compelling nature of the European political, social and economic model. The main agents for change are within neighbouring countries themselves. Experience suggests that a pragmatic approach, based on a realistic assessment of mutual interests, is more likely to achieve results than a somewhat mechanistic model of rewards for good performance.

The degree of engagement with individual countries should not be seen as a kind of ratchet, to be moved up a notch whenever governments introduce a reform that brings them closer to European models of governance. Outside actors, like the EU and the US, need to encourage, to warn and to support the authorities in these countries in line with their own political, economic and security interests. They should warn if it appears that the rule of law and the enjoyment of fundamental freedoms are compromised. They should provide support, when requested, to civil society and state bodies which have a genuine commitment to reform. But they should not seek to impose political change which needs to be generated by political actors and populations within the countries concerned.

Transition countries in Eastern Europe will require a generation at least for regimes based on political and economic freedom to take root. In North Africa

---

28   See also Chapter 11 by Stephan Keukeleire in this volume.

29   The Progress Report of 2013 recognizes 'shifts in the foreign policy orientation of partner countries' and cautions that 'in the Southern Mediterranean, Turkey, countries of the Gulf and organisations such as the Arab League are playing a more prominent role in ... promoting their economic and political interests' and that '[t]he emergence of alternative regional integration schemes in the Eastern neighbourhood presents a new challenge'. JOIN(2013) 4 final, op. cit., 22.

and the Levant it is too early to be confident of the type of regimes likely to emerge. Despite real progress, a post-Soviet aura still envelops Belarus, Ukraine, Moldova and the Southern Caucasus. In most cases it is hard for outsiders to judge the policy mix most likely to obtain the necessary local buy-in.

An enormous amount of political energy was expended in the EU in the first decade of this century in the process leading up to the adoption of the Lisbon Treaty. One of the Treaty's main aspirations is to create the foundations of a European foreign and security policy. Major institutional changes have been made with a view to bringing this about. If the EU is to have an impact on the fast evolving international system, proportionate to the degree of integration it has attained internally, it needs to display both pragmatism and principle. It cannot rely solely on the magnetic appeal of its own political, economic and social model. This model is increasingly questioned internally, in light of the persistent financial and economic crisis. Externally, there are other influences at work which are at least as compelling to vast swathes of people in neighbouring countries. Electoral democracy does not necessarily produce regimes committed to liberal democracy or 'deep democracy' on the Western plan.

It is time for the EU to set aside a foreign policy model based on rewarding countries for becoming more like ourselves. This approach is explicit in the enlargement process, implicit in the neighbourhood policy, and a lingering *leitmotif* in relations with more distant countries. The EU's internal narrative has been so centred on integration, interdependence, and the progressive extension of political and economic freedoms that this colours its approach to foreign policy in general. Yet other countries continue to play by the rules of national interest, spheres of influence, and the balance of power. The situation is further complicated by the influence of religion and sectarian strife.

The EU has placed the promotion of values (democracy, the rule of law, human rights) at the heart of its nascent foreign policy. This reflects the inherent importance of such values, their link with peace and stability, and their emblematic significance as markers of the EU's identity. Democracy and human rights constitute a core of values on which all Member States can agree, even when they differ on the use of force or willingness to confront regional powers that overstep the mark.

But a values-based approach to foreign policy needs to be balanced by pragmatism. Enlightened political realism is the watchword in the chancelleries of Europe and indeed in the West in general. The Member States' own bilateral relations are largely pragmatic while they have become accustomed to outsourcing 'the export of European values' to Brussels. The EU would be more likely to attain its own objectives in neighbouring regions and further afield if it set aside grand schemes in favour of a pragmatic, country-by-country approach. Ambitious 'partnerships' provide a convenient narrative but lose credibility when belied by political and economic realities. Process predominates with impact and effectiveness on the ground relegated to second place.

Effective engagement requires a lucid analysis of EU interests from which more detailed goals and objectives, ways and means can be derived. Brussels will be serving its Member States best by clearly formulating such interests and objectives following close consultation with national capitals.

The deconstruction of the ENP into eastern and southern components is a step towards greater realism. Pragmatic engagement with each country, according to its needs, capacities, and the EU's own interests, would be another step forward. A lighter, more selective approach to engagement with countries on the EU's periphery is more likely to achieve desired outcomes. Such an approach will blur the rather artificial distinction between 'neighbouring' countries and those further afield. Why should Jordan, for example, be considered a 'neighbouring' country while Iraq is not? The fate of Jordan is deeply entwined with that of its neighbours. There should be no taboos in devising effective foreign and security policies to replace the ENP. Above all, a sober assessment should be made of EU interests and all EU policy instruments mobilized in pursuit of those interests.

Bibliography

Council of the European Union 2003. *A Secure Europe in a Better World: European Security Strategy*, 12 December.

Dabrowski, M. and Maliszewska, M. (eds). 2011. *EU Eastern Neighborhood: Economic Potential and Future Development*. Berlin: Springer.

Dekanozishvili, M. 2011. *The European Neighborhood Policy: The South Caucasus Dimension*. Saarbrücken: Lambert Academic Publishing.

Delors, J. 1989. Statement on the Broad Lines of Commission Policy, *Bulletin of the European Communities*, Supplement no. 1, Strasbourg, 17 January.

European Commission 2003. Communication from the Commission to the Council and the European Parliament. *Wider Europe – Neighbourhood: A New Framework for Relations with our Eastern and Southern Neighbours*, COM(2003) 104 final, Brussels, 11 March.

European Commission 2007. Communication from the Commission to the Council and the European Parliament. *Black Sea Synergy – A New Regional Cooperation Initiative*, COM(2007) 160 final, Brussels, 11 April.

European Commission 2008. Communication from the Commission to the European Parliament and the Council. *Barcelona Process: Union for the Mediterranean*, COM(2008) 319, Brussels, 20 May.

European Commission 2008. Communication from the Commission to the European Parliament and the Council. *Eastern Partnership*, COM(2008) 823/4, Brussels, 3 December.

European Commission 2010. The EU agrees to grant Jordan advanced status partnership. *Press release*, IP/10/1388, Brussels, 26 October.

European Commission 2013. *Implementation of the European Neighbourhood Policy in Ukraine Progress in 2012 and recommendations for action*, SWD(2013) 84 final, Brussels, 20 March.

European Commission 2013. *Implementation of the European Neighbourhood Policy in 2012 Regional Report: Eastern Partnership*, SWD(2013) 85 final, Brussels, 20 March.

European Commission 2014. *The EU's Association Agreements with Georgia, the Republic of Moldova and Ukraine*, MEMO/14/430, Brussels, 23 June, http://europa.eu/rapid/press-release-MEMO-14-430-en.htm [accessed: 30 July 2014].

European Commission and High Representative 2011. Joint Communication to the European Council, the European Parliament, the Council, the European Economic and Social Committee and the Committee of the Region. *A Partnership for Democracy and Shared Prosperity with the Southern Mediterranean*, COM(2011) 200 final, Brussels, 8 March.

European Commission and High Representative 2011. Joint Communication to the European Parliament, the Council, the European Economic and Social Committee and the Committee of the Regions. *A New Response to a Changing Neighbourhood*, COM(2011) 303, Brussels, 25 May.

European Commission and High Representative 2013. Joint Communication to the European Parliament, the Council, the European Economic and Social Committee and the Committee of the Regions. *European Neighbourhood Policy: Working towards a Stronger Partnership*, JOIN(2013) 4 final, Brussels, 20 March.

Füle, S. 2013. *Speech: Presentation of the European Neighbourhood Policy package*, European Parliament Foreign Affairs Committee, Brussels, 20 March.

Garçon, J. 2003. Droits de l'homme en Tunisie: Chirac blanchit Ben Ali. *Libération*, 5 December.

Jackson, B.P. 2013. The Post-Soviet Twilight. *Hoover Institution Policy Review*, 177, 1 February.

Lannon, E. 2012 (ed.). *The European Neighbourhood Policy's Challenges/Les défis de la politique européenne de voisinage*. Brussels: P.I.E, Peter Lang.

Leigh, M. 2005. The EU's Neighborhood Policy, in Brimmer E. and Fröhlich S. (eds). *The Strategic Implications of European Union Enlargement*. Johns Hopkins University: Center for Transatlantic Relations, 101–26.

Leigh, M. 2007. Making a Success of ENP: Challenge and Response, in Weber, K., Smith, M.E. and Baun, M. (eds), *Governing Europe's Neighbourhood*. Manchester: Manchester University Press, 209–17.

Leigh, M. 2012. Europe's Response to the Arab Spring. *GMF Policy Brief*, Washington, DC: The German Marshall Fund of the United States, October.

Varwick, J. and Lang, K.O. (eds). 2007. *European Neighbourhood Policy: Challenges for the EU-policy Towards the New Neighbour*. Opladen: Barbara Budrich Publishers.

Puddington, A. 2013. *Freedom in the World 2013: Democratic Breakthroughs in the Balance*. Washington, DC: Freedom House.

Reuters 2013. Armenia says will join Russia-led customs union, 3 September, http://www.reuters.com/article/2013/09/03/us-armenia-russia-customsunion-idUSBRE9820U520130903 [accessed: 4 January 2014].

Whitman, R.G. and Wolff, S. (eds). 2010. *The European Neighbourhood Policy in Perspective: Context, Implementation and Impact*. Basingstoke: Palgrave Macmillan.

Chapter 11

Lessons for the Practice and Analysis of EU Diplomacy from an 'Outside-in' Perspective

Stephan Keukeleire

Introduction[1]

Analysing the broader neighbourhood of the European Union (EU) poses significant challenges in terms of knowledge and understanding of this neighbourhood. Having a good knowledge of the EU's positions and policies towards these regions is not sufficient to detect the challenges Europe is facing in its broader neighbourhood, to evaluate the EU's strategies and frameworks of cooperation with the neighbours of the EU's neighbours, and to assess how further bridges can be built with these various countries and regions as well as with the EU's immediate neighbours covered by the European Neighbourhood Policy (ENP).

This chapter argues that, in order to achieve a genuine understanding of the EU's relationship with and policies towards its broader neighbourhood, it is essential to complement an EU-centred perspective with what is labelled in this chapter as an 'outside-in' perspective. An 'outside-in' perspective means that the analyst or practitioner (diplomat or civil servant) does not take the EU's policy towards a third country or region as the only point of reference, but also tries to look at this EU policy from the perspective of the third countries or regions concerned – in the context of this book the Gulf region, the Sahel region, the Horn of Africa, Central Asia and the Caspian Sea region.

The first section of this chapter provides possible explanations for the recurrent neglect of the 'outside' in the analysis of EU foreign policy. The following section offers several building blocks for adopting an 'outside-in' perspective and applies this on the EU's policy towards the neighbours of its neighbours. This will serve as a basis for the last section, which draws lessons from an 'outside-in' perspective for the various actors involved in EU foreign policy, including the High Representative, the European External Action Service (EEAS) and the EU Delegations.

1 Research on the 'outside-in' perspective in EU foreign policy has been conducted in the framework of the *TOTAL Chair of EU Foreign Policy* at the College of Europe in Bruges. I am grateful to the European and non-European researchers and practitioners who contributed to my learning process about the 'outside' as well as to Raphaël Metais and Charles Thépaut, former Research Assistants of the *TOTAL Chair of EU Foreign Policy*, for their input and critical comments.

The Neglect of the 'Outside'

One of the limitations of the academic analysis of EU foreign policy is that this research predominantly adopts an 'inward-looking' or 'inside-out' perspective, thereby focusing on the EU's foreign policy mechanisms and evaluating EU foreign policy from the perspective of the EU. Less scholarly attention is given to an 'outside-in' perspective in which the 'outside' (or the 'foreign' – see below) is taken as a major point of reference.[2] Such an 'outside-in' perspective implies that the foreign policy analysts examine foreign policy from the perspective and within the context of the region, country, society, elites or populations that are the subject, target, recipient, beneficiary or victim of the given foreign policy. Recent research that emphasizes the 'outside' includes academic work on external perceptions of the EU[3] and on the EU's democratization policy in the Mediterranean.[4]

Before providing building blocks to conceptualize the 'outside-in' perspective, this section looks at possible explanations for the neglect of the 'outside' by foreign policy analysts. In a variation on the statement of Tickner and Wæver that 'the discipline of International Relations (IR) is ironically not "international" at all', it is argued in this chapter that the academic analysis of EU foreign policy and of foreign policy in general is often, ironically, not 'foreign' at all.[5] The presence of non-Western scholars and non-Western approaches in publications on EU foreign policy is rather limited. Analysts and scholars are often specialized in the EU's foreign policy towards a specific country or region, but are in many cases not at all specialized in the country, region or society that is the subject of the analysis. The analysis of foreign policy also suffers from the limited explanatory power of predominant Western perspectives and categories to analyse non-Western contexts.[6]

---

2   Cavatorta and Pace use the label 'inside-out' for what this chapter refers to as 'outside-in'. See Cavatorta, F. and Pace, M. 2010. Special Issue: The Post-Normative Turn in European Union (EU)-Middle East and North Africa (MENA) Relations. *European Foreign Affairs Review*, 15(5), 581–737.

3   See Chaban, N. and Holland, M. (eds) 2013. *Europe and Asia: Perceptions from Afar*. Baden-Baden: Nomos; Chaban, N., Holland, M. and Ryan, P. (eds) 2009. *The EU through the Eyes of Asia: New Cases, New Findings*. Singapore/London: World Scientific; Lucarelli, S. and Fioramonti, L. (eds) 2010. *External Perceptions of the European Union as a Global Actor*. Abingdon: Routledge.

4   See Mayer, H. and Zielonka, J. 2012. Special issue: Europe as a global power: views from the outside. *Perspectives*, 20(2), 1–128; Pace, M. and Seeberg, P. 2009. *The European Union's Democratization Agenda in the Mediterranean*. London: Routledge; and Youngs, R. (ed.) 2010. *The European Union and Democracy Promotion: A Critical Global Assessment*. Baltimore, MD: Johns Hopkins University Press.

5   Tickner, A.B. and Waever, O. (eds) 2009. *International Relations Scholarship around the World*. London: Routledge.

6   Wæver, O. 1994. Resisting the Temptation of Post Foreign Policy Analysis, in Carlsnaes, W. and Smith, S. (eds), *European Foreign Policy: The EC and Changing Perspectives in Europe*. London: Sage Publications, 11; and Tickner, A.B. 2003. Seeing

In their book on *Non-Western International Relations Theory*, Acharya and Buzan explain that, despite their variety, most IR theories are rooted in the Western tradition of social theory and in a Eurocentric framing of world history.[7] IR scholars therefore analyse foreign policy from a Western perspective – based on the Westphalian paradigm and modernization paradigms – and have major problems in overcoming Western ethnocentrism and accepting 'difference' in international relations.[8] In this regard, developing an 'outside-in' approach only makes sense if the ethnocentric bias of the Western perspective is acknowledged and is conceptually overcome. This implies that the existence of different modernization narratives is accepted and that the Western modernization process is seen as only one possible path, instead of taking it for granted and generalizing its applicability to the modernization processes of other parts of the world. The recognition of 'difference' thus implies recognition that other countries or societies can have 'alternative developmental schemas' and can be subject to different transformative mechanisms, processes and contexts.[9]

Constructing an 'Outside-in' Perspective

Constructing an 'outside-in' perspective implies the willingness and capacity to enter into a learning process in order to recognize and analyse 'difference'. In this section, some building blocks for adopting an 'outside-in' approach are proposed, including the geographical 'outside-in', polity 'outside-in', normative 'outside-in', linguistic 'outside-in', and disciplinary and methodological 'outside-in' perspectives.

Geographical 'Outside-in'

On the most basic level, an 'outside-in' approach implies, first, that the analysis and assessment of EU foreign policy starts from a thorough knowledge of the situation in the 'target countries', 'recipient countries', or 'partner countries' of the EU's foreign policy and, second, that this knowledge is constructed from the

---

IR Differently: Notes from the Third World. *Millennium: Journal of International Studies*, 32(2), 295–324.

    7   Acharya, A. and Buzan, B. 2010. *Non-Western International Relations Theory: Perspectives on and beyond Asia*. London: Routledge, 6.

    8   Inayatullah, N. and Blaney, D.L. 2004. *International Relations and the Problem of Difference*. London: Routledge, 93–125; Chabal, P. and Daloz, J-P. 2006. *Culture Troubles: Politics and the Interpretation of Meaning*. London: Hurst & Company; and Kayaoglu, T. 2010. Westphalian Eurocentrism in International Relations Theories. *International Studies Review*, 12(2), 193–217.

    9   Delanty, G. and Rumford, C. 2005. *Rethinking Europe: Social Theory and the Implications of Europeanization*. Abingdon: Routledge, 15.

perspective of and taking into account their contexts (and not only that of the EU or the West). Regarding the subject of this book, the neighbours of the EU's neighbours, this implies that the analysis of the EU's policy towards its broader neighbourhood needs to start from a sound knowledge of the various regions (the Horn of Africa, the Sahel region, the Gulf and Central Asia), with this expertise being acquired from within the perspective and context of these regions. This thorough knowledge is essential in order to contextualize the EU's foreign policy and avoid the EU's policy being evaluated only or mainly on the basis of EU or Western paradigms. Expertise on the various regions can also provide the touchstones needed to evaluate the effectiveness, the impact and particularly the relevance of the EU's foreign policy. This already points to the importance of area studies and area specialists for the analysis and development of EU foreign policy, which will be discussed further in this chapter.

A geographical 'outside-in' perspective requires a thorough understanding of a wide range of both material and immaterial features of the third country or region. The material features can be detected through basic facts with regard to the geographical situation *sensu stricto* (surface area, nature of the terrain, borders, etc.), the economic situation and the societal composition of a country or region (with regard to ethnicity, religion, etc.), the human development situation (basic facts on demography, health, education, literacy rate, gender, violence, etc.), the basic infrastructure and communication networks (roads, electricity, Internet access, etc.), the public sector (the public administration, the judicial sector, public finance, etc.), in addition to the basic facts on the political system, external trade, defence, and security and foreign policy of the country or region concerned.[10] An example demonstrates the relevance of basic facts to evaluate the EU's foreign policy: When evaluating the EU's Common Security and Defence Policy (CSDP) operations as part of its Sahel Strategy – EUCAP Sahel in Niger, EUTM Mali and EUBAM Libya[11] – it is important to keep in mind the sheer surface area, the desert nature of parts of the countries and the length of their borders, as well as of the implications of these facts for the EU's efforts to strengthen the capacity of the security forces in these countries to control their territory and borders.

The immaterial features of a country or region are much more difficult to pin down but are at least as important, as they touch upon the historical, cultural, societal, linguistic, ideational or normative contexts of a country or region.[12] An explanation for, as well as examples of some of these immaterial contexts, are provided in the following sections.

---

10   See CIA 2013. *The World Factbook*; UNDP 2013. *Human Development Reports*; UNSTATS 2013. *United Nations Statistics Division*; and World Bank 2013. *Data*.

11   See also Chapter 3 by Alexander Mattelaer in this volume.

12   Goodin, R.E. and Tilly, C. (eds) 2006. *The Oxford Handbook of Contextual Political Analysis*. Oxford: Oxford University Press.

Polity 'Outside-in'[13]

Related to the ethnocentric biases of IR and of the Westphalian paradigm described by Inayatullah and Blaney, one can observe in many publications on EU foreign policy a one-sided focus on the nation state, often considered as the main level of analysis or point of reference.[14] Western foreign policy analysts as well as Western/European foreign policy actors are mainly interested in structures on the national, regional, international and global levels (with the regional and global level considered as consisting predominantly of state actors), but rarely pay attention to polities or structures on various societal levels which do not fit within Western or 'modern' conceptualizations. However, there are other structures through which groups of people are connected in a persistent way, on the basis of ethnicity or religion[15] or on the basis of kinship or other systems of legitimacy to organize large or smaller groups of people (such as kingdoms, chiefdoms, tribes, clans, neighbourhoods or extended families). In terms of effectiveness, legitimacy and identity, these polities can be complementary or superior to those at the state level.[16] Adopting a polity 'outside-in' approach, and thus including such other polities in our analysis, allows us to overcome the 'territorial trap' in the analysis of foreign policy, being the geographical assumption of IR theory and the particular concept of space that dominated the development of the West and of Western academic thinking.[17] As Agnew explains, this territorial trap includes the misconception of the 'historical relationship between territorial states and the broader social and economic structures and geopolitical order (or form of spatial practice) in which these states must operate'.[18]

When looking at the EU's broader neighbourhood and the analysis provided in various other chapters in this book, the relevance of a polity 'outside-in' perspective and of overcoming the 'territorial trap' becomes very clear. The various tribes in Northern Africa, the Sahel region and the Horn of Africa are polities that, for the population in these regions, are often more important in terms of identity, legitimacy and often also effectiveness in providing public services than the formal state structures that are the EU's main point of reference. The same holds for Islam in its various forms and expressions, with the Quran and the Sharia being the main point of reference for the population at large and for a wide

---

13 I am grateful to Charles Thépaut for the suggestion of this term.

14 Inayatullah, N. and Blaney, D.L. 2004. *International Relations and the Problem of Difference*. London: Routledge.

15 Wæver, O. 1993. Societal security: the concept, in Wæver, O. et al. (eds), *Identity, Migration and the New Security Agenda in Europe*. London: Pinter Publishers, 23.

16 Migdal, J.S. 1998. *Strong Societies and Weak States: State-Society Relations and State Capabilities in the Third World*. Princeton, NJ: Princeton University Press; and Migdal, J.S. 2001. *State in Society: Studying How States and Societies Transform and Constitute One Another*. Cambridge: Cambridge University Press.

17 Agnew, J. 1994. The Territorial Trap: The Geographical Assumptions of International Relations Theory. *Review of International Political Economy*, 1(1), 53–80.

18 Ibid., 77.

variety of groups, movements and currents.[19] This is true not only in the Middle East and Africa, but also in Central Asia and parts of the Caspian Sea region. The pertinence of these different types of polities and societal structures points to the importance of area specialists who also know and understand the various ethnic- and religion-based groups and movements.

Normative 'Outside-in'

Partially related to the polity 'outside-in' perspective is the normative 'outside-in' perspective. This points to the importance of analysing other regions – and the EU's policies towards these regions – not only on the basis of the EU's or the West's value system, but also on the basis of norms that may be equally or even more important for people in those regions. EU foreign policy as well as its analysis are strongly biased towards values that are predominant in the EU's discourse and that are also mirrored in the conceptualization of the EU as a 'normative power',[20] including democracy, human rights, rule of law or gender equality. And this is often mirrored in the absence of any sensibility for and knowledge and understanding of values that are less important in the West.

Examples of values that are important in the EU's immediate neighbourhood – for instance in the ENP – and in its broader neighbourhood and that also inspire a very wide range of political and social movements are the various values related to the Islamic belief system, with the most important and prevalent value being the belief in and submission to Allah as the omnipotent, merciful and unique.[21] Another example is the important value of allegiance to, responsibility for and solidarity with (the members of) the own group or polity – although this may lead to practices which in the West are labelled as discrimination, nepotism or corruption.[22] A third example is a value which also appears in the European discourse, but receives much less attention in the foreign policy of the EU: 'justice'. The importance of this value is mirrored in the various prominent political parties from the Islamist spectrum in countries in the EU's southern neighbourhood which carry 'justice' in their name. A normative 'outside-in' approach implies that the EU foreign policy analyst or practitioner acquires a sound knowledge of and sensibility to the importance of these and other values in countries and regions in the EU's broader neighbourhood.

---

19   See Rubin, B. (ed.) 2013. *Islamic Political and Social Movements*. London: Routledge.

20   Manners, I. 2002. Normative Power Europe: a contradiction in terms? *Journal of Common Market Studies*, 40(2), 235–58; and Whitman, R. (ed.) 2011. *Normative Power Europe: Empirical and Theoretical Perspectives*. London: Palgrave Macmillan.

21   See Rubin, op. cit.

22   See Blundo, G. and de Sardan, J-P.O. 2006. *Everyday Corruption and the State: Citizens and Public Officials in Africa*. London: Zed Books; and de Sardan, J-P.O. 1996. L'économie morale de la corruption en Afrique. *Politique africaine*, 63, 97–116.

Linguistic 'Outside-in'

The dominance of English as the *lingua franca* of IR and as the main language in the analysis of EU foreign policy has substantial consequences for the analysis of the EU's policy. It reinforces both the marginalization of and the indifference to the 'outside'. A very limited number of EU foreign policy scholars are able to read primary and secondary sources or to talk to and conduct interviews in Arabic (in its various forms), Farsi, Turkmen, Kazakh, or the many African languages. Moreover, Arab, Persian, African and Asian scholars are only to a limited extent present in the academic publications read by EU foreign policy specialists.

An additional reason why the 'foreign' is missing in foreign policy analysis is that information, concepts, approaches and concerns that are foreign to the scholars' conceptual lenses and cognitive world are often lacking in the analysis, even though they may be key to understanding the outcome and effect of the EU's foreign policy. This leads to the need for a linguistic 'outside-in' approach: the need to read, understand and use more sources written in non-European languages and to work together with local specialists or at least scholars with a sound knowledge of the local language. It also requires a linguistic openness for words or concepts that are perhaps not important in (and can sometimes not easily be translated into) European languages, as well as a sensibility to the impact of language on the way people and societies think. The above mentioned 'problem of difference' is indeed also related to the problem of 'conceptual difference': words used in various languages and regions can in fact have quite different meanings and connotations, while words and concepts that are part of the discourse in some languages may not exist or be less important in other languages.[23]

Disciplinary and Methodological 'Outside-in'

A good understanding of EU foreign policy requires the incorporation of knowledge and analytical frameworks from other academic disciplines. Firstly, as indicated before, a geographical 'outside-in' perspective requires input from specialized 'area studies' (Middle East Studies, Central Asian Studies, etc.), including expertise not only from Western experts but also from experts from those regions. The EU has a comparative disadvantage vis-à-vis the US, Russia or China in this respect: 'area studies' are much less developed in the university system of most European countries (with the exception of the UK), which also implies that the number of area specialists emerging from European universities is rather limited. Therefore, it would be in the interests of the EU to actively promote and subsidize not only 'European studies' in other parts of the world (as it does),

---

23 See Chabal, P. and Daloz, J-P. 2006. *Culture Troubles: Politics and the Interpretation of Meaning.* London: Hurst & Company; and Laïdi, Z. 1998. *A World without Meaning: The Crisis of Meaning in International Relations.* Abingdon: Routledge.

but also 'Caucasus studies', 'Middle Eastern studies', 'Persian/Iranian studies' and other area studies at European universities and research centres.

Secondly, in view of the multidimensional nature of most foreign policy challenges, there is a need to rely more systematically on the analysis provided by other disciplines such as security studies, international political economy, democracy studies, development studies, anthropology or philosophy. In addition, the systematic integration of insights from the study of complex policy issues (such as corruption, democracy promotion, or Security Sector Reform) can provide the sophisticated knowledge that is needed to examine related dimensions of EU foreign policy. The analyst can borrow from methodological approaches and research techniques that are used in other disciplines in order to overcome what Hudson described as the 'deep and growing methodological discontent' in foreign policy analysis, with many scholars continuing to use 'inappropriate methods, by employing simplifying assumptions that evade the complexity with which the methods cannot cope'.[24] A major obstacle in this regard is related to data collection and data analysis. Adopting an 'outside-in' perspective implies that the analysis cannot just be based on primary and secondary Western literature and data, but that data also have to be obtained in the target country, region or society itself. However, research and fieldwork in many of the countries of the EU's broader neighbourhood involves specific methodological but also linguistic, financial and other practical challenges.

Thirdly, as indicated before, insights from non-Western scholars are essential for a serious assessment of EU foreign policy. On a more theoretical level, although there might not yet be a 'non-Western IR theory'[25] as such, scholars from the Arab world, Africa and Asia bring to the fore concepts, approaches and issues that are important for understanding non-Western regions, countries and societies. These are thus also relevant for studying the EU's foreign policy towards these regions, countries and societies and for bringing 'difference' and the 'outside' into EU foreign policy analysis.[26]

Lessons for EU Diplomacy

Adopting an 'outside-in' approach has implications for the EU's foreign policy architecture: for the High Representative, the EEAS, the EU Delegations and CSDP missions/operations in third countries, the various Directorates-General (DGs) within the Commission with relevance to the EU's foreign policy (such

---

24   Hudson, V.M. 2007. *Foreign Policy Analysis: Classic and Contemporary Theory.* New York: Rowman & Littlefield, 188.

25   Acharya, A. and Buzan, B. 2010. *Non-Western International Relations Theory: Perspectives on and beyond Asia.* London: Routledge.

26   Tickner, A.B. and Blaney, D.L. (eds). 2012. *Thinking International Relations Differently.* Abingdon: Routledge; and Tickner and Wæver, op. cit.

as DG DevCo or DG Trade), the Council of Ministers and the European Council (and the various relevant committees), the European Parliament (and its relevant committees and inter-parliamentary delegations) and the EU's Member States.[27]

Challenges for the EU's Diplomatic System

Various questions can be raised as to whether the EU's foreign policy framework is sufficiently equipped and adapted to think and act outside the (European) box – in terms of expertise, mandate and capacity to feed the EU's foreign policy system with an 'outside-in' perspective.[28] A first question is whether the EU's diplomatic system can rely on sufficient expertise and in-depth knowledge about other countries and societies. The EU not only needs excellent generalists or people with outstanding diplomatic skills, but also country or area specialists with a sound knowledge of and experience in third countries and with a solid network of contacts in these countries. The various relevant EU actors should be able to rely not only on diplomats or civil servants specialized in, for instance, the EU's policy towards the Caucasus or the Arab world, but also on specialists in the Caucasus and the Arab world itself, with an in-depth knowledge of these regions, their history, societies, value systems, dynamics and complexities.

A second question is to what extent the EEAS, EU Delegations, CSDP missions and relevant DGs have sufficient staff who are fluent in the local languages, as a prerequisite for real interaction and dialogue. An inquiry in various EU Delegations learns that this is often not the case.[29] EU diplomats in EU Delegations often depend to a large extent on local staff for following the debates in a country, for translating documents and interpreting conversations with local actors. This dependency on local staff raises particular challenges in various non-democratic countries where the EU Delegation has to rely on local personnel that is selected and proposed by the government of the guest country.

A third question is whether diplomats and civil servants are able in their daily work to invest sufficient time and energy in the interaction and dialogue with actors in third countries – not only with the elites but also with other segments of societies, including those that do not fit well within the EU's value system and conceptualization of 'civil society' (such as religious movements and parties, which are important in the EU's broader neighbourhood). To what extent have the staff members in the EEAS and in the EU Delegations (including the Heads of Delegation) sufficient time for outreach, in view of their considerable management tasks, of their administrative and budgetary responsibilities, and of the time and

---

27 Keukeleire, S. and Delreux, T. 2014. *The Foreign Policy of the European Union.* 2nd edn. Basingstoke: Palgrave Macmillan, 61–93.

28 Keukeleire, S. 2013. European Foreign Policy beyond Lisbon. The Quest for Relevance, in Govaere, I. and Hanf, D. (eds), *Liber Amicorum – Paul Demaret.* Brussels: P.I.E Peter Lang, 829–39.

29 Author's interviews.

energy needed to interact with the many EU actors involved in foreign policy-making? This is particularly problematic in EU Delegations, as the number of EEAS staff in these Delegations responsible for foreign policy and diplomacy is in general only a fraction of the number of people in these Delegations that is working for DG DevCo or DG Trade.

These questions and critical remarks are often dismissed by EU diplomats. The EU's diplomatic system can indeed also rely on a pool of outstanding diplomats and experts, with a sometimes long experience in third countries and a strong sensibility for the 'outside-in' perspectives. The EU also increasingly tries to attract country/region specialists for the EEAS and EU Delegations, which in turn raises the question whether these experts also dispose of sufficient diplomatic skills and experience. However, the challenge of adopting an 'outside-in' perspective becomes evident when inquiring into the number of staff (in the EEAS in Brussels and in the EU Delegations in non-Western countries) who are fluent in the local language(s), have a thorough understanding of the country and society (and not only of the relations between that country or region with the EU), and who also have sufficient time and mandate to interact with broader sections of society. The limited attention to the 'outside' perspectives also appears in the preparation and training of EU diplomats and civil servants that are sent to EU Delegations in third countries.[30] Most attention is dedicated to the internal functioning of the EU and to the bureaucratic procedures. However, with some exceptions, EU staff neither receive serious language training nor serious preparation regarding the specificities of the third country or region before being sent on mission. Taking into account the 'outside' perspectives is also hampered by the EU's general staff policy which prescribes a regular rotation of EU staff from one position to another (and thus also from one EU Delegation to another, or from an EU Delegation to an unrelated country/area desk in the Brussels offices, or vice versa). This explains why for EU staff it is not always worth investing too much time and energy in delving into the specific context and peculiarities of the country or region in which they reside or for which they are responsible in the EEAS or in the Commission.

The fourth question is whether the EU's policy-making system allows EU diplomats and civil servants to transcend the traditional conception of European interest by incorporating the interests of other states and societies within the EU's own definition of interests. This requires that Ministers and national diplomats within the Council of Ministers, COREPER, the Political and Security Committee (PSC), and the various working groups also accept that complementing an 'EU perspective' with a 'third country perspective' is essential to increase the external relevance and effectiveness of EU foreign policy. This also underlines the daunting challenge of promoting an 'outside-in' perspective in an EU of 28 Member States.

---

30   Davis Cross, M. 2011. Building a European Diplomacy: Recruitment & Training to the EEAS. *European Foreign Affairs Review*, 16(4), 447–64; and Mahncke, D. and Gstöhl, S. 2012. Training European Diplomats, in Mahncke, D. and Gstöhl, S. (eds), *European Union Diplomacy: Coherence, Unity and Effectiveness*. Brussels: P.I.E Peter Lang, 241–70.

It indeed implies that, in addition to the interests of the EU in general, the interests of the 28 Member States and of the EU institutions as well as those of the third country and society are to be taken seriously.

Lessons for EU Foreign Policy-Making

The preceding observations lead to a number of recommendations with regard to the staff policy in the EU's diplomatic system. First, in terms of recruitment, the EU should try to attract more country/area specialists to the EEAS and other relevant actors in the EU's external relations. Second, the EU should systematically organize training programmes for its civil servants and diplomats to assure that they have a sufficient knowledge of the regions, countries and societies where they will work or which are the subject of their work in Brussels. Within these training programmes, the unavoidable EU focus (related to the objectives of EU foreign policy, the functioning of the EU's diplomatic and institutional system, etc.) has to be complemented with an explicit 'outside-in' approach to make sure that the EU diplomats and civil servants are able to look outside the (European and Western) box. This can also require the development of systematic cooperation with external experts or research institutes specialized in these regions. Third, and related to the previous point, following the example of major diplomatic services such as in the US, Russia and China, the EU should organize intensive language training for its diplomats. Fourth, the EU should – at least for the civil servants and diplomats involved in the EU's diplomacy and external action – adapt its human resources policy in such a way as to foster and accumulate expertise on third countries and regions. This implies replacing its long-standing system where EU staff are regularly transferred to other posts with a system where they can work for a longer term on (or in) a specific region (such as Central Asia or the Arab world).

Another set of recommendations is related to the functioning of EU diplomacy and EU foreign policy-making. First, diplomats and civil servants should receive the explicit instructions to systematically complement (in their political analyses, reports, briefings and drafts for declarations and decisions) the now predominantly EU-centred perspective with an 'outside-in' perspective, and to explain why and how this is relevant for the EU's foreign policy. This goes against the current practice where documents and briefings are very much adapted to the EU's discourse and where, in the worst case, reports and other documents written by EU staff in EU Delegations or CSDP missions are even rewritten in the EEAS or the relevant Commission DGs in Brussels in order to better fit the EU's points of view, priorities, language, and political and institutional sensibilities. Second, emphasizing more the 'outside-in' perspective requires that EU diplomats and civil servants be able to spend more time and energy than is now the case not only for 'outreach' (contacting other actors and explaining and defending the EU's positions and interests), but also for 'inreach' (gaining insights in the contexts, positions and interests in the third country or region and incorporating these in the EU's foreign policy-making system). Third, in the preparatory documents for the policy-making processes in which Member State representatives are involved (on the level of the working parties, COREPER, the PSC, the Council of Ministers or European Council), the 'outside-in' perspective is to be systematically presented, in order to avoid that the various EU actors mainly focus on internal dynamics and neglect the external relevance, legitimacy and effectiveness of the EU's foreign policy. Adopting an 'outside-in' perspective is indeed not inspired by a merely altruistic wish to take into account the views and context of the 'other', but is to be seen as a way to strengthen the EU in its interactions with other actors in the world.

It is obvious that the realization of some of the recommendations would require additional financial and other resources for the EEAS and the EU Delegations. However, this goes against the practice of the previous years where Member States were reluctant to increase the resources of the EU's diplomatic system – even when creating the EEAS, which had to be a budget-neutral operation.[31] Moreover, adopting these measures would also reinforce EU foreign policy and EU diplomacy, which may precisely be what several Member States and particularly the larger Member States want to avoid.

Conclusions

The main argument of this chapter is that the usually predominant EU-centred perspective in the foreign policy of the EU and in the analysis of EU foreign policy has to be complemented by an 'outside-in' perspective. Such an 'outside-in' perspective implies that the analyst or practitioner takes not only the EU and its policy towards a third country or region as the main point of reference, but also tries to look at this EU policy from the perspective of the third country or region. The chapter proposed several analytical building blocks for constructing an 'outside-in' perspective and for overcoming Western ethnocentrism and recognizing 'difference'. The chapter makes a distinction between a geographical 'outside-in' perspective, a polity 'outside-in' perspective, a normative 'outside-in' perspective, a linguistic 'outside-in' perspective, and a disciplinary and methodological 'outside-in' perspective.

Within the context of the EU's policy towards the neighbours of its neighbours, a geographical 'outside-in' perspective implies a thorough knowledge of the various regions in the EU's broader neighbourhood, with expertise on the various regions being acquired within the perspective and context of these regions. The polity 'outside-in' perspective refers to the need to take into account the various tribes and ethnic- or religion-based groups and movements which are in terms of identity, legitimacy and effectiveness often important in the Gulf, Northern Africa and the Horn of Africa in particular. This is closely related to the normative

---

31   See Council of the European Union 2010. *Council Decision of 26 July 2010 establishing the organisation and functioning of the European External Action Service (2010/427/EU)*, OJ L 201/30, 3 August, preamble 15.

'outside-in' perspective, which points to the importance of analysing the various regions in the EU's neighbours of the neighbours not only on the basis of the EU's value system, but also on the basis of values that are important for the diverse societies in these regions. Alternative value systems are often reflected in a different discourse in the regions concerned, which also is one aspect of the linguistic 'outside-in' perspective. Constructing an 'outside-in' perspective also requires a disciplinary and methodological 'outside-in' perspective. This implies the incorporation of knowledge and analytical frameworks from specialized 'area studies' (such as Middle East Studies or Central Asian Studies) and from other academic disciplines that can lead the analysis of the EU's policy towards its broader neighbourhood to a higher level of sophistication.

The last section of the chapter distinguishes various factors that hamper the capacity of the EU's institutional and bureaucratic framework to feed the EU's foreign policy system with an 'outside-in' perspective and to think and act 'outside the (European) box'. This provides the basis for the formulation of a number of recommendations for EU diplomacy, both for the EU's staff policy and for the daily practice of EU diplomacy and EU foreign policy-making. Taken together, they may contribute to strengthening the relevance and effectiveness of the EU's foreign policy towards the neighbours of its neighbours.

Bibliography

Acharya, A. and Buzan, B. 2010. *Non-Western International Relations Theory: Perspectives on and beyond Asia*. London: Routledge.

Agnew, J. 1994. The Territorial Trap: The Geographical Assumptions of International Relations Theory. *Review of International Political Economy*, 1(1), 53–80.

Balfour, R. and Ojanen, H. 2011. Does the European External Action Service Represent a Model for the Challenges of Global Diplomacy? *IAI Working Papers*, no. 11, Rome: IAI.

Blundo, G. and de Sardan, J-P.O. 2006. *Everyday Corruption and the State: Citizens and Public Officials in Africa*. London: Zed Books.

Cavatorta, F. and Pace, M. 2010. Special Issue: The Post-Normative Turn in European Union (EU)-Middle East and North Africa (MENA) Relations. *European Foreign Affairs Review*, 15(5), 581–737.

Chabal, P. and Daloz, J-P. 2006. *Culture Troubles: Politics and the Interpretation of Meaning*. London: Hurst & Company.

Chaban, N. and Holland, M. 2008. *The European Union and the Asia-Pacific: Media, Public and Elite Perceptions of the EU*. London: Routledge.

Chaban, N. and Holland, M. (eds) 2013. *Europe and Asia: Perceptions from Afar*. Baden-Baden: Nomos.

Chaban, N., Holland, M. and Ryan, P. (eds) 2009. *The EU through the Eyes of Asia: New Cases, New Findings*. Singapore/London: World Scientific.

CIA. 2013. *The World Factbook*, https://www.cia.gov/library/publications/the-world-factbook/fields/2096.html [accessed: 30 August 2013].

Council of the European Union 2010. *Council Decision 2010/427/EU of 26 July 2010 establishing the organisation and functioning of the European External Action Service*, OJ L201/30, 3 August.

Davis Cross, M. 2011. Building a European Diplomacy: Recruitment & Training to the EEAS. *European Foreign Affairs Review*, 16(4), 447–64.

Delanty, G. and Rumford, C. 2005. *Rethinking Europe: Social Theory and the Implications of Europeanization*. Abingdon: Routledge.

Goodin, R.E. and Tilly, C. (eds) 2006. *The Oxford Handbook of Contextual Political Analysis*. Oxford: Oxford University Press.

Grevi, G., Kelly, D. and Keohane, D. 2009. Conclusion, in Grevi, G. et al. (eds), *ESDP: The First Ten Years*. Paris: EUISS, 403–12.

Hudson, V.M. 2007. *Foreign Policy Analysis: Classic and Contemporary Theory*. New York: Rowman & Littlefield.

Inayatullah, N. and Blaney, D.L. 2004. *International Relations and the Problem of Difference*. London: Routledge.

Kayaoglu, T. 2010. Westphalian Eurocentrism in International Relations Theories. *International Studies Review*, 12(2), 193–217.

Keukeleire, S. 2013. European Foreign Policy beyond Lisbon: The quest for relevance, in Govaere, I. and Hanf, D. (eds), *Scrutinizing Internal and External Dimensions of European Law: Liber Amicorum – Paul Demaret*. Brussels: P.I.E Peter Lang, 829–39.

Keukeleire, S. and Delreux, T. 2014. *The Foreign Policy of the European Union*. 2nd edn. Basingstoke: Palgrave Macmillan.

Keukeleire, S. and Thépaut, C. 2012. *Towards an Outside-in Approach in the Analysis of (European) Foreign Policy*. Paper presented at the conference 'The European Union in International Affairs III', Brussels, May.

Laïdi, Z. 1998. *A World without Meaning: The Crisis of Meaning in International Relations*. Abingdon: Routledge.

Lucarelli, S. 2007. Special Issue: The European Union in the Eyes of Others. *European Foreign Affairs Review*, 12(3), 249–429.

Lucarelli, S. and Fioramonti, L. (eds) 2010. *External Perceptions of the European Union as a Global Actor*. Abingdon: Routledge.

Mahncke, D. and Gstöhl, S. 2012. Training European diplomats, in Mahncke, D. and Gstöhl, S. (eds), *European Union Diplomacy: Coherence, Unity and Effectiveness*. Brussels: P.I.E Peter Lang, 241–70.

Manners, I. 2002. Normative Power Europe: A Contradiction in Terms? *Journal of Common Market Studies*, 40(2), 235–58.

Mayer, H. and Zielonka, J. 2012. Special Issue: Europe as a Global Power: Views from the Outside. *Perspectives*, 20(2), 1–128.

Migdal, J.S. 1998. *Strong Societies and Weak States: State-Society Relations and State Capabilities in the Third World*. Princeton, NJ: Princeton University Press.

Migdal, J.S. 2001. *State in Society: Studying How States and Societies Transform and Constitute One Another*. Cambridge: Cambridge University Press.

Paasivirta, E. 2011. The EU's external representation after Lisbon: New rules, a new era?, in Koutrakos, P. (ed.), *European Union's External Relations a Year after Lisbon, CLEER Working Papers*, no. 3, The Hague: T.M.C. Asser Institute, 39–47.

Pace, M. and Seeberg, P. 2009. *The European Union's Democratization Agenda in the Mediterranean*. London: Routledge.

Peters, J. (ed.) 2012. *The European Union and the Arab Spring: Promoting Democracy and Human Rights in the Middle East*. Lanham, MD: Lexington.

Rubin, B. (ed.) 2013. *Islamic Political and Social Movements*. London: Routledge.

de Sardan, J-P.O. 1996. L'économie morale de la corruption en Afrique. *Politique africaine*, 63, 97–116.

Scheipers, S. and Sicurelli, D. 2008. Empowering Africa: Normative Power in EU-Africa Relations. *Journal of European Public Policy*, 15(4), 607–23.

Tickner, A.B. 2003. Seeing IR Differently: Notes from the Third World. *Millennium: Journal of International Studies*, 32(2), 295–324.

Tickner, A.B. and Blaney, D.L. (eds) 2012. *Thinking International Relations Differently*. Abingdon: Routledge.

Tickner, A.B. and Wæver, O. (eds) 2009. *International Relations Scholarship around the World*. London: Routledge.

UNDP 2013. *Human Development Reports*, http://hDr.undp.org/en/reports [accessed: 30 August 2013].

UNSTATS 2013. *United Nations Statistics Division*, http://unstats.un.org/unsd/default.htm [accessed: 30 August 2013].

Wæver, O. 1993. Societal security: The concept, in Wæver, O. et al. (eds), *Identity, Migration and the New Security Agenda in Europe*. London: Pinter Publishers, 17–27.

Wæver, O. 1994. Resisting the Temptation of Post Foreign Policy Analysis, in Carlsnaes, W. and Smith, S. (eds), *European Foreign Policy: The EC and Changing Perspectives in Europe*. London: Sage Publications.

Whitman, R. (ed.) 2011. *Normative Power Europe: Empirical and Theoretical Perspectives*. London: Palgrave Macmillan.

World Bank 2013. *Data*, http://data.worldbank.org [accessed: 30 August 2013].

Youngs, R. (ed.) 2010. *The European Union and Democracy Promotion: A Critical Global Assessment*. Baltimore, MD: Johns Hopkins University Press.

Chapter 12

The Global Players in the EU's Broader Neighbourhood

Jonatan Thompson

Introduction

The preceding chapters in this volume have provided a panorama of the state of play and the EU's role in the Sahel and the Horn of Africa, the Arabian Gulf and Central Asia. They have highlighted the economic, political and security spill-overs between these neighbours of the neighbours and the EU's neighbourhood, and the challenges and opportunities these present for the EU. This chapter focuses on the foreign policies of the other global players in the Sahel and the Horn of Africa, in the Arabian Gulf and in Central Asia, with a view to provide context and highlight the implications for EU policies. The term 'global player' refers here to powers that pursue interests beyond as well as within their own regions. The chapter focuses on the US, China and Russia, in recognition of their geopolitical, military, political and economic weight and the intensity of their interaction with the EU and its broader neighbourhood. It is important to bear in mind that China and Russia are regional players in Central Asia and the Arabian Gulf which they consider part of their extended neighbourhood or 'near abroad'. As will be shown below, each global player pursues its objectives in the regions on the basis of distinct historical ties, capabilities and approaches which lead to complex economic, political and military-strategic interactions or 'games' between global and regional players.[1] These 'games', in turn, contribute to shaping the long-term regional order which can be conceptualized along a continuum between anarchy, a balance of power, a concert of powers, and intra-regional cooperation and integration.[2]

---

1   Cooley, A. 2013. *Great Game, Local Rules: The New Great Power Contest in Central Asia*. Oxford: Oxford University Press.

2   The conception of a 'region' as a strategic space draws on the concept of the 'Regional Security Complex' set out by Buzan, B. and Wæver, O. 2003. *Regions and Powers: The Structure of International Security*. Cambridge: Cambridge University Press. The notion of 'regional order' draws on Kaim, M. 2008. U.S. Policy and the Regional Order of the Persian Gulf: The Analytical Framework, in Kaim, M. (ed.), *Great Powers and Regional Orders: The United States and the Persian Gulf*. Aldershot: Ashgate, 1–12. On regionalization through dominant practices, see Kavalski, E. (ed.). 2010. *China and the Global Politics of Regionalization*. Farnham: Ashgate.

The chapter will first identify the overarching objectives, roles and foreign policies of the US, China and Russia in the EU's broader neighbourhood. As has been shown in the preceding chapters, one of the overarching aims of the EU's external action is to support the development of inclusive intra-regional economic integration, political cooperation and regional institutions, particularly among developing countries.[3] Hence, this chapter will consider the policies of the other players to see to which extent the foreign policy 'games' they play are complementary to, or in tension with, the 'regionalist games' of the EU. It argues that, while these global players pursue a number of region-level diplomacy and policy initiatives, their policy objectives and practices tend to differ markedly from those of the EU and tend to place a higher premium on bilateral relations and the norms of sovereignty and non-interference. The chapter proceeds by looking at the Sahel and the Horn of Africa, the Arabian Gulf, and Central Asia, before drawing some overall conclusions about the roles of the global players in the EU's broader neighbourhood and the challenges their policies present for the EU.

The Global Players in the Sahel and the Horn of Africa

The Sahel and Horn of Africa region, referring to the arc of countries from Mauritania to the Horn of Africa between the Southern Mediterranean and sub-Saharan Africa, is characterized by weak states and strong non-state actors which give rise to common security problems linked to the near-anarchical conditions in the remoter desert areas.[4] There is an almost total absence of regional economic integration and political cooperation in the Sahel and the Horn of Africa. Actors from the extended region, especially Algeria, Libya and Nigeria, play a considerable role in the regional order and security, and new opportunities to exploit energy and mineral resources have in recent years contributed to drawing the attention of external players. As was shown in the preceding chapters, the EU has in recent years played a growing role through development cooperation and humanitarian aid as well as through civilian and military interventions, most recently in reaction to the 2012–13 crisis in Mali.[5]

---

3 See, for instance, European Commission 2012. *Promoting regional poles of prosperity and stability*. Brussels: DG Development and Cooperation – Europeaid, 17 February, http://ec.europa.eu/europeaid/what/economic-support/regional-integration/index-en.htm [accessed: 14 August 2013].

4 See also Chapter 3 by Alexander Mattelaer and Chapter 4 by Alex Vines and Ahmed Soliman in this volume.

5 See also Chapter 2 by Claudia Zulaika and Chapter 3 by Alexander Mattelaer in this volume.

The US in the Sahel and the Horn of Africa: Leading from behind

The US paid relatively little attention to the Sahel and the Horn of Africa in the decade after the end of the Cold War. US interest was rekindled, however, following the 11 September 2001 terrorist attacks in New York and Washington, which sparked concerns that weak and fractured African states could provide a safe haven for transnational terrorist organizations. These concerns prompted the US to introduce programmes to strengthen local state capabilities against terrorism and other threats, while taking pains to avoid any direct involvement in regional conflicts, given memories of the October 1993 'Black Hawk Down' Battle of Mogadishu.[6] US policies include region-wide Security Sector Reform, joint military training, coordination and exercises, non-security sector development assistance, as well as humanitarian aid in response to the 2011–12 regional food crisis. Alongside these programmes the US military has developed the capabilities and agreements for region-wide intelligence collection and the ability to strike suspected terrorists.[7] In 2002 the US launched its first flagship policy initiative, the Pan-Sahel Initiative (PSI) to improve the border management and counterterrorist capabilities of Chad, Niger, Mali and Mauritania. In 2004 the programme was expanded geographically to include Algeria, Morocco, Nigeria, Senegal and Tunisia, and functionally, to include USAID education programmes, Department of State civilian airport security programmes, and Treasury Department fiscal management assistance.[8] The PSI was renamed the Trans-Sahara Counterterrorism Initiative before being turned into the Trans-Sahara Counterterrorism Partnership (TSCTP) in 2008.[9] In addition to these region-wide security initiatives, the US increased its development assistance programmes in Mali from 2008 onwards,[10] and, since the outbreak of the 2011–12 food crisis, USAID has provided substantial humanitarian aid to Mauritania, Mali, Burkina Faso, Niger and Chad, amounting to $231 million for the 2013 financial year.[11] Given the wide thematic and geographical scope but limited budget of the TSCTP (around $100 million

---

6   Lawson, L. 2007. U.S. Africa Policy since the Cold War. *Strategic Insights*, VI(1).

7   Zoubir, Y.H. 2009. The United States and Maghreb-Sahel Security. *International Affairs*, 85(5), 977–95.

8   US initiatives include the training and 'Flintlock' joint military exercises, the African Coastal and Border Security Program, the International Military Education and Training Program, the Excess Defense Articles Program as well as an intelligence collection and fusion programme operating from Burkina Faso, the Joint Task Force Aztec Silence. See Thurston, A. 2012. *On US Bases in Africa*, Sahel Blog, 14 June, http://sahelblog.wordpress.com/2012/06/14/on-us-bases-in-africa [accessed: 1 June 2013].

9   Ibid.

10   USAID 2014. *Interactive map*, http://map.usaid.gov/?l=regional&w=SUB%20SAHARAN%20AFRICA [accessed: 18 January 2014].

11   USAID 2014. *The Sahel*, http://www.usaid.gov/crisis/sahel [accessed: 18 January 2014].

per year on average),[12] some observers argue that an underlying aim of these state-strengthening programmes is to build ties with African military and civilian security forces to facilitate intelligence collection and counterterrorist operations across Africa, including through the use of African military bases when needed.[13] Another underlying objective, some argue, is to facilitate US access to regional hydrocarbon and mineral resources.[14]

How have Washington's policies affected regional inter-state relations and economic integration? The official US objectives in the Sahel and the Horn of Africa are to address and prevent conflicts and humanitarian emergencies by strengthening economic resilience, states and regional institutions, and by encouraging more regional cooperation between Maghreb and Sahel states to coordinate counterterrorism efforts.[15] Yet some observers argue that Washington's prioritization of bilateral US-African security cooperation, reflecting US security concerns, has entailed a relative neglect of intra-regional socioeconomic development and political cooperation. For example, programmes to secure national borders may have further depressed cross-border trade in the region.[16] More recently, the Obama Administration has indicated a renewed focus on promoting development, cross-border trade and building resilience to food crises. However, the fragile security situation in Mali since 2012 and recent official remarks suggest that counterterrorism and crisis management are likely to remain at the top of the US agenda for some time.[17]

China in the Sahel and the Horn of Africa: The Chequebook Challenger

China's role in Africa has evolved considerably from its Mao era support for anti-colonial revolutionaries to Beijing's present-day focus on African natural resources and markets. China presents itself to African countries as 'the largest developing country in the world ... an example of successful government-led development and preservation of sovereignty without submitting to Western conditionality'[18] and seeking 'mutually beneficial engagement, not humanitarian paternalism'.[19] In 2000 Beijing took the initiative to establish the Forum on China-

---

12   Boudali, L.K. 2007. *The Trans-Sahara Counterterrorism Partnership*. West Point: United States Military Academy, The Combating Terrorism Center, 4.

13   *Global Security* 2013. *Trans Sahara Counterterrorism Partnership (TSCTP)*, 24 January http://www.globalsecurity.org/military/ops/tscti.htm [accessed: 2 August 2013].

14   Lawson, op. cit.

15   Thomas-Greenfield, L. 2013. *Keynote Address at the National Defense University*. Washington, DC, 30 October.

16   Zoubir, op. cit.

17   Thomas-Greenfied, op. cit.

18   Kavalski, E. 2010. Making a Region out of a Continent? China's Regionalization of Africa, in Kavalski, E. (ed.), *China and the Global Politics of Regionalization*. Farnham: Ashgate, 178.

19   Lawson, op. cit.

Africa Cooperation to hold summits with African leaders at three-year intervals.[20] Such continent-wide gatherings provide opportunities for multilateral summit diplomacy as well as for strengthening bilateral relations with resource-rich countries such as Sudan and Niger.[21] Chinese policies often comprise a mix of targeted investment, prestigious infrastructure construction projects, large up-front payments and loans in return for advantageous resource extraction deals. These payments are often coupled with development aid programmes, humanitarian assistance, as well as medical, educational and cultural programmes.[22] In the Sahel and the Horn of Africa, Chinese companies have, in recent years, been party to a number of resource exploitation agreements, involving oil fields in Chad, Niger and Mauritania, iron ore in Mauritania, and yellow-cake uranium deposits in Niger, where French companies had previously enjoyed a monopoly on extraction.[23] China has developed a particularly close relationship with Khartoum through trade in arms and energy, purchasing two-thirds of Sudan's oil exports and making large investments in the absence of Western companies which have left the country due to international sanctions.[24]

Given China's reliance on imported African energy and minerals, the growing stock of Chinese investments and ever greater number of Chinese citizens living in Africa, one is struck by the relatively low level of Chinese involvement in regional political and security questions. Beijing's May 2013 commitment of combat troops to a UN peacekeeping operation in Mali (MINUSMA), the first of its kind, appears to indicate the beginning of a more direct involvement in regional security, previously limited to taking part in the anti-piracy naval operations in the western Indian Ocean. In addition, China has long played an important indirect role in security matters as one of the chief suppliers of military weaponry and equipment, particularly small arms, to African states.[25]

---

20   Forum on China-Africa Cooperation 2004. *The First Ministerial Conference of FOCAC*. Forum on China-Africa Cooperation, http://www.focac.org/eng/ltda/dyjbzjhy/CI12009/t157577.htm [accessed: 18 January 2014].

21   Calabrese, J. 2008. Sino-Gulf Relations and the United States: Dark Cloud-Silver Lining?, in Kaim, M. (ed.), *Great Powers and Regional Orders: The United States and the Persian Gulf*. Aldershot: Ashgate, 241–62.

22   For example, China constructed the African Union's $200 million headquarters in Addis Ababa Ethiopia. See *BBC News Africa* 2012. African Union opens Chinese-funded HQ in Ethiopia, 28 January, http://www.bbc.co.uk/news/world-africa-16770932 [accessed: 5 August 2013].

23   Simon, L., Mattelaer, A. and Hadfield, A. 2012. *A Coherent EU Strategy for the Sahel*. Brussels: European Parliament (DG External Policies PE 433.778).

24   Vasiliev, A. 2011. *Russia and Africa : Vying for mineral resources*. Valdai Discussion Club, 10 May, valdaiclub.com/africa/24840/print-edition [accessed: 26 June 2013].

25   *Stratfor* 2013. *Mali: China Commits 500 Soldiers to U.N. Mission*, Stratfor, 24 May, http://www.stratfor.com/sample/analysis/mali-china-commits-500-soldiers-un-mission [accessed: 25 May 2013]. On China's arms sales in the region, see Cabestan,

In light of the above, how does China's presence affect the regional order of the Sahel and the Horn of Africa? In official statements Beijing emphasizes China's equal relationship with African states as partners in development and supports the African Union and other regional institutions. Yet it appears that the Chinese practice of pursuing state-to-state agreements with resource-rich countries, premised on the norms of inviolable state sovereignty and non-interference, benefits some countries more than others, at the risk of deepening regional disparities and discouraging inclusive forms of regional cooperation. Hence, Beijing's stated support for regional integration and institutions such as the African Union appear to some extent to be inconsistent with Chinese 'games' in the region.[26]

Russia in Africa: Back in Business?

Moscow's role in the Sahel and the Horn of Africa fell precipitously in the decade after the dissolution of the Soviet Union. Today, Russia's re-emerging foreign policy in Africa as a whole is based on status considerations and economic pragmatism, including Moscow's interest in hydrocarbon exploitation projects and access to uranium and other raw materials to sustain its domestic industry. Also important is Russia's long-standing role as the chief supplier of arms and equipment to many African militaries. While Moscow can draw on the legacy of Soviet relations with regional powers like Algeria, Egypt, South Africa and Angola, President Vladimir Putin's tour to South Africa and Morocco in September 2006 signalled Russia's ambition to strengthen ties across the continent.[27] Russian firms have in recent years made some inroads in African energy, mining, telecom and other sectors, although they have a relative limited presence in the Sahel and the Horn of Africa. The growing output of hydrocarbons from Africa, and the envisaged construction of a Trans-Saharan gas pipeline to bring Nigerian gas and oil to the EU market, currently heavily reliant on energy imports from Russia, give Moscow a stake in the future development of this region's resources. This has no doubt been a significant consideration behind Gazprom's interest in Nigerian energy exploration and the Trans-Saharan pipeline project.[28]

Russia is a second-tier player in regional security matters with a limited participation in multilateral UN deployments. It had by 2010 contributed 230

J.P. 2010. *La politique internationale de la Chine. Entre intégration et volonté de puissance.* Paris: Presses de Sciences Po Références, 379.

26   Scott, D. 2010. From Brussels to Beijing: Comparing the Regionalization Strategies of the EU and China, in Emilian, K. (ed.), *China and the Global Politics of Regionalization.* Farnham: Ashgate, 109–20.

27   Fidan, H. and Aras, B. 2010. The Return of Russia-Africa Relations. *bilig*, winter 2010, 52, 47–68.

28   *BBC News* 2009. Gazprom seals $2.5bn Nigeria deal, 25 June, http://news.bbc.co.uk/2/hi/8118721.stm [accessed: 5 July 2013].

soldiers and police to peacekeeping operations in the Democratic Republic of Congo, Western Sahara, Sierra Leone, Ethiopia, Eritrea, the Ivory Coast, Liberia and Sudan.[29] As for the overall impact of Russia's 'games' on the regional order, Moscow's prioritization of bilateral business relations with resource-rich countries on Westphalian premises, along with an overarching ambition to re-assert national 'great power' status, seem to fall into a pattern similar to Chinese practices, albeit on a much more limited scale. The overt focus on pragmatic commercial interests and non-interference contrasts with the regional strategic approaches of the EU and the US.

Conclusions: The Global Players in the Sahel and the Horn of Africa

The EU and its Member States are the most prominent external players in the Sahel and the Horn of Africa and pursue the most comprehensive range of policies in the region. The US also pursues a broad range of goals in the spheres of security and development, but on a smaller scale and with counterterrorism as the central theme. Washington notably took a supporting rather than a leading role in the French-led 2013 military intervention in Mali. As for future developments, the trend of the last two decades is telling, with Sino-African trade expanding thirtyfold, US-African trade sevenfold, EU-Africa trade three-and-a-half-fold and Russo-African trade threefold.[30] China's trade with Africa as a whole now surpasses that of the US and rivals that of the EU, implying that China is likely soon to become the dominant external economic power in Africa as a whole, including in the Sahel and the Horn of Africa.[31] However, Beijing is a fairly low-key player in regional politics and security, where the EU and its Member States and the US will most likely remain the most important actors for the foreseeable future.

In addition to the first-tier players dealt with above, other powers, while playing a less comprehensive role, are also increasing their presence in the region. Japan, India and Brazil, in particular, have been expanding their trade and investment across Africa in recent years, although much less rapidly than China. From the Arabian Gulf, Saudi Arabia and Qatar have been promoting the growth of the severe Wahhabi variant of Islam, particularly in Mauritania and Mali, through public and private funding. And on the African continent itself, apart from the Maghreb countries and Nigeria, South Africa is also an important economic player in the Sahel and the Horn of Africa.

As seen in other chapters in this volume, the EU possesses a number of long-term strategies and tools for promoting development, cross-border cooperation and inclusive integration in the region. By way of comparison, US policies tend to frame the region in terms of 'hard' security and humanitarian challenges with

---

29   Fidanand Aras, op. cit.

30   Vasiliev, op. cit.

31   Zoubir, Y.H. 2012. The Sahara-Sahel Quagmire: Regional and International Ramifications. *Mediterranean Politics*, 17(3), 452–8.

relatively less emphasis on long-term regional cooperation and inclusive economic integration.[32] China and Russia both prioritize bilateral economic relationships and the region-level initiatives pursued by China serve above all as a framework for deepening bilateral relations. Hence, the EU has not only to face the considerable challenges present in the Sahel and the Horn of Africa but also the tensions between EU norms and objectives and the 'games' of the major global players in the region.

The Global Players in the Arabian Gulf

To the EU's south-east, the Arabian Gulf has been an arena of foreign power rivalry for centuries, extending back in time to 'Great Game' between Russia and Britain in the nineteenth century. The region possesses around half of the world's proven liquid fuels and over 40 per cent of proven gas reserves, ensuring its continued geopolitical importance in the years ahead.[33] Over the last four decades the Gulf monarchies' petro dollar-driven growth has created new markets for foreign investment and exports, while Gulf investors have made high-profile direct and portfolio investments abroad. Since the post-colonial era the regional order has been shaped by the triangle of Iran, Iraq and Saudi Arabia, whose affiliations with external powers has raised the stakes, and at times the volatility, of a regional order characterized by inter-state anarchy.[34] Regional security problems, such as the disruption of energy production or exports; the proliferation of weapons of mass destruction; and the growth of extremist militant groups with ambitions beyond the Gulf and the Middle East, reverberate far beyond the Arabian Gulf itself and are prominent items on the international agenda.

The Gulf Cooperation Council (GCC), established in 1981 by the six Gulf monarchies (Bahrain, Kuwait, Oman, Qatar, Saudi Arabia and the United Arab Emirates), has been developed alongside other regional and bilateral integration projects. However, given the disparities and rivalries between the Gulf monarchies and their strong bilateral economic and military ties with the US, described below, the GCC has seen only modest gains in uniting the six states politically and economically. The EU aspires to have an inter-regional EU-GCC free trade agreement beyond the 1988 Cooperation Agreement, but negotiations have been on hold since 2008.[35] The GGC states' ratification in 2013 of a plan to form a unified military command and move towards a Gulf Union suggests a new impetus for integration amidst the regional turmoil and GCC concerns about the negotiations

---

32   USAID, op. cit.

33   US Energy Information Administration 2013. *International Energy Outlook 2013.* Washington, DC, 25 July.

34   See also Chapter 6 by Silvia Colombo and Chapter 7 by Clément Therme in this volume.

35   Ibid.

over Iran's nuclear programme and their implications for the US commitment to the Gulf states' security.[36]

Of course, the Arabian Gulf region cannot be analysed independently of developments in the wider Middle East. Since 2011 the wave of uprisings and conflicts gripping the region has drawn in the Gulf countries as active players in the struggles between incumbent Sunni autocratic regimes, militaries, the Muslim Brotherhood, the *Ba'ath* regime in Syria, Shiites and Salafist movements as well as more liberal parties, further raising the stakes of regional rivalries.

The US in the Arabian Gulf: The Security Guard

The US has been the dominant global player in the Arabian Gulf since the first Gulf War in 1991, and Washington maintains a substantial military presence with bases and port facilities in all countries except Yemen and Iran and aircraft carriers patrolling the Gulf's maritime routes.[37] The US's overarching objectives in the Gulf have been, on the one hand, to maintain regional stability and counter regional security externalities – the disruption of energy supplies; the proliferation of weapons of mass destruction; and transnational terrorism – and, on the other, to promote liberal and democratic reforms. The relative weight of, and tensions between, these objectives give rise to pendulum swings in US policies in the Gulf. Since 1979 the US has aimed to contain the Islamic Republic of Iran's regional influence, and over the past decade, its ability to produce a nuclear bomb. The US has maintained a commitment to the security of Saudi Arabia, the region's biggest oil producer, since the 1990–91 Gulf War, although Washington began to view the Saudi Kingdom with greater circumspection after the 11 September 2001 terrorist attacks.[38] Since the 2003 US-led invasion of Iraq, the project of fostering a self-sustaining democratic Iraqi political system entered the list of US foreign policy objectives.

At the time of writing, after decade-long counter-insurgency campaigns in Afghanistan and Iraq, there is a widespread desire among the US public and policymakers to scale back US military commitments in the wider Middle East.[39] The North American shale gas boom and the 2011 announcement of a 'pivot' to Asia also indicate the shift of US attention away from the Arabian Gulf and a reduced willingness to intervene in the region unless core US security interests

---

36   See also Chapter 6 by Silvia Colombo in this volume.

37   Baldor, L.T. 2013. US boosting naval presence in Persian Gulf. *The Globe and Mail*, 28 August.

38   Olimat, M. 2010. Playing by the rules? Sino-Middle Eastern relations, in Breslin, S. (ed.), *The Handbook of China's International Relations*. London: Routledge, 184.

39   Pew Research Center 2013. *Americans want to mind their own business*, 29 July, http://www.pewresearch.org/fact-tank/2013/07/29/americans-want-to-mind-their-own-business/ [accessed: 16 January 2014].

are at stake.[40] The arrival of a new government in Tehran in August 2013 seemed to improve the odds for an agreement on Iran's nuclear programme, which might allow the US to divert its attention elsewhere. It appears unlikely, however, that the US will be able to extract itself completely from dealing with the interrelated conflicts and security threats in the wider region – including the Israeli-Palestinian conflict, the rivalry between Iran and the Sunni Gulf monarchies, the continuing centrifugal violence in Iraq, and the civil conflict waging in Syria since 2011 – not least because of the risk of losing credibility beyond the region itself. Still, in the context of the uprisings and turmoil engulfing the wider Middle East since 2011, Washington has steadily scaled back its commitments and adopted a cautious stance, as illustrated by the relatively modest US role in the 2011 NATO intervention in Libya and Washington's backtracking in September 2013 over whether to intervene militarily in the war in Syria.

How do US policies affect prospects for greater regional cooperation and economic integration in the Arabian Gulf? The bilateral defence agreements established with the Gulf states in the early 1990s to contain Iran and Iraq may have stymied the development of regional security dialogues and a collective security arrangement between the Gulf monarchies. Likewise, the US has in recent years concluded bilateral free trade agreements with individual Gulf countries,[41] encouraging stronger trade and investment with the US, while having an uncertain impact on economic integration within the Arabian Gulf itself. In large part this approach seems attributable to, but arguably also reinforces, the dynamics of rivalry and asymmetry within the GCC, as well as the tensions in the wider region.[42]

China in the Arabian Gulf: Well-Oiled Relations

In deepening its role in a region of high-stake rivalries with reverberations far beyond the region itself, and in which the US has firmly established security and economic interests, China's growing presence in the Middle East is a foray into global politics.[43] As a permanent member of the UN Security Council and

---

40   Clinton, H.R., Secretary of State. 2011. America's Pacific Century. *Foreign Policy*, November.

41   The US has free trade agreements in force with Bahrain and Oman, in force since 2006 and 2009, respectively. See US Department of State 2014. Existing U.S. Free Trade Agreements, http://www.state.gov/e/eb/tpp/bta/fta/fta/index.htm [accessed: 19 January 2014].

42   Fedorchenko, A.V. 2012. Economic integration in the Arabian world: Results and perspectives, in *Yearbook of the Institute for International Studies – 2012*. Moscow: Moscow State Institute of International Relations.

43   In 2002 Beijing nominated a special envoy for the Israeli-Palestinian process. As for security, to date China has contributed troops to the United Nations Interim Force in Lebanon (UNIFIL) and sent a few ships to fight piracy off the coast of Somalia. See Schenker, D. 2013. *China-Middle East Relations: A Change in Policy?* Beijing: Carnegie-

of the 'E3+3' group on the Iranian nuclear programme, China is in some way involved in the efforts to address every major security question facing the region. Today, the Arabian Gulf region accounts for around 45 per cent of China's oil imports, with Saudi Arabia, Iran, Oman, Kuwait and the United Arab Emirates as its major suppliers.[44] Beijing took the initiative in 2003 to establish a China-Gulf Cooperation Council Forum, and strategic dialogues were held in this framework in 2010 and 2014.[45] China also established, during a 2004 visit by the Chinese president Hu Jintao to the League of Arab States headquarters in Cairo, a China-Arab States Cooperation Forum, and in 2010 the parties announced the consecration of a 'China-Arab strategic cooperative relationship'.[46] While building deep relations with the Arab Gulf states, China has also fostered close ties with Iran, which provides around 13–14 per cent of its oil imports.[47] In the shadow of Tehran's withering economic ties with the West due to US and EU sanctions, Beijing has built close relations in a range of areas, including energy, infrastructure construction, military and no doubt also nuclear cooperation.[48] China also enjoyed good relations with Saddam Hussein's Iraq, trading arms and oil (including under the UN oil for food programme), and Beijing's criticism of the 2003 US-led invasion was tempered by a pragmatic manoeuvring to obtain contracts with the new government to reconstruct the country and develop its oilfields.[49] Beijing has an ambivalent relationship with the third regional power, Saudi Arabia, China's number one oil supplier and a major customer for Chinese arms. While Saudi Arabia aims to deepen their bilateral trade, Beijing conversely seeks to diversify its energy imports, while Saudi support for restive Muslim populations within China is a sore point in bilateral relations.

Given China's dependence on uninterrupted shipments of Gulf oil, the US's dominant role in regional security, and in particular the US navy's guarding of its crucial maritime lanes, inspire unease in Beijing.[50] Meanwhile, China's closeness to Iran and ambiguous position with regard to the proliferation of ballistic

---

Tsinghua Center for Global Policy, http://carnegietsinghua.org/2013/03/18/china-middle-east-relations-change-in-policy/g0uk [accessed: 2 August 2013].

44   Cabestan, op. cit., 374.

45   Aluwaisheg, A.A. 2014. China-GCC strategic dialogue resumes. *Arabnews*, 19 January, http://www.arabnews.com/news/511401 [accessed: 19 January 2014].

46   Yang J., Foreign Minister of China. 2012. Deepen strategic cooperation, promote common development. *People's Daily Online*, 30 May, http://english.peopledaily.com.cn/90883/7831062.html [accessed: 19 January 2014]

47   Calabrese, op. cit., 248.

48   Since the late 1980s, Chinese companies have agreed to substantial long-term investments and exploitation contracts, continuing in spite of the 1996 US Iran and Libya Sanctions Act. See, for example, ibid.

49   Currier, C.L. and Dorraj, M. 2010. Reconstructing the Silk Road in a New Era: China's Expanding Regional Influence in the Middle East, in Emilian, K. (ed.), *China and the Global Politics of Regionalization*. Farnham: Ashgate, 172–3.

50   Calabrese, op. cit., 244.

missiles and weapons of mass destruction have caused considerable concerns among the US and likeminded countries.[51] However, while Beijing trades with and protects, to a certain extent, the Iranian regime, it has generally abstained from blocking US-led initiatives outright and has tempered its criticism of US policy in the region.[52] Some analysts argue that Beijing is not contesting the basic order of US hegemony, although Beijing tries to constrain what Chinese policymakers perceive as excessive US unilateralism.[53] In the wider regional context of the 'Arab Spring', Beijing has acted quite pragmatically, supporting the new governments in Egypt and Libya after the fall of their authoritarian regimes in 2011 (the latter following a NATO air campaign). On the other hand, Beijing has joined Russia in opposing humanitarian intervention against Bashar al-Assad's regime in Syria, reflecting China's continuing concern to uphold the principles of inviolable state sovereignty and non-interference.

How do Chinese policies affect the regional order in the Arabian Gulf? On the one hand, the different diplomatic configurations established in recent years provide forums for high-level summit diplomacy, while, on the other, creating opportunities for bilateral diplomacy and economic agreements. China and the GCC launched free trade negotiations in 2004 which have since stagnated, although in September 2013 Chinese President Xi Jinping called for renewed efforts to reach an agreement.[54] As for cross-border economic integration in the Arabian Gulf, Beijing's mercantilist approach to secure resources through joint equity deals between Chinese state-owned energy companies and the Gulf host states (*fen'e you* or *equity oil*) has been criticized in many quarters for undermining efforts to open the region's energy markets.[55] Hence, in sum, Beijing pursues its policy objectives – to increase China's leverage towards the US and ensure continued energy and two-way investment in energy and other sectors – through a mix of formats in which Beijing nevertheless accords primacy to bilateral relations with its oil-rich Arabian Gulf counterparts, reflecting and arguably reinforcing existing fault-lines in the region.

51   Kan, S.A. 2014. *China and Proliferation of Weapons of Mass Destruction and Missiles: Policy Issues*. Washington DC: Congressional Research Service. http://www.fas.org/sgp/crs/nuke/RL31555.pdf [accessed: 19 January 2014].

52   China allowed the UN Security Council to pass resolution 1441 (2002) on Iraq and has supported UN sanctions against Iran.

53   Currier, and Dorraj, op. cit., 175–6.

54   Li X. 2013. Xi seeks to resume FTA talks with GCC. *People's Daily USA*, 17 September, http://usa.chinadaily.com.cn/china/2013–09/17/content-16974340.htm [accessed: 19 January 2014]

55   Olimat, M. 2010. Playing by the rules? Sino-Middle Eastern relations, in Breslin, S. (ed.), *The Handbook of China's International Relations*. London: Routledge, 180.

Russia in the Arabian Gulf: Great Power Politics

Russia's foreign policy in the Gulf, where the US is the dominant external power, is mainly defensive, and focused on projecting the status of a great power while seeking to maintain stability within its own adjacent territory and Muslim populations. The Soviet Union shared a border with the Gulf (Iran) through the now independent states of Armenia and Azerbaijan, and present-day Russia borders the Gulf through its Caspian coastline, making the region a historic arena of Russian interests. During Vladimir Putin's first decade in power, Russia built pragmatic partnerships with all key powers in the region, centred on Russian exports of arms, technology and expertise in hydrocarbon exploitation and nuclear power, as well as political cooperation in some multilateral contexts.[56] However, Moscow's efforts over the past decade to befriend all the regimes in the region have been thrown into question by the Russian reaction to the 'Arab Spring', particularly Moscow's steadfast support for Bashar al-Assad in Syria since the outbreak of civil conflict in 2011, which have damaged relations with the Sunni monarchies as well as the new post-revolution governments in the region. As a major exporter of hydrocarbons outside the Organization of Petroleum Exporting Countries (OPEC), Russia enjoys considerable economic leverage against the major Gulf exporters. Russian interests in the energy sphere centre on opportunities to exploit and export Middle Eastern and Mediterranean energy resources and maintaining steady energy prices.[57] Vladimir Putin floated the idea of an OPEC-like cartel for natural gas with Iran and Qatar in 2008, although the global economic slow-down, US shale gas boom and regional instability have since cooled interest on all sides.[58]

As the US role in regional security has grown over the last two decades, Russia has consistently opposed what it sees as US unilateral behaviour which ignores Moscow's views on major security questions. In reaction to the invasion of Iraq and the US policy on Libya and Syria, Moscow has sought to constrain Washington's freedom to act by invoking international law and preventing Western-led resolutions from passing in the UN Security Council. However, for many observers, Moscow's juggling of power play and security matters, in particular its support for the Syrian and Iranian regimes and willingness to sell them arms and nuclear technology, raises questions about the compatibility between these tactical anti-US alignments and Russia's own long-term security

---

56   Katz, M. 2012. *Moscow and the Middle East: Repeat Performance?*, Russia in Global Affairs, 7 October, http://eng.globalaffairs.ru/number/Moscow-and-the-Middle-East-Repeat-Performance-15690 [accessed: 13 June 2013].

57   Due to under-investment and lack of capacity, partly as a result of the forcible 2003 dismantlement of Yukos, Russia is unable to expand domestic production significantly, giving Moscow an interest in stable energy prices.

58   Blank, S. 2008. Pax Americana in the Persian Gulf and the Contradictions of Russian Foreign Policy, in Kaim, M. (ed.), *Great Powers and Regional Orders: The United States and the Persian Gulf*. Aldershot: Ashgate, 226.

and interests in the region. Moscow's policies have severely damaged relations with the Gulf states and Sunni Islamist and liberal movements in the wider Middle East, as well as with the US and EU. Some analysts see here a potential replay of Moscow's earlier manoeuvring over Iraq, which undermined relations not only with the US, but with the new Iraqi authorities as well.[59]

As for regional integration, Russia declares itself for multilateral solutions bringing in all major players in full respect of international law, and has among other initiatives in 2008 proposed a multilateral security regime for the Gulf.[60] However, given that Moscow at the same time 'openly favors hegemonic spheres of influence and "zero-sum games", all within a context of traditional Realpolitik', such proposals are perceived by many observers as opportunistic designs to dilute US influence and secure Moscow a seat at the table of the big powers.[61] In practice, Russian foreign policy over the last decade has consisted of attempting to build and maintain bilateral relations with the main actors in the region to promote Russian interests and hamper US policies, without really altering the regional constellation of tense inter-state relations.

Conclusions: The Global Players in the Arabian Gulf

The relations between the EU and the Arabian Gulf countries have been characterized by strategic and commercial interests, particularly Gulf energy exports, but also broader geopolitical factors, which have risen in prominence since the eruption of the 'Arab Spring' in 2011.[62] There have been efforts to deepen relations between the EU and the GCC, for which the relevant framework remains the 1988 Cooperation Agreement, as long as plans for a free trade agreement are on hold.

In spite of the announced 'pivot' to Asia, the US remains the undisputed dominant global player in the region through its bilateral relationships, military presence, commercial ties and investments. China has built strong bilateral relationships focused on trade and investment in energy and armaments with the Gulf monarchies, while building close ties with Iran. Beijing has dealt

---

59   Whatever Moscow's interest in challenging US dominance, Russia does surely not have an interest in nuclear proliferation in the Gulf, as is made clear by Russia's willingness to cooperate in the UN on sanctions against Iran; nor in a drawn-out Syrian war threatening to engulf the whole region; in state-sponsored terrorism; in antagonizing Israel; or in making enemies in the Sunni Arab world. See Trenin, D. 2013. Russia's Middle East Gambit. *Tablet*, 30 May; and Kaim, M. 2008. Challenges for the Next U.S. Administration, in Kaim, M. (ed.), *Great Powers and Regional Orders: The United States and the Persian Gulf*. Aldershot: Ashgate, 268.

60   Embassy of the Russia Federation in the State of Qatar. *Russia's concept of security in the Gulf area*, http://www.qatar.mid.ru/mer_e_08.html [accessed: 19 January 20134].

61   Blank, op. cit., 233.

62   See Chapter 5 by Andrew Bower and Raphaël Metais and Chapter 6 by Silvia Colombo in this volume.

pragmatically with the 'Arab Spring' with the overall goal of maintaining stability to safeguard Chinese investments and trade. Russia's cooperation with Iran and strategic support for the Syrian regime has eroded Moscow's relations with the Gulf states, Turkey and Israel and have lost Moscow much of the ground won in the region over the last decade.[63]

The US has prioritized bilateral partnerships and military alliances with the GCC states, while China has prioritized commercial bilateral relations on both sides of the Arabian Gulf as well as a free trade agreement with the GCC as a whole. Russia has mainly sought to preserve its status as a power in the Arabian Gulf, including through grand multilateral initiatives with little chance of materializing. Hence, the objectives and 'games' of the global players in the Arabian Gulf complicate regional efforts, of which the EU has been a supporter, to achieve greater political and economic integration in the Arabian Gulf amidst growing regional turmoil.

The Global Players in Central Asia

Historically a space of great power rivalry, the Central Asian states of Kazakhstan, Uzbekistan, Turkmenistan, Tajikistan and Kyrgyzstan have forged independent foreign policies since gaining independence from the Soviet Union, giving rise to what one recent book termed a new 'great game, [with] local rules'.[64] Notwithstanding growing inequality in economy and population, inter-state relations between the five Central Asian 'stans' are marked by diffidence rather than dominance, which many observers attribute to the weaknesses in identity and state formation in the region.[65] Central Asia's large hydrocarbon reserves, concentrated in Kazakhstan, Uzbekistan and Turkmenistan, have drawn the interest of regional and global powers since the states became independent in 1991.[66]

A number of initiatives have been taken to foster greater regional security cooperation, giving rise to a regional order resembling, in some respects, a 'concert of powers' in which external players play the dominant roles. The Central Asian republics interact regularly through Russian and Chinese-led initiatives: the Russian-led Commonwealth of Independent States (CIS), the Collective Security Treaty Organization (CSTO), and the Shanghai Cooperation Organization (SCO). Beyond these frameworks, economic integration and political cooperation are scant: Soviet-era infrastructure has over the years crumbled and been replaced

---

63   Katz, op. cit.

64   Cooley, A. 2013. *Great Game, Local Rules: The New Great Power Contest in Central Asia*. Oxford: Oxford University Press.

65   Lanteigne, M. 2010. Security, strategy and the former USSR. China and the Shanghai Cooperation Organisation, in Breslin, S. (ed.), *The Handbook of China's International Relations*. London: Routledge, 166–76.

66   See also Chapter 9 by Alexander Warkotsch in this volume.

by hardened borders, and Central Asian governments have failed to cooperate on regional environmental, political and security problems, while crude ethno-nationalist politics have increased the dangers of internal and regional conflicts. The EU has gradually increased its involvement in Central Asia in the form of trade and investment, development cooperation, Security Sector Reform and policy dialogues, since 2007 within the framework of the Strategy for Central Asia.[67] As with the European Neighbourhood Policy, two overarching goals of the EU's Strategy are to deepen political and economic cooperation with the EU and to promote greater intra-regional cooperation and economic integration. This section will consider the objectives and approaches of other players and their impact on the regional order.

The US in Central Asia: Aiding Transition or in Transit?

The 2001 NATO invasion of Afghanistan brought US troops to military bases in Uzbekistan and Kyrgyzstan and heightened the US's role in regional stability. While European policymakers today tend to frame Central Asia as part of the EU's broader Eurasian neighbourhood and an extension of the EU's Eastern Partnership, US planners consider the region through the lens of a set of broader geopolitical considerations revolving around the war in Afghanistan on the one hand, and the US's security interests and presence in the Arabian Gulf and Middle East on the other.

Since the 1990s the US has sought to encourage the political autonomy, economic development and stability of the new Central Asian republics, primarily through the diversification of their hydrocarbon exports to European and South Asian markets. Since the 2001 US-led invasion of Afghanistan, Islamic extremism and terrorism,[68] as well as continued access to the military bases, have taken centre stage in US policy. Washington has nudged the region's autocratic regimes to respect liberal democratic principles, but has prioritized stability. This 'securitization' approach has tended to support the Central Asian regimes' narrative that the main threats are the spread of violence and extremism from Afghanistan, rather than internal tensions and poor governance. With both the EU and the US engaged in Security Sector Reform, the EU tends to promote long-term border security and institutional development, while the US tends to focus more on short-term efforts to bolster the five Central Asian states' 'hard' security

---

67   See also Chapter 8 by Francesca Fenton and Chapter 9 Alexander Warkotsch in this volume.

68   Islamic militant groups are active across Central Asia, with a locus in the Fergana valley straddling Uzbekistan, Kyrgyzstan and Tajikistan. See Petersen, A. and Barysch, K. 2011. *Russia, China and the Geopolitics of Energy in Central Asia*. London: Centre for European Reform, 33.

capabilities by training and equipping them to counter cross-border militancy.[69] The withdrawal of international troops from Afghanistan in 2014 will see long-term US involvement shrink again and leave an economic, political and military vacuum which other players, foremost among them Russia and China, may move to fill.

How have the US presence and policies affected the regional order? In 2011 the Department of State set out a vision for a 'New Silk Road' of infrastructure and economic agreements connecting Afghanistan and the wider region to European and global markets (while apparently bypassing Iran, China and Russia) to help foster regional integration and stability after the 2014 troop withdrawal.[70] However, it seems to have had limited impact on the ground, and the US continues to engage with Central Asian states mostly on a bilateral basis through development programmes, Security Sector Reform and policy dialogues. Overall, US policies have arguably given priority to security concerns, such as strengthening border management and policing, as well as bilateral relations and agreements on US military bases and troop movements, with relatively less emphasis on encouraging intra-regional economic and political cooperation.

Russia in Central Asia: The Legacy of Power

In the post-Soviet period, Moscow has sought to bind the former Soviet Union republics to Russia through bilateral links and a series of regional initiatives: the Commonwealth of Independent States, launched in 1991;[71] the Collective Security Treaty of 1992, which was given legal status as an organization in 2002;[72] and the Eurasian Economic Community,[73] launched in 2000 and recently revived as a more ambitious Eurasian Union building on the fledgling Customs Union launched in 2011 by Russia with Belarus and Kazakhstan.[74] Through these various

---

69   The relative elevation of 'hard' over 'soft' security can be attributed, in part, to the division of labour between the Department of Defense and the Department of State, in which the former's focus on external threats tends to prevail in the Annual Bilateral Consultation process with Central Asian countries. See Boonstra, J. and Laruelle, M. 2013. *EU-US cooperation in Central Asia: Parallel lines meet in infinity? EUCAM Policy Brief*, no. 31, Brussels: EUCAM.

70   Clinton, H.R., Secretary of State 2011. *Remarks at the New Silk Road Ministerial Meeting*. New York, 22 September.

71   Commonwealth of Independent States 2014. *About Commonwealth of Independent States*, http://www.cisstat.com/eng/cis.htm [accessed: 20 January 2014].

72   Collective Security Treaty Organization 2014. *Basic facts,* http://www.odkb.gov.ru/start/index-aengl.htm [accessed: 20 January 2014].

73   Eurasian Economic Community 2014. *About EurAsEC*, http://www.evrazes.com/en/about [accessed: 20 January 2014].

74   Heritage, T. 2013. *Ukraine holds key to Putin's dream of a new union, Reuters*, http://www.reuters.com/article/2013/11/29/us-ukraine-eu-putin-idUSBRE9AS0F320131129 [accessed: 20 January 2014].

frameworks Russia plays a role of stabilizer between the different forces of the region – albeit an uneasy one due to Russia's unwillingness to take on weighty security commitments in the region and, more importantly, to the Central Asian states' wariness of Russian dominance. Since the mid-1990s China's growing economic and political clout has increased the pressure on Russia's position, as illustrated by President Islam Karimov's 2012 decision to suspend Uzbekistan's membership of the CSTO shortly before travelling to a SCO summit in China.[75]

Moscow's security policy is guided by an overriding concern to preserve Russia's dominance of the region against the inroads made by the US and China, especially in energy exports, which until recently relied almost entirely on pipelines passing through Russian territory. Moscow has attempted to maintain control over Caspian resources through strategic, rather than commercial, bids for pipeline construction and energy production, in particular to counter competing projects to bring Turkmen and Azeri gas to the EU, Russia's own captive market.[76] The US-led campaign in Afghanistan was initially embraced by Moscow as an opportunity to cooperate with Washington as an equal in the 'Global War on Terror', also seen as a suitable narrative for Russia's suppression of separatists in the North Caucasus. However, Moscow soon hardened its stance against the US and began to pressure Central Asian states to evict the US military from the region to re-establish its own pre-eminence. Meanwhile, Russia's legacy of regional dominance in security and commerce has been challenged by other developments. On one hand, Moscow's claims to a 'sphere of influence' and 2008 war with Georgia sowed new doubts among Central Asian states about Russia's respect for the principles of sovereignty and territorial integrity.[77] On the other hand, Russia's mute response to the violence in Kyrgyzstan in 2010 illustrated Moscow's limited willingness and ability to intervene militarily in a crisis situation within the CSTO.[78] Russia is an active participant in the SCO, but the organization is perceived by many Russian policymakers and observers as a vehicle for Chinese interests in Central Asia, and Moscow is wary about China's ambitions to broaden its scope of activities. In future, Uzbekistan, Kyrgyzstan and Tajikistan, in particular, are likely to look to the US for security and eventually to rapidly growing China.[79]

The impact of Russian policies on regional integration is twofold. In seeking to establish lasting ties with Kazakhstan, Kyrgyzstan and Tajikistan, in particular,

---

75   Laruelle, M. 2012. *Factoring the Regional Impact of Uzbekistan's Withdrawal from the CSTO*. Washington, DC: The German Marshall Fund of the United States. http://www.gmfus.org/wp-content/blogs.dir/1/files-mf/1345830436Laruelle_Uzbekistan_Aug12.pdf [accessed: 20 January 2014].

76   Petersen and Barysch, op. cit., 31.

77   Cabestan, op. cit., 295.

78   Délétroz, A. 2013. A new Central Asia security set-up. *EUCAM Watch*, no. 15, Brussels: EUCAM, 2.

79   Petersen, A. 2012. After CSTO Withdrawal Uzbekistan also Looks East, *China in Central Asia*, 2 July.

Moscow has seemingly been a driving force for regional integration through the CIS, CSTO and SCO. However, the Russian 'zero-sum approach' to its neighbourhood has thrust upon the Central Asian republics a stark choice between Moscow and other partners such as China, the US and/or Europe.[80] The tensions between 'spheres of influence' and Westphalian norms in Russian policy, and the seemingly short-term calculations and interests inherent in Russia's regionalist projects make them unlikely to provide a durable framework for political and economic integration in the region.

China in Central Asia: The Giant Neighbour

China is the upcoming power in Central Asia, on track to become the region's top trading partner, with a growing Chinese presence in regional energy production.[81] The Chinese ascent has taken place in the context of the development of the SCO, whose member countries (China, Russia and the five Central Asian republics minus Turkmenistan) hold regular summits, organize biennial military exercises and cooperate, to a limited degree, on regional security and economic issues. China's security interests in Central Asia revolve around three pre-occupations: (1) diversifying energy imports to ensure a stable supply of energy; (2) quelling external and domestic support for Uyghur separatists in the Xinjiang province; and (3) nurturing the relationship with former Cold-War rival Russia and firming up China's position in its neighbourhood against rival powers.[82] Beijing has aimed to contain the growing US role in the region and prevent an eastward expansion of NATO in the shadow of Russia's weakening over the 1990s. However, while calling for NATO troops to leave the region, Beijing also worried about the security vacuum their departure might create.[83] Although Moscow's and Washington's commitment to regional security seems to be flagging, Beijing does not appear willing or able to bid for a role as security guard in this volatile region.

With its vociferous demand for energy and strategic aim to diversify imports, China is becoming a major player in the exploitation and export of Central Asian hydrocarbons. China has in recent years executed large deals, orchestrated at the top political level, involving huge portfolio and direct investments in hydrocarbon fields with long-term supply agreements coupled with generous loan packages and agreements on political cooperation.[84] Few if any other powers can match the Chinese offer, free also of conditions such as good governance. Although China's share in the

---

80   Russia has attempted in particular to maintain close relations with Kazakhstan, Kyrgyzstan, and Uzbekistan. Fidan and Aras, op. cit.

81   Laruelle, M. 2013. Goodbye to the idea of a region. *EUCAM Watch*, no. 15, Brussels: EUCAM, 2.

82   Cabestan, op. cit., 90.

83   Petersen. and Barysch, op. cit., 39.

84   In addition to the 1,800 km Central Asia-China Gas Pipeline, in 2009 China signed a $10 billion 'loan for oil' deal with Kazakhstan; committed $10 billion to members of the

region's total output of hydrocarbons is still relatively modest, it is set to rise as new exploitation projects enter operation. Apart from energy, Chinese investors have also entered other sectors, including agriculture and telecoms, while goods manufactured in China have flooded Central Asian markets, aided by high-level diplomacy to facilitate market access and assuage worries of Chinese dominance. Since 2002, China's trade with Central Asian has grown to the point of China overtaking Russia's bilateral trade with Kazakhstan, Kyrgyzstan and Tajikistan.[85]

With regard to regional integration, the SCO reflects a particular Chinese approach to regional cooperation as a community of practice without formal institutions or hierarchical alliances. While the organization serves as a forum for coordinating a common front against US and EU-led liberal interventionism, such as the NATO intervention in Libya, and for striking bilateral deals, its outputs in terms of regional economic integration are meagre and mainly declarative.[86] Indirectly, this mode of interaction serves to promote China's Westphalian norms of state sovereignty and non-interference, a 'game' which clearly clashes with the EU interest in promoting internal and regional political reforms and encourage inclusive regional integration.

Conclusions: The Global Players in Central Asia

EU policies increasingly draw links between Central Asia and the EU's Eastern Partnership, with the EU's 2007 Strategy for Central Asia a first tangible step towards a comprehensive approach to the broader Eurasian region. With the US reducing its military presence and Moscow focused on the Eurasian Customs Union with Kazakhstan and Belarus, China looks set to become the dominant player overall over the next decades, while Russia will likely retain great influence, particularly in the security sphere and through its close relations with Kazakhstan. However, China does not appear willing or able to take on much greater security commitments, leaving open the possibility of a relative vacuum in an increasingly volatile region.[87] As for other players in Central Asia, Turkey and Iran both sought in the 1990s to expand existing ties with Central Asian countries, especially to the energy sphere, but subsequently scaled back their ambitions. India and Pakistan also have important commercial ties with Central Asia, and there are plans to construct a Turkmenistan–Afghanistan–Pakistan–India pipeline. Gulf Arab monarchies are important trading partners and sponsor Islamic organizations

SCO and $4 billion to Turkmenistan for developing the South Yolotan gas field, followed in 2011 by another $4.1 billion loan. See ibid., 42–3.

85   Cabestan, op. cit., 308.

86   La rédaction 2013. *A Bichkek, l'OSC attractive et en devenir – sécurité et* économie *au menu*, September, http://www.francekoul.com/articles/a-bichkek-losc-attractive-et-en-devenir-securite-et-economie-au-menu [accessed: 15 September 2013].

87   Kassenova, N. 2013. Central Asia: Now as in 2030, at the crossroads. *EUCAM Watch*, no. 15, Brussels; EUCAM, 2.

which some observers argue are likely to become increasingly powerful in Central Asian politics.[88] Major industrial and emerging economies, for example those of Eastern and South-East Asia, are also increasing their trade with the region, particularly in energy.

Given the EU's ambition to promote intra-regional integration, the Russian and Chinese-led regional organizations in Central Asia merit attention. Still, as we have seen, questions remain over the extent to which the SCO and the envisaged Eurasian Union are capable of durably strengthening the ties between the Central Asian states. Meanwhile, bilateral relations with external powers, particularly trade and investment in energy with the more resource-rich states in the region, seem to outshine various multilateral constellations and initiatives in shaping the regional order.

Conclusions: The Global Players in the EU's Broader Neighbourhood

The preceding analysis has identified the overarching objectives, roles and foreign policies of the US, China and Russia, as well as of other important players, in the EU's broader neighbourhood. A recurring theme is the external players' interest in hydrocarbon exports, strategic raw materials and investment opportunities in the regions. A second recurring theme are the uneasy synergies between these players' policies towards the serious security problems afflicting the broader neighbourhood, including banditry, drug and human smuggling, ethnic and religious extremism, terrorism, inter-state tensions and the proliferation of weapons of mass destruction.

This chapter has also considered the extent to which the foreign policy 'games' of the other players support or hamper the EU's interest in promoting greater intra-regional integration in its broader neighbourhood. Of the three global players dealt with here, the US continues to play, in terms of diplomatic influence, military force, military and non-military aid, trade and investment, a prominent role across the regions. However, around the time of the arrival of the first Obama Administration in 2009, Washington began to reduce its ambitions and commitments, moving towards an approach of 'leading from behind' in crisis management. As for the impact of US policies on the development of the regional order, we have seen that the US supports greater integration by strengthening cross-border infrastructure and trade. However, on balance the US tends to privilege bilateral relations in these regions and has generally tended to offer relatively less active support to regional initiatives and institutions, such as the African Union, than the EU has done.

China has a growing stake in economic and political developments and threats to stability in the EU's broader neighbourhood, and Beijing has in recent years adopted a wide variety of pragmatic approaches in pursuit of its objectives. Propelled by rapid domestic economic growth China seems poised, in the medium

---

88   Ibid.

term, to extend its prominent role in the economic sphere to a greater involvement in political and security questions, where it has so far remained modest. Meanwhile, China is contributing to shaping regions through multilateral policies and practices which favour bargaining between 'hard shell' sovereign states for mutual advantage. This aspect of Chinese 'games' in the EU's broader neighbourhood raises challenges to efforts to promote inclusive regional integration by pooling state sovereignty to reap medium-and-long-term benefits.[89]

As for Russia, Moscow's claim to a special 'sphere of influence' in the former Soviet Central Asia jars with Russia's otherwise conservative approach to international law and insistence on the inviolability of state sovereignty – invoked inter alia to oppose UN Security Council resolutions on the civil conflict waging in Syria since 2011. This inconsistency, which also sets Russia apart from China, reflects what some identify as an overarching opportunism in Russian foreign policy. Hence, the Russian 'games' are likely to lead to instability and deepen divisions rather than the creation of durable alternative configurations of regional integration in the EU's broader neighbourhood.

In sum, as has been shown in this chapter and in other contributions to this volume, the neighbours of the EU's neighbours present important challenges which call for a comprehensive approach that takes into account actual and potential inter-linkages with the EU's immediate neighbourhood. To do so requires EU policymakers to be cognizant of the 'games' played by other major regional and global players and to anticipate when these align or conflict with the EU's own interests.

Bibliography

Aluwaisheg, A.A. 2014. China-GCC strategic dialogue resumes. *Arabnews*, 19 January, http://www.arabnews.com/news/511401 [accessed: 19 January 2014].

Baldor, L.T. 2013. US Boosting Naval Presence in Persian Gulf. *The Globe and Mail*, 28 August.

BBC News 2009. Gazprom Seals $2.5bn Nigeria Deal, 25 June, http://news.bbc.co.uk/2/hi/8118721.stm [accessed: 5 July 2013].

BBC News Africa 2012. African Union Opens Chinese-Funded HQ in Ethiopia, 28 January, http://www.bbc.co.uk/news/world-africa-16770932 [accessed: 5 August 2013].

Blank, S. 2008. Pax Americana in the Persian Gulf and the contradictions of Russian foreign policy, in Kaim, M. (ed.), *Great Powers and Regional Orders: The United States and the Persian Gulf*. Aldershot: Ashgate, 223–40.

Boonstra, J. and Laruelle, M. 2013. EU-US Cooperation in Central Asia: Parallel Lines Meet in Infinity? *EUCAM Policy Brief*, no. 31, Brussels: EUCAM.

Boudali, L.K. 2007. *The Trans-Sahara Counterterrorism Partnership*. West Point: United States Military Academy, The Combating Terrorism Center.

---

89   European Commission 2012, op. cit.

Buzan, B. and Wæver, O. 2003. *Regions and Powers: The Structure of International Security*. Cambridge: Cambridge University Press.

Cabestan, J-P. 2010. *La politique internationale de la Chine. Entre intégration et volonté de puissance*. Paris: Presses de Sciences Po Références.

Calabrese, J. 2008. Sino-Gulf relations and the United States: Dark cloud-silver lining?, in Kaim, M. (ed.), *Great Powers and Regional Orders: The United States and the Persian Gulf*. Aldershot: Ashgate, 241–62.

Clinton, H.R., Secretary of State 2011. *Remarks at the New Silk Road Ministerial Meeting*. New York, 22 September.

Clinton, H.R., Secretary of State 2011. America's Pacific Century. *Foreign Policy*, November.

Collective Security Treaty Organization 2014. *Basic facts,* http://www.odkb.gov.ru/start/index_aengl.htm [accessed: 20 January 2014].

Commonwealth of Independent States 2014. *About Commonwealth of Independent States*, http://www.cisstat.com/eng/cis.htm [accessed: 20 January 2014].

Cooley, A. 2013. *Great Game, Local Rules: The New Great Power Contest in Central Asia*. Oxford: Oxford University Press.

Currier, C.L. and Dorraj, M. 2010. Reconstructing the Silk Road in a new era: China's expanding regional influence in the Middle East, in Emilian, K. (ed.), *China and the Global Politics of Regionalization*. Farnham: Ashgate, 165–76.

Délétroz, A. 2013. A New Central Asia Security Set-up. *EUCAM Watch*, no. 15, Brussels: EUCAM.

Embassy of the Russia Federation in the State of Qatar 2014. *Russia's concept of security in the Gulf area*, http://www.qatar.mid.ru/mer_e_08.html [accessed: 19 January 2014].

Eurasian Economic Community 2014. *About EurAsEC*, http://www.evrazes.com/en/about [accessed: 20 January 2014].

European Commission 2012. *Promoting regional poles of prosperity and stability*, DG Development and Cooperation – Europeaid, 17 February:http://ec.europa.eu/europeaid/what/economic-support/regional-integration/index_en.htm [accessed: 14 August 2013].

Fedorchenko, A.V. 2012. Economic integration in the Arabian world: results and perspectives, in *Yearbook of the Institute for International Studies – 2012*. Moscow: Moscow State Institute of International Relations.

Fidan, H. and Aras, B. 2010. The Return of Russia-Africa Relations. *bilig*, winter 2010, 52, 47–68.

Forum on China-Africa Cooperation 2004. *The First Ministerial Conference of FOCAC*, http://www.focac.org/eng/ltda/dyjbzjhy/CI12009/t157577.htm [accessed: 18 January 2014].

Gause, F.G. and Lustick, I.S. 2012. America and the Regional Powers in a Transforming Middle East. *Middle East Policy*, 19(2), 1–9.

Global Security 2013. *Trans Sahara Counterterrorism Partnership (TSCTP)*, 24 January, http://www.globalsecurity.org/military/ops/tscti.htm [accessed: 2 August 2013].

Heritage, T. 2013. *Ukraine holds key to Putin's dream of a new union.* *Reuters*, http://www.reuters.com/article/2013/11/29/us-ukraine-eu-putin-idUSBRE9AS0F320131129 [accessed: 20 January 2014].

Kaim, M. 2008. U.S. Gulf policy: Challenges for the next U.S. administration, in Kaim, M. (ed.), *Great Powers and Regional Orders: The United States and the Persian Gulf*. Aldershot: Ashgate, 263–70.

Kaim, M. 2008. U.S. policy and the regional order of the Persian Gulf: The analytical framework, in Kaim, M. (ed.), *Great Powers and Regional Orders: The United States and the Persian Gulf*. Aldershot: Ashgate, 1–12.

Kan, S.A. 2014. *China and Proliferation of Weapons of Mass Destruction and Missiles: Policy Issues*. Washington, DC: Congressional Research Service, http://www.fas.org/sgp/crs/nuke/RL31555.pdf [accessed: 19 January 2014].

Kassenova, N. 2013. Central Asia: Now as in 2030, at the Crossroads. *EUCAM Watch*, no. 15, Brussels: EUCAM.

Katz, M. 2012. *Moscow and the Middle East: Repeat Performance?*, Russia in Global Affairs, 7 October, http://eng.globalaffairs.ru/number/Moscow-and-the-Middle-East-Repeat-Performance-15690 [accessed: 13 June 2013].

Kavalski, E. (ed.) 2010. *China and the Global Politics of Regionalization*. Farnham: Ashgate.

Kavalski, E. 2010. Making a region out of a continent? China's regionalization of Africa, in Kavalski, E. (ed.), *China and the Global Politics of Regionalization*. Farnham: Ashgate, 177–90.

La rédaction 2013. A Bichkek, l'OSC attractive et en devenir – sécurité et économie au menu, September, http://www.francekoul.com/articles/a-bichkek-losc-attractive-et-en-devenir-securite-et-economie-au-menu [accessed: 15 September 2013].

Lanteigne, M. 2010. Security, strategy and the former USSR: China and the Shanghai Cooperation Organisation, in Breslin, S. (ed.), *The Handbook of China's International Relations*. London: Routledge, 166–76.

Laruelle, M. 2012. *Factoring the Regional Impact of Uzbekistan's Withdrawal from the CSTO*. Washington, DC: The German Marshall Fund of the United States, http://www.gmfus.org/wp-content/blogs.dir/1/files_mf/1345830436Laruelle_Uzbekistan_Aug12.pdf [accessed: 20 January 2014].

Laruelle, M. 2013. Goodbye to the Idea of a Region. *EUCAM Watch*, no. 15, Brussels: EUCAM.

Lawson, L. 2007. U.S. Africa Policy since the Cold War. *Strategic Insights*, 6(1).

Li, X. 2013. Xi Seeks to Resume FTA Talks with GCC. *People's Daily USA*, 17 September, http://usa.chinadaily.com.cn/china/2013-09/17/content_16974340.htm [accessed: 19 January 2014]

Olimat, M. 2010. Playing by the rules? Sino-Middle Eastern relations, in Breslin, S. (ed.), *The Handbook of China's International Relations*. London: Routledge, 177–86.

Petersen, A. 2012. After CSTO Withdrawal Uzbekistan also Looks East. *China in Central Asia*, 2 July.

Petersen, A. and Barysch, K. 2011. *Russia, China and the Geopolitics of Energy in Central Asia*. London: Centre for European Reform, 22.

Pew Research Center 2013. *Americans want to mind their own business*, 29 July, http://www.pewresearch.org/fact-tank/2013/07/29/americans-want-to-mind-their-own-business [accessed: 16 January 2014].

Schenker, D. 2013. *China-Middle East Relations: A Change in Policy?*, Carnegie-Tsinghua Center for Global Policy, 18 March, Beijing, http://carnegietsinghua.org/2013/03/18/china-middle-east-relations-change-in-policy/g0uk [accessed: 2 August 2013].

Scott, D. 2010. From Brussels to Beijing: Comparing the regionalization strategies of the EU and China, in Emilian, K. (ed.), *China and the Global Politics of Regionalization*. Farnham: Ashgate, 109–20.

Simon, L., Mattelaer, A. and Hadfield, A. 2012. *A Coherent EU Strategy for the Sahel*. Brussels: European Parliament (DG External Policies PE 433.778).

Stratfor 2013. *Mali: China Commits 500 Soldiers to U.N. Mission*, 24 May, http://www.stratfor.com/sample/analysis/mali-china-commits-500-soldiers-un-mission [accessed: 25 May 2013].

Thomas-Greenfield, L. 2013. *Keynote Address at the National Defense University*. Washington, DC, 30 October.

Thurston, A. 2012. *On US Bases in Africa*, 14 June, http://sahelblog.wordpress.com/2012/06/14/on-us-bases-in-africa [accessed: 1 June 2013].

Trenin, D. 2013. Russia's Middle East Gambit. *Tablet*, 30 May.

US Department of State 2014. *Existing U.S. Free Trade Agreements*, http://www.state.gov/e/eb/tpp/bta/fta/fta/index.htm [accessed: 19 January 2014].

US Energy Information Administration 2013. *International Energy Outlook 2013*. Washington, DC, July.

USAID 2014. *Interactive map*, http://map.usaid.gov/?l=regional&w=SUB%20SAHARAN%20AFRICA [accessed: 18 January 2014].

USAID 2014. *The Sahel*, http://www.usaid.gov/crisis/sahel [accessed: 18 January 2014].

Vasiliev, A. 2011. *Russia and Africa: Vying for mineral resources*. Valdai Discussion Club, 10 May, valdaiclub.com/africa/24840/print-edition [accessed: 26 June 2013].

Yang J., Foreign Minister of China 2012. Deepen Strategic Cooperation, Promote Common Development. *People's Daily Online*, 30 May, http://english.peopledaily.com.cn/90883/7831062.html [accessed: 19 January 2014].

Zoubir, Y.H. 2009. The United States and Maghreb-Sahel Security. *International Affairs*, 85(5), 977–95.

Zoubir, Y.H. 2012. The Sahara-Sahel Quagmire: Regional and International Ramifications. *Mediterranean Politics*, 17(3), 452–8.

Chapter 13

Conclusion: Models of Cooperation with the Neighbours of the EU's Neighbours

Sieglinde Gstöhl

Introduction: Extending the European Union's 'Neighbourhood'

The European Security Strategy stresses the need 'to promote a ring of well governed countries to the East of the European Union and on the borders of the Mediterranean'.[1] Yet, should this ambition stop with the countries of the European Neighbourhood Policy (ENP)? As this volume shows, the challenges in the broader neighbourhood of the European Union (EU) are manifold: political stability, radical ideologies, poverty, population growth, irregular immigration, energy security, and the prospect of geopolitical competition to name but a few.

The EU is founded on certain values such as democracy, the rule of law and the respect for human rights, and the Lisbon Treaty emphasizes that the EU's external action in general shall be guided by these principles (see articles 3.5 and 21.1 TEU). In light of the EU's 2004 enlargement, the ENP aimed 'to avoid new dividing lines in Europe and to promote stability and prosperity within and beyond the new borders of the Union'.[2] Hence, one could argue that in light of the ENP 10 years later, the EU should also focus on avoiding new dividing lines between the ENP countries and their neighbours. Indeed, as various observers have pointed out, '[t]he common goal of achieving stability and prosperity by means of peaceful inter-action makes Europe and Central Asia partners for increased cooperation',[3] 'the Sahara will become stable only when it becomes more prosperous',[4] and, in order to avoid irrelevance in the Middle East, the EU needs to shift 'the balance of diplomatic effort to deepen the linkages between the Mediterranean, the Gulf, Iran and Iraq'.[5]

---

1 European Council 2003. *European Security Strategy: A Secure Europe in a Better World*, Brussels, 12 December, 8.

2 European Council 2002. *Presidency Conclusions*, Copenhagen, 12–13 December, point 22.

3 Council of the European Union 2007. *The European Union and Central Asia: Strategy for a New Partnership*, Brussels, 21–22 June, 2.

4 *The Economist* 2013. Afrighanistan? 26 January-1 February, 11.

5 Youngs, R. and Echagüe, A. 2010. Europe, the Mediterranean, the Middle East and the Need for Triangulation. *The International Spectator*, 45(3), 38.

Hence, the EU can in the long run not afford to keep out of its broader neighbourhood. In fact, the European Commission had already in 2006 called to work with 'the neighbours of our neighbours' in Central Asia, the Gulf or Africa.[6] Yet, this appeal has subsequently not been followed up with a systematic policy approach. Underscoring the need for a strategy going beyond the ENP countries was one of the main objectives of the conference on which the contributions of this volume are based.[7] The insight into the importance of the EU's broader neighbourhood is slowly gaining ground. Grevi, for instance, recently argued that 'the neighbourhood should be framed as an extended strategic space stretching from West Africa and the Sahel to Central Asia and Russia, via the broader Middle East'.[8]

A value added of the concept of the 'neighbours of the EU's neighbours' is that it encourages to think about the connections that could link the EU, the ENP partners and their neighbouring countries as well as about the need to engage these neighbours in a more systematic and comprehensive approach in the face of numerous security, political, economic and social challenges. The concept invites the EU to define its role in the broader neighbourhood, also in relation to the other global players such as the United States, Russia and China.[9] The strong heterogeneity of the neighbours of the EU's neighbours thereby poses a particular challenge to the consistency of the EU's external action.

This concluding chapter asks to what extent the EU's current models of cooperation with the neighbours of its neighbours can be considered adequate and what further bridges could be built across this broader neighbourhood. It is argued that the EU's policy frameworks, which range from bilateral to inter-regional and multilateral approaches, lack not only an overarching strategic framework but could and should strengthen the interconnections between the regions. The chapter first reviews the EU's current models of cooperation and points at their major shortcomings before considering how they could be rendered more suitable by tying them closer to each other and embedding them in a strategy for the neighbours of the EU's neighbours.

---

6   European Commission 2006. *Communication from the Commission to the Council and the European Parliament on Strengthening the European Neighbourhood Policy*, COM(2006) 726 final, Brussels, 4 December, 11. See also Chapter 1 by Erwan Lannon in this volume.

7   College of Europe 2012. *The Neighbours of the EU's Neighbours: Diplomatic and Geopolitical Dimensions beyond the ENP – Conference Summary*. Bruges: College of Europe, 15–16 November, https://www.coleurope.eu/sites/default/files/uploads/page/conference-summary.pdf [accessed: 10 December 2013].

8   Grevi, G. 2014. Re-defining the EU's Neighbourhood, in Grevi, G.and Keohane, D. (eds), *Challenges for European Foreign Policy in 2014: The EU's Extended Neighbourhood*. Madrid: FRIDE, 16.

9   See Chapter 12 by Jonatan Thompson in this volume.

Current EU Models of Cooperation with the Neighbours' Neighbours

All neighbours of the EU's neighbours have in various forms concluded or envisaged cooperation agreements with the EU, political dialogues are in place, and the EU provides financial and technical assistance. In terms of trade, they all benefited from the EU's unilateral Generalized System of Preferences (GSP) until the end of 2013. The GSP reform which entered into force in 2014 focuses on fewer beneficiaries: high and upper-middle income countries have been excluded, thus leaving only Iraq, Kyrgyzstan, Tajikistan, Turkmenistan and Uzbekistan in the 'standard GSP'. Together with Iran these countries would qualify to apply for the 'special incentive arrangement for sustainable development and good governance' ('GSP+') which offers additional tariff reductions in return for more political conditionality in terms of international conventions to be ratified and implemented.[10] In addition, 11 least developed countries (LDCs), as defined by the United Nations, benefit from the 'Everything-But-Arms initiative' (EBA) which grants duty-free and quota-free market access to the EU.[11] With the exception of Yemen, these LDCs among the neighbours of the EU's neighbouring countries are all situated in Africa.

Other instruments of the EU to deal with the challenges posed by the neighbours of its neighbours have been missions carried out under the Common Security and Defence Policy (CSDP) in Iraq, Sudan and South Sudan, the Sahel (Mali, Niger and Chad) and the Horn of Africa (Djibouti, Kenya, Somalia, Seychelles and Tanzania).[12] There are or have recently been EU Special Representatives (EUSRs) for the African Union, for the Middle East peace process, for the Southern Mediterranean region, for Sudan and South Sudan, for the Sahel, for the Horn of Africa and for Central Asia. Finally, some regions benefit from special external assistance instruments and regional strategies or Strategic Partnerships, while others do not.

On an abstract level, the principal models of cooperation are (1) bilateralism, either pure or with a regional dimension; (2) multilateralism, (3) inter-regionalism between the EU and another institutionalized region; and (4) sub-regionalism[13] promoted by the EU, either with the EU being a member – like in the case of

---

10   See Beretta, L.C. 2013. Reforming the EU GSP in Europe: Defining the New Map of Tariff Preferences and Supply Options. *Global Trade and Customs Journal*, 8(7/8), 217–23.

11   For the latest version of the preferences scheme, see European Parliament and of the Council of the European Union 2012. *Regulation (EU) No 978/2012 of the European Parliament and of the Council of 25 October 2012 applying a scheme of generalised tariff preferences and repealing Council Regulation (EC) No 732/2008*. OJ L303/1, 31 October.

12   See European External Action Service 2014. *Missions and Operations*, http://eeas.europa.eu/csdp/missions-and-operations/index_en.htm [accessed: 10 March 2014].

13   Sub-regionalism is here understood in terms of 'nested regimes' and refers to a situation where regional integration efforts are fully (or to a substantial part) included within the framework of another regional integration scheme.

the Union for the Mediterranean (UfM) or the Eastern Partnership – or without the EU being a member, as is the case for the Central European Free Trade Agreement (CEFTA)[14] and the Agadir Agreement.[15]

The models of cooperation in the EU's broader neighbourhood appear to be looser from West to East, reflecting historically grown relationships: while in Africa multilateralism and (emerging) inter-regionalism prevail, cooperation in the Middle East is characterized by inter-regionalism and bilateralism and in Central Asia solely by bilateralism.

Africa: Multilateralism and (Emerging) Inter-Regionalism

The Joint Africa-EU Strategy adopted in 2007 defines the long-term policy orientations between the two continents and aims in particular 'to bridge the development divide between Africa and Europe through the strengthening of economic co-operation and the promotion of sustainable development in both continents, living side by side in peace, security, prosperity, solidarity and human dignity'.[16] The Africa-EU Partnership is driven through formal dialogue at various levels, including EU-Africa Summits. Within this overall political framework, the EU's regional approach towards North Africa and the Near East is defined by the Euro-Mediterranean Partnership, the Union for the Mediterranean and the European Neighbourhood Policy, while relations with sub-Saharan African countries take place under the policy framework of the Cotonou Agreement with the African, Caribbean and Pacific (ACP) states. Whereas the Mediterranean partners have benefited from the European Neighbourhood and Partnership Instrument (ENPI),[17] the main geographical financial instrument for the ACP countries is the European Development Fund (EDF). In addition, both groups benefit from various thematic financial instruments of the EU.

At the bilateral level, the EU has concluded association agreements and is in the process of negotiating so-called deep and comprehensive free trade areas (DCFTAs) with the Southern ENP countries. At the multilateral level, the Euro-Mediterranean Partnership foresees the establishment of a Euro-Mediterranean Free Trade Area. With regard to South-South integration, Tunisia, Morocco,

---

14   The current CEFTA members are the (potential) EU candidate countries Albania, Bosnia and Herzegovina, the former Yugoslav Republic of Macedonia, Montenegro, Serbia and the United Nations Interim Administration Mission in Kosovo (UNMIK) on behalf of Kosovo as well as the ENP country Moldova.

15   The current contracting parties to the Agadir Agreement are the ENP countries Egypt, Jordan, Morocco and Tunisia.

16   Council of the European Union 2007. *The Africa-EU Strategic Partnership: A Joint Africa-EU Strategy.* Lisbon, 9 December, 16344/07 (Presse 291).

17   As of 2014 the ENPI has been transformed into the European Neighbourhood Instrument (ENI). See European Parliament and Council of the European Union 2014. *Regulation (EU) No 232/2014 of the European Parliament and of the Council of 11 March 2014 establishing a European Neighbourhood Instrument.* OJ, L 77/27, 13 March.

Jordan and Egypt entered the Agadir Free Trade Agreement which remains open to other countries of the region. Also the Economic Partnership Agreements (EPAs) with regional groupings of the ACP countries are to progressively establish free trade areas compatible with the rules of the World Trade Organization (WTO). The ACP countries in the Sahel and the Horn of Africa region have together with other ACP countries been split into four different regional groupings to negotiate EPAs with the EU.[18] The EPAs partly build on pre-existing regional integration schemes in Africa but are as such not, as a kind of sub-regionalism, nested within a larger integration project. The EPA negotiations have encountered many obstacles, in particular because trade would no longer be based on the principle of non-reciprocity with the whole ACP group, but on reciprocal free trade agreements (FTAs) to be concluded with several regions.[19] Moreover, as least developed countries, most countries of the Sahel and the Horn of Africa benefit from the EU's unilateral EBA initiative and have thus little incentive to sign up to a reciprocal regional EPA. It remains thus questionable to what extent the EPAs can be considered as emerging inter-regionalism.

The various free trade projects in the Mediterranean and ACP regions are not (planned to be) hooked up with each other. The difficulty of drawing lines between regions is illustrated by the case of Mauritania: the ACP country is a member of the Euro-Mediterranean Partnership and of the UfM, but – unlike the other countries of the Arab Maghreb Union (Algeria, Libya, Mauritania, Morocco and Tunisia) established in 1989 – it has not been included in the ENP.

The EU has since 2011 developed regional strategies in response to the problems in the Sahel and in the Horn of Africa. The Sahel Strategy recognizes that the challenges facing the three core Sahelian states Mauritania, Mali and Niger also affect neighbouring countries like Algeria, Libya or Morocco whose engagement is necessary to help solve problems such as extreme poverty, climate change effects, food crises, fragile governance, corruption, violent extremism, illicit trafficking and terrorism.[20] The Strategy acknowledges that 'the absence of a sub-regional organisation encompassing all the Sahel and Maghreb states [is likely to] lead to unilateral or poorly coordinated action and hamper credible and effective regional initiatives'.[21] However, Bello argues that '[i]nadequate geographical scope, unclear operational connection with wider regional frameworks and initial

---

18   See also Chapter 2 by Claudia Zulaika in this volume.

19   See, for instance, Pape, E. 2013. An old partnership in a new setting: ACP-EU relations from a European perspective. *Journal of International Development*, 25(5), 727–41.

20   Council of the European Union 2011. *Strategy for Security and Development in the Sahel*, Annex to the Council Conclusions on a European Union Strategy for Security and Development in the Sahel, Brussels, 21 March.

21   Ibid., 3.

reluctance to consider a more serious and direct security commitment have all limited the strategy's impact'.[22]

Another strategy in the region is the Horn of Africa Strategy.[23] It builds on the earlier 'EU Policy on the Horn of Africa' which also emphasized that '[a]ll individual countries of the sub-region have seen their domestic conflicts influenced by, or having implications on, the neighbourhood'.[24] The 2006 Commission Communication suggested including relevant Horn of Africa issues in discussions with key stakeholders in the wider African and Arab region, in particular because the Horn of Africa 'is in close proximity to countries covered by the EU Neighbourhood policy, both in North Africa and the Near East'.[25] The EU is thus aware of the need to link and embed its regional strategies but lacks a policy to address the challenges in a comprehensive manner. The turmoil in Mali in 2013 and the piracy off the coast of Somalia revealed how closely connected the Sahel is to the EU's immediate neighbourhood.[26]

Table 13.1 summarizes the models and instruments for the African neighbours of the EU's neighbours. The EU's approach to this region concentrates on development and security issues. Several EU Special Representatives had been appointed for the region and several CSDP missions carried out. Overall, the relationship is embedded in the EU-Africa Strategic Partnership and characterized by the Cotonou Agreement's multilateral cooperation, including a potential but rather unlikely future inter-regional dimension in the form of EPAs.

---

22   Bello, O. 2012. *Quick Fix or Quick Sand? Implementing the EU Sahel Strategy.* Madrid: FRIDE, 17.

23   Council of the European Union 2011. *A Strategic Framework for the Horn of Africa*, Annex to the Council Conclusions on the Horn of Africa, 3124th Foreign Affairs Council meeting, Brussels, 14 November. It covers the countries belonging to the Inter-Governmental Authority for Development (IGAD): Djibouti, Eritrea, Ethiopia, Kenya, Somalia, Sudan, South Sudan and Uganda.

24   Council of the European Union 2009. *An EU Policy on the Horn of Africa – Towards a Comprehensive EU Strategy*, Annex to the Outcome of Proceedings of the Foreign Affairs Council, Brussels, 8 December, 8.

25   European Commission 2006. *Communication from the Commission to the Council and the European Parliament. Strategy for Africa: An EU regional political partnership for peace, security and development in the Horn of Africa*, COM(2006) 601 final, Brussels, 20 October, 5.

26   See Chapter 4 by Alex Vines and Ahmed Soliman as well as Chapter 3 by Alexander Mattelaer in this volume and Map VI in the Annex.

Table 13.1   Models and instruments: Sahel and Horn of Africa

Models	Instruments
Multilateralism (13 ACP countries in the region of the Sahel and the Horn of Africa)	Group-to-group association with ACP (Cotonou Agreement); special geographical instrument outside the EU budget (EDF)
Potential inter-regionalism under negotiation	Future FTAs (EPAs) within Cotonou framework whose group members do not entirely correspond to the regional integration schemes
EU-Africa Strategic Partnership 2007	Two regional strategies (Horn of Africa 2011, Sahel 2011) within the continental Joint Africa-EU Strategy 2007 CSDP missions EUSRs for the African Union, for the Sahel, for the Horn of Africa and for Sudan/South Sudan

Middle East: Inter-Regionalism and Bilateralism

The ill-fated Euro-Arab Dialogue between the European Community and the League of Arab States, dating back to 1973, was again suspended in 1990 after the Iraqi invasion of Kuwait, which had split the Arab world.[27] Since then Europe has divided the Arab countries into different frameworks of cooperation: in addition to the Euro-Mediterranean Partnership covering most of the Maghreb and Mashreq countries and the Cotonou Agreement with ACP countries such as Sudan, Somalia and Mauritania, the EU maintains since over two decades an inter-regional relationship with the Gulf Cooperation Council (GCC).[28] The 1988 Cooperation Agreement between the European Economic Community (EEC) and the GCC inter alia committed them to enter negotiations on a FTA. Although these negotiations were initiated in 1990 they soon reached a standstill. In spite of their resumption in 2002, they still have not led to an agreement.[29] Antkiewicz and Momani argue that the EU's motives for inter-regional negotiations with the GCC are explained by geopolitical rather than economic interests and by the desire to export its regional model.[30] The EU also favours an accession of Yemen to the GCC but this considerably poorer country has so far not been accepted by the

---

27   The term 'Arab world' is used to describe the 22 countries that belong to the League of Arab States.

28   The GCC members are Bahrain, Kuwait, Oman, Qatar, Saudi Arabia and the United Arab Emirates.

29   See Chapter 6 by Silvia Colombo in this volume.

30   Antkiewicz, A. and Momani, B. 2009. Pursuing Geopolitical Stability through Interregional Trade: The EU's Motives for Negotiating with the Gulf Cooperation Council. *Journal of European Integration*, 31(2), 217–35.

GCC.[31] Unlike the other Gulf countries, Yemen is not a monarchy and qualifies as a least developed country that benefits from the EU's EBA initiative.

This proliferation of unrelated policies has left Arab countries like Iraq and Yemen out of any multilateral institutional arrangement with the European Union.[32] The EU instead relies on bilateral relations with Yemen, Iraq and (non-Arab) Iran. The EU and Yemen signed a Cooperation Agreement in 1998, and the EU–Iraq Partnership and Cooperation Agreement (PCA) was signed in 2012. By contrast, negotiations for a Trade and Cooperation Agreement between the EU and Iran have been put on hold since 2005, when Iran started to intensify its nuclear activities.[33] The three countries benefit from the Development Cooperation Instrument (DCI), whereas the framework for financial cooperation between the EU and the GCC countries (as well as other high-income countries) is the Instrument for Cooperation with Industrialized Countries (ICI).[34]

The 2004 'EU Strategic Partnership with the Mediterranean and the Middle East' (SPMME) was a first step in the direction to overcome the fragmentation of frameworks.[35] This Strategic Partnership was taking shape at the same time as the ENP. Although it embraced the countries of North Africa, the GCC, Yemen, Iraq and Iran, it still relied on existing instruments and mechanisms and clearly distinguished between the countries of the Euro-Mediterranean Partnership and those east of Jordan. Nevertheless, it considered the progressive future establishment of regional free trade agreements, such as a linking of the Euro-Mediterranean and EU-GCC FTAs. However, the original proposal from the European Commission and High Representative to envisage a regional strategy for the Wider Middle East was not followed up in the SPMME.[36] With the launching of the Union for the Mediterranean in 2008, 'the EU's Strategic Partnership with the Mediterranean and the Middle East was being quietly forgotten'.[37] Instead of embedding the UfM in the Strategic Partnership, which would have allowed to connect Europe, the Arab Mediterranean

---

31   Ibid., 229. For the difficulties which a Yemenite accession faces, see Burke, E. 2012. 'One Blood and One Destiny'? Yemen's Relations with the Gulf Cooperation Council. *Research Paper, Kuwait Programme on Development, Governance and Globalisation in the Gulf States*, 23, London: LSE.

32   See Chapter 5 by Andrew Bower and Raphaël Metais in this volume.

33   See Chapter 7 by Clément Therme in this volume.

34   As of 2014 the ICI has been transformed into the Partnership Instrument (PI). The PI focuses on cooperation with industrialized countries and emerging economies on core EU interests and common challenges of global concern. See European Parliament and Council of the European Union 2014. *Regulation (EU) No 234/2014 of the European Parliament and of the Council of 11 March 2014 establishing a Partnership Instrument for cooperation with third countries.* OJ, L 77/77, 15 March.

35   European Council 2005. *Final Report on an EU Strategic Partnership with the Mediterranean and the Middle East*, Brussels, 17 June.

36   European Commission and High Representative 2003. *Strengthening EU's Relations with the Arab World*, D(2003) 10318, Brussels, 4 December, 7.

37   Youngs and Echagüe, op. cit., 28.

and the Gulf, the EU's policy remained compartmentalized. The SPMME did not succeed in producing greater coherence for the EU's policy towards this region.

Table 13.2 provides a synopsis of the EU's relations with the Arabian Peninsula, Iraq and Iran. The approach combines bilateral and inter-regional aspects and focuses so far mainly on security, ranging from containment to reconstruction and economic cooperation. There is no specific EUSR for this region, except more generally for the Middle East peace process.[38] The Strategic Partnership with the Mediterranean and the Middle East has not been complemented by a tailor-made regional strategy.

Table 13.2   Models and instruments: Arabian Peninsula, Iraq and Iran

Models	Instruments
Inter-regionalism with GCC	EEC-GCC Cooperation Agreement 1988 and FTA under negotiation
Bilateralism with non-GCC countries	Cooperation Agreements with Yemen 1998 and Iraq 2012 (Iran on hold) CSDP mission (Iraq)
Strategic Partnership with the Mediterranean and the Middle East 2004 (GCC, Yemen, Iraq, Iran)	No strategy for the Wider Middle East No special geographical instruments: DCI (Yemen, Iraq, Iran) and ICI/PI (GCC countries)

Central Asia: Bilateralism

The EU's trade relations with Kazakhstan, Kyrgyzstan, Tajikistan and Uzbekistan are governed by bilateral Partnership and Cooperation Agreements signed in the late 1990s (respectively 2010 in the case of Tajikistan). The PCA concluded with Turkmenistan in 1998 has still not been ratified because of human rights concerns. Kazakhstan is since 2011 negotiating an enhanced PCA which will provide for a reinforced political dialogue, trade and investment, cooperation in justice, freedom and security, as well as energy, and cooperation in the field of foreign and security policy, transport, development, agriculture and health.[39]

In 2007 the EU adopted with a view to these countries its 'Strategy for a New Partnership'. According to the Central Asia Strategy, '[t]he strong EU commitment towards its Eastern neighbours within the framework of the European

---

38   Yet the mandate of Bernardino León, the EUSR for the Southern Mediterranean region, inter alia includes close coordination with the African Union, the GCC, the Organization of Islamic Cooperation, the League of Arab States, and the Arab Maghreb Union in its policy objectives. See Council of the European Union 2012. *Council Decision 2012/327/CFSP of 25 June 2012 extending the mandate of the European Union Special Representative for the Southern Mediterranean region.* OJ L 165/56, 26 June, article 2.

39   See Chapter 8 by Francesca Fenton in this volume.

Neighbourhood Policy will also bring Europe and Central Asia closer to each other'.[40] An EU Special Representative was appointed to promote good relations between the EU and Central Asian countries and to oversee the implementation of the EU strategy. Nevertheless, the EU attempted no multilateral approach towards the five republics, nor any sub-regional initiatives.

The Black Sea region occupies a strategic position between Europe, Central Asia and the Middle East and is rich in natural resources. The EU's Black Sea Synergy initiative of 2007 aimed at cooperation with the Organization of the Black Sea Economic Cooperation, which comprises Albania, Armenia, Azerbaijan, Bulgaria, Georgia, Greece, Moldova, Romania, Russia, Serbia, Turkey and Ukraine. The Black Sea Synergy was to complement the EU's Strategic Partnership with Russia, the pre-accession strategy and the Eastern Partnership: 'There would be a close link between the Black Sea approach and an EU Strategy for Central Asia. Black Sea co-operation would thus include substantial inter-regional elements'.[41] However, the initiative did not fulfil these expectations and failed to set up any sectoral partnerships.[42] In view of 'the rather limited results' of the Black Sea Synergy and the fact that 'the Black Sea region is a strategic bridge connecting Europe with the Caspian Sea area, Central Asia and the Middle East', the European Parliament had in 2011, so far in vain, called for a proper 'EU Strategy for the Black Sea'.[43]

The TACIS programme (Technical Assistance to the Commonwealth of Independent States) which ran from 1991 to 2006 covered Armenia, Azerbaijan, Belarus, Georgia, Kazakhstan, Kyrgyzstan, Moldova, Mongolia, the Russian Federation, Tajikistan, Turkmenistan, Ukraine and Uzbekistan. Hence, it had covered the ENP East and Central Asia plus Russia and Mongolia. In 2007, TACIS was replaced by the DCI which comprises 47 countries in Latin America, Asia and Central Asia, the Gulf region (Iran, Iraq and Yemen) and South Africa.

The former Soviet republics, except for the Baltic states, have been united in the Commonwealth of Independent States (CIS) founded in 1991. However, Ukraine and Turkmenistan have not ratified the charter and Georgia withdrew in 2009. Instead, the Eurasian Economic Community is increasingly becoming a more important organization for the countries of the CIS. The Treaty on the establishment of the Eurasian Economic Community was signed in 2000 by Russia, Belarus,

---

40   Council of the European Union 2009. *The European Union and Central Asia: The New Partnership in Action*, Brussels, June, 10, http://eeas.europa.eu/central_asia/ docs/2010_strategy_eu_centralasia_en.pdf [accessed: 10 December 2013].

41   European Commission 2007. *Communication from the Commission to the Council and the European Parliament, Black Sea Synergy – A New Regional Cooperation Initiative*, COM(2007) 160 final, Brussels, 11 April, 3.

42   See Duhot, H. 2012. The Black Sea Synergy Initiative: The Reflection of EU's Ambitions and Limitations in the Region, in Lannon, E. (ed.), *The European Neighbourhood Policy's Challenges/Les défis de la politique européenne de voisinage*. Brussels: P.I.E. Peter Lang, 323–44.

43   European Parliament 2011. *An EU Strategy for the Black Sea (2010/2087(INI))*. Brussels, P7-TA(2011)0025, 20 January.

Kazakhstan and Tajikistan.[44] Uzbekistan joined in 2005 but withdrew three years later. It is in fact in reaction to the EU's Eastern Partnership that Russia, Belarus and Kazakhstan established in 2010 the customs union of the Eurasian Economic Community. By 2015, they aim to create the Eurasian Union, based on the model of the European Union. The Armenian government's announcement in late 2013 to join the customs union and the decision of the Ukrainian government to suspend the signature of its Association Agreement and DCFTA with the EU have shown that 'the EU is no longer the only actor promoting deep economic integration premised on regulatory convergence in the post-Soviet space'.[45] It also clearly demonstrated that the EU cannot escape geopolitical rivalry in its neighbourhood.

Table 13.3 gives an overview of the main elements of the EU's relations with Central Asia. They are based on bilateralism, accompanied by a regional strategy, and a strong focus on energy security.

Table 13.3   Models and instruments: Central Asia

Models	Instruments
Bilateralism	PCAs (Turkmenistan on hold, enhanced PCA with Kazakhstan under negotiation)
with a regional strategy	Central Asia Strategy 2007 EUSR for Central Asia No special geographical instruments: DCI

A comparison of the three regions reveals that the EU's relations with the Sahel and the Horn of Africa, despite all their shortcomings, are currently based on the most elaborate and comprehensive model among the neighbours of the EU's neighbours, although the multilateral approach in place is not exclusive for the region. This region is also the most challenging one for Europe. By contrast, the EU's bilateral relationship with Central Asia is the least institutionalized and least developed one. The Gulf region is placed in between with a combination of inter-regionalism and bilateralism. All three relationships are largely concerned with security issues and to a much lesser extent with socioeconomic issues or political reform. Trade relations are currently still based on Partnership and Cooperation Agreements or the GSP rather than free trade, and compared to the ENP countries, political conditionality has been weak.

---

44   Eurasian Economic Community 2013. *Treaty on the Establishment of the Eurasian Economic Community*, http://www.evrazes.com/docs/view/95 [accessed: 10 December 2013].

45   Delcour, L. and Wolczuk, K. 2013. Eurasian Economic Integration and Implications for the EU's Policy in the Eastern Neigbhourhood, in Dragneva, R. and K. Wolczuk, K. (eds), *Eurasian Economic Integration: Law, Policy, and Politics.* Cheltenham: Edward Elgar, 180.

Shortcomings of the Current EU Models of Cooperation

Among the main shortcomings of the current models of cooperation between the EU and the neighbours of its neighbours are, on the one hand, the fragmentation within the regions (except for Central Asia) and, on the other hand, the lack of tailor-made linkages with the ENP and thus with the EU's immediate neighbours. In response to these shortcomings, the EU is confronted with several questions. First of all, how is a region best defined? Should it be defined geographically (such as the Arabian Peninsula), historically (like the ACP group), culturally (for instance, the Arab world) or geopolitically (like the Horn of Africa plus Yemen)? For example, the EU policy towards the Mediterranean and Middle East is often described as suffering from division: while the EU's policy towards the Southern Mediterranean has become highly institutionalized (Euro-Mediterranean Partnership, ENP, UfM), the policy frameworks with the Gulf states as well as with Iran and Iraq are still in the making. Such fragmentation risks leading to 'patchiness and policy vacuums' and 'fails to leverage regional connections'.[46] As a result, the EU punches below its weight in the Arab world: its own construction of the Mediterranean – also as a sphere of influence for Europe – overlooks the increasingly strong relations of this region with the Gulf and fails to embed it in a broader Middle East strategy. As argued by Colombo, the EU's neglect of the GCC in its reaction to the 'Arab Spring' reveals its short-sightedness.[47]

Even more so than in the Gulf, the European Union has remained a marginal player in Central Asia. The EU's Central Asia Strategy appears to have been largely inspired by concerns for energy security and the future of Afghanistan rather than by the concerns of the populations in the region such as prosperity and respect for their human rights.[48] Stephan Keukeleire argues in general that the EU's view on the neighbours of its neighbours should be complemented by an 'outside-in' perspective which looks at EU policy from the perspective of the third countries or regions concerned.[49] This implies a thorough knowledge of the regions, their actors, interests and value systems.

As several contributions in this volume show, the European (or Western) model is not necessarily the driving motivation for many leaders in the EU's broader neighbourhood. Therefore, Leigh argues that the EU should adopt a more pragmatic approach, inspired by classic foreign policy rather than the enlargement experience.[50] This means combining support for democratic and market-oriented economic reforms with the pursuit of security, energy and commercial interests. Such an approach will help overcome the distinction between the ENP countries and the neighbours of the EU's neighbours. A lesson to be drawn from the 'Arab

---

46 Youngs and Echagüe, op. cit., 27.
47 See Chapter 6 by Silvia Colombo in this volume.
48 See also Chapter 9 by Alexander Warkotsch in this volume.
49 See Chapter 11 by Stephan Keukeleire in this volume.
50 See Chapter 10 by Michael Leigh in this volume.

Spring' for Central Asia is that the EU's engagement with authoritarian leaderships for the sake of political stability should not side-line its commitment to democracy, rule of law and human rights if it wants to remain a credible actor. This is why Melvin argues with regard to Central Asia in favour of a 'values-based realism'.[51]

Second, what is the European Union's broader strategic vision with regard to the neighbours of its neighbours? The Central Asia Strategy, for instance, has helped increase the EU's presence but '[i]t lacks a clear political vision of Europe's interests and comparative advantages in the region'.[52] The definition of regions and regional strategies must be coherent with the EU's overall foreign policy strategy. Without taking into account the interconnections between the regions, conflicts might arise between different regional strategies. For instance, the Sahel Strategy emphasizes security cooperation with Algeria, while the ENP stresses political conditionality with regard to democracy and human rights standards in this country.[53] This is why some authors argue in favour of a 'grand strategy' for EU external action which would allow, if necessary, to make choices at a higher level.[54] A 'grand strategy' would define the long-term objectives and their priorities as well as the instruments. It would take into account both values and interests, as requested by the Lisbon Treaty. Strategies can help improve the horizontal coherence between competing policy areas as well as the vertical coherence between the national and European levels.

Third, and linked to the two previous questions, how far does the neighbourhood of the European Union extend? As far as its vital interests are concerned? While the EU is an important power in the Mediterranean, it is operating below its potential in the Middle East and at best a 'second tier' player in Central Asia compared to China, Russia or the US.[55] Duke argues that 'the concept of geopolitics should be employed to suggest a clear strategic focus for the Union and that this, in turn, will help make the EU a more credible and influential international partner'.[56] If the EU is going to join in the geopolitical game in its broader neighbourhood, it must address the growing expectations regarding the export of stability, peace and prosperity. The logical focus then falls upon the membership candidates, the ENP countries, the Sahel and Horn of Africa, Central Asia and the Gulf countries.[57] The latter countries influence the EU's relations with the ENP partners and with the global players.

---

51   N. Melvin 2012. The EU Needs a New Values-Based Realism for its Central Asia Strategy. *EUCAM Policy Brief*, no. 28, Brussels: EUCAM, October, 3.

52   Ibid., 3.

53   See Chapter 3 by Alexander Mattelaer in this volume.

54   S. Biscop 2012. Raiders of the Lost Art: Strategy-Making in Europe. *Egmont Security Policy Brief*, no. 40, Brussels: Egmont.

55   See Chapter 12 by Jonatan Thompson in this volume.

56   Duke, S. 2011. Pax or Pox Europeana after the Lisbon Treaty? *The International Spectator*, 46(1), 83.

57   Ibid.

Building Bridges across EU Policy Frameworks

From a cross-regional perspective, a lesson that can be learned from the EU's ENP experience is that less importance should be attached to the 'process' and more to the 'substance' of cooperation, that is, to the content of the relationships that the EU intends to build with the 'neighbours of its neighbours' and their expected impact.[58] For the future, the EU needs to create stronger connections between the different strands of its policies in order to avoid inconsistencies and take advantage of political synergies. In other words, the current compartmentalization of the neighbours of the EU's neighbours should be replaced by a 'variable geometry' approach within an overarching strategic framework. Such an overarching framework should focus on building sustainable bridges across the regions despite their undeniable diversity. These bridges could consist of (1) inserting regional cooperation clauses as interfaces in the various regional instruments and perhaps even envisaging an own 'neighbours of neighbours' cross-border cooperation programme; (2) connecting infrastructure and trade networks across the regions and developing synergy initiatives; and (3) linking the EU strategies in a region and embedding them in an overall strategy for the neighbours of the EU's neighbours. They are further developed below. In addition, existing tools could be renewed or expanded, for instance by reviving political dialogue such as with the Arab world or by enlarging the membership of the UfM or of the ENP. The various EUSRs for the broader neighbourhood could also coordinate amongst themselves within the framework of a broader neighbourhood strategy.

Inter-Regional Interfaces in Instruments

The term of 'the neighbours of the EU's neighbours' was first used by the European Commission when pointing to the possibility of financial instruments (such as the ENPI and DCI) to fund regional cooperation activities which include both ENP countries and their neighbours.[59] This is of particular importance in sectors such as energy, transport, environment or migration. Some cross-regional programmes already exist, in particular for infrastructure networks. The INOGATE programme (Interstate Oil and Gas Transport to Europe) supports the development of energy cooperation between the European Union, the littoral states of the Black and Caspian Seas and their neighbouring countries.[60] Since 2007 INOGATE is funded by the ENPI and the DCI (instead of the TACIS programme). Another example is

---

58   See also Chapter 10 by Michael Leigh in this volume.

59   European Commission 2006. *Communication from the Commission to the Council and the European Parliament on Strengthening the European Neighbourhood Policy*, COM(2006) 726 final, Brussels, 4 December, 11.

60   INOGATE covers the European Union, Armenia, Azerbaijan, Belarus, Georgia, Kazakhstan, Kyrgyzstan, Moldova, Tajikistan, Turkmenistan, Ukraine and Uzbekistan. See www.inogate.org.

the TRACECA programme (Transport Corridor Europe-Caucasus-Asia), initiated in 1993 to develop the international transport between Europe and Asia across the Black Sea, the South Caucasus, the Caspian Sea and Central Asia, which is also funded through the DCI and ENPI.[61] The revised Cotonou Agreement as well as the ENPI and DCI regulations already contain 'passerelle clauses' for cooperation between countries, regions and territories eligible under the DCI, ENPI and EDF.[62]

In addition to unilateral instruments for regional cooperation, such 'passerelle clauses' could also be inserted in bi- and multilateral agreements. In its 1998 Cooperation Agreement with Yemen, for instance, the EU explicitly foresaw that economic and other cooperation may extend to activities under agreements with other countries of the same region and encouraged activities to develop cooperation between Yemen and its neighbours, including coordination with its own programmes with the Mediterranean and GCC countries.[63] Such interfaces in agreements could be used more systematically.

Connecting Trade and Infrastructure Networks

With the European Neighbourhood Policy the EU has primarily created a 'hub-and-spoke bilateralism' between the itself and its neighbours.[64] It still needs to reinforce the connections 'between the spokes' and with the neighbours of the neighbours. When the European Council of March 2009 adopted the Eastern Partnership, it underlined the 'effective complementarity between the Eastern Partnership and existing regional initiatives in the EU's neighbourhood, in particular the Black Sea Synergy' and that third countries would be eligible for participation on a case-by-case basis in concrete activities.[65] Drawing on the strengths and weaknesses of the Black Sea Synergy, a Caspian Sea Synergy could be considered to better exploit the cooperation potential.

The ENP's model of 'bilateralism-within-regionalism' could to some extent also be useful within the broader Middle East[66] or Central Asia. The different initiatives should reinforce pan-regional dynamics instead of cross-cutting them,

---

61   The current full parties of TRACECA are Armenia, Azerbaijan, Bulgaria, Georgia, Iran, Kazakhstan, Kyrgyzstan, Moldova, Romania, Tajikistan, Turkey, Ukraine and Uzbekistan. See www.traceca-org.org. Due to the UN and EU sanctions, no EU technical assistance is provided to the Islamic Republic of Iran.

62   See Chapter 2 by Claudia Zulaika in this volume.

63   Council of the European Union 1998. *Cooperation Agreement between the European Community and the Republic of Yemen* 1998. OJ L 72/18, 11 March, article 9.

64   Gstöhl, S. 2012. What Is at Stake in the Internal Market? Towards a Neighbourhood Economic Community, in Lannon, E. (ed.), *Challenges of the European Neighbourhood Policy/Les défis de la politique européenne de voisinage*. Brussels: P.I.E. Peter Lang, 100.

65   European Council 2009. *Declaration by the European Council on the Eastern Partnership, Presidency Conclusions of the Brussels European Council*, 19–20 March, Annex 2.

66   Youngs and Echagüe, op. cit., 28.

resulting in what Youngs and Echagüe call a 'graduated regionalism'.[67] For example, sectoral agreements (for instance, in the fields of energy and transport) could be extended to the neighbouring region or trade and cooperation agreements could be interconnected. The SPMME of 2004, which included the countries of North Africa, the GCC, Yemen, Iraq and Iran, had envisaged the possibility to link the future Euro-Mediterranean and EU-GCC FTAs. This is a potential bridge to keep in mind.

Moreover, sectoral partnerships across regions in the broader neighbourhood could be developed. The Energy Community can serve as an example of an open regional building block for sectoral integration. The Energy Community Treaty, which entered into force in 2006, extends the EU's internal market for electricity and gas to South Eastern Europe, Moldova and Ukraine (with Armenia, Georgia, Norway and Turkey as observers). The members agreed to adopt the relevant *acquis* on energy, environment, competition and renewables and they have the right but not an obligation to follow the evolution of the *acquis*. Other potential examples of 'sectoral multilateralism' are the European Common Aviation Area with the Western Balkans, Iceland and Norway (with the possibility of ENP countries joining) signed in 2006; and the planned Transport Community Treaty with South Eastern Europe.[68] Compared to these cases, the forms of cooperation with the broader neighbourhood could remain looser.

Linking and Embedding Regional Strategies

The SPMME has so far not followed up on the proposal to envisage a regional strategy for the Wider Middle East. This idea should be reconsidered. Moreover, the European Union could renew the Euro-Arab Dialogue by strengthening its relations with the Arab League, where all the countries of the Mediterranean and Middle Eastern region are present (except for Israel and Iran). According to Baabood, it is 'surprising and odd given the European passion for promoting regional integration that the EU has no formal dialogue with the League'.[69] The first ministerial meetings of the Ministers of Foreign Affairs of the EU and of the League of Arab States took place in 2008 and 2012.[70]

---

67   Ibid.

68   Blockmans, S. and Van Vooren, B. 2012. Revitalizing the European 'Neighbourhood Economic Community': The Case of Legally Binding Sectoral Multilateralism. *European Foreign Affairs Review*, 17(4): 577–604. They refer with regard to the ENP countries to 'legally binding sectoral multilateralism', aiming at treaty-based legal integration in selected areas between the EU and (able and willing) neighbours and between the latter themselves.

69   Baabood, A. 2010. What an Effective Arab Strategy for the EU Should Look Like. *Europe's World*, spring, http://www.europesworld.org/NewEnglish/Home-old/Article/tabid/191/ArticleType/articleview/ArticleID/21591/language/en-US/Default.aspx [accessed: 10 December 2013].

70   Council of the European Union 2012. *Cairo Declaration, Second European Union-League of Arab States Foreign Affairs Ministerial Meeting*, Cairo, 13 November

Bello argues that in spite of its shortcomings, the EU Sahel Strategy 'is gradually evolving into a project that could help mobilize fragmented regional actors around shared security objectives'.[71] Furthermore, the EU should strive to better connect its Southern ENP partners and their neighbouring ACP countries, as well as the regional strategy for Central Asia and the policy towards the Eastern ENP partners.

Moreover, the EU should pay more attention to its relations with the regional powers as well as potential geopolitical rivalries between regional players. For instance, the Sahel Strategy largely neglected the role of Nigeria, the Economic Community of West African States (ECOWAS) and Algeria,[72] while in the Middle East Saudi Arabia requires attention as a pivotal player and in Central Asia Kazakhstan.

To conclude, the European Union could promote bridge-building between the ENP countries and their neighbours on several levels: (1) unilaterally through the funding of cross-framework and cross-regional cooperation on the basis of specific clauses in financial instruments and/or an own 'neighbours of neighbours' cross-border cooperation programme and through the linkage of its regional strategies while embedding them in a broader common strategic framework; (2) bilaterally through regional cooperation clauses in partnership and free trade agreements and through enhanced political dialogue; and (3) multilaterally through enhanced cooperation with the neighbours of the EU's neighbours in regional and global fora.

Conclusion: An EU Strategy for the Neighbours of the Neighbours?

The regions of the Middle East, the Sahel and the Horn of Africa as well as Central Asia represent poles of strategic interest for the EU. These regions face crucial challenges such as the spill-over of the 'Arab Spring', regional conflicts, state failures, food crises, terrorism, trafficking, organized crime and undemocratic regimes. This chapter examined, on the basis of the preceding chapters, the EU's models of cooperation with the neighbours of its neighbours. It argued that the EU's current policy models, ranging from bilateral to inter-regional and multilateral approaches, are inadequate in terms of the interconnections between the regions and the lack of an overarching strategic framework.

The 2003 Commission Communication on 'Wider Europe', the first communication on the ENP, had proposed that 'the EU should aim to develop a zone of prosperity and a friendly neighbourhood – a "ring of friends" – with whom

---

2012, http://www.consilium.europa.eu/uedocs/cms-data/docs/pressdata/EN/foraff/133465. pdf [accessed: 10 December 2013].

71   Bello, op. cit., 17.

72   Ibid., 1.

the EU enjoys close, peaceful and co-operative relations'.[73] An 'EU Strategy for the Neighbours of its Neighbours' would in the long run aim at the creation of a 'second ring of friends' beyond the ENP, transforming the 'arc of crisis' in the broader neighbourhood.[74] Such a long-term objective can only be tackled in a pragmatic manner. Compared to the ENP countries, values tend to be less shared with the EU in the neighbours of its neighbours and the challenges are bigger and more diverse.

While a 'grand strategy' for all EU external action might be too ambitious, an 'EU Strategy on the Neighbours of the Neighbours' which draws on the existing instruments of cooperation and focuses on building bridges across the regions concerned appears more realistic. This would imply overcoming the compartmentalization of the neighbours of the ENP countries by a pragmatic, functional 'variable geometry' approach within an overarching strategic framework that would allow for the necessary flexibility. 'Variable geometry' permits different (groups of) countries to cooperate (or integrate) in different policy areas and at varying degrees. A certain ad hoc variable geometry is to a limited extent already practiced, yet it needs to be addressed in a more systematic manner, embedding the regional strategies in an overall strategy, while avoiding a mere *à la carte* participation.

It should be kept in mind though that in a multipolar system, the major powers may have overlapping and sometimes conflicting neighbourhood policies. For example, the EU's pursuit of normative objectives may face the Russian and Chinese non-interference doctrines. Moreover, 'countries that are the subject of more than one neighbourhood policy may become adept in playing off the competition between them, as illustrated by Belarus and Azerbaijan – as well as Ukraine – in their policies towards the EU and Russia'.[75]

As a result, the EU's broader neighbourhood policy needs to become more geopolitical, while still striving to reconcile values and interests.

Bibliography

Antkiewicz, A. and Momani, B. 2009. Pursuing Geopolitical Stability through Interregional Trade: The EU's Motives for Negotiating with the Gulf Cooperation Council. *Journal of European Integration*, 31(2), 217–35.

---

73   European Commission 2003. *Communication from the Commission to the Council and the European Parliament, Wider Europe – Neighbourhood: A New Framework for Relations with Our Eastern and Southern Neighbours*, COM(2003) 104, Brussels, 11 March, 4.

74   See Chapter 1 by Erwan Lannon in this volume.

75   Emerson, M. 2011. Just Good Friends? The European Union's Multiple Neighbourhood Policies. *The International Spectator*, 46(4), 59.

Baabood, A. 2010. What an Effective Arab Strategy for the EU Should Look Like. *Europe's World*, spring, http://www.europesworld.org/NewEnglish/Home_ old/Article/tabid/191/ArticleType/articleview/ArticleID/21591/language/en-US/Default.aspx [accessed: 10 December 2013].

Bello, O. 2012. *Quick Fix or Quick Sand? Implementing the EU Sahel Strategy.* Madrid: FRIDE.

Beretta, L.C. 2013. Reforming the EU GSP in Europe: Defining the New Map of Tariff Preferences and Supply Options. *Global Trade and Customs Journal*, 8(7/8), 217–23.

Biscop, S. 2012. Raiders of the Lost Art: Strategy-Making in Europe. *Egmont Security Policy Brief*, no. 40, Brussels: Egmont.

Blockmans, S. and Van Vooren, B. 2012. Revitalizing the European 'Neighbourhood Economic Community': The Case of Legally Binding Sectoral Multilateralism. *European Foreign Affairs Review*, 17(4), 577–604.

Burke, E. 2012. 'One Blood and One Destiny'? Yemen's Relations with the Gulf Cooperation Council. *Research Paper, Kuwait Programme on Development, Governance and Globalisation in the Gulf States*, 23, London: LSE.

College of Europe 2012. *The Neighbours of the EU's Neighbours: Diplomatic and Geopolitical Dimensions beyond the ENP – Conference Summary.* Bruges: College of Europe, 15–16 November, https://www.coleurope.eu/sites/default/ files/uploads/page/conference_summary.pdf [accessed: 10 December 2013].

Council of the European Union 1998. *Cooperation Agreement between the European Community and the Republic of Yemen 1998.* OJ L 72/18, 11 March.

Council of the European Union 2007. *The European Union and Central Asia: Strategy for a New Partnership*, Brussels, 21–22 June.

Council of the European Union 2007. *The Africa-EU Strategic Partnership: A Joint Africa-EU Strategy*, 16344/07 (Presse 291), Lisbon, 9 December.

Council of the European Union 2009. *The European Union and Central Asia: The New Partnership in Action*, Brussels, June, http://eeas.europa.eu/central_asia/ docs/2010_strategy_eu_centralasia_en.pdf [accessed: 10 December 2013].

Council of the European Union 2009. *An EU Policy on the Horn of Africa – Towards a Comprehensive EU Strategy*, Annex to the Outcome of Proceedings of the Foreign Affairs Council, Brussels, 8 December.

Council of the European Union 2011. *Strategy for Security and Development in the Sahel*, Annex to the Council Conclusions on a European Union Strategy for Security and Development in the Sahel, Brussels, 21 March.

Council of the European Union 2011. *A Strategic Framework for the Horn of Africa*, Annex to the Council Conclusions on the Horn of Africa, 3124th Foreign Affairs Council meeting, Brussels, 14 November.

Council of the European Union 2012. *Council Decision 2012/327/CFSP of 25 June 2012 extending the mandate of the European Union Special Representative for the Southern Mediterranean region.* OJ L 165/56, 26 June.

Council of the European Union 2012. *Cairo Declaration, Second European Union-League of Arab States Foreign Affairs Ministerial Meeting*, Cairo,

13 November 2012, http://www.consilium.europa.eu/uedocs/cms_data/docs/pressdata/EN/foraff/133465.pdf [accessed: 10 December 2013].

Delcour, L. and Wolczuk, K. 2013. Eurasian Economic Integration and Implications for the EU's Policy in the Eastern Neigbhourhood, in Dragneva, R. and Wolczuk, K. (eds), *Eurasian Economic Integration: Law, Policy, and Politics*. Cheltenham: Edward Elgar, 179–203.

Duhot, H. 2012. The Black Sea Synergy Initiative: The Reflection of EU's Ambitions and Limitations in the Region, in Lannon, E. (ed.), *The European Neighbourhood Policy's Challenges/Les défis de la politique européenne de voisinage*. Brussels: P.I.E. Peter Lang, 323–44.

Duke, S. 2011. Pax or Pox Europeana after the Lisbon Treaty? *The International Spectator*, 46(1), 83–99.

Emerson, M. 2011. Just Good Friends? The European Union's Multiple Neighbourhood Policies. *The International Spectator*, 46(4), 45–62.

Eurasian Economic Community 2013. *Treaty on the Establishment of the Eurasian Economic Community*, http://www.evrazes.com/docs/view/95 [accessed: 10 December 2013].

European Commission 2003. *Communication from the Commission to the Council and the European Parliament, Wider Europe – Neighbourhood: A New Framework for Relations with Our Eastern and Southern Neighbours*, COM(2003) 104, Brussels, 11 March.

European Commission 2006. *Communication from the Commission to the Council and the European Parliament. Strategy for Africa: An EU regional political partnership for peace, security and development in the Horn of Africa*, COM(2006) 601 final, Brussels, 20 October.

European Commission 2006. *Communication from the Commission to the Council and the European Parliament on Strengthening the European Neighbourhood Policy*, COM(2006) 726 final, Brussels, 4 December.

European Commission 2007. *Communication from the Commission to the Council and the European Parliament, Black Sea Synergy – A New Regional Cooperation Initiative*, COM(2007) 160 final, Brussels, 11 April.

European Commission and High Representative 2003. *Strengthening EU's Relations with the Arab World*, D(2003) 10318, Brussels, 4 December.

European Council 2002. *Presidency Conclusions*, Copenhagen, 12–13 December.

European Council 2003. *European Security Strategy: A Secure Europe in a Better World*, Brussels, 12 December.

European Council 2005. *Final Report on an EU Strategic Partnership with the Mediterranean and the Middle East*, Brussels, 17 June.

European Council 2009. *Declaration by the European Council on the Eastern Partnership, Presidency Conclusions of the Brussels European Council*, 19–20 March, Annex 2.

European External Action Service 2014. *Missions and Operations*, http://eeas.europa.eu/csdp/missions-and-operations/index_en.htm [accessed: 10 March 2014].

European Parliament 2011. *An EU Strategy for the Black Sea (2010/2087(INI))*. Brussels, P7-TA(2011)0025, 20 January.

European Parliament and Council of the European Union 2012. *Regulation (EU) No 978/2012 of the European Parliament and of the Council of 25 October 2012 applying a scheme of generalised tariff preferences and repealing Council Regulation (EC) No 732/2008*. OJ L303/1, 31 October.

European Parliament and Council of the European Union 2014. *Regulation (EU) No 232/2014 of the European Parliament and of the Council of 11 March 2014 establishing a European Neighbourhood Instrument*. OJ, L 77/27, 13 March.

European Parliament and Council of the European Union 2014. *Regulation (EU) No 234/2014 of the European Parliament and of the Council of 11 March 2014 establishing a Partnership Instrument for cooperation with third countries*. OJ, L 77/77, 15 March.

Grevi, G. 2014. Re-defining the EU's Neighbourhood, in Grevi, G. and Keohane, D. (eds), *Challenges for European Foreign Policy in 2014: The EU's Extended Neighbourhood*. Madrid: FRIDE, 15–22.

Gstöhl, S. 2012. What Is at Stake in the Internal Market? Towards a Neighbourhood Economic Community, in Lannon, E. (ed.), *Challenges of the European Neighbourhood Policy/Les défis de la politique européenne de voisinage*. Brussels: P.I.E. Peter Lang, 85–108.

Melvin, N. 2012. The EU Needs a New Values-Based Realism for its Central Asia Strategy. *EUCAM Policy Policy Brief, no. 28, Brussels: EUCAM, October.*

Pape, E. 2013. An Old Partnership in a New Setting: ACP-EU Relations from a European Perspective. *Journal of International Development*, 25(5), 727–41.

The Economist 2013. Afrighanistan? 26 January – 1 February, 11.

Youngs, R. and Echagüe, A. 2010. Europe, the Mediterranean, the Middle East and the Need for Triangulation. *The International Spectator*, 45(3), 27–39.

Annex
List of Agreements and Maps

Table A.I   **Agreements between the EU and its neighbours and between the EU and the neighbours of its neighbours (italics), June 2014**

Country	Agreement	References (OJ) (EU accession status)
Albania	Stabilization and Association Agreement	L 107/166 (28/04/2009)
Algeria	Euro-Mediterranean Association Agreement	L 265/2 (10/10/2005)
Andorra	Cooperation Agreement	L 135/14 (28/05/2005)
Armenia	Partnership and Cooperation Agreement	L 239/3 (09/09/1999)
Azerbaijan	Partnership and Cooperation Agreement & Protocol extending the PCA to trade in textile products	L 246/3 (17/09/1999) L 17/14 (24/01/2007)
Bahrain	Cooperation Agreement EEC-GCC	L 54/3 (25/02/1989)
Belarus	Partnership and Cooperation Agreement signed in 1995 Agreement on trade in textile products	Ratification frozen since 1997 L 123/120 (17/05/1994) + L 345/23 (28/12/2005)
Bosnia and Herzegovina	Stabilization and Association Agreement	Signed in 2008, but not yet in force
Chad	Cotonou Agreement	L 317/287 (15/12/2000), revised in 2005 (L 209/27) and 2010 (L 287/3)
Egypt	Euro-Mediterranean Association Agreement Agreement on scientific and technological cooperation Agreement in the form of the exchange of letters concerning reciprocal liberalization measures on agricultural products, processed agricultural products and fish and fishery products	L 304/39 (30/09/2004) L 182/12 (13/07/2005) L 106/41 (28/04/2010)
FYROM	Stabilization and Association Agreement	L 84/3 (20/03/2004) EU candidate country since 2005
Georgia	Partnership and Cooperation Agreement Association Agreement (incl. DCFTA) Common Aviation Area Agreement	L 205/3 (04/08/1999) Signed in June 2014 L 321/3 (20/11/2012)

Iceland	Agreement on the European Economic Area	L 1/3 (03/01/1994) EU candidate country since 2009, accession negotiations since 2010
Iran	(negotiations on a Trade and Cooperation Agreement on hold since 2005)	–
Iraq	Partnership and Cooperation Agreement	Signed in 2012, L 204/20 (31/07/2012), but not yet in force
Israel	Euro-Mediterranean Association Agreement & amendment in order to achieve greater liberalization in trade of agricultural products	L 147/3 (21/06/2000) L 346/67 (31/12/2003)
	Agreement on scientific and technical cooperation Agreement in the form of the exchange of letters concerning reciprocal liberalization measures on agricultural products, processed agricultural products and fish and fishery products	L 154/80 (21/06/2003) L 313/3 (28/11/2009)
	Euro-Mediterranean Aviation Agreement Agreement on Conformity Assessment and Acceptance of Industrial Products Agreement on mutual recognition of OECD principles and good laboratory practice (GLP)	L 208/3 (02/08/2013) L1/2 (04/01/2013) L 263/7 (09/10/1999)
Jordan	Euro-Mediterranean Association Agreement Agreement in the form of an Exchange of Letters between the European Community and the Hashemite Kingdom of Jordan concerning reciprocal liberalization measures and amending the EC-Jordan Association Agreement as well as replacing Annexes I, II, III and IV and Protocols 1 and 2 to that Agreement	L 129/3 (15/05/2002) L 41/3 (13/02/2006)
	Euro-Mediterranean Aviation Agreement Agreement on scientific and technological cooperation Agreement in the form of the exchange of letters concerning reciprocal liberalization measures	L334/3 (06/12/2012) L 159/108 (17/06/2011) L 41/3 (13/02/2006)
Kazakhstan	Partnership and Cooperation Agreement (Enhanced PCA under negotiation since 2011)	L 196/3 (28/07/1999)
Kosovo	(Stabilization and Association Agreement under negotiation since 2013)	– Potential EU candidate country since 2008
Kyrgyz Republic	Partnership and Cooperation Agreement Agreement on certain aspects of air services	L 196/48 (28/07/1999) L 179/39 (07/07/2007)
Kuwait	Cooperation Agreement EEC-GCC	L 54/3 (25/02/1989)
Lebanon	Euro-Mediterranean Association Agreement Agreement on certain aspects of air services	L 143/2 (30/05/2006) L 215/17 (05/08/2006)
Libya	(negotiations on a Framework Agreement on hold since 2011)	–
Liechtenstein	Agreement on the European Economic Area	L 1/3 (03/01/1994) + L86/58 (20/04/1995)

Mali	Cotonou Agreement	L 317/287 (15/12/2000), revised in 2005 (L 209/27) and 2010 (L 287/3)
Moldova	Partnership and Cooperation Agreement Association Agreement (incl. DCFTA) Agreement on certain aspects of air services	L 181/3 (24/06/1998) Signed in June 2014 L 126/24 (13/05/2006)
Mauritania	Cotonou Agreement	L 317/287 (15/12/2000), revised in 2005 (L 209/27) and 2010 (L 287/3)
Monaco	Agreement on application of certain Community acts on the territory of Monaco	L 332/42 (19/12/2003)
Montenegro	Stabilization and Association Agreement	L 108/3 (29/04/2010) EU candidate country since 2008, accession negotiations since 2012
Morocco	Euro-Mediterranean Association Agreement Agreement in the form of an Exchange of Letters between the European Community and the Kingdom of Morocco concerning reciprocal liberalization measures and the replacement of the agricultural protocols to the EC-Morocco Association Agreement	L 70/2 (18/03/2000) L 345/119 (31/12/2003)
	Agreement on scientific and technical cooperation Fisheries Partnership Agreement Agreement on certain aspects of air services Euro-Mediterranean Aviation Agreement Agreement in the form of the exchange of letters concerning reciprocal measures on agricultural products, processed agricultural products and fish and fishery products	L 37/9 (10/02/2004) L 141/4 (29/05/2006) L 386/18 (29/12/2006) L 386/57 (29/12/2006) L 241/4 (07/09/2012)
Norway	Agreement on the European Economic Area	L 1/3 (03/01/1994)
Niger	Cotonou Agreement	L 317/287 (15/12/2000), revised in 2005 (L 209/27) and 2010 (L 287/3)
Oman	Cooperation Agreement EEC-GCC	L 54/3 (25/02/1989)
Palestinian Authority	Euro-Mediterranean Interim Association Agreement on Trade and Cooperation Agreement in the form of the exchange of letters on reciprocal liberalization measures Agreement in the form of the exchange of letters concerning reciprocal measures on agricultural products, processed agricultural products and fish and fishery products	L 187/3 (16/07/1997) L 2/6 (05/01/2006) L 238/5 (10/12/2011)
Qatar	Cooperation Agreement EEC-GCC	L 54/3 (25/02/1989)
Russia	Agreement on Partnership and Cooperation Agreement on trade in textile products Agreement on cooperation in science and technology Agreement on trade in certain steel products	L 327/1 (28/11/1997) L 222/2 (10/08/1998) L 299/21 (18/11/2003) L 303/39 (22/11/2005)
San Marino	Agreement on Cooperation and Customs Union	L 84/43 (28/03/2002)
Saudi Arabia	Cooperation Agreement EEC-GCC	L 54/3 (25/02/1989)

Serbia	Stabilization and Association Agreement	L 278/16 (18/10/2013) EU candidate country since 2012
Somalia	(Accession to Cotonou Agreement pending)	L 317/287 (15/12/2000), revised in 2005 (L 209/27) and 2010 (L 287/3)
South Sudan	(Accession to Cotonou Agreement pending)	–
Sudan	Cotonou Agreement	L 317/287 (15/12/2000), revised in 2005 (L 209/27) and 2010 (L 287/3) Signed the Agreement but did not ratify its first revision in 2005
Switzerland	EEC-Switzerland Free Trade Agreement	L 300/189 (31/12/1972) More than 120 sectoral bilateral agreements, protocols, etc.
Syria	Cooperation Agreement (legally speaking Association Agreement based on former article 238 EEC) (Negotiations on Association Agreement on hold since May 2011)	L 269/2 (27/09/1978)
Tajikistan	Partnership and Cooperation Agreement	L 350/3 (29/12/2009)
Tunisia	Euro-Mediterranean Association Agreement Agreement in the form of an Exchange of Letters between the European Community and the Republic of Tunisia concerning reciprocal liberalization measures and amendment of the Agricultural Protocols to the EC/ Tunisia Association Agreement Agreement of scientific and technical cooperation	L 97/2 (30/03/1998) L 336/93 (30/12/2000) L 37/17 (10/02/2004)
Turkey	Association Agreement Additional Protocol (23 November 1970) Decision 1/95 of the Association Council (final phase of the customs union)	L 217/3687 (29/12/1964) L 293/1 (29/12/1972) L 35/50 (13/02/1996) EU candidate country since 1997, accession negotiations since 2005
Turkmenistan	Partnership and Cooperation Agreement signed in 1998 Interim agreement on trade and trade related matters	Not yet ratified L 80/21 (26/03/2011)
Ukraine	Partnership and Cooperation Agreement Agreement on trade in textile products Agreement on trade in certain steel products Agreement on certain aspects of air services Association Agreement (incl. DCFTA)	L 49/3 (19/02/1998) L 81/294 (30/03/1996) L 384/23 (28/12/2004) L 211/24 (01/08/2006) Signed in June 2014 (political provisions in March 2014)
U.A. Emirates	Cooperation Agreement EEC-GCC Agreement on certain aspects of air services	L 54/3 (25/02/1989) L 28/21 (01/02/2008)
Uzbekistan	Partnership and Cooperation Agreement	L 229/3 (31/08/1999)
Yemen	Cooperation Agreement	L 72/18 (11/03/1998)

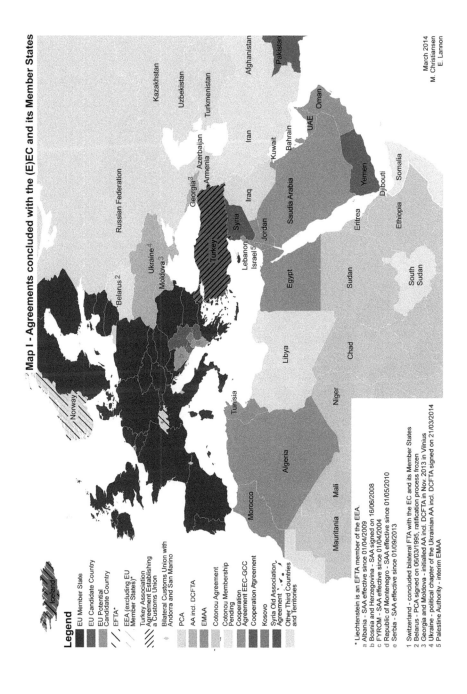

Map I - Agreements concluded with the (E)EC and its Member States

Legend

- EU Member State
- EU Candidate Country
- EU Potential Candidate Country
- EFTA*
- EEA (excluding EU Member States)*
- Turkey Association Agreement Establishing a Customs Union
- Bilateral Customs Union with Andorra and San Marino
- PCA
- AA incl. DCFTA
- EMAA
- Cotonou Agreement
- Cotonou Membership Pending
- Cooperation Agreement EEC-GCC
- Cooperation Agreement
- Kosovo
- Syria Old Association Agreement
- Other Third Countries and Territories

* Liechtenstein is an EFTA member of the EEA.
a Albania - SAA effective since 01/04/2009
b Bosnia and Herzegovina - SAA signed on 16/06/2008
c FYROM - SAA effective since 01/04/2004
d Republic of Montenegro - SAA effective since 01/05/2010
e Serbia - SAA effective since 01/09/2013

1 Switzerland - concluded bilateral FTA with the EC and its Member States
2 Belarus - PCA signed on 06/03/1995, ratification process frozen
3 Georgia and Moldova - initialled AA incl. DCFTA in Nov. 2013 in Vilnius
4 Ukraine - political chapter of the Ukrainian AA incl. DCFTA signed on 21/03/2014
5 Palestine Authority - interim EMAA

March 2014
M. Christiansen
E. Lannon

Map II - Pan Euro-Mediterranean Area and SPMME

Legend

- EU Member State
- EU Candidate Country
- EU Potential Candidate Country
- EEA (excluding Member States)*
- EFTA*
- NATO Member Country
- ENP
- Potential ENP Partner
- Bilateral Customs Union with Andorra and San Marino
- EMP
- Potential EMP Partner
- UfM (excluding EU Member States)
- EU Russia Strategic Partnership**
- Eastern Partnership***
- SPMME
- Kosovo
- Other Third Countries and Territories

* Liechtenstein is an EFTA member of the EEA.
** Russia is not included in the ENP but benefitted from the ENPI (2007-2013).
*** Belarus (that is under EU restrictive measures) and Kazakhstan are members of the Eurasian Customs Union with Russia. Armenia announced in 2013 its decision to join as well. These countries thus cannot conclude an Association Agreement including a Deep and Comprehensive Area with the EU but can be included in the ENP.

March 2014
M. Christiansen
E. Lannon

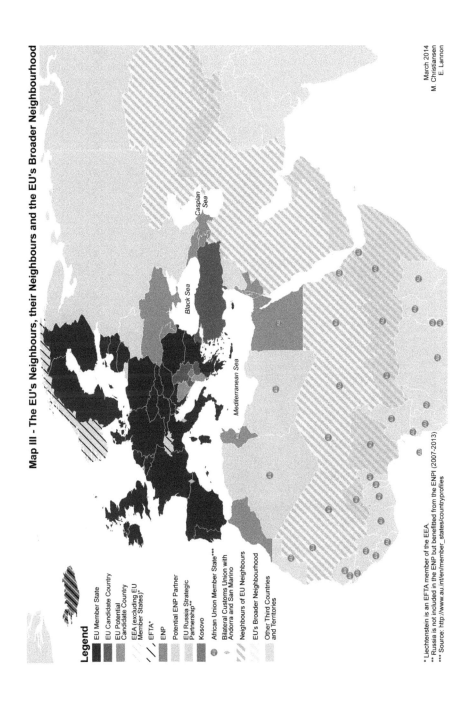

Map III - The EU's Neighbours, their Neighbours and the EU's Broader Neighbourhood

Legend

- EU Member State
- EU Candidate Country
- EU Potential Candidate Country
- EEA (excluding EU Member States)*
- EFTA*
- ENP
- Potential ENP Partner
- EU Russia Strategic Partnership**
- Kosovo
- African Union Member State ***
- Bilateral Customs Union with Andorra and San Marino
- Neighbours of EU Neighbours
- EU's Broader Neighbourhood
- Other Third Countries and Territories

* Liechtenstein is an EFTA member of the EEA.
** Russia is not included in the ENP but benefitted from the ENPI (2007-2013)
*** Source: http://www.au.int/en/member_states/countryprofiles

March 2014
M. Christiansen
E. Lannon

Caspian Sea

Black Sea

Mediterranean Sea

298

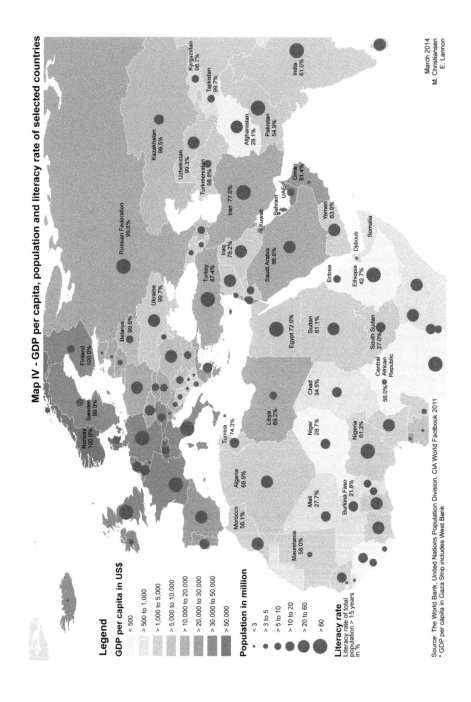

Map IV - GDP per capita, population and literacy rate of selected countries

Legend

GDP per capita in US$

< 500
500 to 1,000
> 1,000 to 5,000
> 5,000 to 10,000
> 10,000 to 20,000
> 20,000 to 30,000
> 30,000 to 50,000
> 50,000

Population in million

< 3
3 to 5
5 to 10
10 to 20
20 to 60
> 60

Literacy rate
Literacy rate of total
population > 15 years
in %

March 2014
M. Christiansen
E. Lannon

Source: The World Bank, United Nations Population Division, CIA World Factbook 2011
* GDP per capita in Gaza Strip includes West Bank

Norway 100.0%
Sweden 98.0%
Finland 100.0%
Belarus 99.6%
Russian Federation 99.6%
Ukraine 99.7%
Kazakhstan 99.5%
Uzbekistan 99.3%
Turkmenistan 99.7%
Tajikistan 99.7%
Kyrgyzstan 98.7%
Afghanistan 28.1%
Pakistan 54.9%
India 61.0%
Iran 77.0%
Oman 81.4%
Turkey 87.4%
Iraq 78.2%
Kuwait
Bahrain
UAE
Saudi Arabia 86.6%
Yemen 63.9%
Tunisia 74.3%
Libya 89.2%
Egypt 72.0%
Sudan 61.1%
Eritrea
Djibouti
Somalia
Ethiopia 42.7%
South Sudan 27.0%
Central African Republic 56.0%
Chad 34.5%
Niger 28.7%
Nigeria 61.3%
Algeria 69.9%
Mali 27.7%
Burkina Faso 21.8%
Morocco 56.1%
Mauritania 58.0%

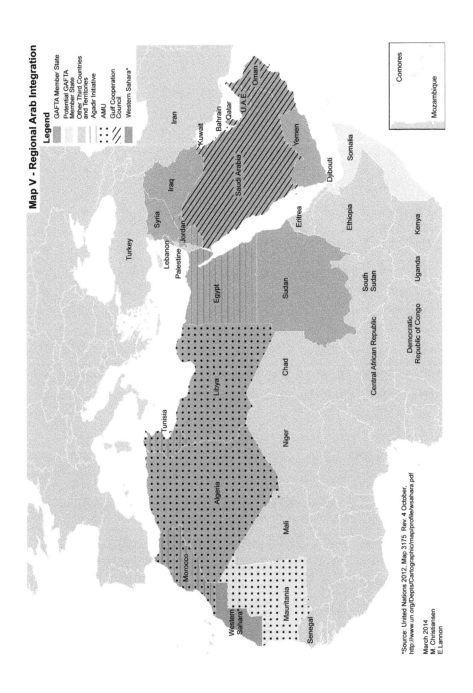

Map V - Regional Arab Integration

Legend
- GAFTA Member State
- Potential GAFTA Member State
- Other Third Countries and Territories
- Agadir Initiative
- AMU
- Gulf Cooperation Council
- Western Sahara*

*Source: United Nations 2012, Map 3175 Rev. 4 October, http://www.un.org/Depts/Cartographic/map/profile/wsahara.pdf

March 2014
M. Christiansen
E.Lannon

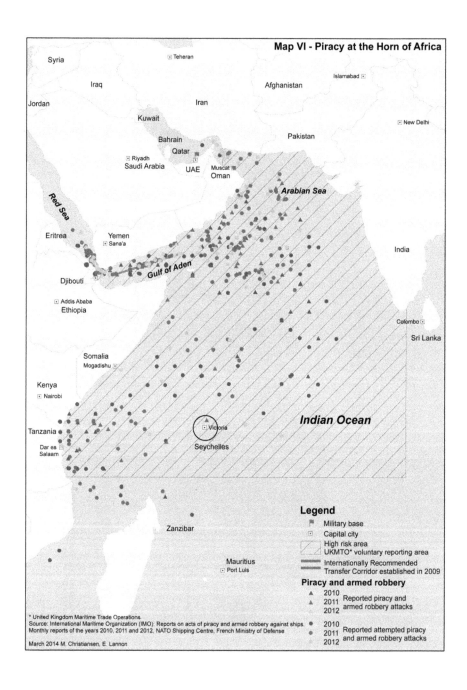

Map VI - Piracy at the Horn of Africa

Legend

- Military base
- Capital city
- High risk area
- UKMTO* voluntary reporting area
- Internationally Recommended Transfer Corridor established in 2009

Piracy and armed robbery

2010	Reported piracy and
2011	armed robbery attacks
2012	

2010	Reported attempted piracy
2011	and armed robbery attacks
2012	

* United Kingdom Maritime Trade Operations
Source: International Maritime Organization (IMO): Reports on acts of piracy and armed robbery against ships.
Monthly reports of the years 2010, 2011 and 2012, NATO Shipping Centre, French Ministry of Defense

March 2014 M. Christiansen, E. Lannon

Index

Bold page numbers indicate figures, *italic* numbers indicate tables.

www.ingramcontent.com/pod-product-compliance
Ingram Content Group UK Ltd.
Pitfield, Milton Keynes, MK11 3LW, UK
UKHW020401010325
455677UK00021B/566